UNLEASHING PROSPERITY

UNLEASHING PROSPERITY

Productivity Growth in Eastern Europe and the Former Soviet Union

Asad Alam
Paloma Anós Casero
Faruk Khan
Charles Udomsaph

THE WORLD BANK
Washington, D.C.

1818 H Street, NW
Washington, DC 20433
Telephone: 202-473-1000
Internet: www.worldbank.org
E-mail: feedback@worldbank.org

1 2 3 4 11 10 09 08

ISBN: 978-0-8213-7279-1

eISBN: 978-0-8213-7280-7

DOI: 10.1596/978-0-8213-7279-1

Library of Congress Cataloging-in-Publication Data

Alam, Asad

Unleashing prosperity: productivity growth in eastern europe and the former soviet union/by Asad Alam, Paloma Anós Casero, Faruk Khan, and Charles Udomsaph.

p. cm.

ISBN 978-0-8213-7279-1 (alk. paper) — ISBN 978-0-8213-7280-7

1. Industrial productivity—Europe, Eastern. 2. Industrial productivity—Former Soviet republics. I. Anós Casero, Paloma. II. Khan, Faruk A. III. Title.

HC244.Z9I52A43 2008

338′.060947—DC22

2007041802

Cover photo by: Mikhail Malyshev/iStockphoto.

Cover design: Naylor Design, Inc.

Contents

Foreword xvii
Acknowledgments xix
Abbreviations xxi

Overview **1**

Introduction 1
What Are the Patterns of Productivity Growth? 9
What Are the Sources of Productivity Growth? 13
Which Policies Drive Productivity Growth? 35
Going Forward: Productivity Growth Requires a Differentiated Policy Agenda across Countries 42
Conclusion 43

1. Patterns of Aggregate Productivity Growth **45**

Patterns of Growth 46
Sources of Growth: The Role of Productivity 48
The Overall Record of Policy Reform 56
The Impact of Policy Reform 58
Conclusions 63

2. Sectoral Patterns of Productivity Growth **65**

Cross-Sectoral Shifts 65

Productivity Growth within Sectors: A Bird's-Eye View 72
Agricultural Productivity 74
Manufacturing Productivity 80
Service Productivity 97
The Role of ICT in Productivity Growth 103
Conclusions 108

3. Firm Productivity Growth 113

Firm Dynamics and Productivity Growth 114
Firm Dynamics and Job Flows 129
Policy Drivers of Firm Productivity Growth 134
Conclusions 152

4. The Future Role of Public Policy 155

Sustained Productivity Growth Will Accelerate the Convergence toward Advanced Economies 155
Fostering Productivity Growth Requires a Differentiated Policy Agenda across Countries 156
Governance and Macroeconomic Stability 159
Competition and Market Entry 160
Labor, Infrastructure, and Technology Development 162
Financial Development 163
Conclusions 165

Appendix 1: Macro Analysis of Productivity: Data and Methodology 167

A. Growth Accounting 167
B. Estimating the Impact of Structural Reforms: Cross-Country Growth Regressions 169

Appendix 2: Sectoral Analysis of Productivity: Data and Methodology 175

A. Benchmarking the Structural Transformation of Transition Economies 175
B. Shift-Share Analysis: Decomposing Aggregate Labor Productivity Growth 176
C. Estimation of Service Input Usage in the Agriculture Sector 181
D. Manufacturing Productivity 184
E. Service Productivity 190
F. The Role of ICT in Productivity Growth 195

Appendix 3: Micro Analysis of Productivity: Data and Methodology 205

A. Firm Productivity Dynamics and Demographics 205
B. Policy Drivers of Firm Productivity Growth 215

Bibliography 247

Index 257

Boxes

1.1 The Growth Accounting Methodology 50
1.2 Estimating the Impact of Structural Reforms 60
2.1 Shift-Share Analysis: Decomposing Aggregate Labor Productivity Growth 69
2.2 The Product Space in Russia and Poland 95
3.1 The Decomposition of Productivity Growth Using Firm-Level Data 115
3.2 Empirical Analysis of Policy Drivers of Firm Productivity Growth 135
3.3 Competition, Productivity, and Distance to the Technological Frontier 141
3.4 Innovation Leads the Catching-Up Process 152

Figures

1 A Large Income Gap Divides the Region, Which Also Lags behind the EU-15, 1999–2005 3
2 Productivity and Progress in Reform in the Region 6
3 Gross Domestic Product Rose, and Poverty Fell Dramatically 10
4 TFP, More Than Labor or Capital, Has Boosted Growth 11
5 TFP Has Rebounded across the Region Since 1990 11
6 Labor Productivity, More Than Employment or Population Growth, Raised per Capita Income, 1999–2004 12
7 The Share of Workers in the Working-Age Population Has Fallen 12
8 Investments in ICT Contributed to Labor Productivity Growth, 1995–2004 13
9 TFP in the Poorest Countries in the Region Is Only Half the Level in the EU-10 14

10	The Share of Services in Value Added and Employment Has Risen	15
11	Higher Value Added per Worker in Services Raised Overall Labor Productivity in Most Countries, 1999–2004	15
12	Labor Productivity Growth Was High, Particularly in the CIS, 1999–2004	17
13	As Transition Proceeds, Productivity Growth Is Driven Mainly by Efficiency Gains within Firms	21
14	Business Start-Ups Have Exceeded Business Exits in Most Countries	23
15	Hungary's Reforms Led to Increased Firm Entry, While the 1998 Crisis Prompted Firm Exit in the Russian Federation	24
16	In Slovenia, the Largest Manufacturing Firms Have Shrunk, While in Mexico, They Have Expanded	25
17	Entrants' Survival Rates Are Higher in the Region Than in Advanced Economies	26
18	Entrants with Higher Labor Productivity Are More Successful at Maintaining the Workforce	27
19	The Role of Reallocation and Firm Turnover in Productivity Growth in Early Reformers Is Now Similar to That in Advanced Market Economies	28
20	In Late Reformers, Firm Turnover Has Not Spurred Productivity Gains in Existing Firms	30
21	Allocative Efficiency Remains Low in the Region	31
22	Labor Shedding at Existing Firms Was the Main Source of Job Destruction	32
23	Sometimes Unsynchronized Job Flows Gave Rise to Net Employment Losses	33
24	In Services, Job Creation Outpaced Job Losses	34
25	Policy Reforms Boost Firm Productivity	36
26	Privatization Has Raised TFP, Especially in Countries That Attracted FDI	39
1.1	Recent Growth Has Been Strong in the Region	47

1.2	Growth Has Rebounded across All Country Groups	48
1.3	TFP Growth Is the Primary Driver of Growth in Transition Countries	51
1.4	Higher Capacity Utilization Partly Explains High TFP Growth Rates	53
1.5	TFP Levels and Growth Vary across the Region	54
1.6	Productivity Growth Rates Are Now Converging in the Region	55
1.7	The Region Is Catching Up with Comparators	55
1.8	The Record on Policy Reform Is Mixed	57
1.9	The Region Lags behind Comparators in Several Key Structural Reforms	59
1.10	Infrastructure and Financial Depth Improvements Would Do the Most to Boost Productivity	61
1.11	Productivity Gains from Policy Improvements Vary across Countries	62
1.12	Infrastructure Upgrading Shows High Returns	62
2.1	A Substantial Shift of Output and Employment to Services	66
2.2	During Transition, Labor Shifted to Agriculture in the Low Income CIS Countries	67
2.3	Labor Shifted to Services in the Middle Income CIS and the EU-10	68
2.4	Higher Value Added per Worker in Services Raised Overall Labor Productivity in Most Countries, 1999–2004	68
2.5	Within-Sector Productivity Is the Main Driver of the Productivity Surge, 1999–2004	70
2.6	The Share of Services in Valued Added and Employment Has Risen	72
2.7	Relative to the EU-15, Labor Productivity Gains Were High, but Levels Lagged, 1999–2004	73
2.8	Labor Productivity in Agriculture Is a Problem	76
2.9	Average Farm Efficiency Is Highest in the EU-10	76
2.10	The Efficiency of Service Industries Is Important in Agricultural Productivity	79

2.11	Average Labor Productivity in the EU-8 Was Less Than 30 Percent of That in the EU-15	81
2.12	Labor Productivity Growth in Manufacturing Is Higher in the EU-8 Than in the EU-15, 1999–2004	82
2.13	Only a Few Manufacturing Industries Sustained Strong Productivity Growth	83
2.14	Policy Drivers of Manufacturing TFP Growth, 1999–2004	84
2.15	ICT Industries Showed More Rapid Productivity Growth, 1999–2004	85
2.16	Industries with High-Skilled Workers Displayed Higher Productivity, 1999–2004	85
2.17	Human Capital Moved from Less- to More-Productive Activities in Early Reformers	86
2.18	The Supply of ICT-Skilled Labor Was Expanding and Was Used More in Services	86
2.19	The ECA Region Still Lags behind the OECD in Labor Market Flexibility, and Late Reformers Lag Even Further	88
2.20	Trade and FDI Have Grown	90
2.21	Poland: FDI and Exports Are Linked to Productivity Growth in Manufacturing	91
2.22	The Technology Differentiation in Exports Was Stark across Countries	91
2.23	The EU-10 and Turkey Are Developing Producer-Driven Networks	92
2.24	Early Reformers Also Display More Export Discoveries	93
2.25	A Gap in Export Sophistication and Capabilities Remains between Early and Late Reformers, 1990–2005	94
2.26	The Gap in Productivity Was Associated with a Gap in Export Sophistication, 1999–2005	96
2.27	Service Labor Productivity in the EU-8 Increased, but Still Lagged Behind the EU-15	98
2.28	Variations Were Wide in Productivity Performance across Service Industries	99
2.29	ICT Service Industries Displayed Higher Productivity, by ICT Taxonomy, 2000–04	100

2.30	Service Industries with Skilled Workers Show Higher Productivity, by Skill Taxonomy, 2000–04	100
2.31	Service Inputs into Manufacturing Vary across Countries	102
2.32	ICT Capital, Labor Productivity Growth, and GDP per Person Employed	104
2.33	ICT Capital Contribution to Labor Productivity Growth, 1995–2004	104
2.34	The Contribution of ICT-Producing Industries to Labor Productivity Growth, 1995–2004	105
2.35	ICT-Using Services Contribute Less to Productivity Growth Than Do ICT-Using Manufacturing	106
3.1	The Sources of Productivity Growth Differ Substantially across Countries and Sectors	118
3.2	Productivity Gains Have Arisen Primarily from Improvements within Firms	119
3.3	Firm Start-Ups Have Exceeded Exits in Most Countries over the Past Decade	122
3.4	Hungary and the Russian Federation Have Varied in Rates of Firm Churning	122
3.5	Entrants Showed Higher Productivity than Incumbents	123
3.6	Transition Economies Show Higher Survival Rates Than Many Advanced Economies	124
3.7	As the Transition Matures, Markets Grow Harsh, and Entrant Survival Rates Drop	125
3.8	Large Manufacturing Firms Are Not Expanding in Slovenia, but They Are in Mexico	126
3.9	Net Entry and Reallocation Are Declining, Converging toward Advanced Market Patterns	127
3.10	New Firms Tend to Spur Productivity Growth in Early Reformers	128
3.11	Entry of New Firms Is Not Always Correlated with Productivity Growth in Existing Firms	129
3.12	Labor Allocative Efficiency in Manufacturing Lags Even in Advanced Reformers	130

3.13	Labor Shedding at Existing Firms Was the Main Source of Job Destruction	130
3.14	Sometimes Unsynchronized Job Flows Gave Rise to Net Employment Losses	131
3.15	Job Creation Exceeded Job Destruction in Services	132
3.16	Firms with Higher Labor Productivity Were More Successful in Creating Jobs	133
3.17	The Recovery in Capacity Utilization Spurred Productivity Growth in the Russian Federation	137
3.18	Privatization Raised Productivity Growth, Particularly in Countries that Attracted FDI	138
3.19	Market Competition Fosters Innovation and Productivity Growth	139
3.20	Firms with External or Private Domestic Financing Showed Higher Productivity Growth, 2001–04	143
3.21	Labor Market Flexibility Yields Productivity Gains, 2001–04	143
3.22	Larger Innovative Firms Are More Likely to Provide Training	145
3.23	On-the-Job Training Yields Firm Productivity Gains, 2001–04	145
3.24	Improvements in Governance Were Associated with Higher Firm Productivity, 2001–04	147
3.25	Infrastructure Quality Was Important to Firm Productivity Growth, 2001–04	148
4.1	A Path toward Convergence	156
4.2	Early Reformers Exhibit a Higher Absorptive Capacity for Innovation, 2006	163
2.D1	Export Sophistication and GDP per Capita, 2005	186
2.D2	Export Sophistication and Subsequent Growth	187
2.D3	Open Forest and GDP per Capita, 2005	189
2.D4	Open Forest and Subsequent Growth	190
2.E1	Intensity of the Use of Service Subsector Inputs in Manufacturing	193

Tables

1	Late Reformers Must Complete the Transition; Early Reformers Must Foster Innovation	43
4.1	Late Reformers Must Complete the Transition; Early Reformers Must Sustain Productivity Growth and Foster Innovation	157
1.B1	Definitions and Data Sources	171
1.B2	Structural Determinants of Productivity Growth: Panel Regression Analysis	172
2.A1	Benchmarking Regressions	176
2.B1	The Contribution of Sectors to Aggregate Labor Productivity	180
2.B2	The Contribution of Manufacturing Industries to Aggregate Manufacturing Labor Productivity	180
2.B3	The Contribution of Service Industries to Aggregate Service Labor Productivity	181
2.C1	Regressions in First-Differences of Productivity in Agriculture Firms and Reform in Services, 2000–04	183
2.E2	The Effects of Service Liberalization on Manufacturing Productivity	195
2.F1	Labor Productivity and ICT Capital, 1995–2004	198
2.F2	Labor Productivity Growth and ICT-Producing Industries, 1995–2004	199
2.F3	Labor Productivity Growth, 1995–2003	199
2.F4	Contributions to Total Labor Productivity Growth, 1995–2000	199
2.F5	Panel Regression for Labor Productivity Growth in Manufacturing (*A*1)	201
2.F6	Panel Regression for Labor Productivity Growth in Manufacturing (*A*2)	201
2.F7	Panel Regression for Labor Productivity Growth in Market Services (*A*1)	201
2.F8	Panel Regression for Labor Productivity Growth in Market Services (*A*2)	201
2.F9	Data Definitions and Sources	202
3.A1	Data Sources	208
3.A2	Sample Coverage, Georgia	209

3.A3 Coverage of the Hungarian and Romanian Samples 210
3.A4 Coverage of the Russian Federation and Ukrainian Samples 211
3.A5 Definitions of Variables 213
3.B1 Descriptive Statistics of Log TFP Growth Estimates, 2001–04 215
3.B2 Baseline Regressions (Amadeus Only), 1999–2004 217
3.B3 Correlation of the Infrastructure Quality Indicator and Underlying BEEPS Variables 222
3.B4 Correlation of Financial Development Indicator and Underlying BEEPS Variables 222
3.B5 Correlation of the Governance Indicator and Underlying BEEPS Variables 222
3.B6 Correlation of the Labor Market Flexibility Indicator and Underlying BEEPS Variables 223
3.B7 Correlation of the Labor Quality Indicator and Underlying BEEPS Variables 223
3.B8 TFP Growth and BEEPS Full Model Regression Results, 2001–04 226
3.B9 Partial Correlations of BEEPS Finance Variables and TFP Growth, 2001–04 227
3.B10 Partial Correlations of BEEPS Infrastructure Variables and TFP Growth, 2001–04 228
3.B11 Partial Correlations of BEEPS Competition Variables and TFP Growth, 2001–04 228
3.B12 Partial Correlations of BEEPS Governance Variables and TFP Growth, 2001–04 229
3.B13 Partial Correlations of BEEPS Labor Variables and TFP Growth, 2001–04 229
3.B14 Partial Correlations of BEEPS Firm Management Variables and TFP Growth, 2001–04 230
3.B15 First-Difference Regressions: Downstream Manufacturing Productivity and Reform in Services, 1999–2004 231
3.B16 First-Difference Regressions: Downstream Manufacturing Productivity and Upstream Service Competition, Herfindahl-Hirschman Indexes, 1999–2004 232

3.B17	First-Difference Regressions: Downstream Manufacturing Productivity and Upstream Service Competition, Lerner Indexes, 1999–2004	234
3.B18	Financial Development and TFP Growth, 1999–2004	237
3.B19	Export Sophistication and TFP Growth, 1999–2004	238
3.B20	Import Penetration Rates and TFP Growth, 1999–2004	239
3.B21	Product Market Regulation and TFP Growth, 1999–2004	240
3.B22	FDI Inflows and TFP Growth, 1999–2004	240
3.B23	R&D and TFP Growth, 2001–04	241
3.B24	ICT Skills and TFP Growth, 2001–04	242
3.B25	Labor Market Rigidities and TFP Growth, 2001–04	242
3.B26	Telecommunications Reform and TFP Growth, 2001–04	244
3.B27	Innovation and Proximity to the Frontier, 2001–04	244
3.B28	TFP Growth and Annual Changes in Shares of Exports in Producer and Buyer Networks, 1999–2004	245

Foreword

Over the past few years, the countries of Eastern Europe and the Former Soviet Union have enjoyed strong economic growth that has been spurred by both domestic and external factors. In the countries in the Region that are new member states of the European Union, domestic reforms and the process of integration into the Union have broadened markets and attracted more investment. In the western Balkans, the cessation of war and domestic reforms have rendered the economic environment more conducive to investment and growth. In the countries of the Former Soviet Union, economic growth has rebounded from the depths of the Russian financial crisis in 1998. For many countries, accession into the World Trade Organization has helped lock in domestic reforms and improve confidence in the policy environment among investors.

Productivity growth is the single most important indicator of an economy's long-term health. Increases in productivity enhance enterprise profitability. With higher profits, enterprises are able to invest in new technologies, develop new products, expand markets, hire more workers, pay higher wages, enhance working conditions, and raise living standards. At the same time, higher profits, when they occur in a competitive market, help attract new firms and spur technological innovations, which can then force existing enterprises to become more efficient. This virtuous cycle raises overall economic efficiency and boosts growth and living standards.

For most countries of Eastern Europe and the Former Soviet Union, the transition from a command economy to a market economy has involved restructuring and reallocating resources to foster greater efficiency in resource use. Countries have enjoyed substantial productivity gains from the reallocation of labor and capital to more productive sectors and enterprises, from the entry of new firms and the exit of obsolete firms, and from the more efficient use of resources. The microeconomic analysis of productivity conducted for this study demonstrates the relative importance of these drivers of productivity change.

The analysis presented in this report assembles, for the first time, evidence from a variety of sources in the countries of Eastern Europe and the Former Soviet Union to show that policy and institutional reforms are important in achieving higher productivity growth. However, significant challenges remain in sustaining that growth. Many countries that started the reform process early, such as the new member states of the European Union, have come to resemble advanced market economies and face challenges in competing successfully in the global economy that are similar to the challenges faced by other European countries. For these new European Union members, the report argues, policies that facilitate innovation and firm expansion will be key. But for other countries that started the reform process later, such as the countries of southeastern Europe and the Former Soviet Union, there is still a need to address the legacy of transition. For these countries, policies that accelerate restructuring and ease the entry and exit of firms will continue to be essential.

This report—part of a series of regional studies of the World Bank's Europe and Central Asia Region that has already covered poverty and inequality, the enhancement of job opportunities, trade and integration, migration and remittances, and the challenges posed by aging populations—is intended as a contribution to our thinking about how the World Bank may work more effectively with client states and other partners in the Region to promote growth and foster higher living standards in a rapidly changing world.

I hope that this report, like others in the series, will stimulate debate, enhance understanding, and encourage action to help realize prosperity for all.

Shigeo Katsu
Vice President
Europe and Central Asia Region
World Bank

Acknowledgments

This report was prepared by a core team comprising Asad Alam, Paloma Anós Casero (task manager), Faruk A. Khan, and Charles Udomsaph. In addition to the analyses performed by the core team, the study drew on background papers prepared by a large cross-sectoral team of World Bank staff and external researchers. These contributions are acknowledged below.

The Overview was written by Asad Alam and Paloma Anós Casero.

Chapter 1 was written by Faruk A. Khan. César Calderón wrote a background paper on the policy drivers of productivity growth. Christine Kessides provided overall guidance on the role of infrastructure in productivity growth.

Chapter 2 was written by Paloma Anós Casero, with contributions from Charles Udomsaph. Zvi Lerman, Jo Swinnen, and Liesbet Vranken wrote background papers on agricultural productivity under the overall guidance of John Nash. Ana Fernandes wrote a background paper on service productivity. Marcin Piatkowski and Bart van Ark wrote a background paper on the role of information and communication technology in productivity. Bailey Klinger provided data on export sophistication and product space. Mark Schaffer provided data on sectoral shares of employment. Ondrej Rigval wrote background papers on education and productivity under the guidance of Edmundo Murrugarra. Victor Sulla and Erwin Tiongson made contributions on the role of human capital in productivity growth. Francis Ng provided data on trade and foreign investment.

Chapter 3 was written by Paloma Anós Casero, with contributions from Charles Udomsaph. The analysis benefited from background papers on firm demographics and productivity dynamics written by Eric J. Bartelsman, David J. Brown, John S. Earle, Stefano Scarpetta, and Almos Telegdy. These authors drew on data collected by local researchers, including Mihails Hazans, Ylva Heden, Jaan Masso, and Saso Polanec.

Chapter 4 was written by Asad Alam.

The report benefited from the support of Pradeep Mitra, chief economist of the Europe and Central Asia Region of the World Bank, who provided essential guidance throughout its preparation. Cheryl Gray also provided valuable support and suggestions. Useful comments were received from Philippe Aghion, Arup Banerji, Fabrizio Coricelli, Shahrokh Fardoust, Marianne Fay, Bernard Funck, Itzhak Goldberg, Daniela Gressani, Sergei Guriev, Carlos Felipe Jaramillo, Homi Kharas, Johannes Linn, Mamta Murthi, Andre Sapir, Luis Serven, and Roberto Zagha.

The report also benefited from the comments of participants in internal and external consultations, including (a) a World Bank workshop in Washington, DC (January 2007), and a brown bag lunch presentation involving country economists of the Europe and Central Asia Region (March 2007); (b) external consultations in March and April 2007 with the European Bank for Reconstruction and Development, the European Central Bank, the European Commission, the Organisation for Economic Co-operation and Development, and the Center for Strategic Studies (Moscow); and (c) the World Bank Growth Commission workshop (April 2007).

Judy Wiltshire formatted the report and helped prepare it for publication. Bruce Ross-Larson assisted in editing. Denise Bergeron, Paula Scalabrin, and Dina Towbin of the World Bank's Office of the Publisher coordinated the book design, final editing, and production.

The financial support of the Office of the Chief Economist of the Europe and Central Asia Region and of the World Bank Research Committee is gratefully acknowledged.

Abbreviations

BEEPS	Business Environment and Enterprise Performance Survey (and Database)
CIS	Commonwealth of Independent States
EAP	East Asia and Pacific
EBRD	European Bank for Reconstruction and Development
ECA	Eastern Europe and Central Asia
EU	European Union
EU-8	the Czech Republic, Estonia, Hungary, Latvia, Lithuania, Poland, the Slovak Republic, and Slovenia
EU-10	the EU-8, plus Bulgaria and Romania (also referred to as *the early reformers*)
EU-15	Austria, Belgium, Denmark, Finland, France, Germany, Greece, Ireland, Italy, Luxembourg, the Netherlands, Portugal, Spain, Sweden, and the United Kingdom
FDI	foreign direct investment
G-7	Group of Seven
GDP	gross domestic product
ICT	information and communication technology

ILO	International Labour Organization
IMF	International Monetary Fund
ISIC	International Standard Industrial Classification of all Economic Activities
LAC	Latin America and the Caribbean
low-CIS or CIS-low	low income CIS countries: Armenia, Azerbaijan, Georgia, the Kyrgyz Republic, Moldova, Tajikistan, Turkmenistan, and Uzbekistan (also referred to among *the late reformers*)
MENA	Middle East and North Africa
mid-CIS or CIS-mid	mid income CIS countries: Belarus, Kazakhstan, the Russian Federation, and Ukraine (also referred to among *the late reformers*)
NACE	Statistical Classification of Economic Activities in the European Community
OECD	Organisation for Economic Co-operation and Development
PCA	principal component analysis
PPP	purchasing power parity
R&D	research and development
RCA	revealed comparative advantage
SAP	South Asia and Pacific
SEE	Southeastern Europe: Albania, Bosnia and Herzegovina, Croatia, the former Yugoslav Republic of Macedonia, Serbia and Montenegro (now separate and independent) (also referred to among *the late reformers*)
TFP	total factor productivity
UN	United Nations
UNCTAD	UN Conference on Trade and Development
UNIDO	UN Industrial Development Organization

Note: All dollar amounts are U.S. dollars ($) unless otherwise indicated.

Overview

Productivity isn't everything, but in the long run it is almost everything.
—Paul Krugman

Introduction

The countries of Eastern Europe and the Former Soviet Union (the Region, hereafter) experienced a productivity surge over 1999–2005 that drove up living standards and reduced poverty. Productivity growth is probably the single most important indicator of a country's economic progress. It is only through increases in productivity that firms may enjoy good prospects for higher profits so they may invest in new technologies, create jobs, and pay more in wages and dividends. The efficiency of labor and capital rose rapidly in the Region, especially in the middle-income countries of the Former Soviet Union (averaging 6 percent during 1999–2005). Output growth during this period was mainly driven by increased productivity, whereas the accumulation of labor and capital played a small role. The surge in productivity drove up living standards. The Region's real income per capita (in constant dollar equivalents of purchasing power parity [PPP]) rose from

US$5,903 in 1998 to US$8,411 in 2005, lifting about 50 million people out of poverty.

Part of the productivity gains derived from increased capacity utilization, especially in the Commonwealth of Independent States (CIS—Armenia, Azerbaijan, Belarus, Georgia, Kazakhstan, Kyrgyz Republic, Moldova, Russian Federation, Tajikistan, Turkmenistan, Ukraine, and Uzbekistan). After a deep fall in output in the early phase of the transition, output per capita recovered in many countries. As firms began using their excess labor and capital, which had become idle during the deep transitional recession, output increased, and this is captured in TFP estimates.

Part of the productivity gains also derived from major structural changes in the economies of the Region, as resources were progressively shifted to higher-productivity uses in response to changed economic and institutional incentives. The transition to a market economy involved a substantial reallocation of factors (labor and capital) across sectors. Many workers moved out of manufacturing and into services, a sector that had been underdeveloped under central planning. In the low income CIS countries, however, labor shifted out of manufacturing into agriculture and there was little progress in the development of a modern service sector.[1]

But most of the productivity surge was driven by firm dynamics. From a microeconomic perspective, productivity growth may be decomposed into three main sources: productivity gains within existing firms, the reallocation of resources across existing firms, and firm turnover (the entry of new, more-productive firms and the exit of obsolete firms). Faced with radical changes in the Region's economies, firms were forced to adapt their behavior. Some seized new opportunities, occupying new market niches that had not been available during central planning. Many obsolete firms that were supported by state subsidies were restructured or closed down. Firms that survived managed to enhance productivity by investing in worker skills and adopting new technologies, abandoning old production lines and introducing new ones, producing new products, and accessing new markets.

Domestic reforms and external factors contributed to the productivity surge. Macroeconomic stability, a better governance and business environment, stronger competition, skill development, financial deepening, and investments in infrastructure, particularly in information and communication technology (ICT), were key drivers of productivity growth. Globalizing factors also contributed to the increase in productivity, especially in the new European Union (EU) member states (the EU-10: Bulgaria, the Czech Republic, Estonia, Hungary, Latvia, Lithuania, Poland, Romania, the Slovak Republic, and Slovenia). In these countries, trade and foreign investment played a significant role in productivity growth by stimulating technological transfers and innovation.

Notwithstanding the recent gains, significant challenges remain in sustaining productivity growth. This is especially evident in the wide disparities in annual per capita income in the Region, ranging from US$950 in Tajikistan to US$17,991 in Slovenia over 1999–2005 (international US$), as well as the disparities in income per capita between the early reformers—the EU-10—and the EU-15 (Austria, Belgium, Denmark, Finland, France, Germany, Greece, Ireland, Italy, Luxembourg, the Netherlands, Portugal, Spain, Sweden, and the United Kingdom, see figure 1). Narrowing these income gaps calls for more rapid productivity growth.

But the room for more rapid productivity growth may be constrained by the limited ability of firms to adopt new technologies (driven by deficiencies in the education system, labor market rigidities, skill shortages, weak private sector involvement in research and development (R&D), and shallow financial markets), the out-migration of labor, and declining populations in many countries (World Bank forthcoming). In addition, while investment rates are comparable with those in advanced market economies, the countries of the Region lag in the quality of infrastructure. New vintages of capital are needed to expand the Region's technological frontier. Policy shortcomings—particularly with respect to macroeconomic management (to cope with volatility, real exchange appreciation, and

FIGURE 1

A Large Income Gap Divides the Region, Which Also Lags Behind the EU-15, 1999–2005

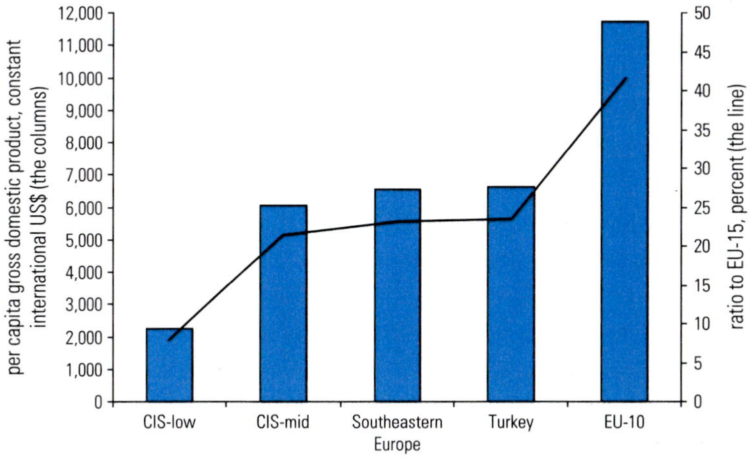

Sources: World Bank staff calculations; World Development Indicators Database 2007.

inflationary pressures), the weak investment climate, and the inadequacy of social safety nets to protect and train workers adversely affected by firm restructuring and closures—may also limit the ability of policy makers to sustain productivity growth.

Addressing these challenges will require sustained, even accelerated policy and institutional reforms. The heterogeneity of the Region means that the specific mix of policy reforms needed to sustain productivity growth varies across countries. This report argues that, for the late reformers (most of Southeastern Europe [SEE: Albania, Bosnia and Herzegovina, Croatia, the former Yugoslav Republic of Macedonia, Serbia and Montenegro (now separate and independent)] and the CIS), policy reforms aimed at accelerating reallocation are a top priority, whereas, for the early reformers (most of the EU-10, plus Turkey), policy reforms aimed at improving the ability of firms to innovate and compete in global markets are a top priority. Though reform priorities vary significantly even within the two broad groups of countries, the evidence is clear: the intensity and speed of reforms matter for productivity growth.

Measuring productivity growth is difficult. The measure most commonly used is labor productivity because it is easy to calculate and interpret. It captures how much output is produced, on average, by each unit of labor employed in production. Labor productivity growth thus gauges the increase in the amount (or value) of output generated per worker. Another measure is total factor productivity (TFP) growth, which refers to increases in output not attributable to increases in labor or capital inputs. TFP growth captures efficiency gains from the technological progress embodied in firm-level improvements, such as better production management methods, better customer support, and better distribution channels for the delivery of goods and services. Both labor and TFP growth may be estimated for the economy as a whole, for a sector of the economy, or for an individual firm.

This report integrates an impressive array of data sets to assess the macro, sectoral, and micro underpinnings of productivity growth in the Region. It builds on aggregate estimates of productivity comparable across countries and over time. It then explores industry and firm-level heterogeneity to understand more clearly the roots of observed aggregate economic performance. Its creative use of new firm-level data sets provides fresh insights into the policy and microeconomic foundations of growth in the Region. The new data include corporate financial data on more than 60,000 firms in 14 countries of the Region (the Amadeus Database) and a harmonized firm-level database drawing on a manufacturing census for 8 countries.[2] These microeconomic data sets permit productivity dynamics to be studied through a decomposition of aggregate productivity growth into the reallocation of labor across firms, firm turnover, and internal firm efficiency. They also permit the evolution of firm demographics to be examined over time, such as firm survival rates, average firm size among entering firms, and the rates of the creation and destruction of firms and jobs. Other data derived from international reviews of policy reforms (the Doing Business Database, the Economic Freedom of the World Database, the European Bank for Reconstruction and Development [EBRD] transition indicators) and from enterprise surveys (the Business Environment and Enterprise Performance Survey [BEEPS] Database) shed light on the policy and regulatory constraints to reallocation and firm productivity growth.

The analysis in this report exploits these data to answer the following questions:

- *What can we learn from the productivity patterns in the Region?* What are the roles of capital accumulation and labor participation and the combined efficiency of these factors in driving output growth?
- *What are the sources of productivity growth in the Region?* How important has the reallocation of resources across and within sectors been in explaining the productivity surge in the Region?
- *Is the transition process over in some countries?* Are countries still struggling to restructure their economies?
- *What is the role of policy reforms in productivity growth?* How do policy drivers influence the pace of reallocation and firm productivity growth? What are the remaining barriers to sustained productivity growth? Which policy reforms will be needed to sustain productivity growth?

The Region shows great diversity in productivity performance and progress in reform (figure 2). Two broad groups of countries emerge from the analysis: the more productive, early reformers (the EU-10 and Turkey) and the less productive, late reformers (most of the CIS and the SEE). The main challenge in the EU-10 and Turkey is to boost innovation to compete successfully in global markets, while the primary challenge in the CIS and SEE is to accelerate reallocation to address the legacy of the transition.

The more-productive early reformers: the EU-10 and Turkey. The EU-10 recovered earlier from the initial economic collapse and pursued deep and pervasive structural reforms. Most of these countries display higher productivity levels and are now well-functioning market economies. In these early reformers, the role of firm turnover and

FIGURE 2

Productivity and Progress in Reform in the Region

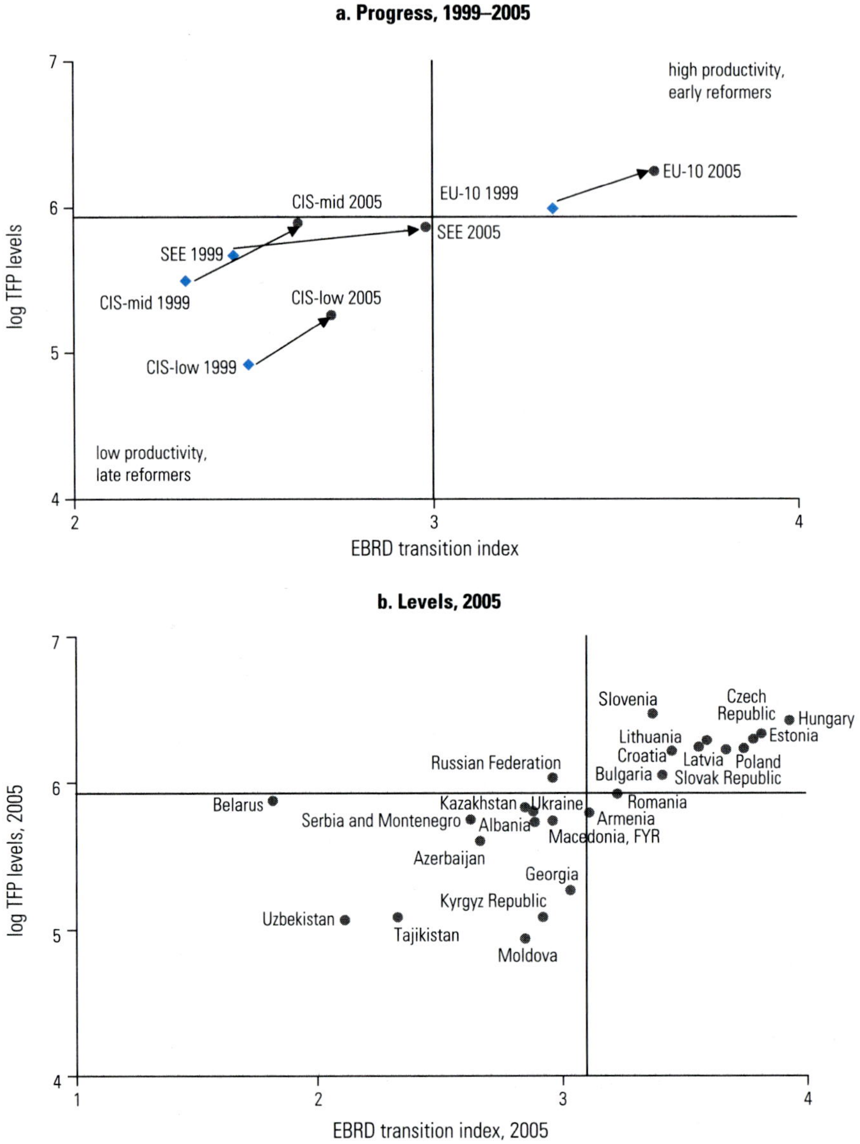

Sources: EBRD 2006; Amadeus Database 2006.

reallocation in productivity growth has declined. The productivity surge is now mainly driven by firm efficiency gains stemming from technological innovation, robust competition, and the penetration of new export markets. After more than a decade of sustained policy reforms, resources have shifted from lower- to higher-productivity uses. Existing firms have been restructured, shed excess labor, and acquired foreign technologies. New productive firms have emerged, and obsolete firms have closed down. Turkey, the only nontransition country in the Region, is in a group by itself, but it reflects many of the productivity trends shown by the EU-10. Since the 2001 financial crisis, Turkey has been going through its own economic transformation and has undertaken bold reforms to stimulate productivity growth and integrate with the global economy. As in the EU-10, domestic and import competition, export penetration in new markets, and innovation have spurred increases in firm efficiency.

The less-productive late reformers: SEE, CIS-mid, and CIS-low. These countries show lower levels of productivity; most of them undertook reforms in the late 1990s and are still dealing with the substantial misallocation of resources inherited from central planning. Among the late reformers, the contributions of firm turnover and reallocation to productivity growth are increasing. Firm efficiency is also playing an important role in aggregate productivity growth, but is mainly driven by transitory factors, especially the utilization of excess capacity and labor shedding. Most CIS and SEE countries continue to face significant resource misallocation and are still some way from the end of the transition. Rapid productivity gains were fairly easy to achieve during the first years of recovery from the deep transitional recession. The scope for productivity-enhancing reallocation was then large. In addition, firms in these countries were so far from the technology frontier that the acquisition of foreign machinery and equipment, combined with favorable terms of trade and the utilization of excess capacity, made extremely large productivity gains possible within a short time. Sustained and strong productivity growth over the longer term will prove more difficult as excess capacity is used up. Recent efforts to promote privatization and firm restructuring are steps in the right direction.

Three central messages emerge from our analysis:

- *For some countries in the Region, recognizing that the transition is over is now important.* As markets develop and resources are allowed to flow to more productive uses, the legacy of transition progressively weakens. This is reflected in the productivity patterns in countries. In most of the EU-10, the contributions of reallocation and firm turnover to aggregate productivity growth have declined. Productivity is mainly driven by efficiency gains within individual firms. The productivity patterns in these countries resemble those of advanced market economies. This is not to suggest that differences in productivity across firms disappear altogether as countries move out of transition. These differences will always exist as a result of technological innovation, the penetration of new export markets, and other factors. But the drivers of firm productivity growth will no longer be specific to the transition. Reallocation and firm turnover will continue to play a role, but they will tend to be associated with the business cycle as in advanced market economies.

- *Accelerating reallocation and removing barriers to firm entry and exit are top priorities among the late reformers in sustaining strong productivity growth.* In most of the CIS and SEE, but also in some EU-10 countries, such as Romania, the contributions of the reallocation of resources and of firm turnover (or net entry) to productivity growth are quite substantial; they are larger than those in advanced market economies. The fact that productivity dispersion across firms is still higher in these countries than in advanced market economies suggests that there is ample room for productivity gains derived from reallocation and firm turnover. But reallocation does not occur automatically. Its nature and speed depend on factor mobility, which, in turn, is affected by the policy environment. Trade openness may facilitate shifts of labor from agriculture toward higher-productivity activities in the manufacturing and service sectors. Greater access to finance may also promote the movement of labor toward industry and services by alleviating liquidity constraints in firms that are hiring. Investments in human capital and greater labor market flexibility may accelerate the reallocation process by increasing worker mobility. Such a set of policies, combined with streamlined regulations for start-ups to encourage the entry of new, more-productive firms and stronger product market competition to spur the exit of obsolete firms, may also contribute to sustaining productivity growth. These efforts to improve firm-level efficiency should be complemented by adequate social safety nets to help mitigate the short-term costs of reallocation among workers who are displaced or pushed out of the workforce.

- *Fostering innovation and international competitiveness is a top priority among early reformers in sustaining productivity growth.* Turkey and most of the EU-10 have achieved impressive results in economic liberalization, the privatization of state-owned enterprises, and opening up their economies to international trade and capital flows. But the integration of goods, services, and capital markets into the world economy is only a first step. Globalization calls for new forms of organization in production to compete in international markets. Innovation, a key driver of productivity growth, requires firms that are less vertically integrated, as well as greater integration into global production chains. It requires greater mobility within and across firms and more flexible labor markets. And it requires greater reliance on market finance and higher investment in R&D and in tertiary education. Innovation-led productivity growth thus calls for policies that increase private sector participation in R&D so as to support skill-based industries and move up the value chain in exports. It also calls for deeper financial sectors that are able to facilitate the financing of new capital. Service sector regulations that facilitate the entry of new players, particularly in services and network industries, will prove important in fostering innovation. Promoting greater competition in financial services and infrastructure-related services, such as telecommunications and transport, will also be important.

What Are the Patterns of Productivity Growth?

Although output, productivity, and prosperity have all risen significantly in the Region since 1999, large gaps remain among countries and sectors. Rapid productivity gains have driven economic growth and helped eliminate some disparities across the Region. But productivity still varies from country to country because of differences in production structures and firm strategies.

Productivity-Driven Output Growth Has Brought Unprecedented Prosperity

Across the Region, strong output growth since 1999 has reversed much of the economic decline that occurred during the early days of the transition. The transition started in the early 1990s with a dramatic recession; the deeper contractions occurred in the CIS and SEE (figure 3). Output declined in virtually all transition economies in the initial years. Output fell by about 15 percent in the EU-10 and by 35–40 percent in the CIS. The speed and extent of the economic recovery that followed varied widely across the Region. The EU-10 reached the nadir in 1993, while the CIS reached the nadir in 1998 when the financial crisis unfolded in the Russian Federation.

Brisk growth, particularly in the CIS, led to a rapid increase in living standards. By the end of 2005, the per capita gross domestic product (GDP) in the CIS was about 50 percent higher than it had been in 1998, though some of the countries had not yet reached pretransition income levels (figure 3). In the EU-10, GDP per capita was about 15 percent higher than the level in 1993. Annual income per capita in the Region, in constant PPP dollars, went from US$5,903 in 1998 to US$8,411 in 2005. By this measure, the Region is now richer than Latin America. This strong growth lifted about 50 million people out of absolute poverty (defined as US$2.15 a day in 2000 PPP dollars) within a population of over 400 million (figure 3).

Economic growth was mostly driven by productivity gains; TFP growth accounted for over 80 percent of total output growth in the Region over 1999–2005, much higher than other regions (figure 4).[3] In some countries, but particularly in the CIS, part of the productivity gains derived from the utilization of excess capacity, which is normal during a recovery. Since 1990, TFP growth has surged, particularly in the CIS (figure 5). This is mainly a reflection of the growth rebound in these countries from the deep contractions of the 1990s. In most of the EU-10, in contrast, productivity growth has been steady since the mid-1990s. These countries were early reformers and made the strongest strides in building the institutional foundations of a market economy, developing a vibrant private sector, and opening up to international trade and foreign finance.

However, the contribution of capital and labor accumulation to the Region's growth performance has been disappointing. The small role of capital stock accumulation and employment growth in the Region's growth performance contrasts with the experience of rapidly growing economies in East Asia, where factor accumulation is the main driver of output growth (figure 4). A similar message emerges from the

FIGURE 3

Gross Domestic Product Rose, and Poverty Fell Dramatically

a. Index of gross domestic product **b. Population by poverty status**

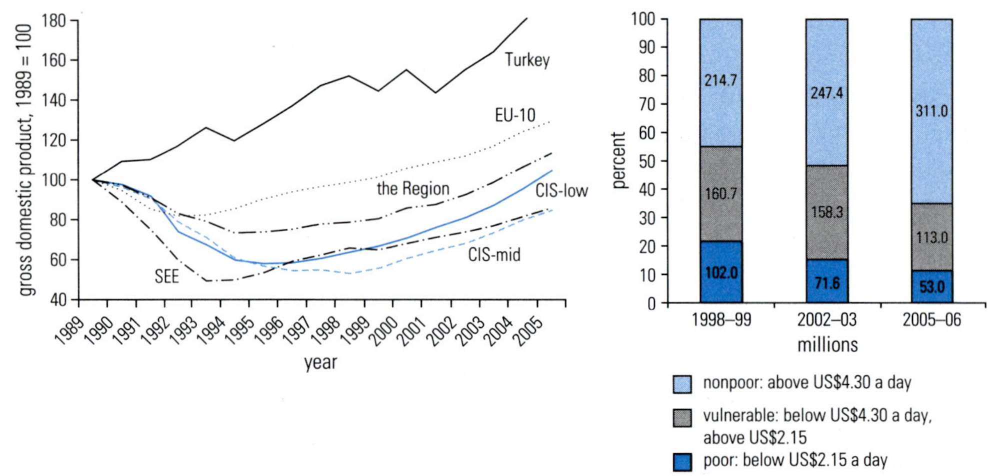

Sources: World Bank staff calculations; World Development Indicators Database 2007; household budget surveys; poverty lines in 2000 PPPs.

FIGURE 4
TFP, More Than Labor or Capital, Has Boosted Growth

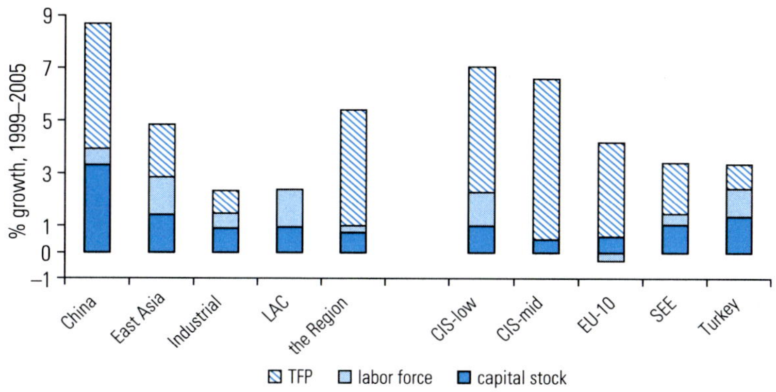

Source: World Bank staff calculations (see appendix 1A).

Note: CIS = Commonwealth of Independent States; EU = European Union; LAC = Latin America and the Caribbean; SEE = Southeastern Europe.

FIGURE 5
TFP Has Rebounded across the Region Since 1990

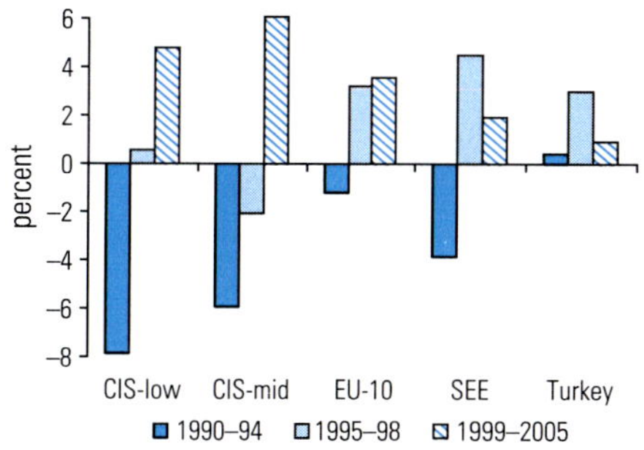

Source: World Bank staff calculations (see appendix 1A for data sources).

decomposition of the growth of GDP per capita. Growth in income per capita from 1999 to 2004, (figure 6) owes more to growth in labor productivity than to employment growth (the share of the working-age population to total population) or favorable demography (the employment share of the total population).

Labor supply and demand factors explain the small contribution of labor input to total output growth. A shrinking working-age population, out-migration, declines in labor participation, and high unemployment rates stifled labor supply, thereby contributing to disappointing labor outcomes. Indeed, the employment rate has continued to fall in many countries since 1998 (figure 7). While the employment rate is generally higher in the CIS (relative to the

FIGURE 6

Labor Productivity, More Than Employment or Population Growth, Raised per Capita Income, 1999–2004

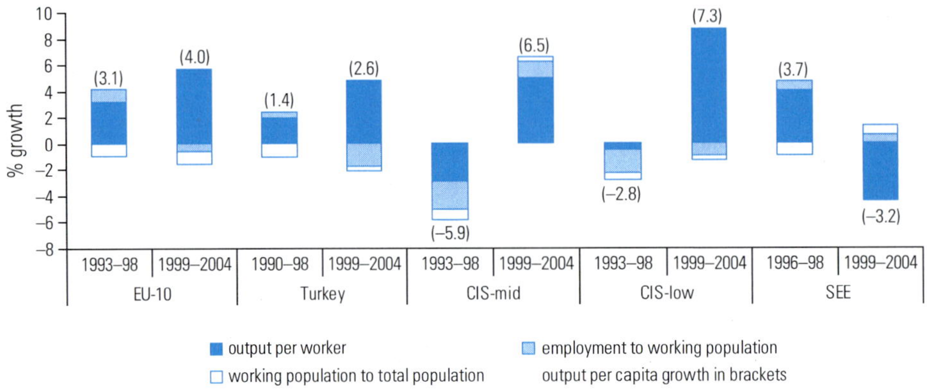

Source: World Bank staff calculations.

FIGURE 7

The Share of Workers in the Working-Age Population Has Fallen

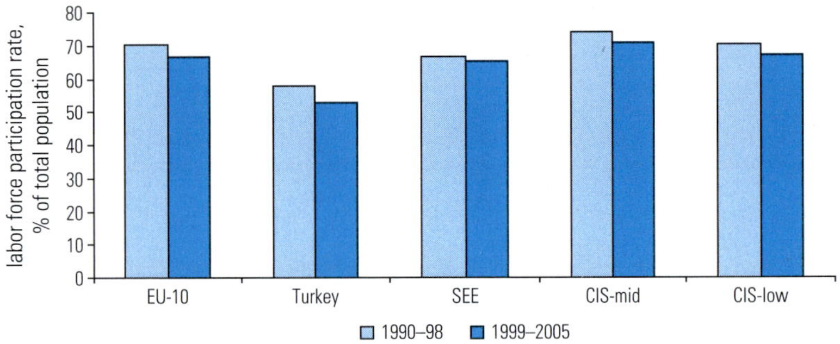

Sources: World Bank staff calculations; World Development Indicators Database 2007.

EU-10, where the rate is short of the Lisbon target of 70 percent), many jobs in the CIS are in low-productivity occupations. These constraints are compounded by deficiencies in the higher education system, which worsen skill mismatches, and rigidities in labor market regulations, which make it difficult for firms to hire workers and slow the pace of the reallocation of workers.

The small role of capital accumulation in the Region's growth partly reflects inefficiencies and low investments in new vintages of capital. In the context of a declining labor force, sustaining per capita income growth will depend on capital deepening (increasing the physical capital per worker) and on additional productivity gains. The small impact of capital accumulation on output growth, particularly in the CIS, also reflects adjustments in the corporate sector that have delayed new investments and led to the disposal of old capital stock. In the EU-10, investment rates have not been low, but depreciation rates are high, and infrastructure provision still lags considerably relative to the EU-15. Even more critical than the quantity of capital investments is the quality of the investments. The EU-10 countries have invested the most in ICT. The use and production of ICT have propelled labor productivity growth (figure 8).

A Substantial Gap in Productivity Remains across the Region

Despite the productivity surge, wide gaps in productivity still divide the Region. Productivity levels in the EU-10 in 2005 were more than twice those in poorer CIS countries (figure 9). Narrowing this gap in productivity calls for sustained productivity growth in these countries.

What Are the Sources of Productivity Growth?

The economic transition from central planning brought gains in efficiency throughout the Region. Many countries saw a dramatic shift of resources toward the service sector, which was underdeveloped under centralized regimes. This shift increased labor productivity in agriculture and manufacturing partly because of labor shedding. While these structural changes contributed to increased productivity growth, firm efficiency gains accounted for most of the surge in productivity and

FIGURE 8

Investments in ICT Contributed to Labor Productivity Growth, 1995–2004

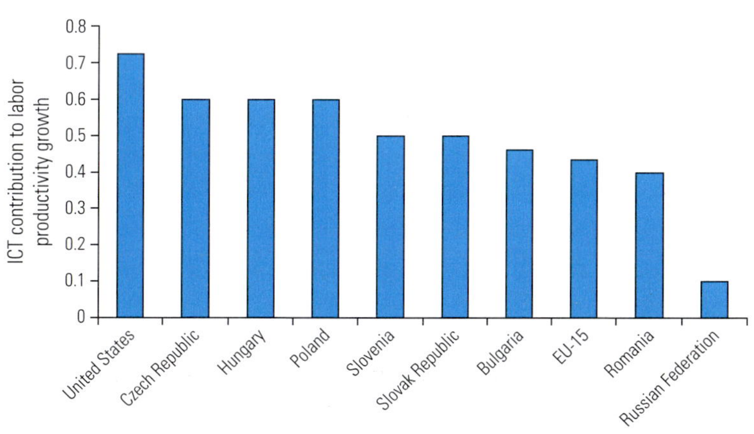

Source: Piatkowski and van Ark 2007.

FIGURE 9

TFP in the Poorest Countries in the Region Is Only Half the Level in the EU-10

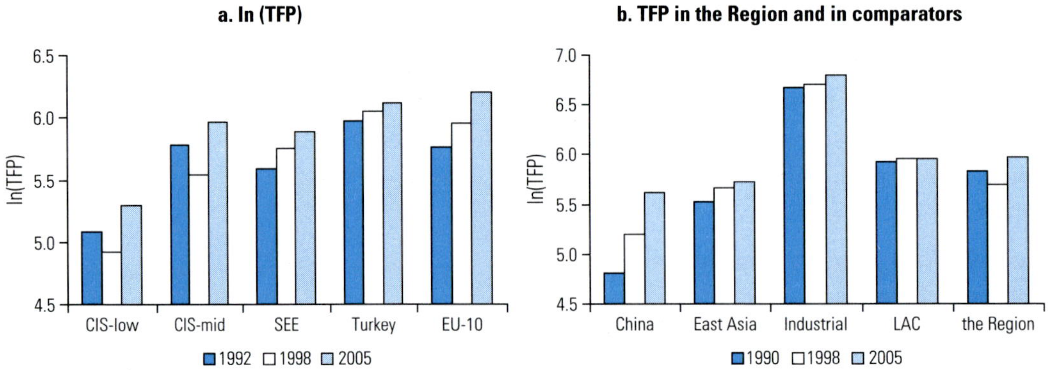

Source: World Bank staff calculations.

brought about a remarkable boost in job flows, although the net employment impact varied across countries, subregions, and industries.

The Reallocation of Resources toward Services Has Boosted Aggregate Productivity

There has been substantial resource reallocation toward services (figure 10). The economies of the Region faced significant challenges in resource allocation at the start of the transition because of serious structural distortions inherited from central planning, namely, an oversized manufacturing sector and an underdeveloped service sector. The service sector has grown relative to agriculture and industry across the Region. In the EU-10, the share of services in total value added rose dramatically, from 40 percent in 1999 to 60 percent in 2005. Labor also shifted toward services.

These sectoral shifts were related to the overindustrialization of the economies, especially in the CIS, although the magnitude of labor reallocation differed across countries. First, many workers moved out of manufacturing as industries adjusted to market forces. This is reflected in significant declines in the share of employment in industry, especially in the CIS, where it fell by around 13 percentage points. Second, workers shifted to market-based services in both the EU-10 and the CIS. At the beginning of the transition, these economies had small service sectors. These sectors grew in response to demand and increased their share in employment by around 16 and 9 percentage points in the EU-10 and the CIS, respectively, moving closer to the patterns observed in advanced market economies. Third, labor in the low income CIS countries shifted to agriculture, which increased its employment share by around 20 percentage points. This occurred because agriculture played the role of a social safety net and absorbed displaced labor from urban industries.

The broad shift to services drove up overall productivity levels. Since value added per worker is the lowest in agriculture and the highest in services in most countries (the exception is the CIS), the shift in employment away from agriculture and manufacturing into services raised labor productivity (figure 11).

FIGURE 10

The Share of Services in Value Added and Employment Has Risen

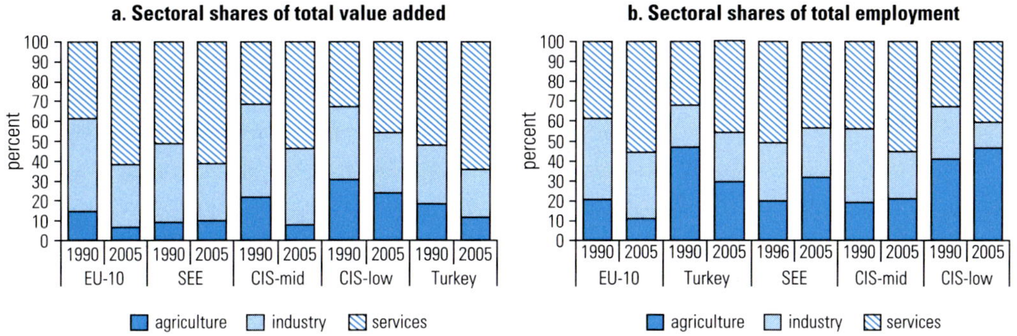

Sources: World Bank staff calculations; World Development Indicators Database 2007.

Note: Employment is proxied by labor force participation. The definition of services in the World Development Indicators Database includes government services and market services. The definition of industry covers manufacturing, construction, electricity, gas, and water.

FIGURE 11

Higher Value Added per Worker in Services Raised Overall Labor Productivity in Most Countries, 1999–2004

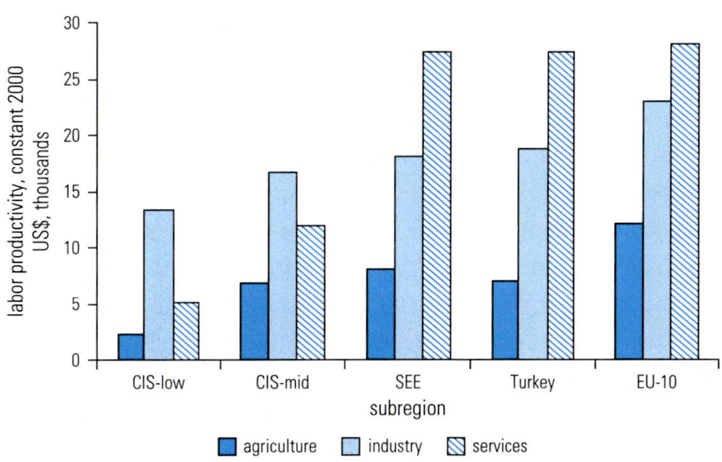

Sources: World Bank staff calculations; World Development Indicators Database 2007.

Efficiency Gains within Sectors Have Been More Important Than Cross-Sectoral Shifts

The sources of aggregate productivity growth may be divided into three components, as follows:

- The *within* effect captures the impact of productivity growth in individual sectors on aggregate productivity in the economy.
- The *between* effect captures the impact of the reallocation of employment across sectors. A positive between effect means that aggregate productivity rises because the sector displays higher than average productivity and labor is moving into the sector or because the sector has lower than average productivity and labor is leaving the sector.
- The *cross* effect captures the impact of the reallocation of employment into sectors exhibiting growing productivity. A positive cross effect means that aggregate productivity increases because employment has moved to sectors showing positive productivity growth (or out of sectors with negative productivity growth).

The sectoral reallocation effects have been substantial in the Region, but they tend to cancel each other out. Labor is generally moving to sectors with high productivity levels (services) and out of sectors with low productivity levels (agriculture). This is reflected in a positive between term. At the same time, labor is moving out of sectors with increasing productivity growth (agriculture, manufacturing) and into sectors with decreasing productivity growth (services). This is reflected in a negative cross term.

Productivity growth in manufacturing and agriculture exceeded productivity growth in services, although the patterns varied across countries. In Turkey and the SEE, agricultural productivity growth exceeded productivity growth in manufacturing and services (figure 12). In the EU-10, productivity grew more rapidly in manufacturing and agriculture than in services. Productivity growth in the CIS has been the highest in the Region, particularly more recently, and has followed a similar pattern across all three sectors, reflecting a broad-based economic recovery after the deep recession.

In agriculture, labor shedding seems to be the main driving force behind the strong productivity surge in the Region. In labor-intensive regions (typically in countries such as Albania, Armenia, Georgia, and the Kyrgyz Republic), a shift from large-scale collective farming to small-scale individual farming caused dramatic gains in technical efficiency, but relatively small losses in scale efficiency. In capital- and land-intensive regions (in countries such as the Czech Republic,

FIGURE 12

Labor Productivity Growth Was High, Particularly in the CIS, 1999–2004

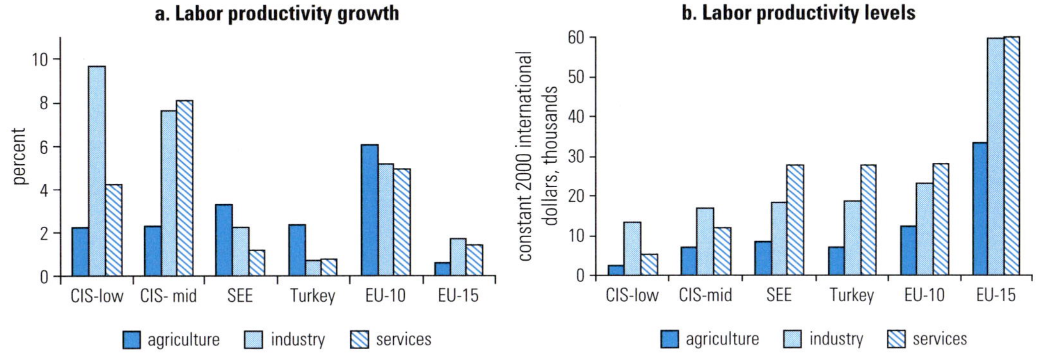

Sources: World Bank staff calculations; World Development Indicators Database 2007.

Hungary, and the Slovak Republic), gains in labor productivity arose primarily because large farms shed labor as they were privatized and because of intersectoral labor reallocation as workers moved away from agriculture to more rapidly growing industries in manufacturing and services. In countries in which neither type of reform was implemented vigorously, productivity gains were generally modest. During the first stage of transition, trade liberalization, the elimination of subsidies, price liberalization, and land reforms were required to accelerate farm restructuring and facilitate the sectoral reallocation of labor. As countries progress along the transition path, an improved investment climate and stronger competition in services are needed to improve within-farm productivity growth and provide off-farm job opportunities.

Productivity growth in manufacturing has been driven by efficiency gains in industries with higher capacity for innovation.[4] High-technology manufacturing industries led the productivity growth in the manufacturing sector, exhibiting the highest annual average productivity growth rates. This group of manufacturing industries employs a large share of highly skilled workers, produces ICT goods, or uses a relatively large amount of ICT capital. The high-technology group includes manufacturers of office machinery, electrical and electronic equipment, and optical instruments. Low-technology manufacturing industries, such as traditional consumer goods manufacturing, posted a lower average productivity growth. Not surprisingly, high-technology industries display higher TFP growth in countries showing more progress in the liberalization of key service industries, deeper financial markets, a more highly skilled workforce, more flexible labor markets, and more R&D investments by the private sector.

Productivity growth in services has been driven by backbone industries such as transport, telecommunications, and financial intermediation. These industries have shown higher productivity levels and a greater propensity to use or produce ICT such as retail trade, transport, telecommunications, and financial intermediation services. The productivity growth in these sectors during 1997–2004 surpassed the average productivity growth achieved among the EU-15. Nevertheless, a substantial gap remains in productivity levels.

The strong performance of these service industries suggests that there is a potential for growth driven by services. The efficiency of backbone services is crucial to the productivity of other sectors in the economy and for integration into global markets. It also enables firms to participate in the global fragmentation of the production of services, which leads to increased service exports.

The potential gains will not be achieved automatically, however. The penetration and efficient use of ICT in services are still limited. Investments in ICT in services will bring about large productivity gains. Policy makers in the Region can play a major role in sustaining the momentum of growth in the service sector by pursuing service liberalization across the board, removing regulatory barriers that limit competition in various service industries, and attracting more foreign direct investment (FDI) and greater trade flows.

Firm Dynamics Contributed to Productivity Growth More Than Sectoral Changes Did

The analysis of cross-sectoral shifts hides substantial firm dynamism within industries. The reallocation of workers and firms from less-productive activities to more-productive activities is important in promoting productivity growth in any market economy, but it assumed a greater role in transition economies because of the highly distorted industrial structures inherited from central planning. Faced with the radical transformation of the economy, firms in all countries were forced to adapt their behavior. Some firms increased productivity through *defensive* restructuring (labor shedding), while others did so through *strategic* restructuring (the adoption of new technologies). New firms entered the market, occupied emerging niches and displaced obsolete firms that had been forced to exit the market.

Evidence at the firm level reveals how individual enterprises managed to reallocate resources, improve efficiency, and enter or exit business operations. It also sheds light on the obstacles that firms face in these tasks. Drawing on firm-level data, one may decompose aggregate productivity growth into three main components, as follows:

- The *within* component accounts for the productivity growth taking place within firms.
- The *reallocation* component captures the productivity gains derived from the reallocation of labor across firms. It is the sum of two terms: between and cross. The between component reflects gains that arise as high-productivity firms acquire greater market share or as low-productivity firms lose market share. The cross component reflects increases in aggregate productivity that arise as firms showing high productivity growth gain market share (or as firms showing low productivity growth lose market share).
- The *net entry* component (also known as firm turnover or firm churning) reflects the productivity gains resulting from the creation of new, more productive firms and the exit of obsolete firms. This component is calculated as the sum of two terms: firm entry and firm exit.

This decomposition of labor manufacturing productivity growth draws on empirical work carried out by Bartelsman and Scarpetta (2007) and Brown and Earle (2007). Their findings suggest the following:[5]

- *Productivity gains within existing firms account for the bulk of productivity growth, especially in early reformers.* In some early reformers, within-firm productivity growth accounts for more than 80 percent of total manufacturing productivity growth. In late reformers, it accounts for between 30 and 60 percent of overall manufacturing productivity growth.
- *The reallocation of labor across existing firms plays a significant role in productivity growth, especially in late reformers.* Reallocation rates are particularly large in countries that are still addressing the resource misallocations inherited from central planning. Reallocation amounts to 15–20 percent of total manufacturing productivity growth in early reformers, but may account for up to 70 percent of total manufacturing productivity growth in some late reformers. Reallocation rates are higher in the latter group of countries, ranging from 15 to 30 percentage points. In early reformers, reallocation rates are only about 6 percentage points. In late reformers, the cross term tends to be negative. This implies that firms experiencing an increase in productivity have also lost employment share (that is, the productivity growth of these firms

has been associated with restructuring and downsizing rather than expansion).

- *Firm churning is also an important driver of productivity growth in transition economies, especially among the late reformers.* Firm turnover is also an important driver of total productivity growth in advanced market economies, accounting for 20–50 percent of total productivity growth. In these countries, the exit effect is positive (that is, the least productive firms exit the market, thereby helping to raise the average productivity of firms that survive), whereas the entry term has tended to be negative.[6] In late reformers, in contrast, the entry term tends to be positive and contributes about 10 percent to aggregate manufacturing productivity growth.

Efficiency Gains within Firms Drive the Bulk of Productivity Growth

The bulk of productivity growth arises from efficiency gains within existing firms. This is axiomatic in regard to healthy market economies, but it is also true in transition economies. Nonetheless, firms improve their productivity in different ways, reflecting variations in the broader country business environment in which they operate. In late reformers, within-firm productivity growth is mostly driven by the utilization of excess capacity and by defensive restructuring (shedding labor and adopting other cost-cutting strategies). In Russia, the available survey data suggest that capacity utilization rates in manufacturing industries have increased appreciably since 1999. In contrast, in early reformers, firms improve their productivity through strategic restructuring, that is, by investing in new technologies and improving the value added content of products and exports. Figure 13 compares the contributions to manufacturing productivity growth (expressed in percentage points) in Hungary and Ukraine.

The available empirical evidence shows a great deal of firm heterogeneity. Firm manufacturing productivity patterns vary according to several factors, including location, firm size, ownership, and industry.

- *Location.* Firms located in rapidly reforming areas enjoy higher productivity growth than those located in laggard areas reforming slowly. This is the case in Ukraine. Similarly, firms located in areas with better transport infrastructure tend to exhibit higher productivity growth relative to firms located in areas with greater transport deficiencies.
- *Firm size.* Among large firms (250 or more employees), within-firm productivity gains are larger relative to small firms (less than

FIGURE 13
As Transition Proceeds, Productivity Growth Is Driven Mainly by Efficiency Gains within Firms

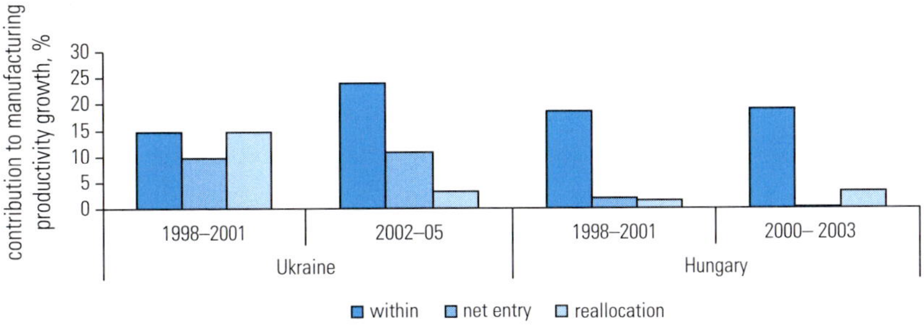

Source: Brown and Earle 2007.

50 employees) and medium firms (50 to 249 employees), although the reallocation effects are larger among small firms. Among large firms, the net entry contribution to total productivity growth is often negative.

- *Firm ownership.* In the new private sector (private firms established since the beginning of transition), manufacturing productivity growth is higher relative to the old private sector (firms established prior to the transition). Within-firm productivity growth is nearly twice as high in the new firms relative to the old firms in Hungary and Russia. In Russia and Ukraine, the reallocation effects are larger among the new firms relative to the old firms. There are also different productivity patterns among state-owned firms and private firms. Reallocation tends to contribute more to productivity growth among private firms relative to state-owned firms. This is the case in Hungary and Romania. However, in Russia and Ukraine, private firms are still less productive, on average, than state-owned firms. The contribution of the reallocation of resources among incumbent firms is also much greater among private firms in Hungary and Romania than among private firms in Russia and Ukraine. These differences are related to the modes of privatization and the degree of market competition (see the next section). Foreign-owned firms tend to show higher productivity growth than domestic private or state firms, except in Russia. The large productivity growth enjoyed by foreign firms is driven mainly by within-firm productivity growth.
- *Industry.* Firms operating in ICT-related industries display higher productivity growth. Firms operating in ICT-related industries rely on strategic restructuring, thereby improving their productivity by

adopting new and better ways to produce goods. In contrast, firms in non-ICT industries tend to engage in defensive restructuring to increase productivity, mostly by shedding labor. Overall, firms in non-ICT industries tend to show lower productivity growth than firms operating in ICT industries. Firm entry also plays an important role in boosting productivity in ICT-related industries, whereas the contribution of new firms to productivity growth is negative in non-ICT industries. This is particularly the case in the early reformers, where a large number of new firms emerged in industries with greater opportunities for innovation. The better performance of companies operating in ICT-intensive sectors may be considered evidence of the presence of technological spillovers. If a firm operates in a high-technology environment, it is more likely to absorb new developments quickly and to boost productivity more extensively. Similarly, firms in industries that depend on external financing tend to enjoy higher productivity growth, particularly in countries with deeper financial markets. In late reformers, there is also a productivity growth gap between industries that are highly reliant on external financing and those that depend little on external financing, although the gap is similar across countries.

Firm Churning Contributes to Productivity Growth

The process of creative destruction, whereby a significant number of businesses start up or close their operations, encourages firms to experiment and learn. It rewards success, and it punishes failure. Healthy market economies exhibit fairly high rates of firm entry and exit; from 5 to 20 percent of firms enter or exit the market every year. In the Region, about 20 percent of firms have been created or destroyed during the past decade (figure 14).

Firm turnover is an important driver of productivity growth in transition economies, especially in late reformers. In early reformers at the start of the transition, the contribution of net entry was large and accounted for between 20 and 40 percent of total productivity growth. Over time, the relative contribution of net entry declined and converged to levels similar to those observed in advanced market economies. In late reformers, the contribution of firm churning to total productivity growth is still substantial and has been increasing in recent years. In Russia, net entry accounted for over 17 percent of total manufacturing productivity growth in 1998–2001 and increased to 46 percent in 2001–04. In most late reformers, where low-productivity firms—because they are sheltered from competitive pressures—have managed to contain job destruction, the effect of firm entry also tends to be larger

FIGURE 14
Business Start-Ups Have Exceeded Business Exits in Most Countries

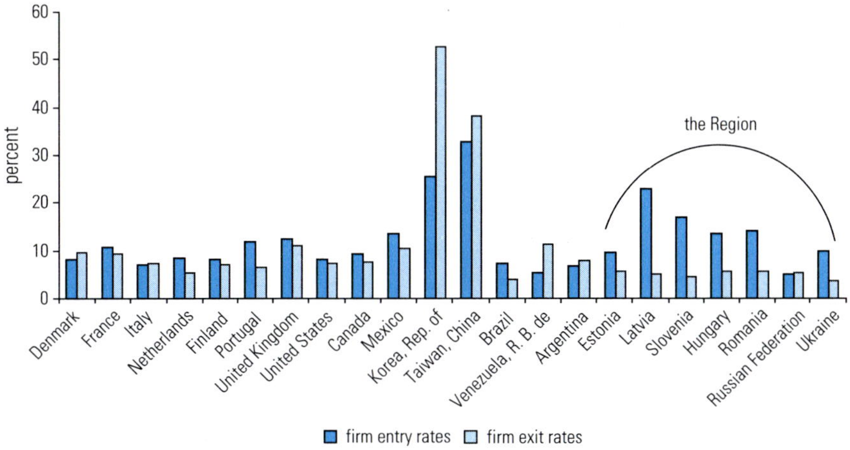

Sources: Bartelsman and Scarpetta 2007; Brown and Earle 2007.

than the effect of firm exit. This suggests that entering firms may still have to undergo downsizing and restructuring.

The size and timing of firm churning vary across countries. In Hungary, at the onset of the transition, a large share of firms closed down and were replaced by new, small ventures, largely as a response to privatization reforms (figure 15). Over time, net firm flows declined to values fairly close to those observed in advanced market economies. In late reformers, such as Russia, firm turnover flows were remarkably low, and, during the second half of the 1990s, firm exit rates exceeded firm entry rates. After the 1998 crisis, this trend was reversed, and the number of new firms exceeded the number of firms that disappeared. The size of firm churning also varies across industries. Firm turnover rates (especially if they are weighted by employment) are higher in service industries (especially in trade) than in manufacturing industries. However, in most countries, some high-technology industries experiencing rapid technological change and market experimentation showed relatively high entry rates in the 1990s (for example, office computing and office equipment, as well as radio, television, and communications).

The productivity performance of entrants relative to incumbents varies across countries:

- *Entrants tend to show higher productivity than incumbents* in countries where reforms are lagging, while, in early reformers, the relative productivity is lower among entrants than among incumbents, though it tends to rise among entrants as they age. In Hungary and

FIGURE 15

Hungary's Reforms Led to Increased Firm Entry, While the 1998 Crisis Prompted Firm Exit in the Russian Federation

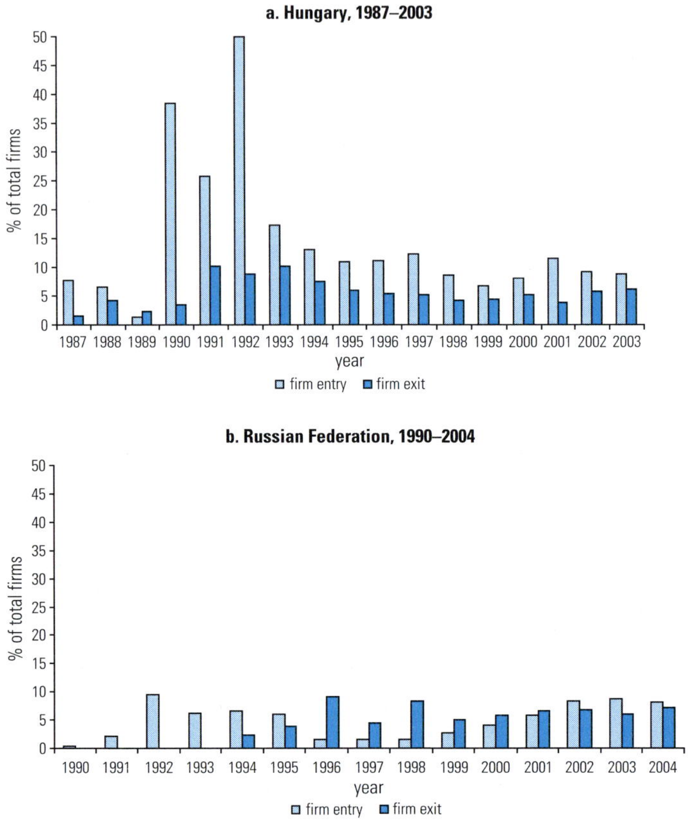

Source: Brown and Earle 2007.

Note: Firm flow data in the early years of the transition may be affected by data quality issues.

Romania, entrants are less productive than the average incumbent, which might signal that they are experimenting more. This pattern is similar to the one observed in the Organisation for Economic Co-operation and Development (OECD), where entrants often lack experience, and small size often makes new firms less productive. In contrast, in Georgia, Russia, and Ukraine, entrants are (on average) more productive than incumbents. They have been able to fill niches, mostly in market services, that were underdeveloped or nonexistent during central planning (figure 16).

- *Entrants tend to be small relative to incumbents in most countries.* Under the centrally planned system, there were relatively few small firms, but, during the transition, the number of small firms shot up, particularly in business service activities. At the same time, many of the entrants that failed during the initial years were also relatively small.

FIGURE 16

In Slovenia, the Largest Manufacturing Firms Have Shrunk, While in Mexico, They Have Expanded

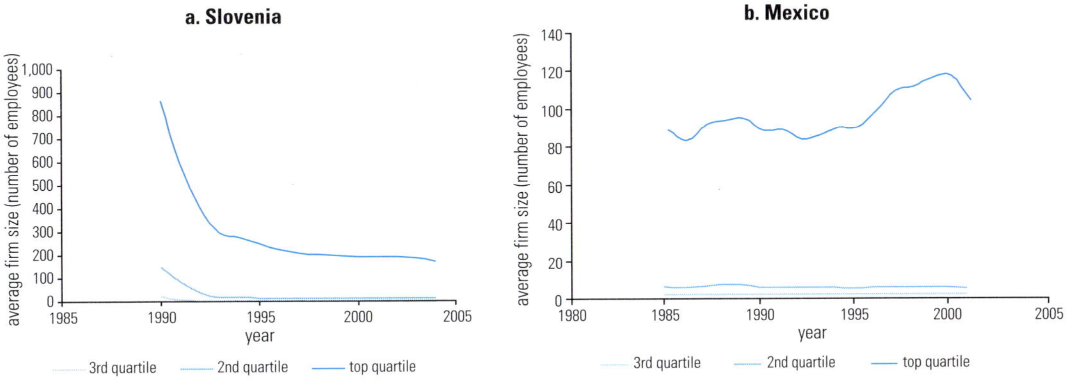

Source: Bartelsman and Scarpetta 2007.

- *Entrants tended to exhibit high survival rates at the beginning of the transition.* An understanding of post-entry performance sheds light on the market selection process, which separates successful entrant firms that survive and prosper from entrant firms that stagnate and eventually exit. Survival rates after entry are higher in Russia and Ukraine. In Estonia, Latvia, and Slovenia, but also in Romania and Hungary, around 70 percent of entering firms survive at least four years. In contrast, in Mexico, firm survival rates are much lower, pointing to harsher market selection or higher variance in the quality of entrants. It may also be that entrants in the transition economies were actually restructured firms that reentered the market with employees who possessed experience and with established connections with customers and suppliers. Such an advantage is likely to diminish over time (figure 17).
- *As countries progress along the transition path, the market becomes harsher and the survival rate of entrants drops.* Entrants show rapidly declining probabilities of survival (especially in Russia, where less than 10 percent of entrants are still in business after seven years). In Hungary, 25 percent of entrant firms are no longer active in the market after two years; the figure is 50 percent after five years, and, after seven years, about 70 percent of new firms have exited. Failure rates among young businesses are high in all market economies, but, in industrial countries, about 50–60 percent of new firms are still in business after seven years. In the Baltic states (Estonia, Latvia, and Lithuania), entrants face an environment that is slightly less harsh than the environment in the EU; about

FIGURE 17

Entrants' Survival Rates Are Higher in the Region Than in Advanced Economies

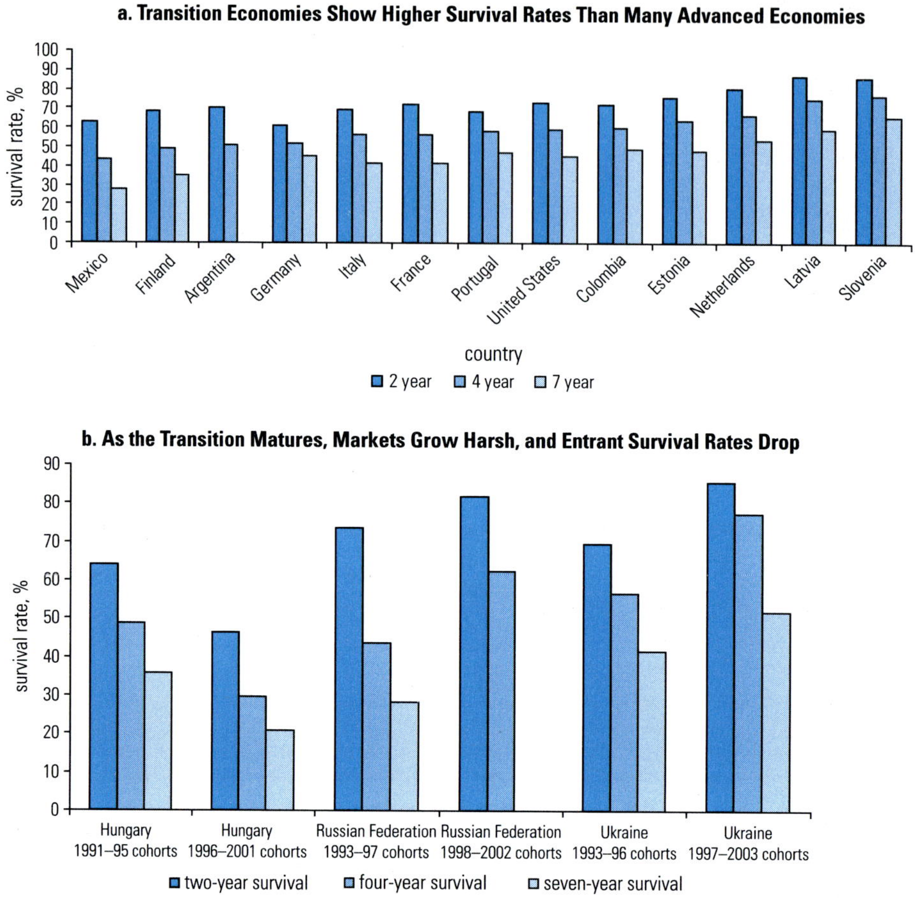

Source: Brown and Earle 2007.

70 percent of entrants survive at least four years, and 50–60 percent survive at least seven years.

- *Successful entrants that exhibited higher initial productivity tend to create more jobs.* The probability of employment growth is strongly associated with a firm's initial productivity performance. In many countries in the Region, the most productive entrants provided the most stable employment over the first three years of firm operations (figure 18).

- *But, even successful entrants have not expanded significantly in the Region; this is especially true of large firms in manufacturing.* At the start of the transition, firms in Estonia, Latvia, and Slovenia exhibited substantial declines in size, especially in manufacturing. The largest

FIGURE 18

Entrants with Higher Labor Productivity Are More Successful at Maintaining the Workforce

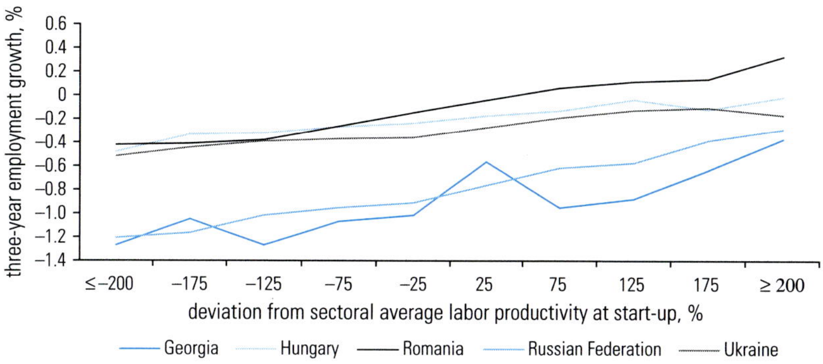

Source: Brown and Earle 2007.

quartile of firms in manufacturing was particularly affected. In Slovenia, the average size among firms in the largest quartile had dropped from more than 800 to 200 employees by the early 2000s. In the Baltic states, no sign of an increase in firm size has been apparent. Indeed, the size of the largest firms in Estonia, Latvia, and Slovenia declined during the transition. The question remains whether firms in these countries are able to benefit fully from the opportunities of economic integration into the EU and an enlarged market. The lack of growth in large manufacturing firms contrasts with the case of Mexico. In Mexico, there has been a rapid expansion in the mean size of manufacturing firms in the largest quartile from 80 to 120 employees per firm (figure 16), and the average size of the largest firms grew rapidly during the first years following the adoption of the North American Free Trade Agreement.

Resource Reallocation across Existing Firms Contributes to Productivity Growth

The reallocation of labor across existing firms also contributed to productivity growth, and its role was particularly large at the start of the transition. In countries at the early stages of transition, the between term tended to be large and positive, indicating that firms with higher than average productivity levels were gaining market share. At the same time, the contribution to total productivity growth of the cross term (shifts of resources toward firms with higher than average productivity growth) is negative. This suggests that firms experiencing an increase in productivity were also losing employment shares, that is, their productivity growth was associated with restructuring and downsizing rather than with expansion.

The rapid pace of restructuring in transition economies is not evidence of the competitive conditions observed in healthy market economies. The pace of entry and exit and the contribution of reallocation to productivity in mature economies point to an ongoing, steady-state process that exerts pressure on incumbents to perform well. In late reformers, which are not so far along in the transition process, reallocation is less an indicator of the overall state of competitiveness of the market and more a reflection of a major change in the supply side of the economy. In early reformers, the pattern is different. Once the net entry rate has become settled, a lack of correlation between the net entry component of growth and incumbent growth may be more indicative of problems in competition.

As the transition matures, the role of reallocation and firm turnover in aggregate productivity growth declines, converging toward the patterns observed in advanced market economies. Not surprisingly, the contributions of reallocation and net entry (or firm churning) to overall productivity growth decrease as countries move along the transition path. After the major distortions inherited from the central planning period have been addressed and after the pre-transition void in certain activities has been filled, productivity decompositions in advanced reformers tend to converge toward those observed in advanced market economies (figure 19).

Reallocation, Firm Turnover, and Within-Firm Productivity Growth Reinforce Each Other

The analysis above focuses on the direct contributions of firm productivity gains within existing firms, labor reallocation across existing

FIGURE 19

The Role of Reallocation and Firm Turnover in Productivity Growth in Early Reformers Is Now Similar to That in Advanced Market Economies

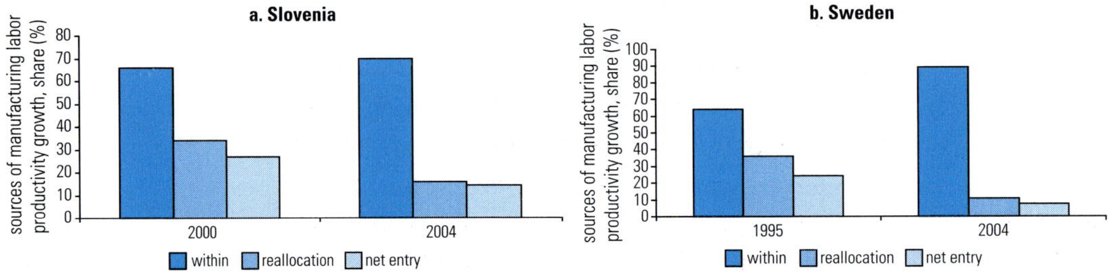

Sources: Bartelsman and Scarpetta 2007; Brown and Earle 2007.

firms, and firm churning to overall productivity growth. The contributions of labor reallocation and firm turnover are often interpreted in the literature as a reflection of a process of creative destruction, while the within-firm contribution is interpreted as a reflection of more traditional sources of productivity growth (the average firm becomes more productive with advancing technology). But, rather than alternatives, these effects (within-firm productivity growth, labor reallocations, and firm churning) may be closely related. A stronger pace in firm creation and destruction may also influence the decisions of domestic firms about efficiency-enhancing investments. The entry of productive firms may increase the contestability of the market, forcing some firms to exit, but also raising the pressure on incumbents to perform more effectively.

Notwithstanding the observed decline in the role of labor reallocation and firm turnover among early reformers, the process of creative destruction is still active in the Region. Among the early reformers, the transition is over, but the Schumpeterian process of creative destruction is not. The large contributions of reallocation across sectors and firm turnover have now declined to the levels observed in advanced market economies. But this does not mean that reallocation and firm turnover will be unimportant for productivity growth. In advanced market economies, these factors tend to be correlated with the business cycle, and this is likely to be the case in the early reformers as well. The fact that productivity dispersion in the Region is still greater than it is in the United States suggests that there is plenty of room in the Region for significant productivity growth via reallocation and firm turnover.

While, in advanced market economies, new entrants exert pressure on incumbents to perform more efficiently, this is not the case in the Region. This is so for the following reasons:

- In advanced market economies, the greater competitive pressure exerted by entrants induces incumbents to perform more efficiently. In the OECD, there is a strong, positive, and statistically significant correlation between the contribution of net entry and the productivity growth of incumbents (Bartelsman and Scarpetta 2007). There is also evidence that sectors with many entrants push incumbents in these sectors to increase their productivity. But, even in the OECD, the impact of entry on the productivity of incumbents varies across industries. Based on data on firms in the United Kingdom over 1987–93, a study by Aghion (2006) finds that the effect of entry on productivity growth is more positive in industries that are close to the technological frontier than in industries that are not close to the frontier.

- In the Region, firm churning does not exert pressure on incumbents to improve productivity. Particularly among late reformers, the relationship between the performance of incumbents and net entry is weaker (figure 20). The lack of pressure from new firms on incumbents reflects weaker market competition. It may also be partly caused by the high failure rates among new businesses.

Distortions in market structure and institutions also affect productivity growth. Allocative efficiency has improved in the Region, although it remains low by international standards. Early in the transition, resources were locked in lower-productivity firms, on average, but the allocation rapidly improved over time with the exit of poor firms and the movement of resources toward more-productive firms. But even early reformers—the EU 10—still display lower allocative efficiency than the EU-15 and the United States, suggesting that there is room for additional adjustments (figure 21).

Firm Dynamics Have Brought About a Remarkable Surge in Job Flows

At the beginning of the transition, gross and net firm flows were large relative to industrial and other emerging economies. Firm-level data on a sample of countries in the Region and a number of comparator countries provide insights on the size of firms and job dynamics. In modern economies, gross rates of job creation and destruction range between 5 and 20 percent, adding up to job turnover of up to 40 percent. A significant part of this job turnover (often 30–50 percent) is due to the entry and exit of firms. In the Region, job reallocation rates across

FIGURE 20

In Late Reformers, Firm Turnover Has Not Spurred Productivity Gains in Existing Firms

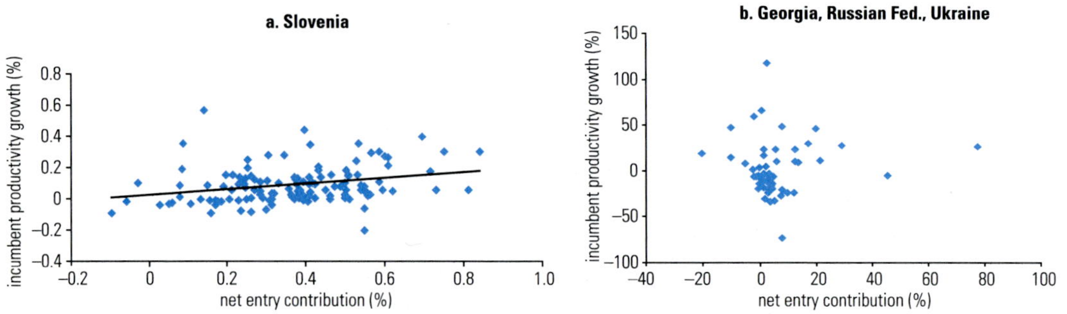

Sources: Bartelsman and Scarpetta 2007; Brown and Earle 2007.

FIGURE 21

Allocative Efficiency Remains Low in the Region

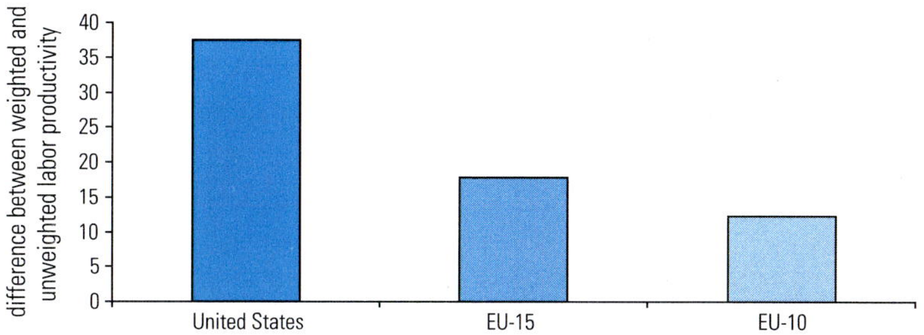

Source: Bartelsman and Scarpetta 2007.

Note: The figure shows the average Olley-Pakes cross term in manufacturing.

firms surged rapidly in response to transition. Job reallocation (the sum of job creation and destruction) increased dramatically, from less than 10 percent of the workforce before the transition to about 20 percent in the 1990s. As the transition moved forward, net firm flows declined and, at the end of the 1990s, had reached values fairly close to those observed in other countries.

Firm turnover contributed substantially to overall job creation during the earlier stages of the transition, but the contribution declined over time. Firm entry outpaced firm exit at the start of the transition, contributing significantly to job creation (25 to 50 percent). New firms not only displaced obsolete incumbents during the transition phase, but also filled markets that had previously been either nonexistent or poorly populated. After firms had filled these pretransition voids, job creation arose increasingly from the expansion of surviving firms.

The contribution of firm exit to job destruction followed different trends across countries. In the OECD, firm exit is strongly correlated with job destruction. This is not the case in the Region, particularly among the late reformers. In these countries, the share of job destruction by continuing firms is much larger than the share of job destruction resulting from firm exit (figure 22). These patterns confirm earlier findings that existing firms in late-reforming countries resorted to defensive restructuring to improve productivity by downsizing and shedding redundant labor.

In countries where job flows were not synchronized, job creation lagged behind job destruction. Job destruction generally surged first, but the response of job creation varied across countries; it caught up rapidly with job destruction in the leading reformers, but remained

FIGURE 22

Labor Shedding at Existing Firms Was the Main Source of Job Destruction

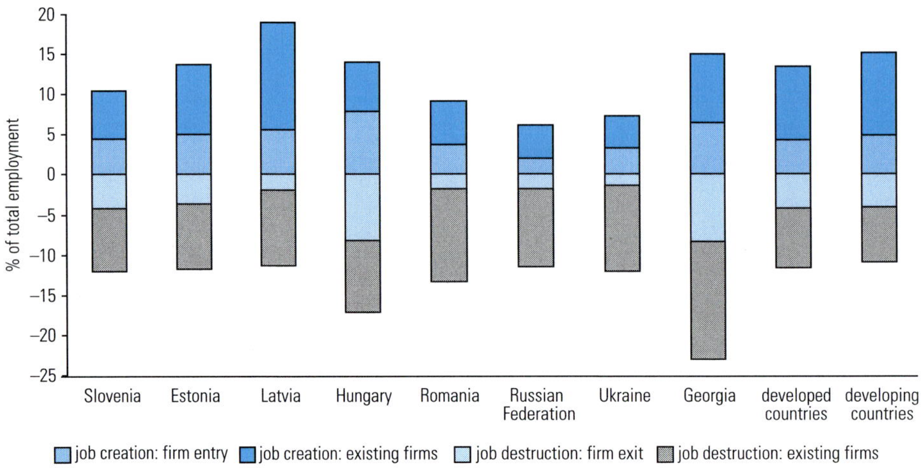

Sources: Bartelsman and Scarpetta 2007; Brown and Earle 2007.

less consistent than job destruction for prolonged periods in the lagging reformers. In countries lagging in market-oriented reforms, such as Russia, stringent labor market regulations discouraged job creation, and as a result, job destruction rates exceeded job creation. In some instances, these unsynchronized job flows gave rise to unemployment (or underemployment, that is, low-productive employment in the informal sector). In contrast, in early reformers, such as Hungary, job creation rapidly caught up with job destruction, giving rise to synchronized job flows (figure 23).

In services, job creation exceeded job destruction owing to the growing role of services in the Region. The service sector, underdeveloped during the central planning period, grew and gained shares in value added and employment. The growth in the sector also reflected an explosive expansion in new firms in markets that had previously been nonexistent or poorly populated. As a result, there were net employment gains in most countries (figure 24).

In Sum, Policy Reforms Should Stimulate Productivity and Remove Barriers to Firm Expansion

In late reformers, there is still a large misallocation of resources across firms, industries, and locations. This ongoing economic distortion calls for policy reforms to accelerate the pace of reallocation so that resources flow from less- to more-productive uses. The process of creative destruction (that is, the exit of unprofitable firms and the

FIGURE 23

Sometimes Unsynchronized Job Flows Gave Rise to Net Employment Losses

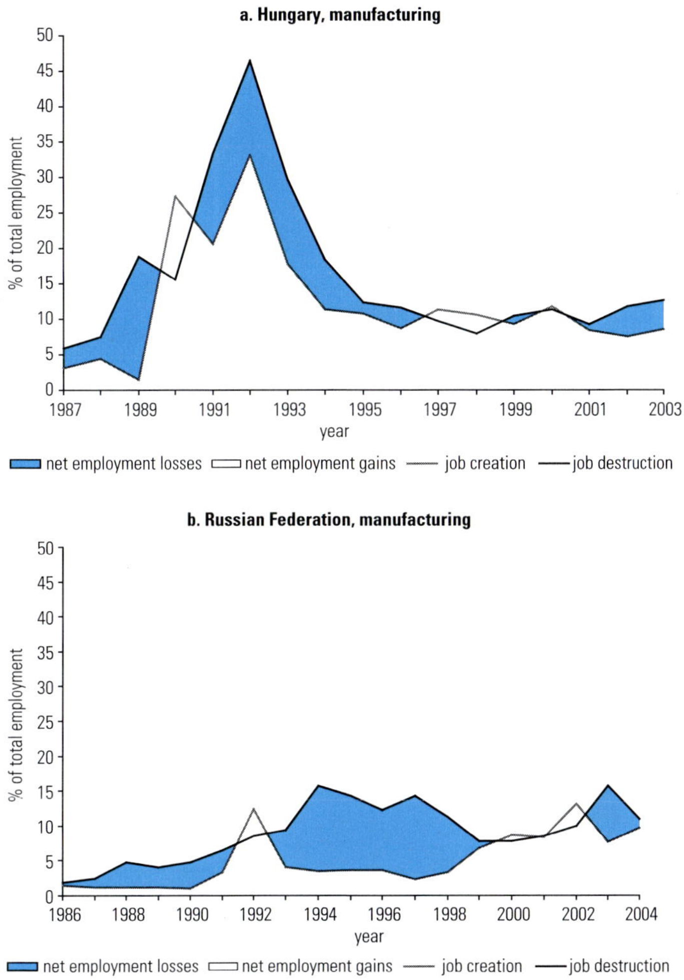

Source: Brown and Earle 2007.

entry of more-productive ones) needs to be invigorated through privatization and stronger market competition.

Although productivity increases are largely driven by within-firm adjustments, firm entry and exit should play an important role in sustaining productivity growth in the years to come. By continuing to protect ailing firms and contain firm exit, the late reformers have not been able to free resources from less-productive uses for more-productive uses. Similarly, restrictive product land factor markets and the uncertain business environment discourage firm entry and

FIGURE 24
In Services, Job Creation Outpaced Job Losses

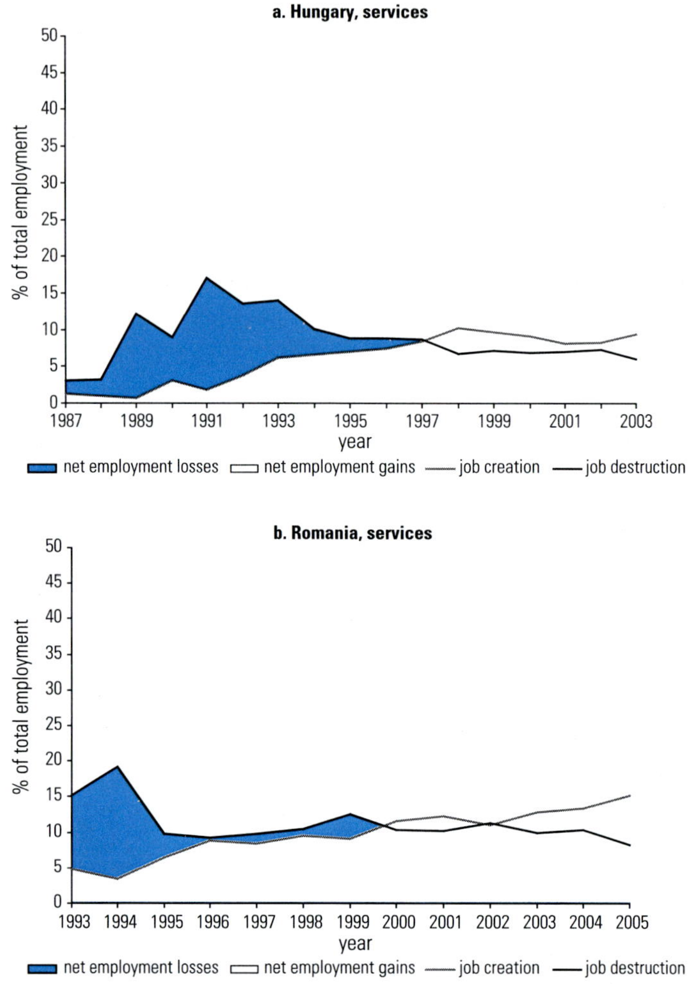

Source: Brown and Earle 2007.

the adoption of better technologies. To foster labor reallocation across and within sectors and firms, policies need to encourage workers to adapt to changing demands for labor and skills, for instance through reforms in the education sector.

In the early reformers, the main challenges revolve around stimulating innovation within firms and encouraging the expansion of successful firms. These countries also need to focus on reducing any remaining barriers to firm entry. In this regard, credit constraints, labor market rigidities, and deficiencies in tertiary and vocational education are likely to act as barriers to entry and innovation. Restrictive product, labor, and service markets may discourage the entry and growth of new firms and may reduce innovative efforts and technology spillovers, and this negatively affects productivity growth.

While entry may be relatively easy for small businesses, firm survival seems to be more difficult. In addition, even though reallocation may enhance productivity in the economy as a whole, there are losers in the process. The losers include owners of obsolete businesses and displaced workers. The high incidence of business failures and job losses in some countries, such as Romania, is a clear source of concern.

The net employment losses observed in some countries of the Region are also the result of policy barriers that slow the pace of the reallocation of resources. The barriers include limited factor mobility (credit market frictions and rigidities in labor markets) and other regulatory constraints affecting firm entry and firm performance. It is, therefore, not surprising to observe that, in these countries, the informal economy still plays an important role as a temporary buffer by creating (less-productive) jobs.

Which Policies Drive Productivity Growth?

The decisions of firms to improve productivity are influenced by the incentive framework in which the firms operate, and the incentives are created or reinforced through government policies and institutions. The strong productivity performance in the Region has been a reflection of improvements in individual sectors and firms. Moreover, firms that have performed well in a particular sector tend to be located in countries that have made the most progress in reforming the policy and regulatory environment. Differences in the productivity performance across firms within the same industries, even during the growth episode in the late 1990s, have revived the debate over which policies drive productivity growth in the Region. What effect has globalization had on productivity? How do government policies and other features of the business environment contribute to firm and industry productivity growth? Which policies should be advocated?

Policy Reforms Boost Firm Productivity

Evidence shows that firm productivity growth is associated with infrastructure quality, financial development, labor market flexibility, the quality of labor, good governance, and market competition (figure 25). The findings presented in this study are consistent with the findings of the large, cross-country empirical literature. Aggregate

FIGURE 25

Policy Reforms Boost Firm Productivity

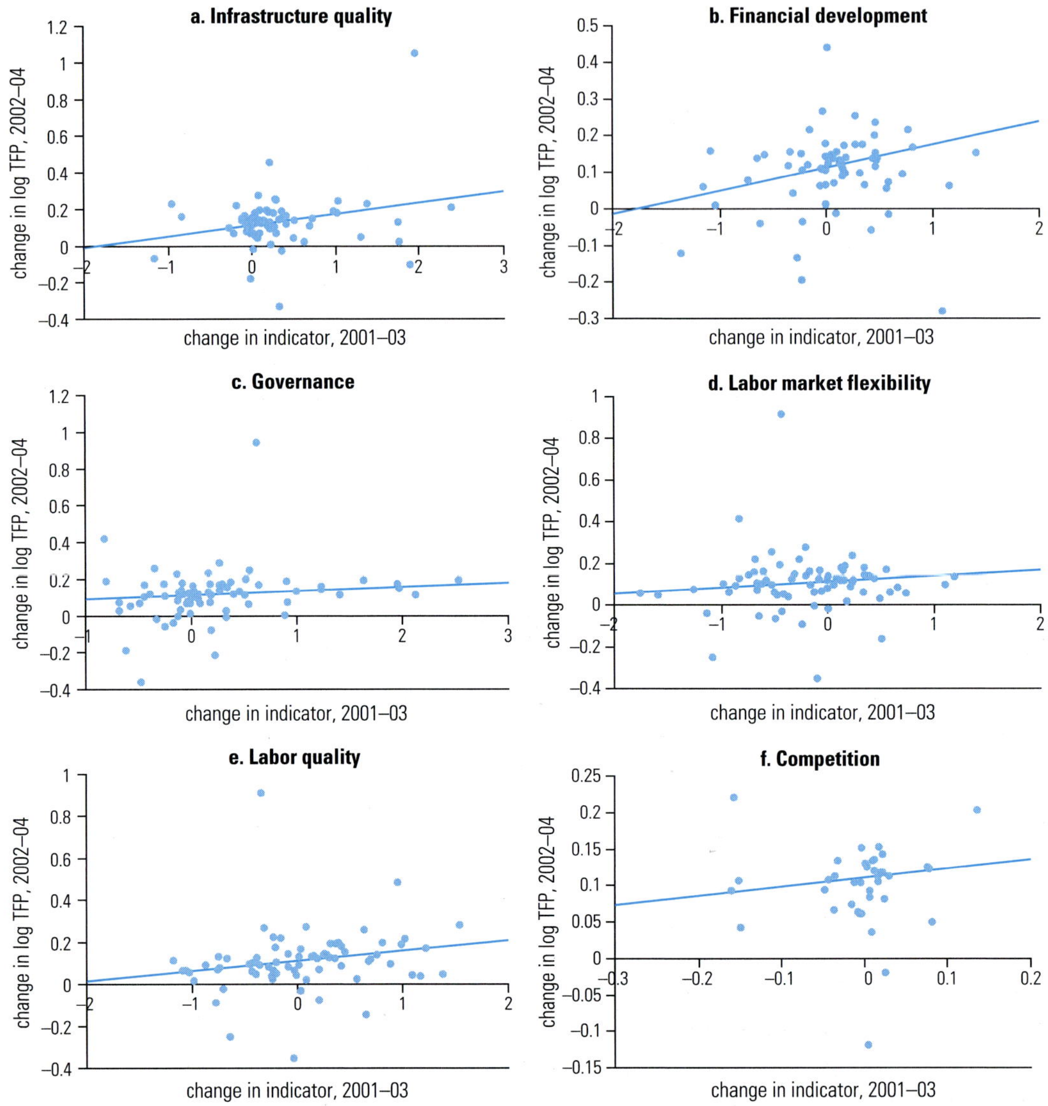

Sources: Amadeus Database 2006; BEEPS 2002, 2005.

Note: The dependent variable is the change in log TFP from 2002 to 2004, subtracting the effects of all other regressors in the full model. See appendix 3 for the estimation methodology and model specification.

cross-country regressions, while generating useful insights, only provide crude indicators of the factors behind the productivity performance of individual countries. This analysis is bound to mask substantial variations within countries and within sectors because of the heterogeneity of firm responses to the policy and business environment in which the firms operate.

The empirical evidence suggests five areas for policy action: promoting good governance and macro stability, strengthening competition, investing in labor and technology, investing in infrastructure, and deepening the financial sector.

Ensuring Good Governance and Macroeconomic Stability

Improvements in governance lower transaction costs among firms by protecting and enforcing property rights, curbing burdensome administrative and judicial rulings, and ensuring good regulatory quality. Sound macroeconomic management holds inflation and fiscal deficits in check to maintain a stable economic environment. More broadly, good governance and macroeconomic management increase predictability and reduce risk in the business environment, which facilitates investment decisions by entrepreneurs. Improvements in corporate governance also contribute to firm productivity growth by increasing the accountability for poor performance.

The transition economies, especially the middle-income ones, must address their remaining macroeconomic vulnerabilities so as to sustain growth momentum. Notwithstanding recent gains in the acceleration of growth, some risks have re-emerged and grown in the light of the recent global credit crunch. Recent rapid growth may slow down. Inflationary and external pressures are building again as a result of the past few years of rapid growth, the quick expansion of credit, and rising food and energy import prices. Current account and budget deficits have grown in some countries. These excess demand pressures have generated concern over macroeconomic vulnerabilities and need to be addressed to provide the necessary, basic macroeconomic stability and governance. Toward this end, prudent fiscal and monetary policies must be maintained to reach stable inflation at low levels, a balance in banking and corporate sector governance regulations, effective supervision, sound competition policies that encourage efficiency, and the development of institutional structures and economic policy processes that permit rapid policy adjustments in response to shocks.

Strengthening Competition

Competition has a pervasive and long-lasting impact on economic performance because it affects the incentive structure among economic actors by encouraging innovative activities and by selecting more-efficient activities over less-efficient activities. At the start of the transition to a competitive market economy, the pressure to increase capacity utilization and institute privatization was the main trigger of firm restructuring and productivity growth. In the longer term, however, productivity improvements need to be sustained through policies aimed at accelerating the reallocation of resources and promoting the introduction of new technologies. The contribution of entrants to productivity growth is thus critical, and it is particularly strong in higher-technology sectors.

Competition is needed in both product and service markets to foster productivity growth. Dynamic efficiency gains from product market competition, however, are unlikely to be achieved without well-functioning service markets. Service liberalization enhances the quality and availability of services through competition and economies of scale. The benefits of service liberalization are not limited to the service sector; they affect all economic activities. Given that services contribute an average of around 10–20 percent to the production cost of products and account for all trading costs (transport, trade finance, insurance, communications, and distribution services), the savings from stronger competition by foreign providers and the gains in competitiveness on international markets among services and goods may be substantial.

Privatization may also play an important role in productivity growth. Privatization reforms have been the main trigger of firm churning and restructuring in transition economies. The net impact of privatization on productivity growth has varied from country to country because transition countries have relied on different methods of privatization and have transferred ownership at a varying pace (figure 26). FDI may also provide domestic firms with access to more efficient technologies and open opportunities for entrants as suppliers, users, or service providers to foreign affiliates.

Policies to strengthen domestic competition are working but need to be reinforced. Since the start of the transition, the promotion of the entry of more-productive firms and the exit of old, less-productive firms has been a focus of public policy and has been seen as a key driver of economic transformation. Entry has best been promoted through the development of a positive investment climate, while the exit of old firms has best been accomplished through the imposition of market discipline. The imposition of market discipline—for example, through the hardening of budget constraints, the introduction of market competition, the enforcement of bankruptcy procedures, and better performance measurement—forces older firms to restructure and become more productive and compete or else face closure. But these policies primarily target reallocation and firm turnover, not within-firm productivity growth. For the latter, competition policies must facilitate integration with global

FIGURE 26

Privatization Has Raised TFP, Especially in Countries That Attracted FDI

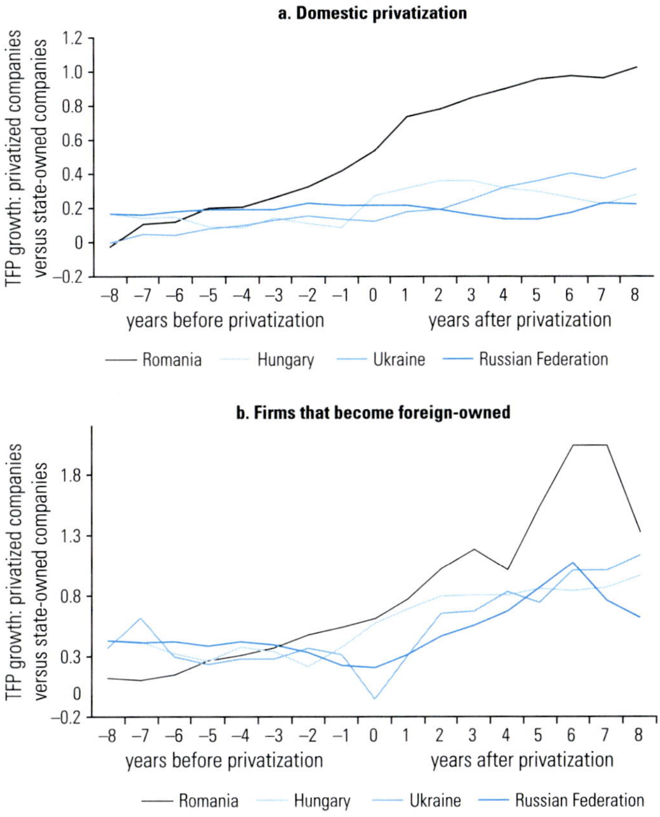

Source: Brown and Earle 2007.

production networks, integrate domestic factor and product markets, and strengthen the regulatory framework for service sector competition. An important new aspect of policies aimed at promoting within-firm productivity growth is the establishment of links between upstream production and downstream services.

Investing in Labor and Technology

A skilled workforce is essential for firm productivity growth because it enables firms to adopt new, better technologies. It also helps in accelerating the reallocation of resources. Skilled workers are more proficient at dealing with rapid change and are more flexible in moving across jobs. In the Region, high-technology sectors are absorbing younger and more highly skilled workers than are low-technology sectors, but many firms are facing increasing shortages in skills. A recent

World Bank report (Desai and Goldberg 2007) on the investment climate in Russia finds that shortages of management and technical skills in Russia have originated in deficiencies in the higher education and public research system and underinvestment in training at the firm level, which are common deficiencies in the Region. Training policies may help improve the productivity of labor across the Region. In some countries (the Czech Republic and Poland, for example), training policies have evolved to accommodate the increased demand for skills. In particular, they have focused on involving private training suppliers and on giving incentives for firms to provide formal training, although evidence on the effectiveness of such programs is patchy.

Countries need to exploit fully their fairly high human capital stock, solid scientific base, and well-developed research institutions to absorb and diffuse new technologies from abroad. Investing more and more effectively in higher education and promoting technological adoption and adaptation are key to catching up with the technological frontier, expediting growth, and accelerating convergence. Globalizing forces provide a substantial opportunity for countries to acquire labor skills and technology though FDI, licensing, and imports of capital goods. The low spending on R&D in the Region—at less than 1 percent of GDP compared with the EU's target of 3 percent—limits the potential for technology development, while the public nature of the spending restricts efficient application. Bringing in more private partnerships in R&D, as is the practice in more advanced countries, may help relieve financing constraints on the absorption and diffusion of new technologies and help any such investment generate higher returns.

Investing in Infrastructure

Improved infrastructure is important for firm productivity growth. Training alone will not suffice to enhance the capacity of firms to innovate. Firms in countries with access to modern telecommunications services, reliable electricity supply, and efficient transport links are more productive that those operating in countries without these advantages. In many countries in the Region, infrastructure deficiencies negatively affect firm productivity growth. Building and maintaining roads, ports, electricity grids, and telecommunications networks are expensive; so, it is not surprising that poor countries in the Region have more problems with infrastructure. Nonetheless, the challenge of modernizing infrastructure is not merely an issue of finding financing. The origin of the difficulties in infrastructure provision in the Region is weak competition, insufficient investments in operations and maintenance, and an inadequate regulatory framework.

Deepening the Financial Sector

Greater financial market sophistication allows firms to take on more innovative and risky projects by offering payment services, mobilizing savings, and allocating financing to firms wishing to invest. If these markets work well, they give firms of all types the ability to seize promising investment opportunities. They reduce the reliance of firms on internally generated cash flows and money from informal sources, such as family and friends, giving the firms access to external equity and facilitating entry into product markets. Constraints to the development of the financial sector—such as entry barriers, restrictions on foreign banks, and state ownership of banks—hurt the financial system and its ability to increase firm productivity growth. Empirical analysis in the Region has shown that firm productivity growth is associated with deeper financial markets and better access to credit from foreign and private banks.

A multipronged financial sector agenda needs to be followed to deepen financial intermediation, promote post-entry firm growth, and strengthen the impact of financial markets on productivity growth generally. Such an agenda, which needs to be tailored to specific country situations, should cover the completion of the privatization of state banks, the strengthening of the prudential framework for bank and nonbank intermediation, the improvement of bank supervision, the strengthening of financial reporting and transparency requirements for bank ownership, and the improvement of credit information systems and collateral regimes. Transition countries have achieved a great deal in the establishment of banks and capital markets, but the contribution of the financial sector to productivity and growth has been uneven. The financial sector in many countries in the Region remains underdeveloped relative to that in other countries at the same level of income. More recently, across the Region, there has been rapid growth in bank credit, much of which is highly skewed toward consumer lending. Whatever firm lending takes place is primarily concentrated in large firms. Indeed, little credit has flowed to new or existing small and medium-sized private enterprises, even though the experience of the EU-10 and Turkey suggests that financial deepening and the development of credit sources located outside firms are essential in promoting expansion and economies of scale within firms after start-up. Financial credit for rural enterprises and farm growth is even scarcer.

Going Forward: Productivity Growth Requires a Differentiated Policy Agenda across Countries

Although all countries in the Region need to continue their reform efforts, their priorities in public policy will depend on their development path. Thus, the primary challenge for the CIS and SEE remains the need to address the transition legacy, while the main challenge for the EU-10 and for Turkey is to boost innovation and productivity growth so as to catch up with the income levels of the EU-15 (table 1).

For the CIS and SEE, the greater initial misallocation of resources and the slower path of transition suggest that productivity gains may still be tapped by facilitating firm restructuring, promoting the net entry of firms, easing access to credit, and simplifying trade practices to capture advantages from trade and greater openness.

For the EU-10, which have largely addressed the legacy of transition, the transition is over. Gains will still accrue from efficient reallocation and churning, as in even the most advanced economies. But the bulk of productivity gains are likely to be tapped through within-firm productivity growth by way of greater competition, more technological imitation and innovation, better absorption of new skills and technology, and additional development of new products and markets. These countries are now competing in the same markets as the more advanced European economies and are catching up with the technological frontier. The success of the EU-10 and of Turkey in moving ever closer to the income levels of the EU-15 largely depends on how well firms and workers are able to move rapidly into new products and markets and make production processes more efficient.

Priorities need to be set in each country based on the relative importance of the three channels of productivity growth at the firm level: within-firm productivity growth, reallocation across firms and sectors, and net entry. Increasing competition, opening the economy to trade, and hardening budget constraints on state enterprises will strengthen the ability of firms to take advantage of each of these channels. But policies may be differentiated across these channels. For instance, financial deepening and the development of sources of credit outside firms are essential in promoting within-firm growth, as the evidence on Turkey suggests.

However, enterprise restructuring and labor reallocation processes might generate some labor costs. This may be mitigated through adequate social safety nets to support workers who have been laid off during firm restructuring (World Bank 2002; Alam et al. 2005; Chawla, Betcherman, and Banerji 2007). In the CIS, where the

TABLE 1
Late Reformers Must Complete the Transition; Early Reformers Must Foster Innovation

Stage	Reforms
First phase of convergence: late reformers in which the initial level of misallocation was greater and transition reforms proceeded slowly	Address the transition legacy: • Facilitate firm entry, restructuring, and exit by – improving the business environment, particularly business licensing, taxation, and legal and judicial reform – hardening the budget constraints to close or privatize loss-making public enterprises • Lower the cost of, and improve access to, credit • Accelerate the behind-the-border agenda to deepen the gains from trade openness, particularly the liberalization of services and the improvement of trade facilitation and logistics such as information technology, infrastructure, port efficiency, and customs regimes
Second phase of convergence: early reformers in which the misallocation of resources has been substantially corrected relative to their peers, but which are still lagging the EU-15	The second- or third-generation reform agenda: sustain productivity gains and foster innovation as a source of growth by • deepening bank and nonbank financial intermediation • adopting competitive product and labor market regulations • improving the quality of human capital (tertiary education) • investing in knowledge (R&D) and new technologies (ICT)

Source: Compiled by the authors.

challenge of restructuring is still relevant and poverty and inequality remain concerns, providing adequate levels of social assistance must be a policy priority. In the EU-10, which can afford more generous safety nets, formal unemployment insurance schemes are being expanded and provide the best way to protect workers displaced by enterprise restructuring. The guaranteed employment, retirement security, and consumer subsidies of the former socialist systems have become obsolete. In many instances, these were fiscally unaffordable, as countries sought to balance expenditure demands with revenues. The best method for protecting the most vulnerable workers involves two steps: removal of the barriers to the entry of new enterprises, thereby creating additional employment opportunities, and the targeting of social assistance on those workers whose skills and experience mean that they are less likely to be employed in the new enterprises.

Conclusion

The countries of the Region have shown strong productivity growth during 1999–2005 that has driven up living standards and reduced poverty. Both domestic and globalizing factors have contributed to this, but significant challenges remain in sustaining productivity growth. Public policies can play an important role but they need to be carefully tailored to each country's situation.

Notes

1. The low income CIS countries (low-CIS or CIS-low) are Armenia, Azerbaijan, Georgia, the Kyrgyz Republic, Moldova, Tajikistan, and Uzbekistan.
2. These data have been collected by independent researchers Eric J. Bartelsman, David J. Brown, John S. Earle, and Stefano Scarpetta. Earlier sets of the data have been used by these researchers in analyses in published papers.
3. The TFP estimates tend to be controversial because of measurement errors. This is particularly true in transition economies, where the quality of the capital stock series remains problematic. Nevertheless, robustness tests applied to the capital stock series ensure that the relative changes indicated in productivity patterns across countries and over time are reliable.
4. The analysis of productivity patterns in manufacturing and service industries focuses on a group of countries (the Czech Republic, Estonia, Hungary, Latvia, Lithuania, Poland, the Slovak Republic, and Slovenia) for which harmonized industry-level deflators are available.
5. A cautionary note is in order on comparisons between productivity growth decompositions across countries. The decomposition of aggregate productivity growth might yield somewhat different results depending on the time horizon (three-year rolling periods or five-year rolling periods). The entry component tends to be larger over longer horizons because more of the entry effect is a within effect over time. Also, the within and entry terms may be influenced by noise and imperfect deflators that might lead to an upward bias in absolute magnitudes. Nevertheless, the broad trends across countries are maintained. Brown, Earle, and Telegdy (2007) correct for this last problem by comparing the productivity of entrants with the sectoral weighted average for the same year.
6. A negative entry effect results if the entrants are less productive than the average incumbents; this does not necessarily point to a lack of dynamism. In vibrant and technologically advanced sectors, many high-risk entrants may exhibit low average productivity, and market selection weeds out all but the most productive entrants, which will eventually overtake incumbents.

CHAPTER 1

Patterns of Aggregate Productivity Growth

For the first time since transition, the countries of Eastern Europe and the Former Soviet Union experienced strong and sustained growth across the board during 1999–2005. This growth drove their convergence toward the income and productivity levels of advanced industrial countries. As a result, it has given way to the optimism surrounding transition that the removal of an array of controls on economic activity would bring about dramatic growth in productivity and output as resources were reallocated to more productive functions. Yet, for almost a decade following the start of the transition, the record on growth was mixed: while some countries did experience rapid growth in output and productivity following a temporary decline, others struggled with the reforms necessary to climb out of a trajectory of protracted decline. The scenario has changed decidedly in recent years: the strong growth across the board since 1999 constitutes a distinct new episode in the growth experience of the Region.

At the same time, significant disparities exist in income and productivity levels and policy challenges across the Region. At the end of 2005, per capita GDP in Slovenia, at $19,797 (in constant 2000 PPP-adjusted prices), was 17 times that in Tajikistan, at $1,170, whereas per capita GDP in Russia, at $9,770, was twice that in Albania, at $4,711. Growth rates in the Kyrgyz Republic and Poland during

1999–2005, at 4 and 3.4 percent, respectively, were sluggish in comparison to the 9.1 and 7.4 percent growth in Kazakhstan and Latvia, respectively. On the policy reform front, while Estonia followed up on its early progress in trade and price liberalization with progress in financial sector reforms and infrastructure reforms, progress in trade and price liberalization has been limited in Uzbekistan. The significant disparities across the Region are likely to be reflected in differences in the trajectory of growth and policy challenges in the years ahead.

This chapter takes a close look at the recent episode of strong growth in output and productivity in the Region. It focuses on the following questions: (a) How has growth in the Region compared with growth in other parts of the world? (b) To what extent has growth been driven by improvements in productivity? (c) How do productivity growth rates and levels vary across countries, and how do they compare with those in other parts of the world? (d) What has been the role of policy reform in driving productivity growth across the Region? and (e) What structural and policy reforms are necessary to sustain and accelerate productivity growth in the years ahead?

The primary findings of the chapter are that the countries of the Region have experienced substantial improvements in productivity that have accelerated their convergence toward the income and productivity levels of the industrial countries. The pattern of productivity growth has been driven by the progress achieved in the policy reforms necessary for the transition to a market economy. At the same time, a sizable gap in income and productivity levels relative to the industrialized world remains. To narrow the gap and continue the process of convergence, sustaining and accelerating productivity growth are important priorities. This will require more progress in the transition policy reform agenda among the lagging reformers, as well as improvements in a range of structural determinants of productivity growth, including infrastructure stock and quality, financial depth, and institutional quality.

Patterns of Growth

The economies of the Region have generated robust growth since the end of the Russian financial crisis in 1998. During the seven-year period 1999–2005, the Region as a whole grew by 5.7 percent. Growth in the Region during this period was higher than that of the advanced industrial countries, Latin America, and East Asia (excluding China and Japan). South Asia experienced modestly higher growth during this period, while China experienced dramatically higher growth than any region (figure 1.1).

Rapid growth in the Region since 1998 has led to convergence toward industrial country levels of GDP per capita, although a large gap remains. Figure 1.1 depicts the evolution of GDP per capita in each region as a share of that of advanced industrial countries between 1990 and 2005. Per capita GDP in the Region increased from $5,903 (constant 2000 PPP-adjusted prices) in 1998 to $8,411 in 2005, which represents a rise from 21.8 percent of the income levels of industrial countries in 1998 to 27.5 percent in 2005. This convergence toward the levels of the industrial countries since 1998 is in sharp contrast to the earlier period in the 1990s when GDP per capita in the Region fell dramatically, from $8,036 in 1990 to $5,903 in 1998 (that is, from 33.8 to 21.5 percent of industrial country per capita GDP). Even though per capita GDP in the Region as a share of the GDP levels in industrial countries has not yet recovered to the corresponding share in 1990, the significantly higher growth rates since 1998 certainly suggest that the Region is moving in that direction. Furthermore, the still large gap in income levels between the countries of the Region and industrial countries suggests that the former have the opportunity to generate high growth by pursuing the policies necessary to close the gap with industrial countries.

Thanks to high growth, the Region has also moved up in the distribution of GDP per capita among developing countries. By 2005, the Region had the highest level of GDP per capita among all developing

FIGURE 1.1

Recent Growth Has Been Strong in the Region

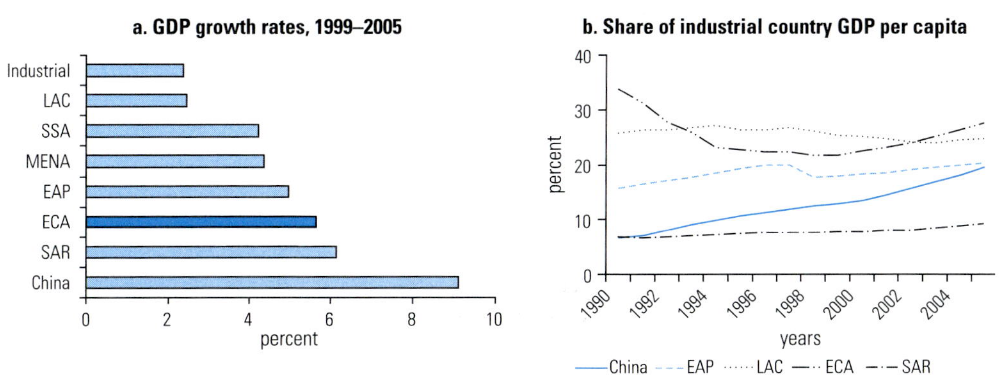

Sources: World Bank staff calculations; World Development Indicators Database 2007.
Note: SAR = South Asia Region.

FIGURE 1.2
Growth Has Rebounded across All Country Groups

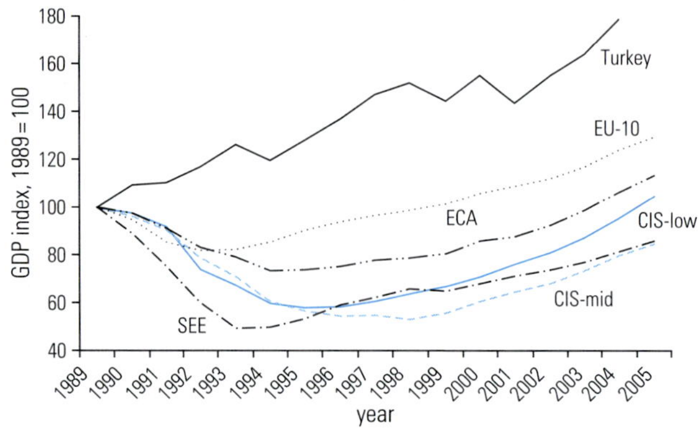

Sources: World Bank staff calculations; World Development Indicators Database 2007.

regions. Between 1998 and 2005, the income level in the Region rose above that of Latin America and pulled further ahead of East Asia (excluding China and Japan).

Even though the Region has experienced strong growth across the board since 1998, countries have followed significantly different trajectories of growth since the start of the transition. During the initial years, 1990–92, the deepest contractions took place in the low income CIS countries, the Baltic states, and the SEE, as shown in figure 1.2. The initial contractions were less severe in Central Europe and the middle income CIS countries. During 1993–98, growth began to take hold in most of the EU-10 and parts of the SEE. Albania and Poland experienced strong growth during this period, while Bulgaria and Romania experienced flat growth. Meanwhile, the CIS countries experienced prolonged and often sharp contractions. During the more recent period, 1999–2005, robust growth took hold across the board. The strongest growth was experienced by the CIS countries that lagged the most during the earlier period.

Sources of Growth: The Role of Productivity

To assess the capacity of countries in the Region to sustain the rapid growth rates of recent years, it is important to determine the extent to which this growth has been accompanied by improvements in productivity. The neoclassical model of growth and a large body of supporting empirical literature have shown that productivity differences are an important determinant of differences in income levels across countries and that productivity growth is the ultimate driver of growth in the long run (see, for example, Bosworth and Collins 2003; Hall and Jones 1999; Klenow and Rodríguez-Clare 1997). To the extent that overall growth is accompanied by productivity growth, the latter is likely to be sustained. However, if productivity growth is sluggish and growth is increasingly driven by accumulation, growth itself is likely to taper off as the returns to accumulation diminish over time.

A growth accounting methodology is thus used to measure the rate of TFP growth in the countries of the Region and assess the extent to which growth in output has been driven by improvements in productivity. Specifically, growth of real GDP is decomposed into (a) the contribution of growth in the capital stock, (b) the contribution of growth in the labor force, and (c) TFP growth.[1]

The analysis in this chapter uses a consistent methodology to account for the sources of growth and compute TFP growth rates that are comparable across the Region, as well as across countries in other parts of the world. A number of previous studies have used the growth accounting methodology to compute productivity growth for the countries of the Region. However, most of these studies have been focused on particular countries or groups of countries, with differences in methodologies making it difficult to compare the numbers obtained across countries and over time. The few studies that have attempted to use a consistent methodology across a large group of countries in the Region have been focused on the period preceding the most recent phase of growth. (For example, see De Broeck and Koen [2000] for growth accounting work on the CIS countries and Campos and Coricelli [2002] for growth accounting work on a number of Eastern European countries.) The analysis in this chapter uses a consistent methodology and the best available data to compute TFP growth rates that are comparable across countries and over time (see box 1.1 and appendix 1.A). Furthermore, the analysis uses the same consistent methodology to implement the growth accounting exercise and measure TFP growth for 96 other countries outside the Region. This enables a fair comparison of TFP levels and growth rates in the Region with those in advanced industrial countries, East Asia, China, Latin America, and other parts of the world (figure 1.3).

Strong growth in the ECA region during 1999–2005 has been driven primarily by a productivity surge, in contrast to most other parts of the world where growth has been driven by a more even

BOX 1.1

The Growth Accounting Methodology

The analysis in this chapter uses a growth accounting methodology to decompose the growth of real GDP into the contributions from growth in the capital stock and in the labor force and TFP growth. As is widely appreciated, the measurement of TFP growth is sensitive to the methodology that is used. In transition economies, the measurement of capital stock also presents special challenges. This box reports on the particular growth accounting methodology used and the techniques employed to address the challenges in capital stock measurement.

Methodology

Starting with the following standard Cobb-Douglas production function:

$$Y_t = A_t K_t^{\alpha} L_t^{1-\alpha}$$

where Y is real GDP, K is the physical capital stock, L is the labor force, A is the level of TFP, and α is the capital share of income. Taking logarithms and differentiating, we obtain the following growth accounting equation:

$$\frac{dY}{Y} = \alpha \frac{dK}{K} + (1-\alpha)\frac{dL}{L} + \frac{dA}{A}.$$

The above equation shows that the growth of real GDP (the first term) may be decomposed into three sources of growth: (a) the contribution from growth in the physical capital stock (the second term), (b) the contribution from growth in the labor force (the third term), and (c) TFP growth (the final term).

Data and Challenges in Measuring Capital Stock in Transition Countries

To implement this decomposition, data on GDP and the labor force have been obtained from the World Development Indicators Database, national statistical offices, and the International Monetary Fund. The basis for constructing the capital stock series is the standard perpetual inventory method:

$$K_{t+1} = (1-\delta) K_t + I_t$$

where I is the level of investment and δ is the depreciation rate. Investment data going back to 1980 for most countries have been obtained from *World Development Indicators* and *World Economic Outlook*, supplemented with data from CISStat and the Vienna Institute for International Economic Studies (see World Development Indicators Database; IMF 2007; CISStat Database; WIIW Database). Estimates of the initial capital stock have been obtained from De Broeck and Koen (2000) for the CIS countries and from the Vienna Institute and national statistical offices for Eastern European countries. The commonly assumed capital share in income of 0.35 percent and a standard depreciation rate of 0.05 percent are used in the baseline analysis.

(*Continues on the following page.*)

BOX 1.1

The Growth Accounting Methodology (*continued*)

Implementing the perpetual inventory method for transition economies presents the particular challenge that, during the initial contraction, a significant portion of the communist capital stock may not only be temporarily idled, but may actually be permanently scrapped. If so, this would cause the contribution of capital accumulation to be underestimated during the subsequent recovery. To address this concern, a one-time adjustment has been applied for the permanent scrapping of a portion of the communist capital stock; in particular, the adjustment contracts the capital stock by the same rate as output during the initial contraction, so that the capital output ratio does not rise during the course of the contraction.

Extensive robustness checks were performed with alternative adjustments for the scrapping of communist capital and with alternative values of the capital share and depreciation rates. While the exact TFP growth numbers obtained do indeed change, the patterns across countries and over time are robust to these alternative techniques.

FIGURE 1.3

TFP Growth Is the Primary Driver of Growth in Transition Countries

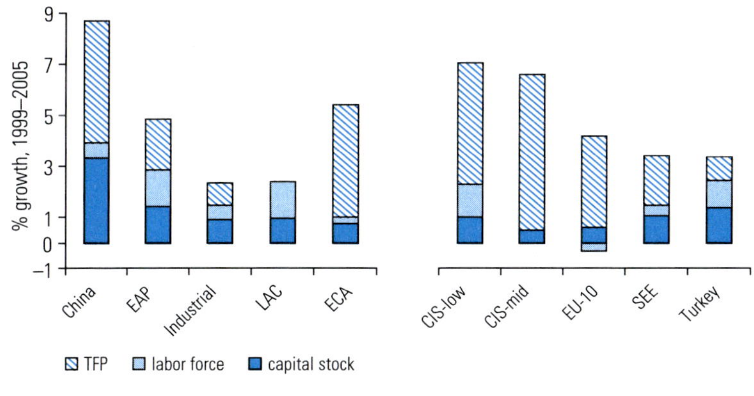

Source: World Bank staff calculations (see appendix 1.A).

mixture of accumulation of inputs and productivity growth. Figure 1.3 shows the contributions of capital accumulation, labor force growth, and TFP growth to aggregate GDP growth in the ECA region as well as in other parts of the world for the period 1999–2005. In the ECA region, out of an overall GDP growth rate of 5.42 percent, TFP growth accounted for 4.43 percentage points. The contribution of the accumulation of inputs was only about 1 percent (of which the contribution of capital accumulation was 0.72 percentage points and that of labor force growth was 0.27 percentage points). By contrast, in East Asia (excluding China), out of an overall GDP growth rate of 4.85 percent during this period, the contribution of TFP growth has been 2 percentage points, whereas the contributions of capital accumulation and labor force growth have accounted for the rest. Even in China, where TFP growth of 4.8 percent has exceeded that of ECA, the accumulation of inputs has accounted for another 4 percentage points of growth. In the industrialized world, the contribution of the accumulation of inputs has exceeded that of TFP growth, whereas Latin America as a whole has not experienced productivity growth during this period, so that all of the growth has been the result of capital accumulation and labor force growth.

The predominant role of productivity growth in driving the growth of GDP is found across the different areas within the Region, although a closer look at the figures reveals a number of differences. The most substantial of these differences is between Turkey and the transition economies. In Turkey, a majority of growth during the most recent period has been a result of the accumulation of inputs, as the labor force has grown at a steady rate and TFP growth has been sluggish. Although the sluggish TFP growth rate in Turkey is influenced by the financial crisis of 2001, a look at a longer time horizon confirms the pattern that growth in Turkey (unlike in the transition economies) has been driven by fairly balanced contributions from the accumulation of inputs and productivity growth.

Across the transition economies of the Region, overall GDP growth was highest in the CIS during 1999–2005. Within the CIS, although overall growth has been higher in the low-income countries, productivity growth has been higher in the middle-income countries. The role of productivity growth in driving growth in the middle income CIS countries has been overwhelming: out of an overall growth rate of 6.6 percent during 1999–2005, TFP growth accounted for 6.1 percentage points, with almost no contribution coming from the accumulation of inputs. In the low income CIS, although TFP growth of 4.8 percent was again the driving force behind the overall growth of 7.1 percent, the accumulation of inputs also contributed 2.3 percentage points (thanks to steady labor force growth in these countries). In the EU-10 group of countries, growth was driven primarily by TFP growth, while, in the SEE, the accumulation of inputs contributed about 1.5 percentage points to the overall growth of 3.4 percent during 1999–2005.

The substantial improvements in productivity accompanying (and, indeed, driving) growth in the Region make it more likely that growth will be sustained in the years ahead. Improved efficiency in the organization of production should attract investment and allow accumulation to play a greater role in contributing to growth over time.

One concern associated with the measurement of productivity in transition economies especially in the CIS, is that high TFP growth rates may simply be a reflection of higher capacity utilization as growth rebounds from the sharp contractions during the early years of transition. Adjusting growth decompositions for capacity utilization is difficult for a broad range of countries in the Region because comparable data on capacity utilization across countries are not available. In Russia, available survey data on capacity utilization permit growth decompositions to be performed using capital stock series adjusted for capacity utilization.[2] The results, displayed in figure 1.4, suggest that the contribution of capital accumulation does, indeed, rise after one adjusts for capacity utilization. But even after adjusting for the utilization of *available* resources, TFP gains from *employed* resources still accounted for nearly two-thirds of the overall growth in Russia during 1999–2005.

Exploring the evolution of productivity growth since the start of the transition in the EU-10 and SEE countries sheds light on what may happen to productivity growth in the CIS countries going forward. We have seen that strong growth in the Region was driven by a surge in productivity, particularly in the CIS. What is likely to happen to productivity and growth going forward? Moreover, how did the substantial rates of productivity growth in the most recent period, 1999–2005, compare with productivity growth during the earlier periods of transition? In the EU-10 (which have had a longer history of postrecovery growth), the initial productivity surge during 1995–98 was sustained and actually increased into the 1999–2005

FIGURE 1.4

Higher Capacity Utilization Partly Explains High TFP Growth Rates

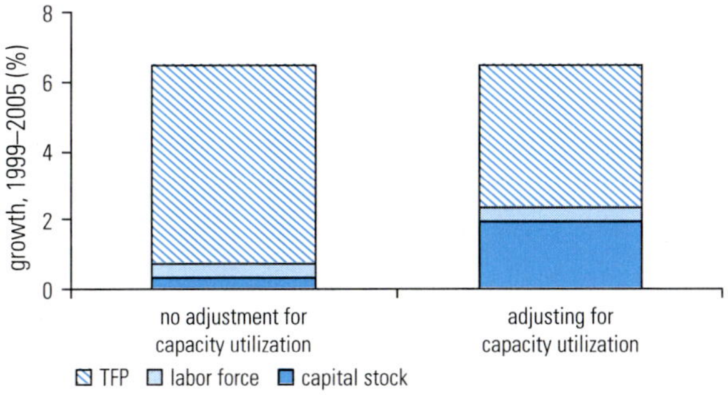

Sources: World Bank staff calculations; Russian Economic Barometer Survey Database, various years.

period (figure 1.5). Conversely, in the SEE countries, the initial spurt of productivity growth during 1995–98 subsided during 1999–2005, although growth was propped up by increasing contributions from the accumulation of inputs. In the CIS, large TFP declines during the earlier years of transition have been followed by high productivity growth since 1999.

While we would expect the contribution from accumulation to increase over time in transition economies, whether or not high productivity growth is sustained over time will ultimately determine how rapidly the countries converge toward the income levels of advanced industrial countries. If the high productivity growth rates in the Region fall off too quickly, then high growth is less likely to be sustained in the long run. Moreover, if improvements in the policy environment lead to sustained high productivity growth over time (as has been the case in China), then rapid growth is likely to continue in the years ahead.

Within the Region, the highest productivity growth during 1999–2005 generally took place in those countries with lower levels of productivity, leading to a convergence in productivity levels during this period. A look at the levels of productivity across the Region points to substantial differences that have been narrowed to some extent in recent years (see figure 1.5). The low income CIS countries, which have levels of productivity far below those in other parts of the Region, have experienced high productivity growth in recent years. Productivity levels in the middle income CIS countries overtook those in the SEE between 1999 and 2005. Similarly, productivity levels in the EU-10 group surged ahead of the level in Turkey during this period. The recent convergence in productivity levels in the Region is in contrast to the divergence in productivity levels during the earlier

FIGURE 1.5

TFP Levels and Growth Vary across the Region

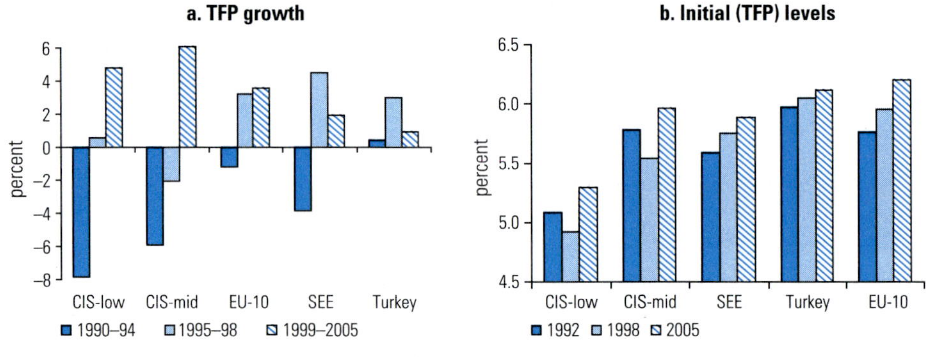

Source: World Bank staff calculations (see appendix 1.A for data sources).

period, when countries with lower productivity levels were generally experiencing sharper contractions (figure 1.6).

The high rate of productivity growth in the Region since 1998 has led to a convergence toward industrial country productivity levels. However, a substantial gap in productivity remains. How have productivity levels evolved over time and how has this compared with the evolution of productivity in other parts of the world? The growth in TFP by 4.4 percent during 1999–2005 is the first episode of strong productivity growth across the board since the start of the transition (figure 1.7). During 1990–94, the Region experienced significant declines in productivity, while productivity levels were essentially flat during 1995–98. Strong productivity growth since 1999 has led to a convergence toward industrial country productivity levels: between 1999 and 2005, the level of productivity as a share of industrial country productivity levels increased from 35 to 44 percent. This contrasts sharply with the earlier period of transition when productivity levels fell from 43 percent of industrial country productivity levels in 1990 to 35 percent in 1998. It is encouraging to note that the level of TFP

FIGURE 1.6

Productivity Growth Rates Are Now Converging in the Region

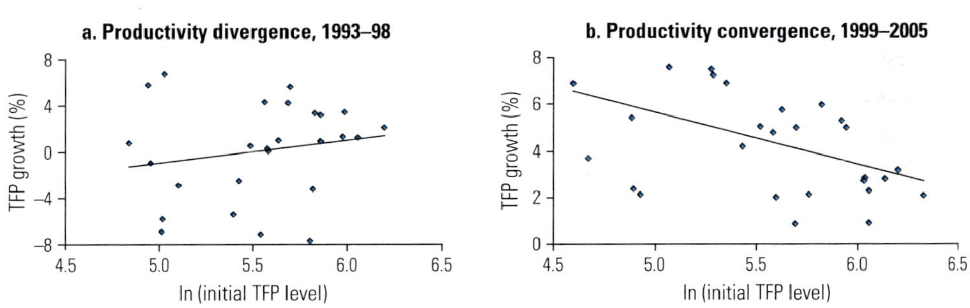

Source: World Bank staff calculations (see appendix 1.A for data sources).

FIGURE 1.7

The Region Is Catching Up with Comparators

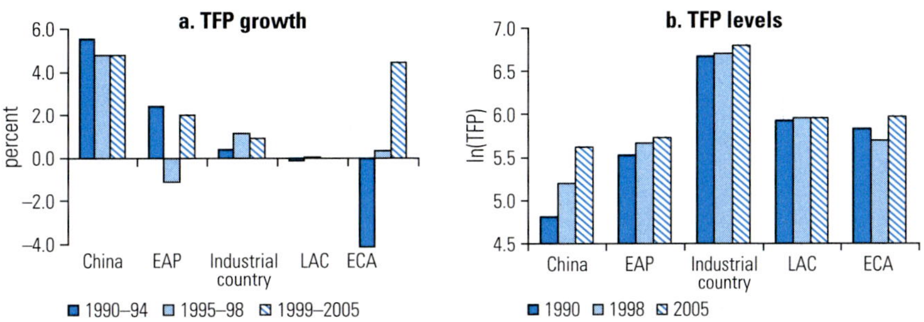

Source: World Bank staff calculations (see appendix 1.A for data sources).

relative to that in industrial countries has recovered to the level at the start of the transition.

The phenomenal record of productivity growth in China during its own transition raises the hope that the countries of Eastern Europe and the Former Soviet Union may be able to sustain high productivity growth going forward. The productivity growth in the Region during 1999–2005 was second only to that in China, which generated productivity growth in excess of 4.5 percent throughout the 1990–2005 period. In fact, looking back even further, we find that China's productivity growth over 1980–2005 was in excess of 4.5 percent per year. The country reaped spectacular gains from the liberalization of repressed sectors, such as agriculture (which had a surplus of labor) and rural industries, and from a massive inflow of foreign investment. This suggests that it is not impossible to sustain high productivity growth during a transition to a market economy.

The large productivity gap between the industrialized world and the countries of Eastern Europe and the Former Soviet Union also offers the opportunity to rapidly gain ground. It is important to bear in mind that China in 1980 (and even in 1990) started from productivity levels that were far below those in the countries of Eastern Europe and the Former Soviet Union today (see figure 1.7, chart b). At the same time, we have seen that productivity levels in the Region today are still substantially behind those in the industrialized world. This suggests that there is significant room to generate high productivity growth in the Region for many years to come by taking advantage of the improved technologies available in the industrialized world. In other words, the high rates of productivity growth in the Region since 1999 should not be viewed merely as a one-time productivity boost during the course of recovery following transition.

Ultimately, of course, sustaining high productivity growth will depend on progress in undertaking the necessary policy reforms. Lagging reformers with a distorted policy environment will require accelerated progress in those reforms necessary during the transition to a market economy. Across the board, improvements will be required in a range of structural determinants of productivity growth. In the rest of this chapter, we explore the role played by policy reforms in sustaining and accelerating productivity growth in the Region.

The Overall Record of Policy Reform

To obtain an overall assessment of progress in the policy reforms necessary for transition to a market economy in the Region, we turn to the European Bank for Reconstruction and Development (EBRD) transition indicators. These indicators rate countries on a scale of 1 to 4+ on nine dimensions of policy reform that are most relevant to transition countries, including trade and price liberalization, privatization, competition policy, financial liberalization, and the liberalization of infrastructure sectors (transportation, telecommunications, electricity, and water). A rating of 1 refers to conditions resembling a controlled economy, whereas a rating of 4+ resembles standards in advanced industrial market economies. We use the average across the nine indicators (figure 1.8).

The progress in reform has been mixed. Policy reforms in the EU-10 have progressed the most rapidly and to the greatest degree. By 2005, the average EBRD rating for the EU-10 was above 3.5, which is approaching the standards in industrial market economies, although a gap persists. In the low income and middle income CIS countries, some early progress in policy reforms through the 1995–98 period was followed by relative stagnation in reform. Between 1995–98 and 1999–2005, little overall progress in reform was achieved in the CIS. Among our subgroups, the low income CIS countries achieved the least progress during 1999–2005, reaching an average score of 2.3 during this period. The SEE countries, meanwhile, followed a path of steady, but slow, progress in reform.

A country's record on growth in output and productivity is broadly consistent with progress in policy reforms. Strong and sustained productivity growth in the EU-10 is consistent with the rapid and sustained pace of policy reform we observe in these countries. Furthermore, the initial progress in policy reform in the CIS through 1998 is consistent with the high rates of productivity growth we observe in these countries after 1999, following a prolonged period of contraction. However, sustaining high productivity growth in the CIS will require an acceleration of the sluggish pace of policy reform since 1999 in these countries.

FIGURE 1.8

The Record on Policy Reform Is Mixed

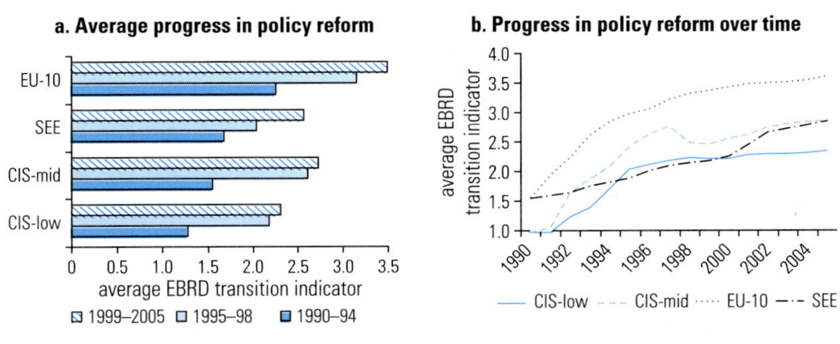

Source: EBRD (European Bank for Reconstruction and Development) 2006.

The Impact of Policy Reform

Sustaining high productivity growth will require further improvements across the Region in a number of structural and policy determinants of productivity. A large body of empirical evidence has shown that cross-country differences in productivity growth are related to differences in macroeconomic stability, human capital, financial depth, trade integration, governance (institutional quality), and infrastructure. Which dimensions of reform are the greatest constraints to sustaining and accelerating productivity growth in the Region? Where should policy makers direct their efforts to generate the greatest impact on productivity in the future? The answer to these questions depends on two factors: first, the extent to which the countries in the Region lag the productivity leader (advanced industrial countries) along each structural or policy dimension and, second, the elasticity of productivity growth with respect to improvements along each dimension of policy. We will look at how the countries in the Region compare with the rest of the world along each structural dimension and then attempt to estimate the impact on productivity growth produced by improvements along each dimension. The measures looked at capture the outcome of an array of reforms along each policy dimension.

The policy reforms in which the Region most lags the industrial countries are financial depth, infrastructure quality and stock, and governance. Figure 1.9 provides a comparison of the levels of education, financial depth, trade openness, institutional quality, and infrastructure stock and quality in the countries in the Region, the industrial countries, and countries in East Asia and Latin America (see box 1.2 for details on the particular measures used to capture these structural determinants of productivity). With regard to financial depth, the Region is on par with Latin America and significantly behind industrial countries and East Asia. The stock of infrastructure in the Region is below levels in industrial countries and East Asia, and the quality of infrastructure in the Region lags that in the industrial countries and East Asia more dramatically. Institutional quality in the Region is better than that in Latin America, somewhat below that in East Asia, and significantly below that in industrial countries. Educational levels in the Region are not dramatically different from those in East Asia and only slightly below those in industrial countries.

We turn next to estimating the impact on productivity growth in the Region of a potential improvement in structural policies to the level of the median advanced industrial country. Attempts to estimate the elasticity of productivity growth with respect to policy in a

FIGURE 1.9

The Region Lags behind Comparators in Several Key Structural Reforms

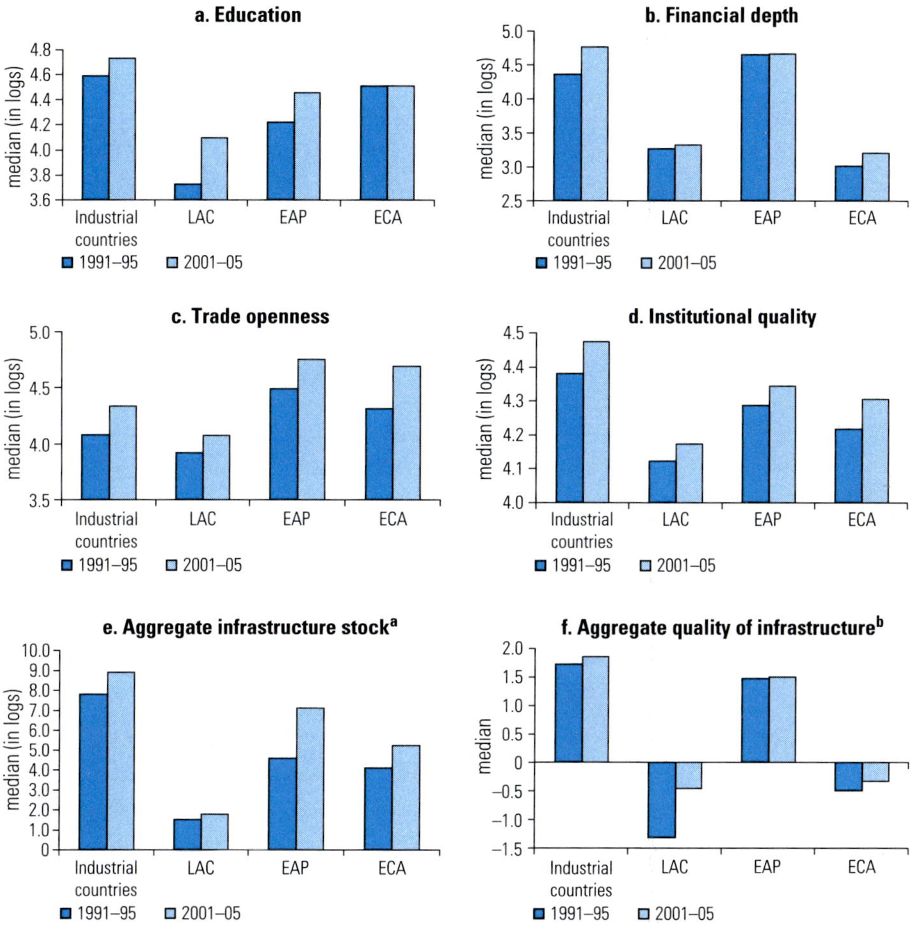

Source: World Bank staff calculations (see appendix 1B for data sources).

a. First principal component of main telephone lines, electricity generating capacity, and total roads.
b. First principal component of telecommunications, electricity, and road quality.

cross-country setting often prove contentious. The most common concerns have to do with omitted variables and the endogeneity of policy. However, the alternative is merely to look at the extent to which a given country lags the cross-country leader along each dimension of policy, without any attempt to obtain a sense of whether the particular policy dimension is related to productivity improvements. In such a scenario, one would need to rely on hunch or assumption to assert that progress along a given dimension of policy should have an effect that equals, is greater than, or is less than the effect of progress along other dimensions. An attempt to instill some rigor in the methodology is clearly a better alternative. Box 1.2

BOX 1.2

Estimating the Impact of Structural Reforms

Estimating the productivity impact of potential structural improvements in a country is a two-step process. The first step involves estimating the relationship between productivity growth and the structural determinants of this growth in a cross-country setting. The second step involves using the estimated elasticities from the cross-country relationship to determine the impact on productivity growth of a potential structural improvement in the country of interest. The estimation of the cross-country relationship often proves contentious. The primary concerns have to do with the endogeneity of independent variables and the sensitivity of the estimates to omitted variables. The analysis recorded in this chapter has involved a number of techniques to address these concerns.

Methodology

A large macroeconomic panel data set has been used that comprises 86 countries and nine nonoverlapping five-year time periods covering 1960–2005. The dependent variable is the growth rate of labor productivity, and the independent variables include a number of structural variables of interest (education, financial depth, trade openness, institutional quality, infrastructure stocks, and infrastructure quality) and a number of control variables (initial level of labor productivity, lack of price stability, government burden, and terms of trade shocks). The estimation technique is the generalized method of moments estimator developed for dynamic panel data models. This technique offers a number of advantages. First, it controls for unobserved time-specific and country-specific omitted variables. Second, it partially controls for the endogeneity of explanatory variables by using the lagged values as instruments.

Measures of Structural Determinants of Productivity

The following measures are used to capture the structural determinants of productivity. Education is proxied by the gross enrollment rate of secondary schooling. Financial depth is measured as domestic credit to the private sector as a percentage of GDP. Trade openness is measured as the sum of exports and imports as a percentage of GDP. Institutional quality is proxied by way of the index of political risk of the *International Country Risk Guide* (PRS Group, various issues). Infrastructure stock is measured using a weighted average of three different measures of physical infrastructure: main or mobile telephone lines per thousand workers, electricity generating capacity per thousand workers, and length of roads per square kilometer of surface area. Similarly, infrastructure quality is a weighted average of three different measures of quality: waiting time for the installation of main telephones lines, percentage of electricity losses in transmission and distribution, and share of paved roads in total roads. The weights used in aggregating the infrastructure indicators are obtained through a principal components analysis that yields weights to maximize the variance of the aggregate index.

Source: Calderón 2007.

provides greater detail on the method used to obtain these estimates and the techniques employed to address the most common concerns.

The greatest boost to productivity growth in the Region would be derived from improvements in infrastructure quality, financial development, infrastructure stock, and institutional quality. Figure 1.10 shows the impact on productivity growth in the Region from raising the level of each dimension of policy to the level of the median industrial country. Thus, if infrastructure quality in the Region were raised to the level of the median industrial country, productivity growth in the Region would be raised by 1.25 percentage points. If infrastructure stock were also raised to the level of the median industrial country, productivity growth would be raised by an additional 0.47 percentage points. Raising financial depth to the level of the median industrial country would provide an additional 0.78 percentage points of productivity growth, while an increase in institutional quality to the industrial country median would provide 0.28 percentage points.

Different countries would respond to the potential improvements in structural indicators depending on their level of progress. The impact of such improvements on productivity growth would be greater in the CIS than in the EU-10. This influence is because, compared with the EU-10, the levels of the various policy indicators in the CIS are further below the median industrial country. Looking at the productivity impact in individual countries in the Region (figure 1.11), one obtains a sense of the policy dimension along which the particular country is relatively further behind the industrial country median. Thus, in Lithuania, the productivity impact of raising financial depth would be greater than the productivity impact of raising infrastructure quality and stock, suggesting that Lithuania lags the median industrial

FIGURE 1.10

Infrastructure and Financial Depth Improvements Would Do the Most to Boost Productivity

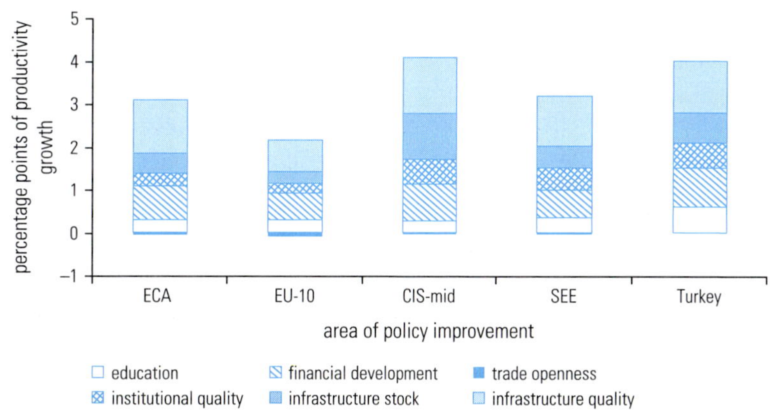

Source: World Bank staff calculations (see appendix 1.B for data sources); Calderón 2007.

FIGURE 1.11

Productivity Gains from Policy Improvements Vary across Countries

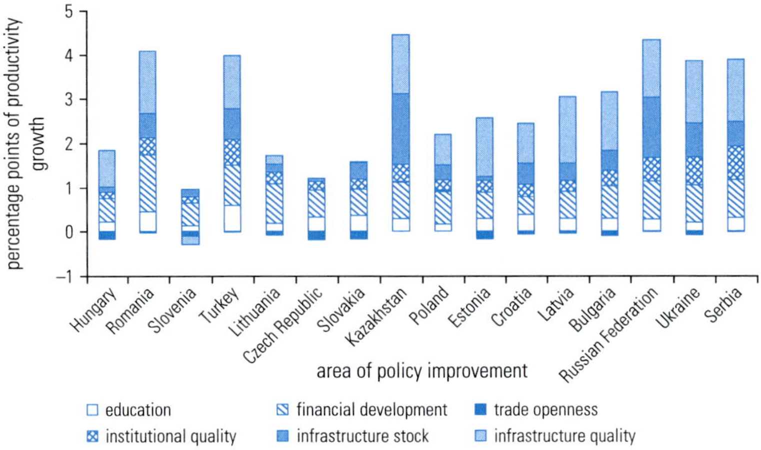

Sources: World Bank staff calculations (see appendix 1.B for data sources); Calderón 2007.

FIGURE 1.12

Infrastructure Upgrading Shows High Returns

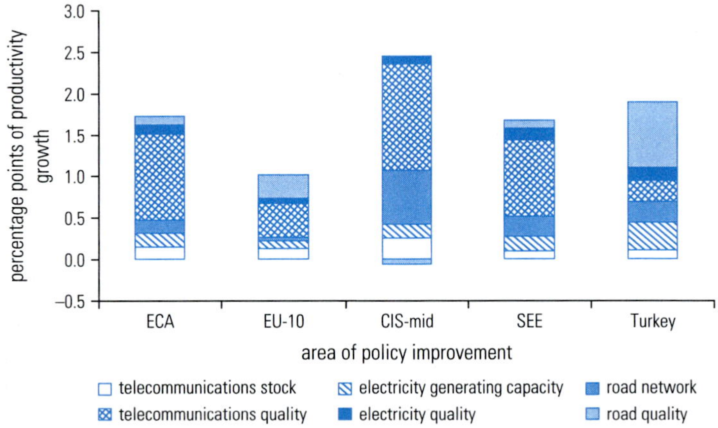

Sources: World Bank staff calculations (see appendix 1.B for data sources); Calderón 2007.

country more along the dimension of financial depth than along the dimension of infrastructure. This suggests that improving financial depth in Lithuania is probably a more pressing need than improving infrastructure in the effort to sustain and accelerate productivity growth. Meanwhile, in Croatia, the productivity impact of improving infrastructure exceeds that of improving financial depth.

The productivity impact from an improvement in infrastructure depends on both the type of improvement and the country group within the Region. Because infrastructure stock and quality jointly have the greatest impact, we disaggregate the impact into different components of infrastructure stock and quality (figure 1.12). We find that telecommunications quality has the greatest impact overall in the Region. Conversely, road density has a large impact in the CIS, while road quality has a large impact in Turkey.

Conclusions

Substantial improvements in productivity have been the driving force behind strong growth in the Region since 1999. This has put the Region on a trajectory of convergence toward industrial country income and productivity levels. These large productivity improvements are not merely a one-time boost in productivity driven by improvements in capital utilization during the course of recovery following the start of the transition. Rather, they reflect real improvements in efficiency in the organization of production. The following chapters will explore in detail how reallocation and restructuring at the sectoral and firm levels have contributed to these improvements in efficiency.

The pattern of productivity growth across the Region has been driven in large part by progress in the policy reforms necessary for transition to a market economy. The rapid and sustained pace of reforms in the EU-10 has led to strong and sustained productivity growth in these countries over time. Progress in policy reforms in the CIS through 1998 set the stage for strong productivity growth after 1999 in these countries following a period of protracted decline.

The still large productivity gap between the Region and the industrialized world reflects an opportunity for sustained high productivity growth through catchup in the years ahead. The adoption of improved production techniques and other productivity-enhancing technologies available in the industrialized world should allow the countries of the Region to close the productivity gap rapidly. Successful adoption of such techniques will, of course, require a supportive policy environment.

Sustaining high productivity growth in the years ahead will require more progress in structural policy reforms. Lagging reformers will need to accelerate the pace of progress in the transition policy reform agenda. Across the Region, the impact of improvements along a range of structural determinants of productivity will depend on the relative progress made by each country along each structural dimension of policy. If the countries of the Region are able to tackle the different sets of policy challenges necessary to sustain high productivity growth going forward, the optimism that accompanied the start of the transition in 1991 will have been justified for many years to come.

Notes

1. This decomposition does not include a separate term for the contribution of human capital accumulation because comparable and reliable data on educational attainment are not available for most countries in the Region for the period of interest (1990–2005). The measured TFP growth will thus include any contribution arising from changes in the stock of human capital. However, because the focus is on a relatively short period (1990–2005), with a greater focus on an even shorter period (1999–2005), it is unlikely that much of the difference in the rate of TFP growth across countries will be due to differences in the evolution of the stock of human capital.
2. Capacity utilization–adjusted TFP growth rates are calculated as follows: The capital stock series (which reflects the stock of *available* capital) is multiplied by the capacity utilization rates (obtained from the Russian Economic Barometer Survey Database) to derive a series reflecting *employed* or *utilized* capital stock. This series on *utilized* capital stock is used to repeat the growth decomposition. Because the capacity utilization rate rises rapidly after 1999, the *utilized* capital stock grows more rapidly than the *available* capital stock, so that the contribution of capital accumulation to growth is higher and the TFP growth rate is lower. Oomes and Dynnikova (2006) obtain similar results. Because the capacity utilization numbers are obtained from a survey of enterprises and the capital stock series is constructed using macroeconomic data, our estimates are accurate only to the extent that the numbers reflect capacity utilization trends in the overall economy.

CHAPTER 2

Sectoral Patterns of Productivity Growth

This chapter aims to describe the patterns of productivity growth across and within sectors (agriculture, manufacturing, and services) and identify the main policy factors driving these patterns. One must look beneath the aggregate numbers presented in chapter 1 to see how sectoral differences explain productivity growth. This chapter shows that the productivity surge in the Region is a reflection of a better allocation of resources across sectors, but, more importantly, of within-sector productivity growth.

The chapter begins with an overview of the sectoral shifts that have taken place since the start of transition. It next analyzes the respective contributions of cross-sectoral reallocation and within-sector productivity growth. It then discusses in detail the patterns of productivity in agriculture, manufacturing, and services and outlines the main policy implications.

Cross-Sectoral Shifts

A Dramatic Shift of Resources to Services

There has been a large resource reallocation into the service sector. The economies of Eastern Europe and the Former Soviet Union faced significant challenges in reallocating resources at the start of the transition as a result of structural distortions inherited from central planning: an oversized manufacturing sector and an underdeveloped service sector. Services have grown relative to agriculture and industry across the Region. For instance, in the EU-10, the share of services in total value added rose dramatically, from 40 percent in 1999 to 60 percent in 2005. Labor also moved to services across all country groups except for the SEE countries (figure 2.1).

These sectoral shifts followed the standard development paradigm, although patterns of labor reallocation differed across countries. The structural gap inherited from central planning narrowed, but this adjustment differed across countries. Following the methodology developed by Raiser, Schaffer, and Schuchhardt (2006) and drawing on updated sectoral shares of employment, this section illustrates country transition paths (with the starting point set in 1990 and the ending point set in 2004). The changes in sectoral employment shares are then benchmarked against the average among 50 industrialized market economies. The main results of this analysis are summarized below (see appendix 2.A for additional details).

- *In all countries, workers moved away from manufacturing.* The move toward market economies was reflected in significant declines in the share of employment in manufacturing. However, the wealthier countries (EU-10) found themselves, in 2004, with shares of manufacturing employment that were still higher than the market economy benchmark (figure 2.2). In contrast, the low income CIS countries had shares of manufacturing employment below the market economy benchmark.

FIGURE 2.1
A Substantial Shift of Output and Employment to Services

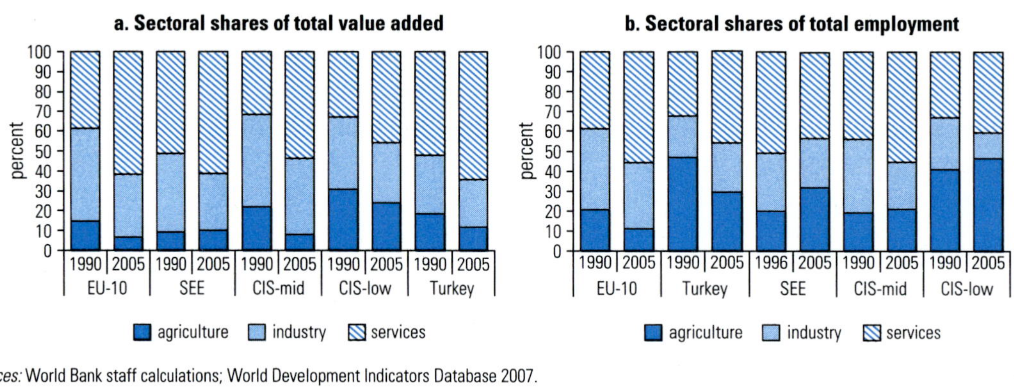

Sources: World Bank staff calculations; World Development Indicators Database 2007.

Note: The definition of services in the World Development Indicators Database includes government services and market services. The definition of industry covers manufacturing, construction, electricity, gas, and water.

FIGURE 2.2

During Transition, Labor Shifted to Agriculture in the Low Income CIS Countries

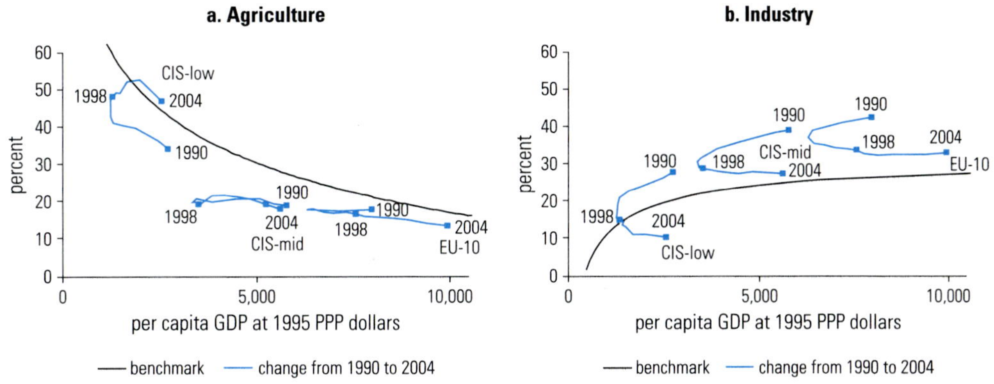

Source: World Bank staff calculations; data are from Raiser, Schaffer, and Schuchhardt 2006.

Note: The definition of industry covers manufacturing, construction, electricity, gas, and water. PPP = Purchasing power parity.

- *Labor shifted to agriculture in most low income CIS countries.* In poorer countries of the Former Soviet Union, labor shifted out of manufacturing toward agriculture, which increased the share of agriculture by around 20 percentage points. Agriculture was the employer of last resort because of the lack of opportunities in services and the absence of adequate social safety nets. As a result, the share of employment in agriculture in 2004 was still well above the corresponding share in the market economies (figure 2.2).

- *Labor shifted to market services in all countries.* All the transition economies started the transition with small market-oriented service sectors. During transition, the EU-10 countries and the middle income CIS countries adjusted by increasing the share of employment in services, moving closer to the patterns in market economies (figure 2.3). In these countries, the share of services in total employment increased by about 5 percentage points during the transition, while the share of manufacturing fell by about 3 percentage points. In contrast, in the low income CIS countries, market services gained little as a share in total employment, and the employment share was still below that in market economies.

The shift to services drove up overall productivity levels in most countries (except the CIS). Value added per worker is the lowest in agriculture and the highest in services. As a result, the shift in employment away from agriculture and manufacturing into services, as occurred in the EU-10, was productivity-enhancing (figure 2.4).

FIGURE 2.3

Labor Shifted to Services in the Middle Income CIS and the EU-10

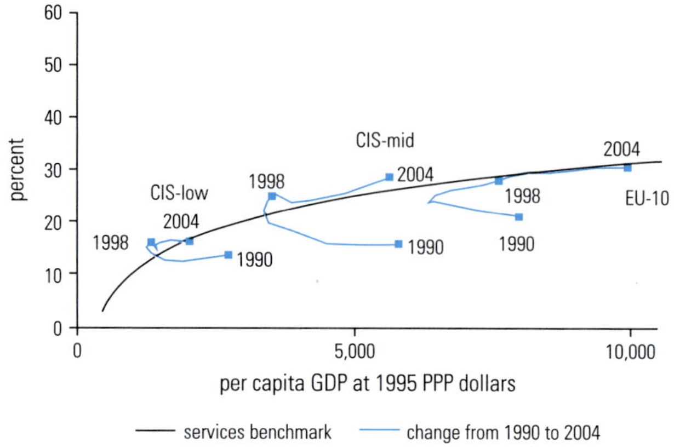

Source: World Bank staff calculations.

FIGURE 2.4

Higher Value Added per Worker in Services Raised Overall Labor Productivity in Most Countries, 1999–2004

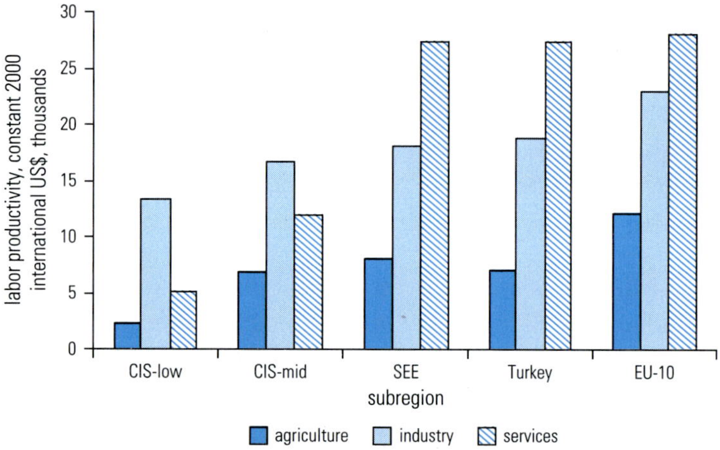

Sources: World Bank staff calculations; World Development Indicators Database 2007.

Within-Sector Productivity Improvements Are Drivers of Productivity Growth

Is overall productivity growth mainly driven by sectoral shifts or by within-sector productivity gains? Answering this question requires performing a shift-share analysis that decomposes aggregate productivity growth into three main components: (a) the *within* effect, which captures the impact of productivity growth within individual sectors on aggregate productivity in the economy; (b) the *between* effect, which reflects the impact of the reallocation of employment from less productive to more productive sectors; and (c) the *cross* effect,[1] which captures the impact of reallocating employment into sectors with growing productivity (see box 2.1 and appendix 2.B).

The analysis conducted in this section decomposes labor productivity growth by sectors.[2] The analysis is first conducted for the entire economy and focuses on the relative contributions of three main sectors—agriculture, industry, and services—to overall labor

BOX 2.1

Shift-Share Analysis: Decomposing Aggregate Labor Productivity Growth

Shift-share analysis permits the decomposition of aggregate labor productivity growth to assess the relative roles of (a) within-sector productivity gains, (b) shifts of employment from sectors with low productivity growth to sectors with high productivity growth, and (iii) shifts of employment from sectors with low productivity levels to those with high productivity levels. Productivity for the entire economy is expressed as the sum of the productivity level of each sector weighted by the sectoral employment shares, as follows:

$$P_m = \frac{Y_m}{L_m} = \sum_{j=1}^{n} \frac{Y_j}{L_j} * \frac{L_j}{L_m} = \sum_{j=1}^{n} P_j * S_j$$

where Y is output, L is employment by sector ($j = 1 \ldots n$) and the total economy (m), P is labor productivity (Y/L), and S is the sectoral employment share. In a discrete time perspective, the expression may be rewritten as follows:

$$\frac{P^t_m - P^0_m}{P^0_m} = \frac{\sum_{j=1}^{n} (P^t_j - P^0_j) * S^0_j}{\sum_{j=1}^{n} P^0_j} + \frac{\sum_{j=1}^{n} P^0_j * (S^t_j - S^0_j)}{\sum_{j=1}^{n} P^0_j} + \frac{\sum_{j=1}^{n} (P^t_j - P^0_j) * (S^t_j S^0_j)}{\sum_{j=1}^{n} P^0_j}$$

for a current year t and a base year 0.

The first term on the right-hand side is the within-industry contribution to overall productivity growth (the within term). The second term may be defined as the static shift effect, which captures the contribution arising from changes in the sectoral composition of employment (the between term). The third term represents the joint effect of changes in employment shares and sectoral productivity (the cross term). It is positive if sectors with above-average productivity growth increase their share in total employment; it is negative if expanding sectors have below-average productivity growth or if the shares in total employment of sectors with high productivity growth are also declining.

Source: Timmer and Szirmai 2000.

productivity growth. It covers all countries in the Region and draws on data from the World Development Indicators Database.

The main finding in this section is that the bulk of the Region's productivity surge over 1999–2004 is explained by within-sector productivity growth. Reallocation effects were also important, but the contribution of these was small. The largest contributor to total productivity growth was the within component (see figure 2.5). The within component is not as large in Turkey as it is in other countries because the period average is affected by the decline in productivity following the currency collapse in Turkey in February 2001. Labor is generally moving to sectors with high productivity (manufacturing and services) and out of sectors with low productivity (agriculture). This change is reflected in a positive between term. Labor is also moving out of sectors with increasing productivity (agriculture and manufacturing) and into sectors with lower productivity (services). This shift is reflected in a negative cross term (figure 2.5). In the CIS and SEE, the cross and between terms tend to cancel each other out. These findings are consistent with the firm-level analysis carried out on a sample of Eastern European and Former Soviet Union countries covering NACE 74 sectors (see chapter 3).

A more disaggregated analysis is then performed for the EU-8 (the Czech Republic, Estonia, Hungary, Latvia, Lithuania, Poland, the Slovak Republic, and Slovenia) across nine broad sectors of the International Standard Industrial Classification of all Economic Activities (ISIC). The data are taken from the EU KLEMS Database (see appendix 2.B

FIGURE 2.5

Within-Sector Productivity Is the Main Driver of the Productivity Surge, 1999–2004

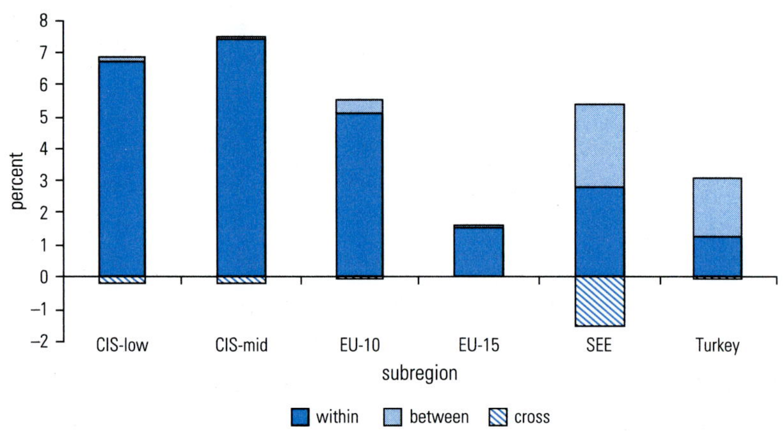

Sources: World Bank staff calculations; World Development Indicators Database 2007.

for more details). The disaggregated shift-share analysis yields three main sets of findings (see appendix 2.B for details):

- First, the within component contributions to aggregate productivity growth were large and increased over time; in contrast, the reallocation effects were small and were mostly driven by labor shifts away from agriculture and manufacturing toward services.
- Second, the largest within component contributions to total manufacturing productivity growth arose from fabricated metals, machinery, and food and beverages. The reallocation effects were small except in a few industries. Medium- and high-technology industries (motor vehicles, electrical machinery, and radio and television) accounted for a large proportion of the reallocation effects. This finding is not surprising. In these industries, the entry of new productive firms contributes the most to total productivity growth (see chapter 3).
- Third, the within component contributions to service productivity growth, aside from construction and real estate, were largely driven by backbone services: electricity and water, transport, telecommunications, and financial services. These industries are called backbone because they have both direct and indirect effects on aggregate productivity growth, providing critical inputs to downstream manufacturing firms. The reallocation effects were small, suggesting small labor shifts across service industries. Business support services and real estate accounted for the largest reallocation effects toward service productivity growth. In these industries, the between component was large and positive.

In sum, the productivity surge seems to have been mostly driven by within-sector productivity improvements, although the reallocation effects were also important. In slow reformers (CIS and SEE), the reallocation effects reflected the response to recent policy reforms aiming at strengthening competition. However, these countries still face deep restructuring. They need to accelerate the reallocation of resources away from low-productive to higher-productivity activities if they are to catch up with more advanced reformers in the Region. The reallocation effects have slowed in the more advanced reformers (EU-8), reflecting the gains already made. However, even in the more advanced reformers, there are some sectors (agriculture, mining, energy, transport services) in which there is still potential for achieving productivity gains from the reallocation of resources toward more productive uses.

Productivity Growth within Sectors: A Bird's-Eye View

The previous section concluded that within-sector productivity growth explained most of the productivity surge in the Region. The focus now turns to the productivity patterns of the main sectors of the economy (agriculture, manufacturing, and services) and the main policy drivers of sectoral performance.[3]

The shares of agriculture and industry in total value added and employment have fallen, while the share of services has grown. The share of industry in total value added averaged 36 percent during 1990–98 and fell to 32 percent during 1999–2004. The share of services in total value added grew from 44 to 54 percent during the same period. The share of industry in total employment averaged 30 percent over 1990–98 and fell to 26 percent over 1999–2004, while the average share of services in total employment increased from 63 to 68 percent (figure 2.6). In the EU-15, these structural changes followed the same pattern.

Productivity growth in both industry and agriculture exceeded that in services, and productivity gains in most countries in the Region were higher than those in the EU-15 during 1999–2005. In Turkey and the SEE, the growth in agricultural productivity exceeded that in manufacturing and services. In the EU-10, productivity grew more quickly in manufacturing and agriculture than in services. In the CIS, productivity growth, particularly in the most recent period, was the highest in the Region, and the growth followed similar patterns across all three sectors, reflecting a broad economic recovery after a deep recession (figure 2.7). However, across sectors, a substantial gap in productivity levels remained between the Region and the EU-15. Labor productivity in the EU-15 is more than three times greater than the average in the Region. To accelerate a convergence toward EU-15

FIGURE 2.6

The Share of Services in Valued Added and Employment Has Risen

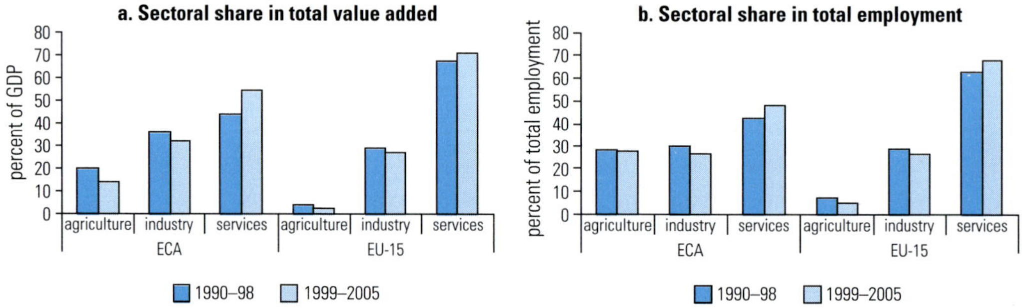

Sources: World Bank staff calculations; World Development Indicators Database 2007.

FIGURE 2.7

Relative to the EU-15, Labor Productivity Gains Were High, but Levels Lagged, 1999–2004

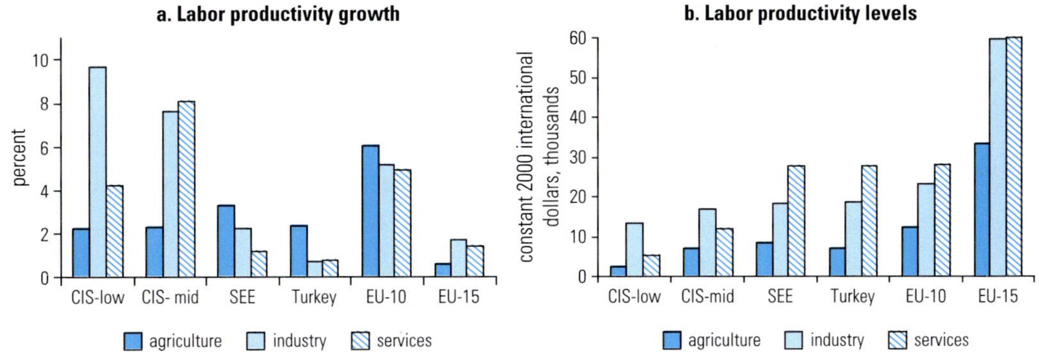

Sources: World Bank staff calculations; World Development Indicators Database 2007.

levels, sustained productivity growth is needed across agriculture, manufacturing, and services.

The next three sections assess in detail the productivity patterns within agriculture, manufacturing, and services. The main findings are as follows:

- *Agricultural productivity growth was driven by labor shedding, though higher farm efficiency was also important.* In labor-intensive countries (Albania, Armenia, Georgia, and the Kyrgyz Republic), a shift from large-scale collective farming to small-scale individual farming led to dramatic gains in technical efficiency, with relatively small losses in scale efficiency. In capital- and land-intensive countries (the Czech Republic, Hungary, and the Slovak Republic), any gains in labor productivity arose primarily because large farms shed labor after privatization. In countries where neither type of reform (privatization and land reforms) was undertaken vigorously, the productivity gains were generally delayed and modest. During the first stage of transition, trade liberalization, privatization, and land reforms were required so as to accelerate farm restructuring and facilitate the sectoral reallocation of labor. As countries progressed along the transition path, a better investment climate and greater efficiency in service sectors are needed to boost within-farm productivity growth and provide off-farm job opportunities.

- *Manufacturing productivity growth was driven by efficiency gains in industries with higher capacity for innovation.* In manufacturing, a group of medium- and high-technology industries seemed to drive productivity growth, exhibiting the highest average annual productivity growth rates. This group employed a large proportion of high-skilled workers, produced ICT goods, or used a relatively large amount of ICT capital. The manufacturing industries in the high-technology group included office machinery, electrical and electronic equipment, and optical instruments. Other industries, such as traditional consumer goods manufacturing, were within the low-technology groups, with lower average productivity growth. Not surprisingly, high-technology industries displayed higher TFP growth in countries that showed more progress in liberalizing key service industries and in financial sector development and that had more skilled workforces, more flexible labor markets, and higher R&D investments financed by the private sector.

- *Service productivity growth was driven by strong performance in backbone industries: transport, telecommunications, and financial intermediation services.* Service productivity growth was driven by backbone industries with higher productivity and a greater propensity to use or produce ICT: the retail trades, transport, telecommunications, and financial intermediation services. Productivity growth in these industries during 1997–2004 outstripped average productivity growth in the EU-15, suggesting that there is a potential for services to drive growth in the Region. Policy makers in the Region can play a major role in sustaining growth momentum in services by pursuing more service liberalization across the board, removing regulatory barriers to competition, and attracting more foreign investment and trade flows.

Agricultural Productivity

Farm systems under central planning targeted production rather than profitability and operated in an environment of highly distorted incentives. Output prices were not set in response to forces of supply and demand. Farms were overdimensioned or uneconomic in size and run under soft budget constraints, with strong subsidies for energy and fertilizer inputs. It was expected that the transition to a market economy would significantly improve productivity in the short to medium term by providing incentives for a more efficient utilization of resources. While many of the expected changes have occurred in many EU-10 countries, the experience of the Region has been uneven, and, in the CIS and SEE, progress has been much slower.

The main finding of this section is that labor reallocation was a key driver of agricultural productivity growth, although within-farm productivity growth was also important. In most countries relying on labor-intensive technologies, agricultural productivity growth arose from within-farm productivity growth ignited by the shift from large-scale collective farming to small-scale individual farming. In land-abundant countries relying on capital-intensive technologies, agricultural productivity gains arose primarily because large farms shed labor following land privatization and farm restructuring. However, the boost provided to labor productivity by land redistribution was a one-time event. Sustained gains in agricultural productivity will require (a) greater trade and foreign investment flows into the sector to support on-farm technology transfer, (b) improved financial and transport sectors to facilitate the development of the sector, and (c) less labor market rigidities and greater education investments to improve the mobility of agricultural workers.

The analysis focuses mainly on labor productivity, though other productivity indicators are also used depending on data availability: (a) yields (output per unit of land) and (b) TFP growth. The latter is estimated for a subset of countries in the Region for which input factor data (land, labor, capital, fertilizer, and animal stock) are available. Drawing on farm-level data, the analysis is also performed on TFP growth.

Agriculture Performance

As we saw in the previous section, agricultural shares in total output declined in most countries in the Region, but employment shares differed across countries. In general, the decline in the terms of trade and the reduction in agricultural output prices were accompanied by dramatic reductions in input use in agriculture. Agricultural shares of output fell across the Region. In contrast, land use remained relatively stable, with the exception of some CIS countries (such as Kazakhstan and the Kyrgyz Republic) where land abandonment has increased in recent years. The trends in agricultural labor use have diverged significantly across countries. Notably, labor use in agriculture declined dramatically in most EU-10 countries, while it remained constant or even increased in low-income CIS and SEE countries.

The Region saw a remarkable recovery in agricultural productivity growth over 1999–2004, but a substantial gap in productivity levels remains. Most CIS countries that experienced the deepest declines in productivity before 1998 have seen a remarkable recovery. Since 1999, labor productivity has been growing throughout the Region, albeit at quite different rates. In the EU-10, strong labor productivity growth in agriculture has been largely due to labor flowing away from agriculture. Nevertheless, a substantial divide in productivity levels remains, with EU-10 at one side of the spectrum, and the low income CIS at the opposite end (figure 2.8).

Agricultural TFP growth follows the same patterns as agricultural labor productivity growth across countries. Data on input factors

FIGURE 2.8

Labor Productivity in Agriculture Is a Problem

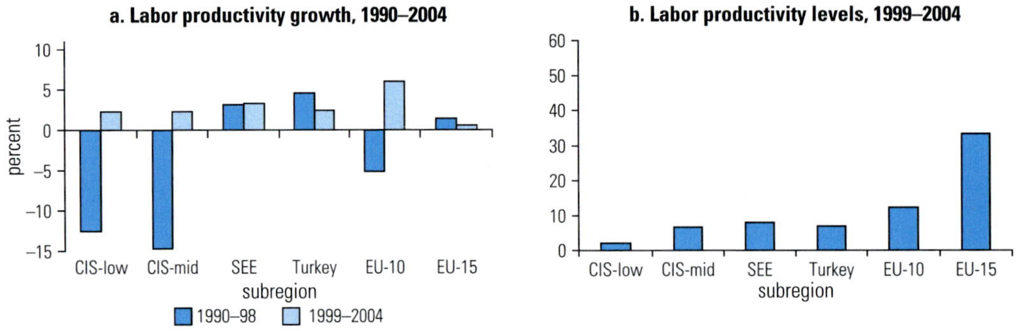

Sources: World Bank staff calculations; World Development Indicators Database 2007.

FIGURE 2.9

Average Farm Efficiency Is Highest in the EU-10

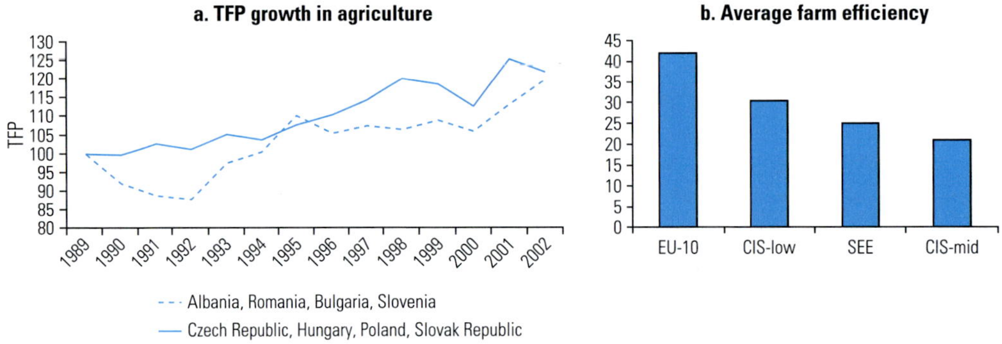

Source: Swinnen and Vranken 2007a.

Note: Farm efficiency score (b) is scaled from 0 to 100, with higher values indicating higher farm efficiency.

(land, labor, capital, fertilizer, and animal stock) from the Food and Agriculture Organization of the United Nations and the OECD permit the estimation of aggregate agricultural TFP growth for eight countries in the Region: Albania, Bulgaria, the Czech Republic, Hungary, Poland, Romania, the Slovak Republic, and Slovenia. TFP growth is higher in early reformers (figure 2.9).

Farm-level data confirm aggregate patterns: the more advanced EU-10 countries enjoy higher average farm efficiency than do the CIS and SEE countries (figure 2.9).[4]

Differences in agricultural productivity across countries reflect the deep divergences in the chosen paths of policy reforms. Three main groups of countries may be distinguished.

- In land- and capital-intensive EU-10 countries, labor productivity growth in agriculture is explained to a greater extent by reallocation (labor shedding) and subsequent capital deepening. In these countries, only about 5 percent of employment was in agriculture. The rapid outflow of labor from agriculture resulted in major gains in labor productivity despite modest yield increases (an average of about 3 percent annually). In some countries, such as the Czech Republic, Estonia, Hungary, Lithuania, and the Slovak Republic, productivity growth was still very strong (an average between 7 and 20 percent per year). A significant share of agriculture in all these countries was organized in large-scale farming companies that had made significant investments in capital. In countries dominated by small-scale individual farms, such as Latvia, Poland, and Slovenia, labor productivity growth was more limited.

- In labor-abundant countries, most low income CIS countries and the SEE, agricultural productivity growth did not arise from labor shedding, but from a shift to small farms following land privatization reforms. In Albania and Azerbaijan, almost half the population is still employed in agriculture, and virtually all agricultural land is cultivated on small individual farms. In these countries, there was no significant outflow of labor away from agriculture, unlike in the EU-10. Productivity growth arose from gains spurred by land reforms that strengthened the incentives of farmers to boost efficiency. However, in most of these countries, land privatization in the absence of a social security mechanism led to the absorption of a typically older labor force into farming. As a result, productivity levels in these countries remained low.
- In countries with strong regional differences in initial technology and farm structures, regional variations in farm restructuring and labor adjustment patterns mimicked cross-country evidence. In Poland, the southern and eastern regions were characterized by small-scale and relatively small intensive production, while the western and northwestern regions were dominated by large-scale farms. In the western and northwestern regions, there was a rapid outflow of labor away from agriculture in the early transition years, with strong increases in labor productivity. In contrast, in the eastern and southern regions, there were fewer such adjustments, and surplus labor stayed on farms.

Policy Drivers of Agricultural Productivity

Uneven progress in reform and the interplay with initial resource intensities contribute in explaining differences in agricultural productivity patterns. Several policy reforms affected agricultural productivity patterns, including trade liberalization, the reduction of agriculture subsidies, and land privatization.

Trade liberalization, removal of or cuts in subsidies, and price liberalization had different effects on productivity and labor use across the Region. The reforms caused a substantial decline in the agricultural terms of trade in all but the poorest countries in the Region. This decline implied a strong reduction in the demand for agricultural labor. But trade and price liberalization also changed the relative factor costs. In many cases, price liberalization caused prices for other inputs, especially capital inputs, to increase relative to wages.

The effect of land privatization on agricultural productivity varied across countries. In labor-abundant countries, the breakup of large-scale farms into smaller individual farms increased the incentives of farmers to improve efficiency. In capital-abundant EU-10 countries, privatized farms, facing hard budget constraints and competition pressures, shed a large number of workers and made substantial technological improvements. In middle income CIS countries with relatively land- and capital-intensive production systems, but with ongoing soft-budget constraints, labor shedding was limited. However, after 1998, labor shedding by large corporate farms in Russia also contributed to labor-productivity increases.

After the initial impact of land privatization and trade liberalization, broader structural reforms are needed to sustain agricultural productivity growth. Policies aimed at strengthening market competition, improving the investment climate, and promoting service liberalization may boost agricultural productivity growth by improving the incentives for farmers to innovate.

Evidence offered by farm-level data shows a positive correlation between farm-productivity growth and reforms in the investment climate and competition. The correlation is closer with the EBRD index (a nonagricultural index capturing progress in the overall investment climate and market competition) than with the agricultural reform index compiled by the World Bank (capturing progress in land reforms, privatization, and other reforms in the sector). This suggests that the main policy drivers of farm-productivity growth are not specific to agriculture. General reforms improving the investment climate stimulate investments in some upstream agricultural sectors (such as agroprocessing) and also create off-farm employment. Trade and the inflow of foreign investments may also bring new technology into agrifood chains, fostering within-farm productivity growth.

The efficiency of service industries is also particularly important for agricultural productivity. Better performance in services as a result of liberalization may be crucial for productivity gains in agriculture. The use of service inputs in agriculture varies across the Region, but some common patterns emerge. Electricity, transport, and financial services have the highest shares of total service inputs in agriculture. Electricity usage in agriculture ranges from 4 percent of total inputs in Estonia and the Slovak Republic to 2 percent in Lithuania. The share of transport, the second most important service input, ranges from 3 percent in Bulgaria and Romania to nearly 5 percent in Lithuania (figure 2.10).

Empirical analysis shows that service liberalization exerts a strong positive effect on farm-productivity growth. The effect of liberalizing backbone services (transport, telecommunications, electricity, water, and financial intermediation) on labor productivity among corporate farms is positive and significant (see appendix 2.C). Farms that rely more on inputs from more liberalized services exhibit higher productivity than do other farms.

Although most countries of the Region have implemented (to a greater or lesser extent) these first-generation reforms, sustaining agricultural productivity growth requires parallel progress on two fronts:

- *Accelerating the pace of reallocation, particularly in the CIS.* State intervention in both price formation and trade policy remains a challenge in many CIS countries. Although there has been significant

FIGURE 2.10

The Efficiency of Service Industries Is Important in Agricultural Productivity

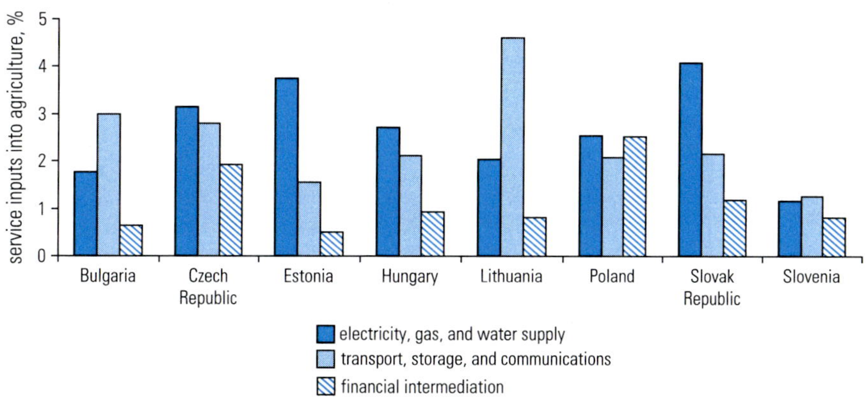

Sources: World Bank staff calculations; input-output tables (see appendix 2.C).

Note: The figure shows the share of the total intermediate consumption of agriculture that is accounted for by service industries, NACE 40–70.

progress toward a more liberal agricultural trade policy in recent years, land privatization and trade liberalization remain a priority in Tajikistan and Uzbekistan. In Russia and Ukraine, although land ownership has been transferred to private hands, the larger farms are still intact. Improvements in the education of rural workers and in social protection systems, by enhancing worker mobility, favor the reallocation of labor away from agriculture. The EU-10 countries also face the challenge of progressively reducing protection to the sector that has increased since EU accession.

- *Boosting within-farm productivity growth through stronger market competition in backbone services.* In the EU-10, backbone services (finance and transport) have improved considerably, but remain weak and mostly dominated by foreign banks that do not extend much credit to the agriculture sector. In most CIS and SEE countries, financial systems have not yet fully adjusted to the needs of a market-based agriculture sector, although, in some countries (Armenia, Georgia, and Moldova), agricultural credit cooperatives have recently emerged.

Manufacturing Productivity

This section focuses on a subset of countries (EU-8) for which disaggregated manufacturing data and comparable industrial PPP deflators are available.

Manufacturing Performance

Average annual labor productivity growth in manufacturing was much higher in the EU-8 than in the EU-15 (figure 2.11). Among the EU-8, the average annual labor productivity growth rate was highest in Lithuania and Poland and lowest in the Czech Republic and Latvia. Average annual labor productivity growth decreased in Estonia, Poland, and Slovenia. But, even in the EU-8, productivity levels lagged behind the EU-15. Although average labor productivity increased in all EU-8 countries from 1995–98 to 1999–2004, average labor productivity in the EU-8 was still less than 30 percent of that in the EU-15. Productivity also varied across the EU-8; it was highest in Poland and Slovenia and lowest in Latvia and Lithuania.

The productivity surge in manufacturing was driven by ICT industries that are often export oriented (figure 2.12). The highest average annual labor productivity growth in the EU-8 was in ICT-producing

FIGURE 2.11

Average Labor Productivity in the EU-8 Was Less Than 30 Percent of That in the EU-15

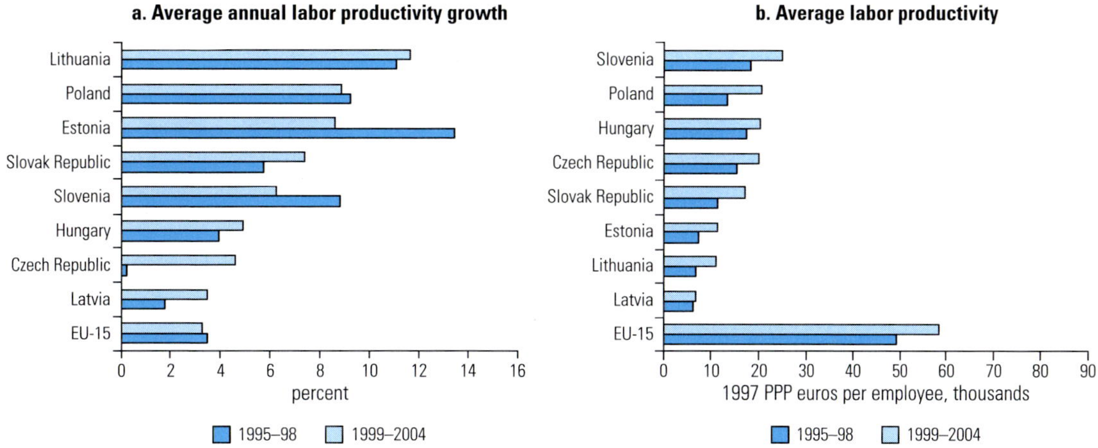

Sources: World Bank staff calculations; EU KLEMS Database 2007.

industries (radios and office machinery), as well as ICT-using industries (rubber and plastics, machinery and electrical apparatuses). In the EU-15, office machinery and electronics showed the highest productivity growth. In these industries, the large productivity gain is not only a reflection of capital deepening, but, more important, a result of rapid technological developments, which increased by several times the utility value of ICT products for the same value of inputs. (In the next section we examine in greater detail the roles of ICT and foreign trade in manufacturing productivity.) The highest labor productivity during 1999–2004 was in office machinery and chemicals. Across most industries, labor productivity is higher in the EU-15 than in the EU-8.

Only a few industries managed to sustain rapid productivity growth. Radio, television, and communication equipment; motor vehicles; and office machinery had the strongest productivity growth after 1995 (figure 2.13). These industries tend to be closely integrated into global production chains. (Later in the chapter we discuss in more detail the role of global production chains and network effects.)

Policy Drivers of Manufacturing Productivity

Wide disparities existed in labor productivity growth across manufacturing industries. Some of these differences were due to different

FIGURE 2.12

Labor Productivity Growth in Manufacturing Is Higher in the EU-8 Than in the EU-15, 1999–2004

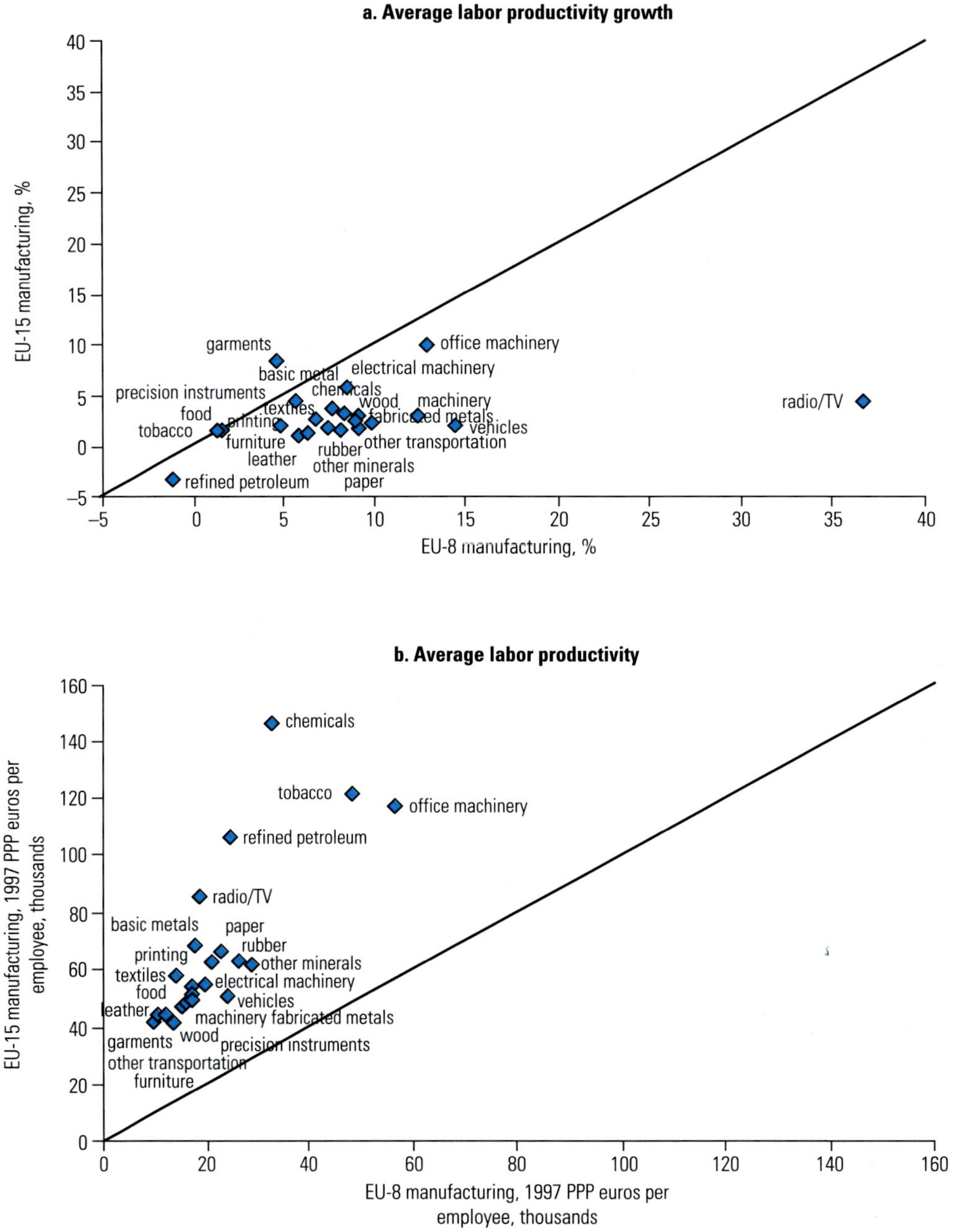

Sources: World Bank staff calculations; EU KLEMS Database 2007.

FIGURE 2.13

Only a Few Manufacturing Industries Sustained Strong Productivity Growth

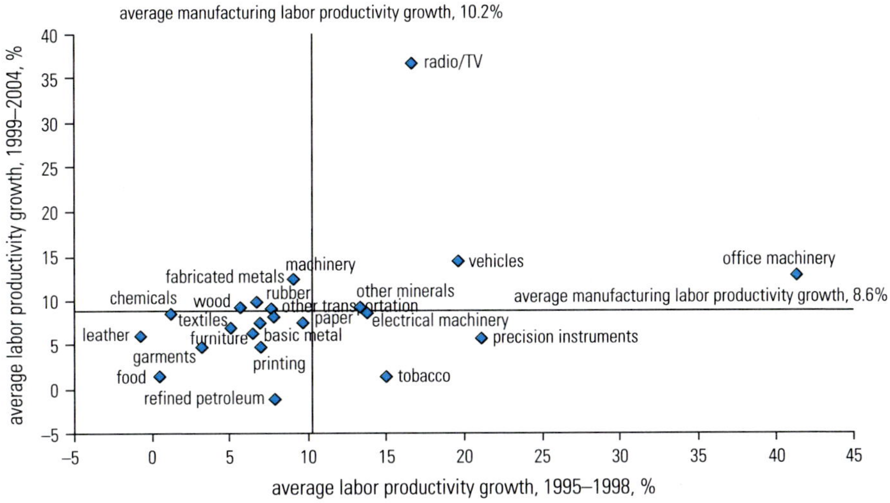

Sources: World Bank staff calculations; EU KLEMS Database 2007.

levels of investment (capital deepening) in capital-intensive industries (such as metals). Capital-intensive industries invested in ICT because the scope to automate plant operations and upgrade equipment to save labor and capital costs is greater. In these high-technology industries, TFP growth tends to be lower than labor productivity growth. But capital deepening is only part of the story. The highest productivity growth was in medium- and high-technology industries that employed highly skilled labor, drew on external financing, were more active in R&D, generated greater export sophistication and more innovation, and were more deeply integrated into global production chains (see figure 2.14).

Investing in ICT

ICT-producing industries showed the highest productivity in manufacturing and more rapid productivity growth over 1999–2004. In the EU-8, ICT-producing industries had the highest labor productivity during 1999–2004 (about 28,000 euros per worker in 1997 PPP terms; see figure 2.15). ICT-producing industries also experienced the most rapid productivity growth over 1999–2004, at more than 12 percent, relative to an average 7 percent labor productivity growth in non-ICT industries over the same period. However, the ICT-manufacturing sector in the EU-8 is still small and is potentially the main driver of convergence with EU-15 productivity levels (see later section on ICT).

FIGURE 2.14

Policy Drivers of Manufacturing TFP Growth, 1999–2004

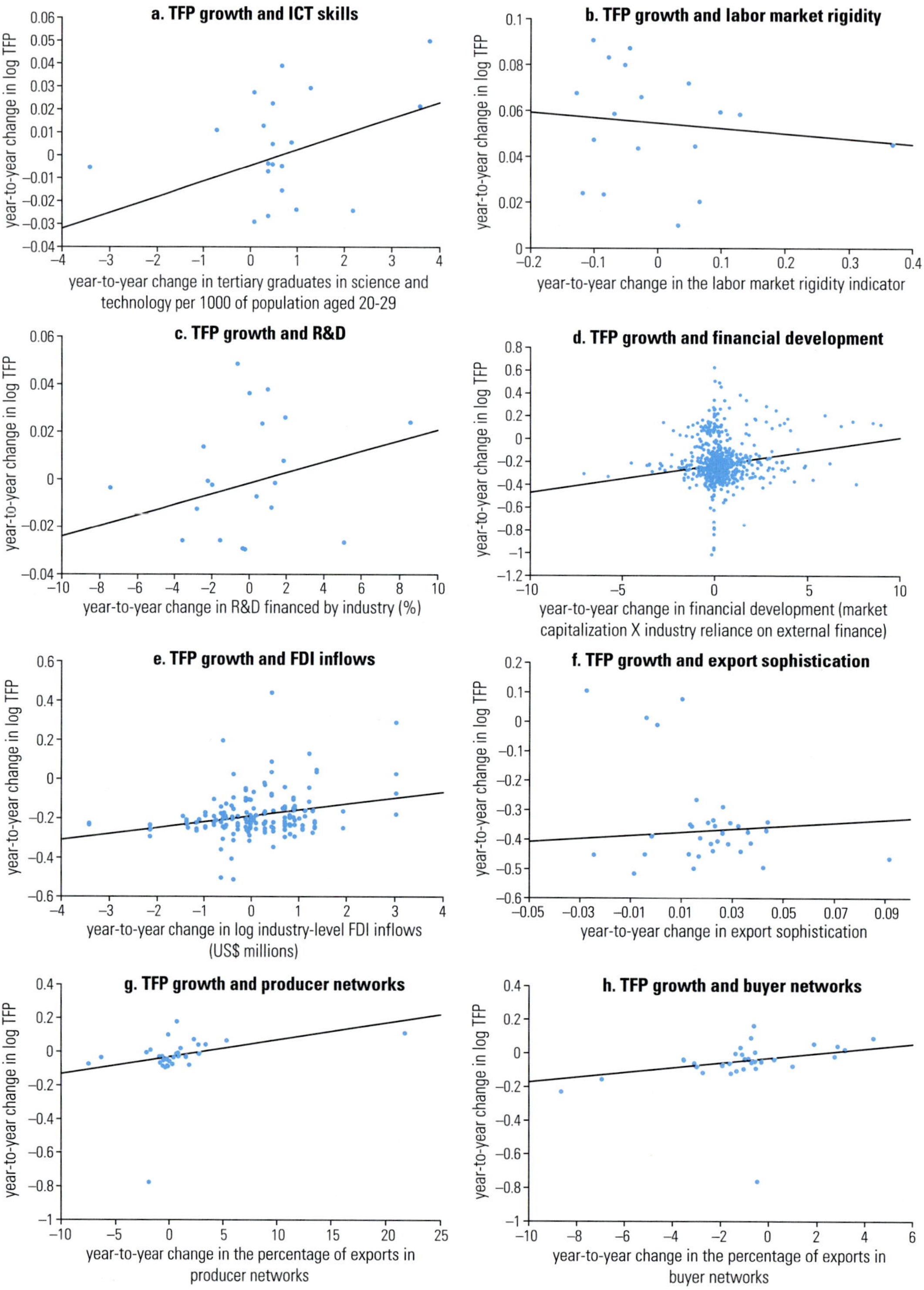

Sources: Authors' calculations; b. Economic Freedom of the World Database.

Note: The dependent variable is the change in log TFP from 1999 to 2004, subtracting the effects of all other repressors. See appendix 3.B for details.

Investing in Skills

Manufacturing industries that drew on high-skilled workers displayed higher productivity and more rapid productivity growth (9 percent annual labor productivity growth over 1999–2004) than industries that relied on low-skilled workers (figure 2.16).

Investing in skills may also help accelerate the pace of reallocation, leading to more productivity improvements. In the Region, high-technology industries were absorbing younger and more highly skilled workers than the low-technology sectors (figure 2.17). In Slovenia, younger and more skilled workers showed a higher probability of transiting into nonagricultural employment, specifically in the service sector (figure 2.18). An increase in the supply of tertiary education and, in particular, ICT-skilled labor, favored the shift of workers from lower- to higher-productivity activities in the EU-8.

FIGURE 2.15

ICT Industries Showed More Rapid Productivity Growth, 1999–2004

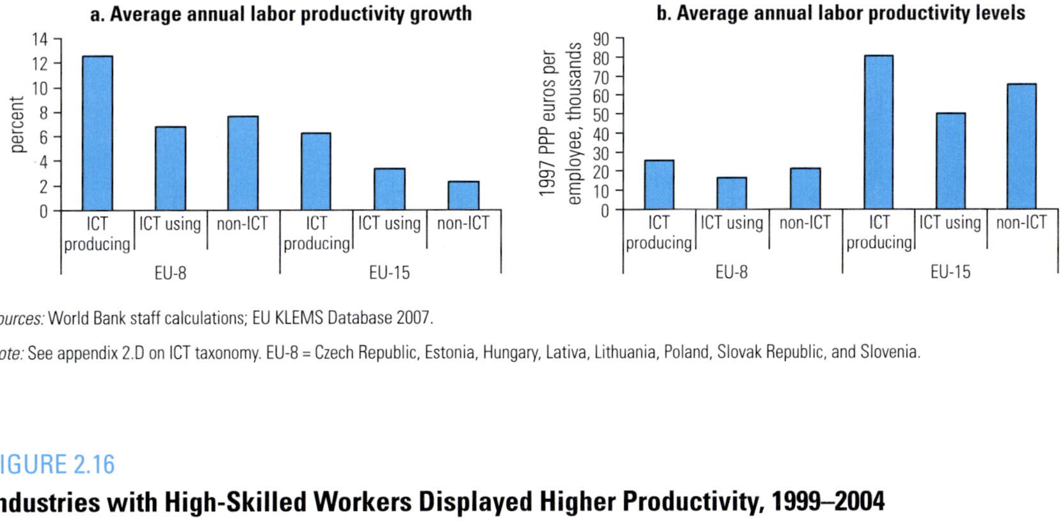

Sources: World Bank staff calculations; EU KLEMS Database 2007.

Note: See appendix 2.D on ICT taxonomy. EU-8 = Czech Republic, Estonia, Hungary, Lativa, Lithuania, Poland, Slovak Republic, and Slovenia.

FIGURE 2.16

Industries with High-Skilled Workers Displayed Higher Productivity, 1999–2004

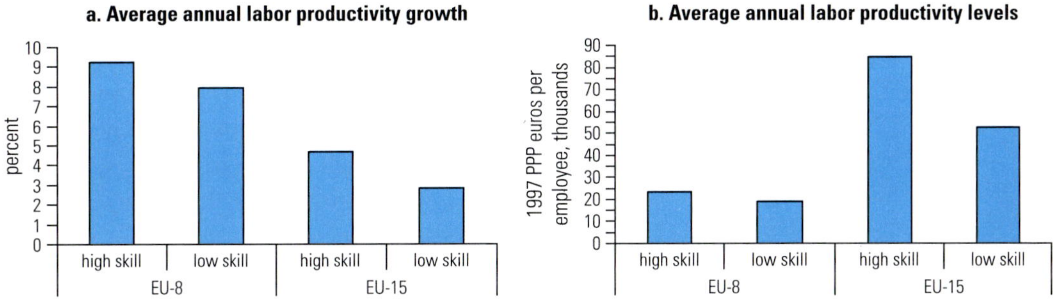

Sources: World Bank staff calculations; EU KLEMS Database 2007.

Note: See appendix 2.D on skill taxonomy.

FIGURE 2.17

Human Capital Moved from Less- to More-Productive Activities in Early Reformers

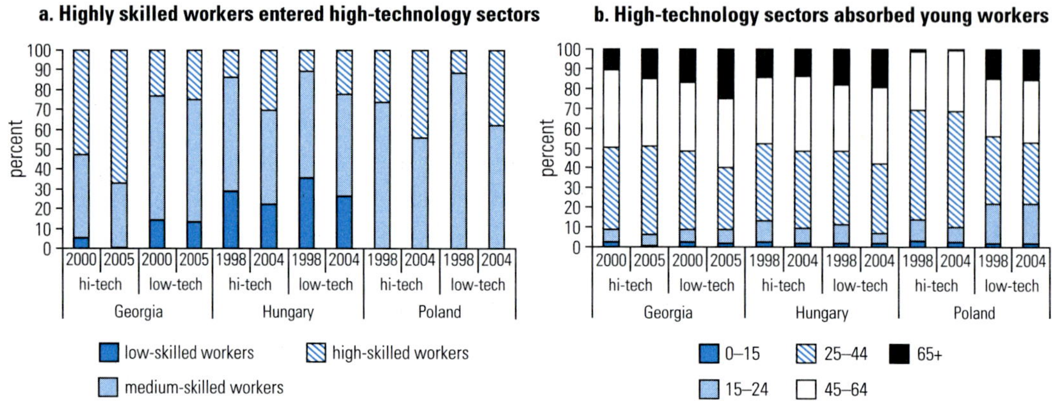

Sources: World Bank staff calculations; labor force surveys.

FIGURE 2.18

The Supply of ICT-Skilled Labor Expanded and Was Used More in Services

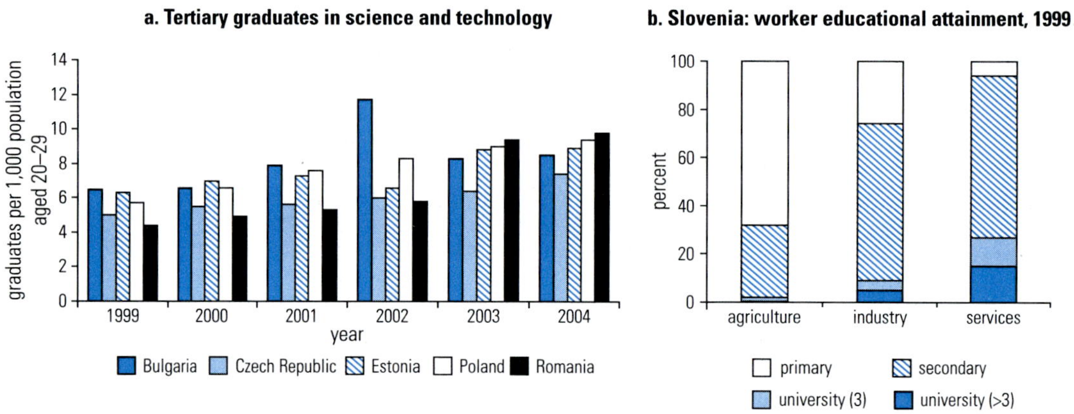

Sources: OECD 2007a; Bojnec and Dries 2005.

Secondary educational attainment was high and tertiary enrollments also started to grow thanks to education reforms beginning in the 1990s that aimed to meet the educational needs of a changing labor market. In upper secondary education, the reforms were geared to providing more work-oriented skills and reinforcing the general educational component of the system, which increased the proportion of students attending general secondary courses. The level of secondary educational attainment tended to be high by international standards. Tertiary enrollments also grew, driven principally by high and rising incomes and employment opportunities. In the Czech Republic, for example, the tertiary education enrollment rate more than doubled, from 7 to 15 percent, between 1995 and 2004.

But tertiary educational attainments are still low by international standards, and diversifying tertiary education toward more vocationally oriented courses is needed to reduce skill shortages and raise productivity. Reflecting demographic decline, the demand for secondary education will soon fall quite rapidly. At the same time, the tertiary education population will increase, and the pressures will stem not only from 19- to 25-year-olds, but also from a backlog in demand from older cohorts.

In addition, population aging in the EU-10 implies that considerable attention will have to be paid to improving the opportunities for lifelong learning. Currently, participation in continuing education is low, at only 5 percent of the working-age population. This is partly because providers have been slow to adapt to economic changes and business needs and partly because the possibilities of transferring individual qualifications across levels and types of institutions have been limited.

Improving Labor Market Flexibility

Onerous labor market regulations may depress productivity in low-technology industries if employers are restricted from shedding labor after the introduction of labor-saving technologies. Strict employment protection legislation is also likely to reduce productivity growth in high-technology industries with relatively low levels of market concentration where technologies tend to evolve or be replaced quickly. But the negative impact of labor market rigidities on industry-level productivity is likely to be less in high-technology industries with higher market concentration, such as in electronic components and aircraft (OECD 2001, 2004).

Greater labor market flexibility may improve worker mobility and facilitate the shift of labor from less- to more-productive activities. The direction of labor market reforms has been toward improving flexibility in hiring and firing regulations (for example, lower direct dismissal costs or the removal of trade union vetoes on dismissals), promoting temporary and part-time employment, and allowing for opting out on collective agreements. The EU-10 countries, as they were approaching entry into the EU, were more aggressive in liberalizing labor markets than others (Ukraine, for example). This development suggests that EU accession may have played a disciplining role in promoting labor market reforms (World Bank 2005a).

However, there is still room for more flexible labor markets. In the EU-10, the protection of permanent workers is better than in the OECD (figure 2.19). While employment protection legislation may help in ensuring secure and decent work, it is also important to balance these

FIGURE 2.19

The ECA Region Still Lags behind the OECD in Labor Market Flexibility, and Late Reformers Lag Even Further

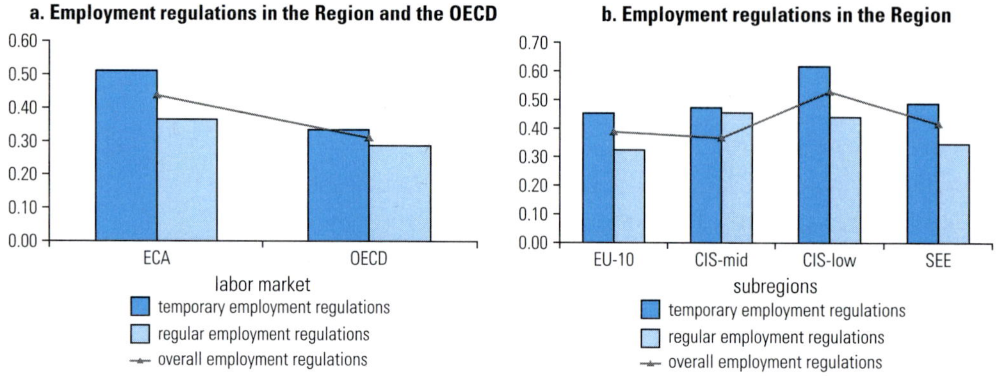

Sources: World Bank staff calculations; World Bank 2005.

Note: The employment regulation index is scaled from 0 to 1, with higher values indicating greater labor market rigidity.

considerations against the need for sufficient flexibility to promote the efficient allocation of labor and boost productivity growth. Allocative efficiency is still much lower in the EU-10 than in the EU-15 and the United States (see chapter 3).

Supporting Private R&D

R&D investments, particularly those financed by the private sector, tend to raise productivity both directly through a firm's own investments and indirectly through spillover effects within industries. Empirical evidence shows that firms operating in industries with higher R&D investments financed by the private sector tend to display higher productivity growth (see appendix 3.B). These findings are consistent with the literature (see Griliches 1988; O'Mahony and Vecchi 2002).

There is more business-financed R&D in industries that obtain higher returns from it. Business-financed R&D intensity differs across countries, but it is higher in medium- and higher-technology industries with high productivity growth and a strong outward orientation. Private R&D investments are still much lower in the EU-10 than in industrialized countries. Almost two-thirds of R&D spending in the EU-10 is financed by government. Less than one-third is financed by industry. In contrast, in countries that are world leaders in R&D (Finland, Japan, Sweden, and the United States), the proportions are reversed: the industry share of R&D spending ranges from 65 to 70 percent, while government spending amounts to only 20–30 percent. Governments in the EU-10 recognize this challenge and have supported business R&D through tax concessions and grants and by encouraging public research agencies and universities to conduct collaborative research with business enterprises (OECD 2004).[5]

Financing Innovation

A large literature emphasizes the positive influence of the development of a country's financial sector on industrial and macroeconomic performance.[6] Empirical analysis conducted for this study confirms the link between financial deepening and productivity growth. Firms operating in industries with higher dependence on external financing exhibit higher productivity growth in countries where financial markets are more developed (see chapter 3 and appendix 3.B for details).

In the Region, the underdevelopment of financial products for the support of innovation hinders productivity growth. Even in the EU-10, it is difficult to find funds to finance intermediate phases of project or product development (such as the preparations to bring a product to market and to market it). Finance may be obtained for earlier phases, such as laboratory work, in the form of research grants. Later development phases, in which a new product is launched on the market, are financed by private equity. But the middle phase is particularly difficult to finance.

Even in advanced reformers, equity markets remain small, and venture capital investments are low. At the end of 2005, with the exception of the Czech Republic, Hungary, Lithuania, and Poland, stock market capitalization was less than 30 percent of GDP in the Region. The ratio of venture capital to GDP was also low. In the Czech Republic and Poland, the venture capital–GDP ratio is about 0.1 percent, whereas in the United Kingdom or the United States, venture capital accounts for 1 percent of GDP. Moreover, private equity investments in mature ventures dwarf venture capital. In Poland, buyout and replacement capital investments represent about 70 percent of total private equity investments, most going to mature companies (Ben-Ari and Vonortas 2005).

Promoting Innovation through Trade and Foreign Investment

Openness to trade and foreign investment improves productivity directly by providing access to new investment capital, technologies, expertise, and export markets and indirectly by speeding up the reallocation process. A key reform at the beginning of the transition from central planning to the market economy was trade liberalization and openness to foreign capital inflows. Total merchandise exports expanded, particularly in the EU-10, reaching about 45 percent over

FIGURE 2.20
Trade and FDI Have Grown

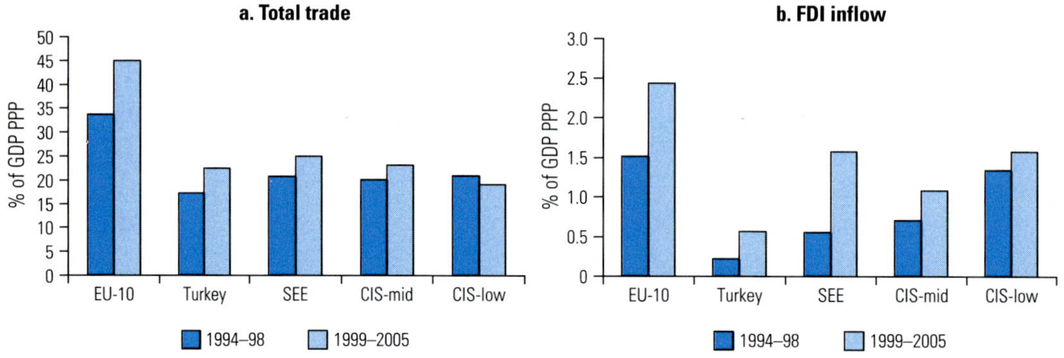

Sources: World Bank staff calculations; UN Comtrade 2007.

1999–2004. Trade in services, which had been considered a low priority under central planning, also rose rapidly in the EU-10, though it still represented a small share of GDP (about 7 percent). Foreign direct investment (FDI) inflows likewise increased dramatically. In the EU-10, these inflows accounted for 2.5 percent of GDP (figure 2.20).

Trade and foreign investment improve productivity growth by providing access to new investment capital, new technologies, expertise, and export markets. Research in the Czech Republic, Latvia, and Lithuania finds that foreign entry in downstream manufacturing industries boosts the productivity of local suppliers upstream (Arnold, Javorcik, and Mattoo 2007; Javorcik 2004). Recent empirical evidence shows that exports and FDI are driving productivity growth in the Czech Republic and Poland (figure 2.21).

Integrating into Global Production Chains

Productivity growth rates were particularly strong in medium- and high-technology industries showing rapid export growth and were well integrated into global production chains. The EU-10 saw rapid growth rates in medium- and high-technology industries and an increase in export products with a world comparative advantage. In contrast, low income CIS countries saw declines in their shares in medium- and high-technology exports. These countries also saw a reduction in the number of export products with a comparative advantage (figure 2.22).

In medium- and high-technology industries, productivity growth is driven by small niche producers who specialize in certain parts, components, or subassemblies (typically in the ICT and automobile sectors). The countries of the Region began by participating in the network trade in clothing and furniture, which are intensive in unskilled labor and embedded in buyer-driven production chains,

FIGURE 2.21

Poland: FDI and Exports Are Linked to Productivity Growth in Manufacturing

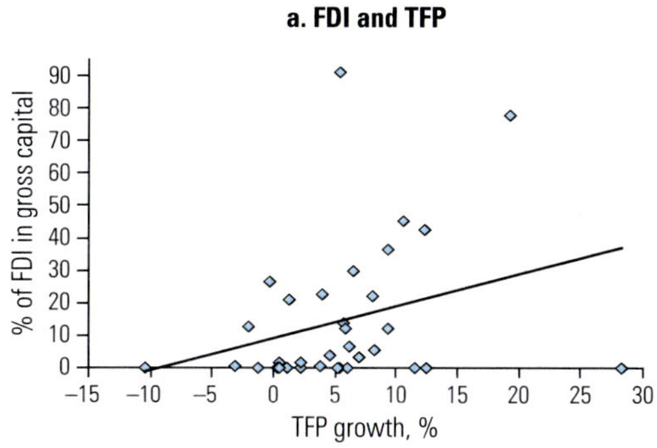

Sources: World Bank 2007.

FIGURE 2.22

The Technology Differentiation in Exports Was Stark across Countries

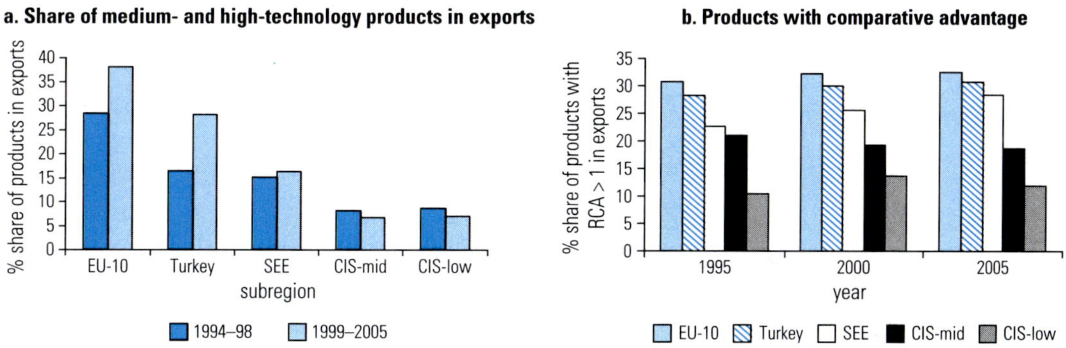

Sources: World Bank staff calculations; UN Comtrade 2007.

Note: Chart *a* shows the share of medium- and high-technology products in the total exports of various groups of countries in the Region. Chart *b* shows the total-exports share of Standard International Trade Classification 3-digit products in which these same groups of countries have a comparative advantage. RCA = revealed comparative advantage.

whereby global buyers create a supply base for production and distribution systems that are built up without their direct ownership. However, the advanced reformers (the EU-10 and Turkey) were able to shift quickly to producer-driven networks in manufacturing industries such as the automotive industry and information technology (figure 2.23). Producer-driven networks divide the value chain into smaller components and move them to countries where production costs are lower. This transition to producer-driven networks has not taken place in the CIS and SEE countries, however; these countries are still involved in the buyer-driven production chains for clothing and furniture.

Empirical analysis conducted for this report confirms the link between manufacturing productivity growth and participation in

FIGURE 2.23

The EU-10 and Turkey Are Developing Producer-Driven Networks

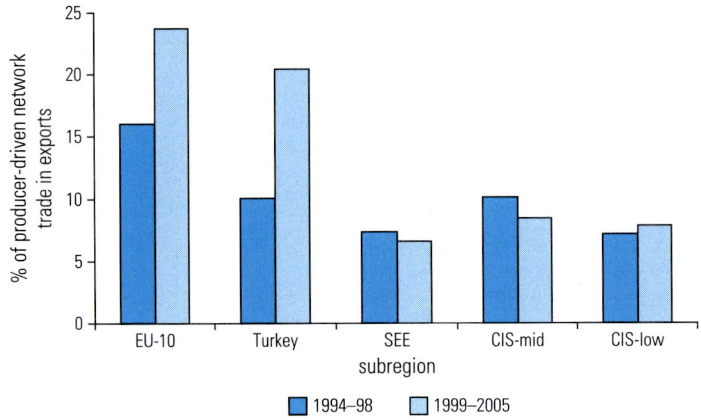

Sources: World Bank staff calculations; UN Comtrade 2007.

Note: The figure shows the percentage share of exports from producer-driven networks in total manufacturing exports. The chemical industry is excluded.

producer-driven network trade. Regression analysis conducted on a group of countries in the Region shows that firms operating in industries with increased participation in producer-driven networks (and buyer-driven networks to a lesser extent) show higher productivity growth than firms in other industries (see appendix 3.B).

Foreign investment has also been instrumental in incorporating local manufacturing capacities into global production networks. Indeed, entry into producer-driven networks appears to be virtually impossible without foreign investment. Two of the largest recipients of FDI—the Czech Republic and Hungary—have also been the best performers in producer-driven network exports. There is a strong positive association between the stock of FDI in manufacturing per capita and producer-driven network exports per capita in the Region (World Bank 2005b). Countries with larger stocks of FDI per capita also show a higher share of skilled labor and capital-intensive products in total exports.

Export Innovation and Sophistication

Productivity patterns are associated with different export strategies: countries with stronger manufacturing performance display higher numbers of export discoveries and export sophistication. The share in new export products in total exports is higher in the EU-10 and Turkey than in the rest of the Region. Most of these new exports are produced with capital-intensive methodologies in medium- and high-technology industries (figure 2.24).

FIGURE 2.24

Early Reformers Also Display More Export Discoveries

a. Share of discoveries in total exports

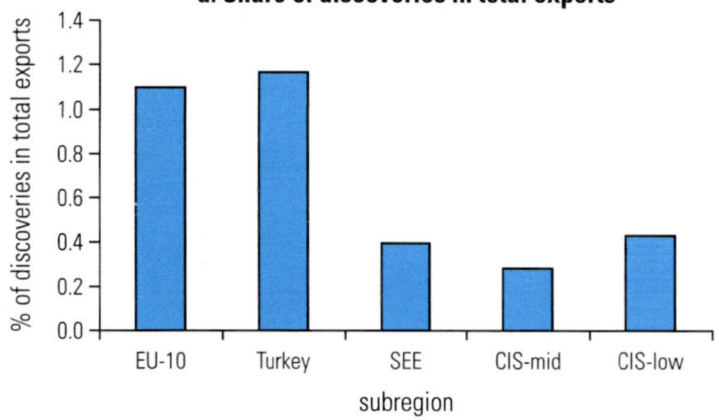

b. Export discoveries, by number

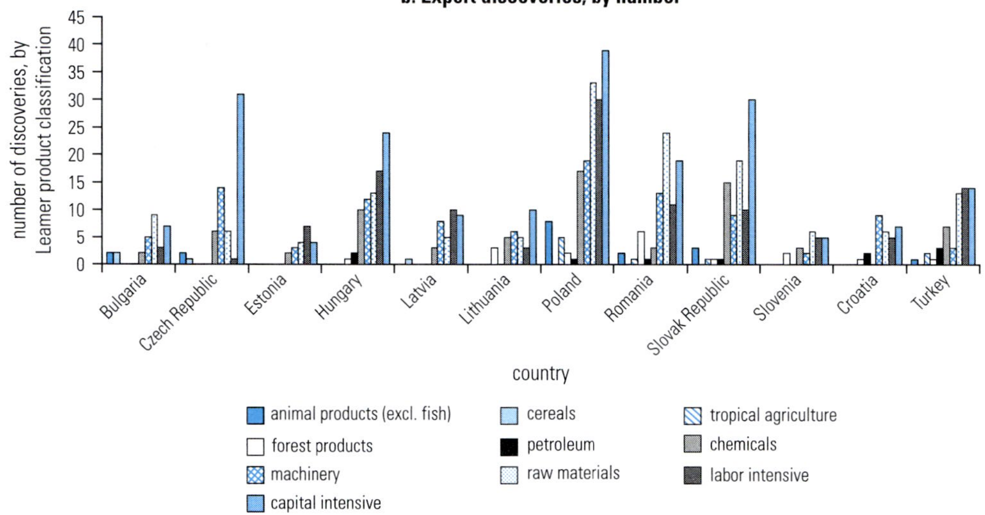

Sources: World Bank staff calculations; UN Comtrade 2007; Klinger and Lederman 2006; Leamer 1984.

Behind the productivity differences are also varying export strategies. Poland and Russia offer an example. Although both countries started the 1990s with export packages of roughly equivalent sophistication (as measured by the export sophistication index developed by Hausmann, Hwang, and Rodrik 2006), Poland's manufacturing sector has been engaged in a continuous upgrading of its export basket toward more sophisticated products, such as automobile components. In Russia, this process has stagnated since 1998, and the country specializes in low-sophistication export products such as metals and petroleum. The degree of export sophistication in Russia is now only 75 percent of that in Poland (figure 2.25). What has been holding back the process of structural transformation in the Russian manufacturing sector? One answer is the structure of production. Russia is specialized in highly peripheral products: goods requiring inputs that have few alternative uses in the development of new products.[7] This is reflected in the low value of its open forest (indicating the small number of new products for which current productive capabilities may be used). Poland, moreover, is specialized in a dense part of the product space. This specialization is reflected in the high value of its open forest, which makes the process of structural transformation and export upgrading much easier because there are many new export products requiring productive capabilities similar to those already existing in the country (figure 2.25; see also box 2.2 and appendix 2.D for more details).

Rendering manufacturing productivity growth sustainable will also require support for the process of structural transformation through the provision of public goods that spur export innovation

FIGURE 2.25

A Gap in Export Sophistication and Capabilities Remains between Early and Late Reformers, 1990–2005

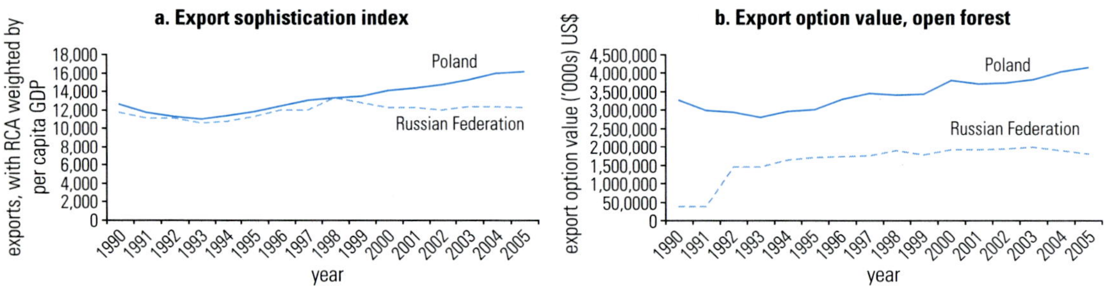

Sources: Klinger 2007a, 2007b.

Note: RCA = revealed comparative advantage.

BOX 2.2

The Product Space in Russia and Poland

The differences in export bundles are reflected in the relative comparative advantage of the product space in each country. The product space is a measure developed by Hausmann and Klinger (2006). Each product not currently exported with a comparative advantage has a particular distance from the country's current export basket (x-axis). In addition, each of these products has a level of sophistication (y-axis). A smaller value of the x and y axes represents a product that is closer to the current productive structure. Products below the line are less sophisticated than the country's export basket as a whole. The colors correspond to Leamer commodity clusters of export products (Leamer 1984).

The product space is relatively dense in Poland and Russia, but the productive capability to export new products differs greatly in these countries. In both countries, there are many new export products above the line (meaning that there are many products that the country is not currently exporting that would generate higher added value than the products currently exported). However, in Russia these products are far away (density of 2) from the country's current export structure. In Poland, in contrast, there are many products that the country is not currently exporting that are close to its current productive capabilities (starting density at 1). The current productive structure of the manufacturing sector in Poland may therefore be adapted for the development of new export products more easily than the productive structure in Russia

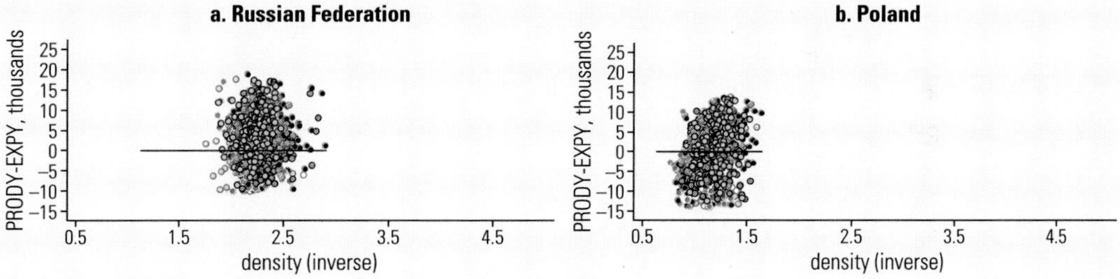

Sources: Klinger 2007a, 2007b.

Note: For explanations of PRODY and EXPY, see appendix 2.D.

either through product innovations (new exports) or through process innovations (improving the sophistication of manufacturing exports). The links between export sophistication, the capability to develop new exports (open forest), and productivity levels are strong and positive in the Region (figure 2.26).

In sum, policies that support innovation through financial deepening, investments in human capital, and outward orientation should be a priority so as to sustain productivity growth in manufacturing.

FIGURE 2.26

The Gap in Productivity Was Associated with a Gap in Export Sophistication, 1999–2005

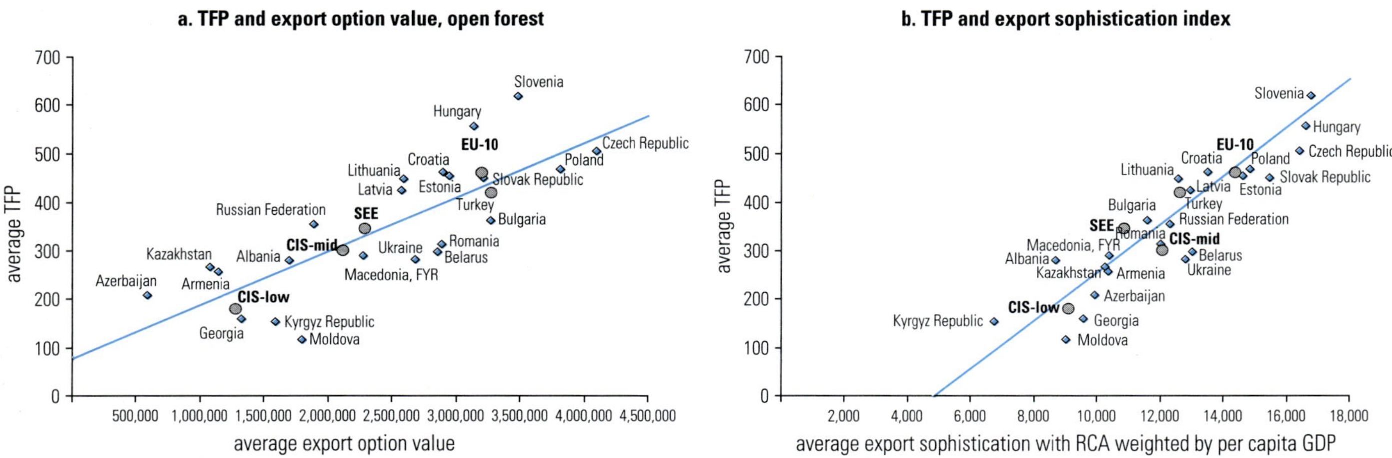

Sources: World Bank staff calculations; Klinger 2007a, 2007b.

Note: RCA = revealed comparative advantage. ● = bloc of countries; ◆ = individual countries.

These policies may also include efforts to attract new FDI inflows and support export diversification, measures to enhance private R&D and support investments in ICT, additional reforms in higher education and training programs, and more efforts to improve the performance of service sectors. The next section explores the link between service performance and manufacturing productivity.

Service Productivity

Improvements in service productivity may affect productivity growth directly and indirectly.[8] We saw earlier that the recent sectoral shift toward services has contributed to an increase in aggregate productivity in the Region. An efficient service sector also has indirect consequences for economic growth through the efficiency of other sectors in the economy (Eschenbach and Hoekman 2006; Arnold, Javorcik, and Mattoo 2007). High-quality market services such as transport or telecommunications affect production costs and, consequently, the competitiveness and the degree of integration into global markets of firms in all sectors. Moreover, high-quality services may also influence the attractiveness of a location for FDI. Service liberalization may help increase average productivity for incumbent firms and may also facilitate the new entry of firms likely to be more innovative and successful in meeting consumer demands and similarly encourage the exit of less-productive firms (see chapter 3).

Service Performance

Labor productivity growth in services was higher in the EU-8 than in the EU-15. Labor productivity growth in services increased substantially in the EU-8 between 1997–2000 and 2001–04 (figure 2.27). There was wide variation of country performance across the EU-8. During 1997–2004, the best EU-8 performer, Hungary, had an unweighted average service labor productivity of 69.7 percent of the EU-15 average (58.2 percent weighted), while Lithuania had an unweighted average service labor productivity of only 25.6 percent of the EU-15 average (26.2 percent weighted).[9]

The EU-15 exhibited substantially higher average labor productivity in the service sector than the EU-8, with a few exceptions. For instance, Estonia and Hungary displayed higher average service labor productivity than the EU-15 in computer and related activities and in legal, technical, and advertising activities.[10]

FIGURE 2.27

Service Labor Productivity in the EU-8 Increased, but Still Lagged Behind the EU-15

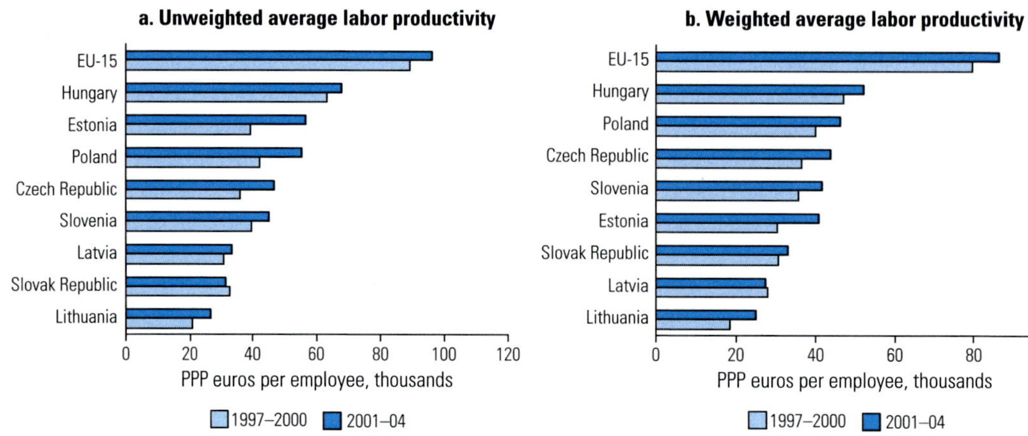

Sources: World Bank staff calculations; WIIW Database 2006.

There was wide variation in EU-8 service productivity performance across industries. Real estate and financial intermediation exhibited the highest average labor productivity; in contrast, tourism services (hotels and restaurants) and wholesale trade exhibited the lowest average labor productivity. Transport, telecommunications, financial intermediation, and retail trade showed the strongest productivity growth in 1997–2000 and 2000–04.[11,12] But the wholesale trade and hotels and restaurants saw declines in productivity (figure 2.28).

If recent service productivity growth rates continue, they will lead to improvements in efficiency among backbone services such as transport, telecommunications, and finance. Any efficiency improvements would be crucial for the competitiveness of other sectors (via reductions in production costs) and would facilitate the participation of the Region in the global service production chains.

Policy Drivers of Service Productivity

A number of factors explain differences in performance across service industries, including capital intensity, market size, the scale at which services may be sold, technological innovations (particularly the use of ICT), skilled labor, and progress in service policy reform.

ICT

ICT service industries showed substantially higher average labor productivity than non-ICT service industries in most EU-8 countries during 2000–04. These findings suggest that there was a progressive penetration and efficient use of ICT in the service industries in the

FIGURE 2.28

Variations Were Wide in Productivity Performance across Service Industries

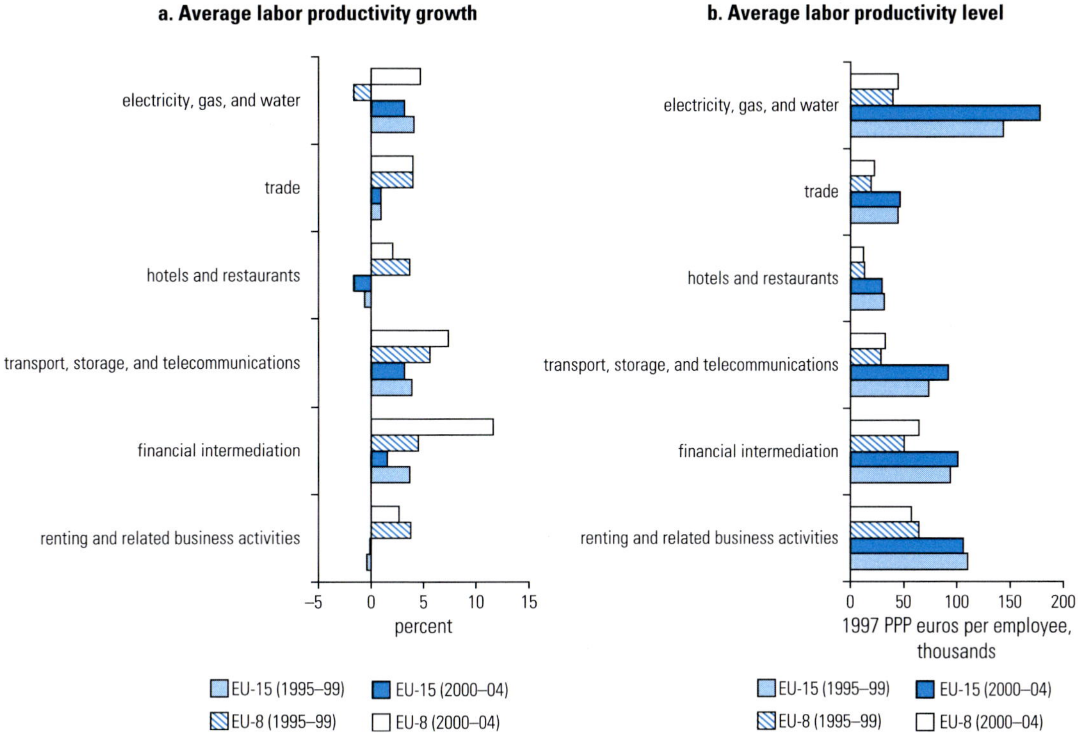

Sources: World Bank staff calculations; EU KLEMS Database 2007.

EU-8 during this period (figure 2.29). ICT users experienced the most rapid productivity growth in all EU-8 countries except Latvia and Lithuania. In Hungary and Poland, ICT producers (in services) also showed more rapid productivity growth than did non-ICT service industries. The high productivity growth in financial intermediation and in transport, storage, and telecommunications documented elsewhere above for these countries may be explained by the introduction of cost-reducing ICT. Productivity growth has been higher among ICT users in most EU-8 countries recently. The next section will explain in detail the potential of ICT to reduce the large productivity gap between the EU-8 and the EU-15.

Skilled Labor

Service industries that draw on a more highly skilled workforce have not only shown higher productivity levels in recent years, but have also achieved more rapid growth. In contrast service industries that have relied mostly on low-skilled workers have experienced declines in productivity growth; their productivity levels are

FIGURE 2.29

ICT Service Industries Displayed Higher Productivity, by ICT Taxonomy, 2000–04

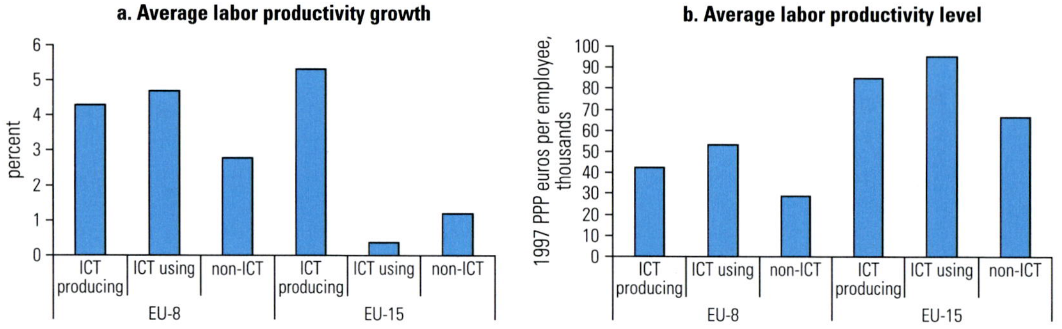

Sources: World Bank staff calculations; EU KLEMS Database 2007.

FIGURE 2.30

Service Industries with Skilled Workers Show Higher Productivity, by Skill Taxonomy, 2000–04

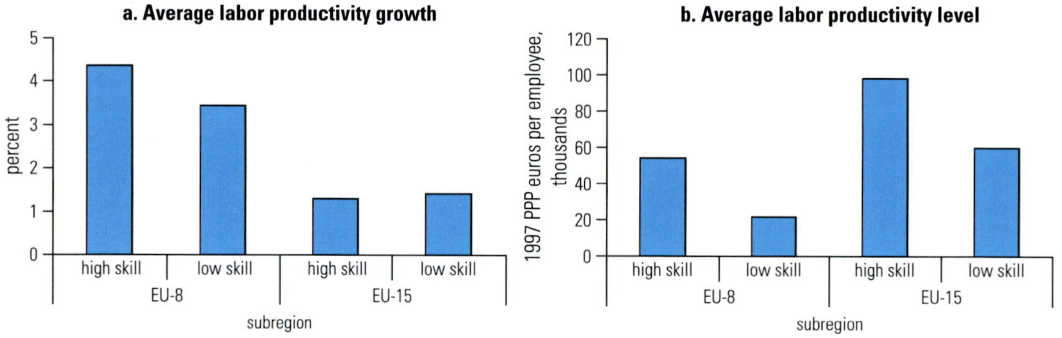

Sources: World Bank staff calculations; EU KLEMS Database 2007.

only about 25 percent of the productivity levels in industries that employ more highly skilled workers (figure 2.30).

Service Liberalization

The performance of service industries is also tied to the progress of the policy reforms leading to liberalization in these industries. Eschenbach and Hoekmann (2006) discuss in detail the content of service policy reforms in the Region and the progress in liberalization. These policy reforms combine deregulation (the dismantling of entry barriers and the promotion of competition) and improved regulation (the establishment of an appropriate legal and institutional environment). On average, more progress in liberalization reform has been achieved in the telecommunications and the electricity industries and in the EU-10.

Despite significant progress, the Region still exhibits high levels of product market regulation that stifles competition, growth, and innovation in the service sector (OECD 2005). Moreover, there is still significant cross-country heterogeneity in the degree of liberalization and the quality of the regulatory framework facing the service sector, which may help explain the differences in performance documented elsewhere above. To capture the extent of service liberalization across the Region, we have used the EBRD index of progress in policy reform (which is industry specific and varies over 1997–2004). The service industries covered by the EBRD index are electricity, water distribution, road transport, telecommunications, banking reform, interest rate liberalization, and nonbanking financial institutions.[13]

Empirical analysis conducted for this report shows that there is a strong association between service liberalization and productivity performance in service sectors. The regressions are estimated using ordinary least squares, including country dummies, industry dummies, year dummies, and an interaction between industry dummies and year dummies, or by using industry fixed effects, including year dummies. Year dummies account for the business cycle or other macroeconomic factors affecting all industries equally, while service industry dummies account for fixed differences in productivity growth across industries. The interaction dummies control for problems in the measurement of output in service industries and problems related to the use of imperfect deflators for real value added (see appendix 2.E for the results).[14]

The liberalization of services may influence the average performance of service industries through its impact on firm productivity and on reallocation. Service liberalization may help increase the average productivity among incumbent firms and facilitate the entry of new firms, which are likely to be more innovative and successful in meeting consumer demand, and the exit of less-productive firms (see chapter 3).

The Effect of Services on Manufacturing Productivity

The efficiency of service industries is important partly because these sectors are increasingly contributing to the economies in the Region and partly because service industries account for critical inputs in downstream manufacturing sectors. Hence, liberalization-related improvements in the performance of the service sector may be crucial in promoting productivity growth. Interestingly, the use of service inputs in manufacturing varies greatly across the Region.

FIGURE 2.31

Service Inputs into Manufacturing Vary across Countries

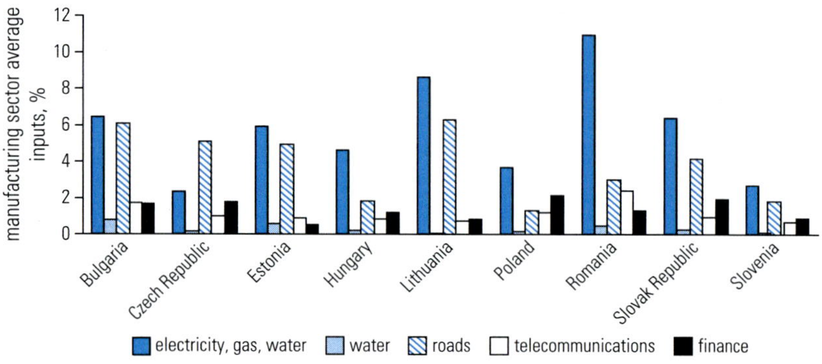

Source: World Bank staff calculations.

Electricity, road transport, and financial services represent the highest shares of total service inputs in manufacturing. Average electricity use in manufacturing ranges from 2 percent of total inputs in the Czech Republic to 11 percent in Romania (figure 2.31). Across the Region (except in Lithuania and Romania), inputs from electricity, gas, and steam represent a higher share of the total inputs used in textiles and textile products than of the inputs used in electrical and optical equipment. The second most important service industry in terms of input provision to manufacturing is road transport, the average share of which in total inputs ranges from 1.3 percent in Poland to 6 percent in Lithuania.

Empirical analysis conducted for this study shows that the effect of service liberalization on labor productivity in downstream manufacturing is strong and positive (see appendix 3.B). More specifically, manufacturing industries that rely more heavily on inputs from more liberalized services exhibit higher productivity than do other manufacturing industries. This is consistent with the findings of Arnold, Javorcik, and Mattoo (2007) on the Czech Republic (see chapter 3 for more analysis on the role of service liberalization in firm productivity).

In sum, the prospects for sustained productivity growth are likely to depend to a large extent on more efficient and more dynamic services. There is clear potential for service-driven productivity growth in the Region if policy makers sustain the momentum of reform by pursuing service liberalization, removing the product market barriers that are still limiting competition in various industries, allowing more FDI, and providing incentives to promote the trade in services. Productivity growth in services would also benefit from the penetration of more ICT, which requires improvements in competition and the continued liberalization of telecommunications.

The Role of ICT in Productivity Growth

This section provides a detailed analysis of the impact of ICT on labor productivity growth in the EU-8—whenever the data allow, the analysis includes Bulgaria, Romania, and Russia—and examines the productivity effects of various types of policy reforms in ICT-related manufacturing and service industries.

Because ICT products and services represent both the outputs of ICT-producing industries and inputs into ICT-using industries, ICT may affect labor productivity through three channels.

- ICT capital is an input in the production of other goods and services.
- Productivity increases in ICT-related industries contribute to aggregate TFP growth in the economy.
- Productivity increases in non-ICT-producing sectors occur through the use of ICT (spillover effects).

The Contribution of ICT Capital to Productivity Growth

Much of the attention on the role of ICT in growth has focused on the contribution of ICT production in growth. However, a number of studies have shown that, as a source of growth in the United States, the G-7 countries, and the EU-15 during the 1990s and early 2000s, ICT capital was more important than ICT-related TFP growth.[15]

The contribution of ICT capital to labor productivity growth in the EU-8 was equal to or greater than that in the EU-15. Piatkowski and van Ark (2007) perform growth accounting and compare the contributions of ICT capital to labor productivity growth in the Region, the EU-15, and the United States during 1995–2003 (figure 2.32). In absolute terms, the contribution of ICT capital to labor productivity growth in the EU-8 was greater or comparable with that in the EU-15.

However, there are substantial differences across the Region. Only the ICT capital contributions in the Czech Republic, Hungary, and Poland were above those in the EU-15 in absolute terms. The ICT capital contributions to labor productivity growth were much lower in slower reformers (Romania and Russia) than in the EU-15 (figure 2.33).

ICT investment in the Region may have been dependent on network effects. Within the EU-8, countries with higher labor productivity

FIGURE 2.32

ICT Capital, Labor Productivity Growth, and GDP per Person Employed

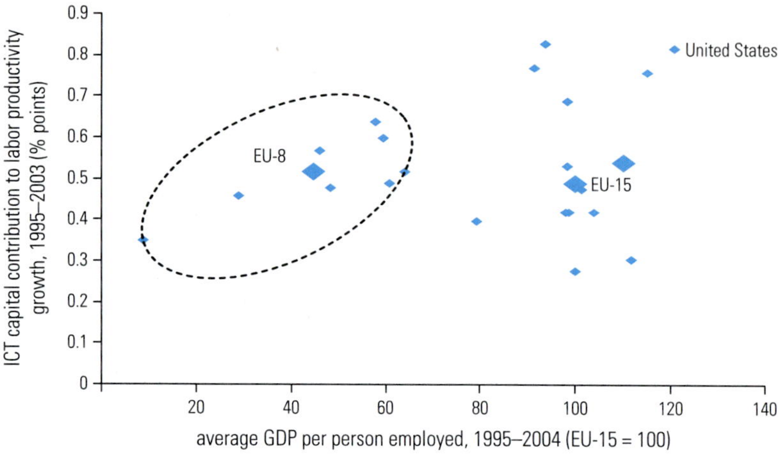

Source: Piatkowski and van Ark 2007.

FIGURE 2.33

ICT Capital Contribution to Labor Productivity Growth, 1995–2004

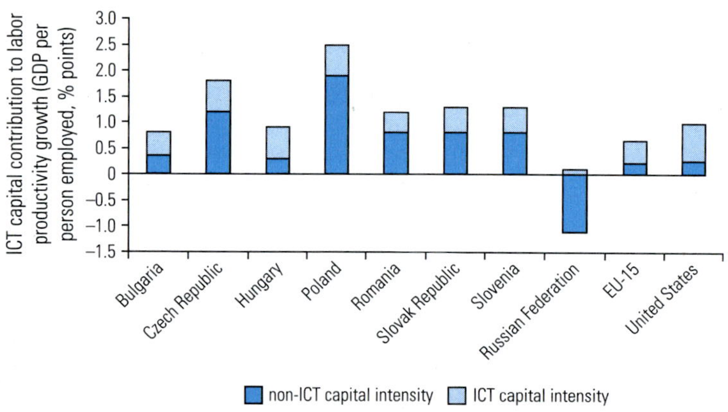

Source: Piatkowski and van Ark 2007.

levels show larger contributions from ICT capital, implying that these countries have successfully used ICT to increase growth in labor productivity to the same degree as the most ICT-intensive countries in the EU-15. This usage suggests that ICT investment in the EU-8 may have been dependent on network effects; in other words, higher levels of development, particularly in ICT infrastructure, have stimulated more rapid growth in the use of ICT through feedback effects.[16] In most EU-8 countries, TFP growth is also driven by productivity effects from the production or use of ICT goods and services.

The Contribution of ICT Production

Although ICT capital has been an important source of productivity growth in the EU-8, there is reason to assume that at least some countries may also have benefited greatly from attracting the production of ICT goods, particularly through FDI.

The growth in ICT-producing industries accelerated the convergence of the EU-8 toward the EU-15 average. ICT production made the largest absolute contribution to labor productivity growth in Estonia, Hungary, and Latvia. The (unweighted) average of the ICT contribution to productivity was higher in the EU-8 than in the United States and the EU-15 (figure 2.34). Hence, the growth in the ICT-producing sector accelerated the convergence between the EU-10 (with the exception of the Slovak Republic and Slovenia) and the EU-15.

What explains the difference between the rapid growth of the ICT sector in some countries and the much slower growth in others? van Ark and Piatkowski (2004) argue that the rise of the ICT sector in the EU-8 may be explained largely by inflows of FDI because domestic industries were not sufficiently competitive to develop. This was so because of technological retardation, lack of access to high-risk financing, and the low level of innovation. In turn, FDI was dependent on the progress made on first-stage reforms (trade openness, development of infrastructure, rule of law, macroeconomic stability) and privatization policies.[17]

Despite its positive contribution to productivity growth, the ICT-producing sector in the Region is still too small. Even in the most

FIGURE 2.34

The Contribution of ICT-Producing Industries to Labor Productivity Growth, 1995–2004

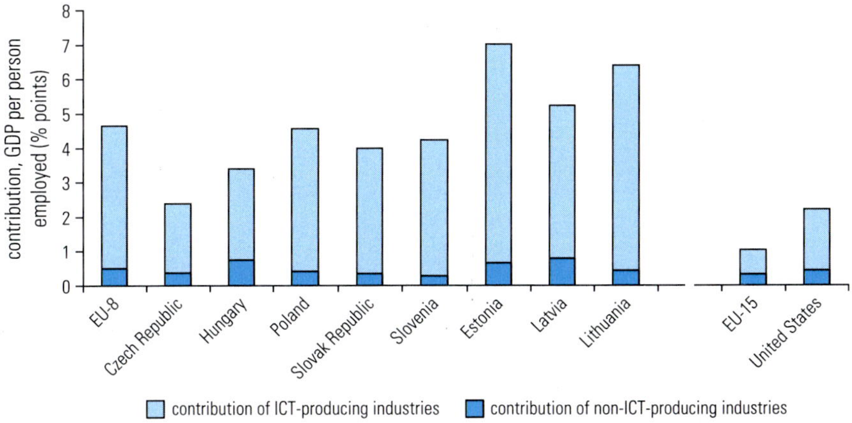

Source: Piatkowski and van Ark 2007.

advanced reformers (the EU-8), the share of ICT-producing industries in GDP is only 5–6 percent. The ICT-related spillover effects are too scant to drive the sustained convergence toward the income levels in the EU-15. So, convergence will have to rely on productivity growth outside the ICT-producing industries.

The Contribution of ICT Use

Given the overwhelming share of ICT-using industries in total GDP, the productive use of ICT in manufacturing and services will be key to more rapid growth and convergence toward the incomes in the EU-15.

Productivity growth in ICT-using manufacturing industries in the EU-8 was substantially higher than that in the EU-15 and the United States.[18] Thanks to high productivity growth, the manufacturing industries in the EU-8 contributed 0.4–1.9 percentage points to aggregate labor productivity growth between 1995 and 2004, substantially more than in the EU-15 or the United States.

However, productivity growth in ICT-using service industries was much lower than that of ICT-using manufacturing industries over 1995–2004 and much lower than the corresponding growth in the United States. So, although market services contributed two-thirds of GDP, their contribution to productivity growth was less than that of manufacturing in most EU-8 countries (figure 2.35).

What explains such large differences in the productivity growth rates between ICT-using industries in manufacturing and services? To answer this question, the empirical analysis in this section studies the

FIGURE 2.35

ICT-Using Services Contribute Less to Productivity Growth Than Do ICT-Using Manufacturing

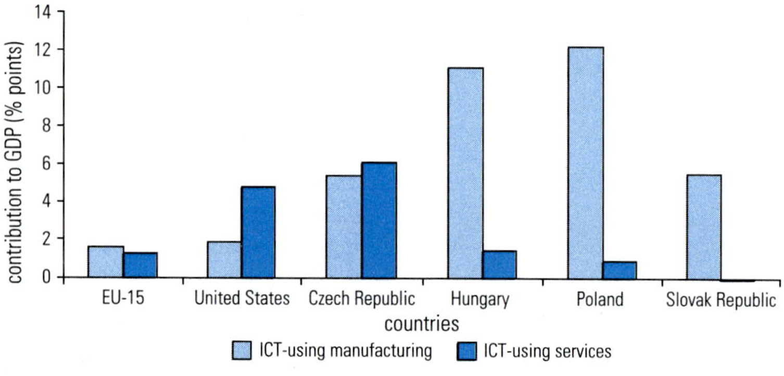

Source: Piatkowski and van Ark 2007.

types of structural reforms that have been most effective in driving productivity growth in manufacturing during the first stage of transition and the reforms that will be key in supporting productivity growth in the future. The higher productivity growth in ICT-using service industries in the United States suggests that only that country has succeeded in moving to the second phase in the productive use of ICT in the service sector. As argued by Piatkowski and van Ark (2007), this is because of the much more conducive business environment in the United States, stemming primarily from the more competitive product markets, the flexible labor markets, organizational innovations, the large investments in R&D, and the availability of high-risk financing.

Labor productivity growth in ICT-using manufacturing industries is more closely correlated with basic fundamental reforms, whereas productivity growth in ICT-using market services is more correlated with a more sophisticated set of reforms. Drawing on a panel data analysis of four EU-8 countries (the Czech Republic, Hungary, Poland, and the Slovak Republic), the EU-15, and the United States, this section explores the policy determinants of labor productivity growth in ICT-using industries in manufacturing and services over 1995–2005 (see appendix 2.F). Despite the low statistical fit because of the small data set and the high volatility of productivity growth rates, the regression results show that labor productivity growth in manufacturing is more closely correlated with basic fundamental reforms (governance quality, trade openness, macroeconomic stability, and financial system development) than with productivity growth in market services. At the same time, we find that more sophisticated reforms (ICT investments, quality of human capital, and labor market and product market flexibility) seem to be more important for productivity growth in market services than in manufacturing.

These findings suggest that the ICT-led convergence in the Region may be divided into two phases. In the first phase, convergence is driven by growth in ICT production and in the ICT-aided reallocation process. In the second phase, convergence must rely on the intensive use of ICT in non-ICT sectors, particularly services.

The completion of the first phase of convergence seems to be mostly dependent on some basic fundamental reforms: market competition, greater openness to trade and FDI, stronger governance, improved access to finance, and sustained macroeconomic stability. It appears on the basis of the available evidence that most EU-10 countries have more or less realized the first convergence phase (though this is less accurate in the case of Bulgaria and Romania) partly through ICT investments and productivity growth in ICT-using manufacturing and partly through productivity growth in ICT production. In contrast, Russia, like many other CIS and SEE countries, has not yet completed the first convergence phase. For these lagging reformers, convergence will depend on continued progress in first-generation reforms.

Success in the second phase of convergence, however, seems to require more sophisticated reform measures: the deregulation of product and service markets, increased labor flexibility, better ICT infrastructure, organizational innovations, improved management practices, access to financing, and investment in a broader palette of human capital and ICT skills.[19] These reforms are especially important for the EU-10 because the productivity effects of the first phase of convergence have been mostly exhausted (Piatkowski and van Ark 2007; Schadler et al. 2006). These reforms are, however, more difficult to achieve than those required during the first stage of convergence.

Conclusions

A large resource reallocation to services raised productivity in the Region. While sectoral reallocation effects were important, the main driver of the productivity surge was within-sector productivity growth. Reallocation effects were important, although, in some countries, such as the CIS countries, they tended to offset each other. Labor was generally moving toward sectors with high productivity levels (services) and out of sectors with low productivity levels (agriculture). At the same time, labor was moving out of sectors showing increasing productivity growth (agriculture and manufacturing) and into sectors showing decreasing productivity growth (services). Most of the productivity growth was arising from gains within each of the sectors (agriculture, manufacturing, and services).

Agricultural productivity growth was driven by labor shedding, though improvements in farm efficiency were also important. In labor-abundant countries, a shift from large-scale collective farming to small-scale individual farming led to dramatic gains in technical efficiency with relatively small losses in scale efficiency. In capital- and land-abundant countries, gains in labor productivity, if any, arose primarily because large farms were shedding labor as farms were privatized. In countries in which land privatization and trade reforms were not implemented vigorously, productivity gains were generally delayed and modest. During the first stage of transition, trade liberalization, price liberalization, subsidy cuts, and land reforms were required to accelerate farm restructuring and facilitate the sectoral reallocation of labor. As countries progressed along the transition path, an improved investment climate and stronger competition in services were needed to raise within-farm productivity growth and provide off-farm job opportunities.

Manufacturing productivity growth was driven by efficiency gains in industries with a higher capacity for innovation. In manufacturing, a group of medium- and high-technology industries seemed to be driving productivity growth. This group of industries employed a large proportion of highly skilled workers, produced ICT goods, or used a relatively large amount of ICT capital. The manufacturing industries in the high-technology group included producers of office machinery, electrical and electronic equipment, and optical instruments. Other sectors, such as traditional consumer goods manufacturing, fell within the low-technology groups and showed lower productivity growth. Not surprisingly, high-technology industries exhibited higher TFP growth in countries with stronger progress in liberalizing key service industries, deeper financial markets, more highly skilled workforces, more flexible labor markets, and greater R&D investments by the private sector.

Service productivity growth was driven by a strong performance in backbone services: transport, telecommunications, and financial intermediation. In addition to trade and real estate, service productivity growth was mainly driven by backbone industries with higher productivity levels and a higher propensity to use or produce ICT: transport, telecommunications, and financial intermediation services. The productivity growth in these industries over 1997–2004 outstripped the average productivity growth achieved in the EU-15. The strong performance of these service industries hints at the potential for service-driven growth in the Region.

The efficiency of backbone services is crucial to the productivity of other sectors. Backbone services enable firms to participate in the global production chains that are associated with productivity gains. But these potential gains will not be achieved automatically. A substantial gap remains in productivity across services. Moreover, the penetration and efficient use of ICT in services remain limited. More investment in ICT in service industries may spur productivity growth. Policy makers in the Region might play a major role in sustaining the growth momentum in services by pursuing service liberalization across the board, removing regulatory barriers to competition in various service industries, and allowing and attracting more FDI and trade flows.

Notes

1. There is a large literature on the impact of changes in sectoral labor composition on aggregate productivity growth in advanced economies and also in the Region (see Timmer and Szirmai 2000; Caselli and Tenreyro 2004; Lenain and Rawdanowicz 2004).
2. A number of studies have also performed the shift-share analysis for EU-8 countries (see the text for the countries), while focusing on TFP growth. The reallocation effects (combining capital and labor shifts) tend to be more dominant in TFP growth decompositions than in labor productivity decompositions. This is mainly attributed to capital shifts across sectors. The stronger the labor productivity growth arising from higher capital-to-labor ratios (capital deepening), the stronger the reallocation effect. This finding is not surprising because capital mobility tends to be greater than labor mobility.
3. The analysis will be conducted at two levels of disaggregation. First, a distinction is made between agriculture, industry, and services that draws on the World Development Indicators Database for all countries of the Region. The analysis on agriculture also covers most countries of the Region. However, detailed analysis of productivity in the manufacturing and service industries is performed on a subset of countries in the Region for which data are available. Aggregate manufacturing and service data draw on the 2006 WIIW Database data set and cover 14 countries in the Region. Second, disaggregated analysis on the manufacturing and service industries is performed only on EU-8 countries with comparable industrial-level purchasing power parity (PPP) deflators available. The analysis draws on the EU KLEMS Database. For both manufacturing and services, an effort is made to distinguish between ICT-related industries and industries not related to ICT and between industries that use skilled labor and industries that rely mostly on low-skilled labor. Throughout, the focus is mostly on labor productivity.
4. Evidence also shows that there is less productivity dispersion across farms. In Kazakhstan, most farmers (80 percent) have an efficiency score lower than 30, and only a very small share of farmers (2 percent) achieve an efficiency score close to 100. In contrast, in Hungary, most farmers have an efficiency score between 40 and 70, and 9 percent have an efficiency score between 90 and 100. A country more advanced in the transition has more farms on the boundary of the production frontier, with farms reaching higher average efficiency.
5. Business R&D intensity at the industrial level tends to be correlated with a high rate of technological progress. Those industries that are currently located on rapidly rising technological paths (such as electronics, pharmaceuticals, aircraft) enjoy high returns to R&D. These returns are likely to be larger than those in industries with lower market concentration (OECD 2004).
6. At the macro-level, the relationship between financial development and economic growth was postulated early by Schumpeter (1911). Empirical evidence has been provided by King and Levine (1993) and Levine and Zervos (1998) using cross-country data and by Rajan and Zingales (1998) using industry-level data across countries. In particular, Beck, Levine,

and Loayza (2000) find that the positive effect of financial intermediation on GDP growth occurs through the impact of financial intermediation on TFP growth rather than through its impact on physical capital accumulation and private savings rates.

7. To capture the readiness of a country to move into new exports, Hausmann and Klinger (2006) develop a measure called open forest. This indicator shows the degree to which a country's export basket is close to other products for the production of which the currently installed productive structure may be easily adapted. High values of the open forest measure indicate lower barriers to the development of new export products that may boost manufacturing productivity growth.
8. The definition of the service sector covers both market services and public utilities, while excluding government services and construction. The section also investigates the effect of service policy reforms on downstream manufacturing productivity. Depending on data availability, the analysis considers Bulgaria, Croatia, FYR Macedonia, Romania, Russia, Serbia, Montenegro, Ukraine, and the EU-8.
9. The exceptions are the Czech Republic and Slovenia, where the average share of wholesale and retail trade and the repair of motor vehicles in total employment was almost unchanged between 1997–2000 and 2001–04.
10. We should note that our data cover only formal economic activities. Subsectors such as retail trade are characterized by high levels of informality, and their contributions to total value added and employment in the Region may, therefore, actually be higher.
11. Given the large number of 2-digit NACE industries, only the share of value added of those industries that (a) represent more than 1 percent of total value added on average in the EU-8 or (b) have a high-technologically or high-skill content are covered.
12. Labor productivity in services for the EU-15 has been obtained as an average of the labor productivity in all subsectors across all EU-15 countries; KLEMS labor productivity for each subsector and country is calculated in a similar way to KLEMS labor productivity for each subsector and country. The consideration of a simple average of labor productivity across the more-advanced and less-advanced EU-15 countries may actually underestimate the true value. The EU-8 may be significantly more distant in terms of labor productivity levels relative to the best performers in the EU-15.
13. To combine the EBRD index with the WIIW Database, we average the index to match the industries covered by the database. Specifically, we average (a) the EBRD index for electric power and the EBRD index for water distribution to match the electricity, gas, and water subsector; (b) the EBRD index for road transport and the EBRD index for telecommunications to match the transport, storage, and telecommunications subsector; and (c) the EBRD index for banking reform and interest rate liberalization and the EBRD index for nonbanking financial institutions to match the financial intermediation subsector.
14. The results based on two-year lagged values of the EBRD index are qualitatively similar.
15. See Jorgenson (2004) for the G-7, Timmer and van Ark (2005) for the EU, and van Ark and Piatkowski (2004) for the EU-8.

16. Röller and Waverman (2001) argue that improvements in telecommunications infrastructure provide for nonlinear network effects.
17. Perminov and Egorova (2005) provide productivity growth estimates for the ICT sector in Russia; yet, their results are not directly comparable with those in this study.
18. The analysis excludes nonmanufacturing industries, including agriculture, forestry, mining and quarrying, and fishing, and nonmarket services, which mostly involve the public sector.
19. For a discussion of the importance of organizational changes in enterprises and of improved management, refer to Brynjolfsson and Hitt (2000) and Dorgan and Dowdy (2002).

CHAPTER 3

Firm Productivity Growth

Chapter 2 shows that overall productivity gains resulted mostly from within-sector productivity growth. However, the sectoral analysis hides significant firm dynamism within individual industries.

The Region's impressive productivity gains within sectors largely reflect substantial dynamism within individual firms. The reallocation of workers and firms from less-productive to more-productive activities contributes to industry-level productivity growth in any market economy, but it has assumed a greater role in transition economies given their highly distorted industrial structures inherited from the central planning period. Faced with the radical transformation of the economies, firms in all countries have been forced to adapt their behavior. Some firms have increased productivity through defensive restructuring (through labor shedding), while others have done this through strategic restructuring (the adoption of new technologies). New firms have entered the market, occupying niches that did not exist until recently (services) and displacing obsolete firms that have been forced to leave the market.

The purpose of this chapter is to identify the drivers of productivity growth at the firm level and to shed light on the role of the creative destruction process (usually ascribed to Joseph Schumpeter) in productivity growth in the Region. The element that distinguishes Schumpeter's theory from standard theories of economic growth is that it recognizes firm heterogeneity across industries and across countries. It also highlights the important role played in productivity growth by the continual changes—entry, exit, expansion, and contraction—in the composition of a population of firms.

Drawing on firm-level data, this chapter also provides fresh insights into the policy drivers of firm productivity growth. The first two sections of the chapter draw on harmonized firm-level data from manufacturing censuses for eight countries in the Region and comparator countries outside the Region (the data have been collected by Eric J. Bartelsman, David J. Brown, John S. Earle, and Stefano Scarpetta). The data permit an examination of the respective roles of the creative destruction process and of productivity gains within firms. The data also permit a study of the evolution of firm demographics over time: rates of the creation and destruction of firms and jobs, the average firm size of entrants, and firm survival rates. In addition to facilitating an understanding of the patterns of firm entry and post-entry performance, firm demographics shed light on the net employment impact resulting from the reallocation process. The last section of the chapter draws on firm-level data included in the Amadeus Database, which contains financial corporate data on more than 60,000 firms in 14 countries in the Region. Amadeus data include details on firm output and factor inputs (material costs, labor data, fixed assets) that allow for the estimation of TFP growth. The last section also draws on enterprise surveys (BEEPS) and international reviews of progress reform indicators (the Doing Business Database, the Economic Freedom of the World Database, and EBRD transition indicators) to shed light on policy and regulatory constraints on good firm performance.

Firm Dynamics and Productivity Growth

What does the microevidence say about the sources of productivity growth? The nature of efficiency gains within firms? The reallocation of workers to more-productive activities? The entry of new firms and the exit of obsolete ones? Answering these questions requires the decomposition of aggregate productivity growth into five components, as follows:

- The *within component,* which accounts for the productivity growth that takes place *within* firms; productivity growth within firms depends on changes in the efficiency and intensity with which inputs are used in production.
- The *between and cross components,* which capture the role of labor reallocation *across* existing firms in aggregate productivity growth. The

between component reflects gains that arise from high-productivity firms that are gaining market share or from low-productivity firms that are losing market share. The cross component reflects increases in aggregate productivity that arise from firms exhibiting high productivity growth that are gaining market share (or from firms exhibiting low productivity growth that are losing market share).

- The *entry and exit components,* which reflect the gains arising from the creation of new firms and the exit of obsolete firms. This is sometimes aggregated into a single component, net entry, which captures the aggregate effect of firm churning (or firm turnover) in total productivity growth.

Aggregate productivity growth may be decomposed in a variety of ways. The decompositions reported in this chapter adopt the approach developed by Foster, Haltiwanger, and Krizan (2001). Box 3.1 and appendix 3.A provide additional details on data sources and methodology. This decomposition may be applied to both labor productivity

BOX 3.1

The Decomposition of Productivity Growth Using Firm-Level Data

Using productivity at the firm level and production factors as building blocks, one may decompose productivity for each industry into the contributions of continuing firms, new entrants, and exiting firms. One defines the sectorwide productivity level in year t, P_t, as

$$P_t = \sum_i \theta_{it} p_{it}$$

where θ_i is the employment share of firm i, and P_t and p_{it} are a productivity measure (in this analysis, labor productivity).

We focus on a common method for decomposing productivity growth. The Foster-Haltiwanger-Krizan method (2001) breaks aggregate productivity growth into five components, commonly called the within effect, the between effect, the cross effect, the entry effect, and the exit effect, as follows:

$$\Delta P_t = \sum_{i \in C} \theta_{it-k} \Delta p_{it} + \sum_{i \in C} \Delta\theta_{it}(p_{it-k} - P_{t-k}) + \sum_{i \in C} \Delta\theta_{it} \Delta p_{it} + \sum_{i \in N} \theta_{it}(p_{it} - P_{t-k}) - \sum_{i \in X} \theta_{it-k}(p_{it-k} - P_{t-k})$$

(Continues on the following page.)

BOX 3.1

The Decomposition of Productivity Growth Using Firm-Level Data (*continued*)

where Δ is changes over the *k*-year interval between the first year (*t–k*) and the last year (*t*); θ_{it} is the share of industry employment in firm *i*; *C*, *N*, and *X* are sets of continuing, entering, and exiting firms, respectively; and P_{t-k} is the aggregate (that is, the weighted average) productivity level of the sector at the first year (*t–k*).

The components of the Foster-Haltiwanger-Krizan decomposition are defined as follows:

- The within-firm effect is within-firm productivity growth weighted by initial output shares.
- The between-firm effect captures the gains in aggregate productivity arising from the expanding market of high-productivity firms or from the shrinking shares of low-productivity firms weighted by the initial shares.
- The cross effect reflects gains in productivity from the expanding shares of high-productivity-growth firms or from the shrinking shares of low-productivity-growth firms. The term is positive if the firms that are gaining market shares are also those with above-average productivity growth; it is negative if the firms that are downsizing are the more productive ones.
- The entry effect is the sum of the differences between each entering firm's productivity and the initial productivity in the industry weighted by the market share of each entering firm.
- The exit effect is the sum of the differences between each exiting firm's productivity and the initial productivity in the industry weighted by the market share of each exiting firm.

The Foster-Haltiwanger-Krizan method uses the first year's values for a continuing firm's share (θ_{it-k}), its productivity level (p_{it-k}), and the average sectorwide productivity level (P_{t-k}). A potential problem with this method is that, in the presence of measurement error in assessing market shares and relative productivity levels in the base year, the correlation between changes in productivity and changes in market share may be spurious, thereby affecting the within- and between-firm effects.

Source: Foster and others 2001.

growth and TFP growth over five- or three-year rolling windows for all periods and industries for which data are available.

Most of this chapter relies on decompositions of labor productivity growth, but, whenever possible, it also draws on TFP growth. TFP estimates tend to be less robust than estimates of labor productivity because of the difficulty of measuring the stock of capital at the firm level. Despite this caveat, the decomposition of TFP has the advantage of being a more comprehensive measure of productivity. The decomposition of TFP growth in the Region yields results that are somewhat different from the results of the decomposition of labor productivity growth. The bulk of TFP growth is also driven by within-firm productivity growth, but the contribution of this term tends to be smaller. The reallocation of labor across existing firms (the between and cross terms) and firm churning (the sum of firm entries and exits) tend to play a more important role. A possible explanation for the discrepancy in the respective roles of within-firm growth and reallocation in labor and TFP growth decompositions may be that incumbent firms have been able to increase labor productivity mainly by substituting capital for labor (capital deepening) or by exiting the market altogether, but not necessarily by improving overall efficiency in production processes. In contrast, new firms entering the market with better combinations of factor inputs and new technologies have generated more rapid TFP growth.

In addition to productivity decompositions, the chapter also reviews firm demographics, focusing on the most easily obtainable statistics, as follows:

- The firm *entry rate* will be calculated as the number of entrants during a certain period, divided by the total number of firms in the sector. Data permitting, the study will also calculate entry penetration rates (where gross sales are used as a measure of the share of entrants) and employment-weighted entry rates.

- The firm *exit rate* will be calculated as the number of exiting firms during a certain period, divided by the total number of firms in the sector. The analogous employment-weighted exit rate will be calculated by dividing the employment levels in existing firms by total employment.

- The firm *turnover rate* is the sum of the entry and exit rates in a given sector over a given period.

To analyze the patterns of exit and survival and of firm growth, several types of regressions will be run that draw on maximum likelihood estimation methods using logit, progit, and tobit functional forms. Explanatory variables will include firm size, age, capital intensity, and ownership structure.

Sources of Productivity Growth

Three main messages emerge from the decomposition of labor productivity growth that draws on firm-level data for a sample of EU-10, CIS countries, and comparator countries outside the Region (see figure 3.1):

- *Productivity growth within each firm accounts for the bulk of overall labor productivity growth.* This is particularly the case if one focuses on

FIGURE 3.1

The Sources of Productivity Growth Differ Substantially across Countries and Sectors

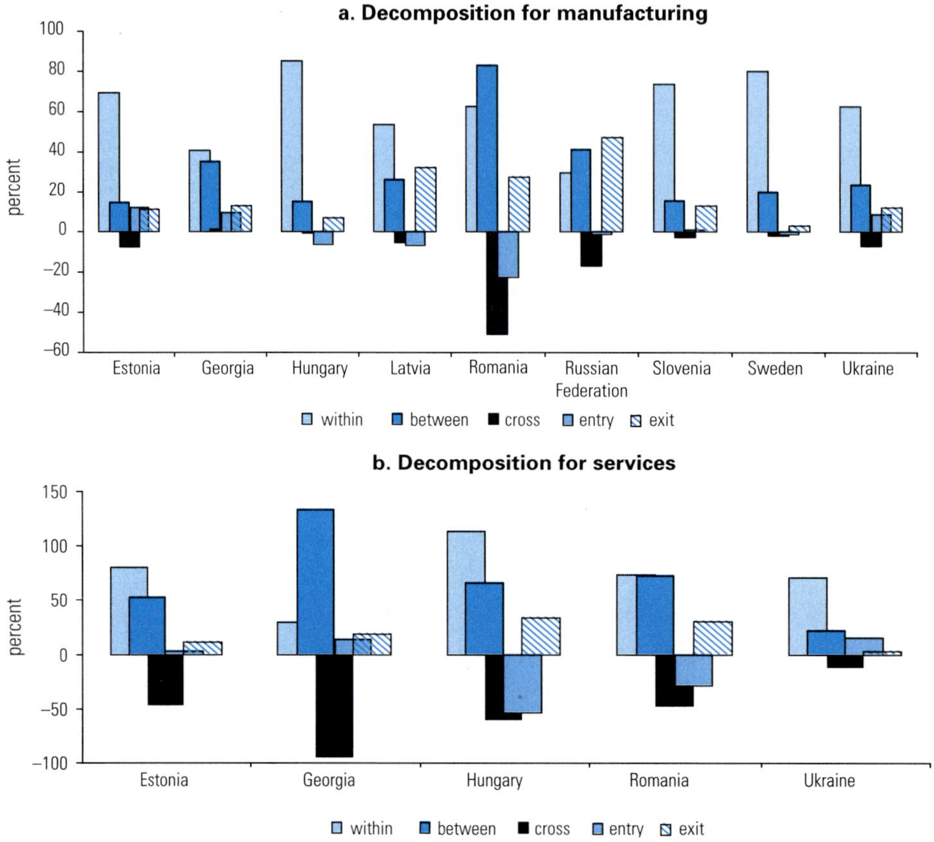

Sources: Bartelsman and Scarpetta 2007; Brown and Earle 2007.

Note: For manufacturing, the years are Estonia, 2002–04; Georgia, 2001–04; Hungary, 2000–03; Latvia, 2003–05; Romania, 2002–05; Russian Federation, 2001–04; Slovenia, 2002–04; Sweden, 2002–04; and Ukraine, 2002–05. For services, the years are Estonia, 2002–04; Georgia, 2001–04; Hungary, 2000–03; Latvia, 2003–05; Romania, 2002–05; and Ukraine, 2002–05.

the three-year horizon; over the longer run (that is, the five-year horizon), reallocation and, in particular, the entry component play a stronger role in promoting productivity growth. Even in advanced reformers, the within component, while sizable, contributes less than it does in advanced industrialized countries.

- *The impact on productivity via the reallocation of resources across existing enterprises or through entries and exits varies across countries.* This reallocation plays a significant role in the transition economies, with a particularly large contribution in laggard reformers. At the same time, however, the cross term is negative. This implies that firms experiencing an increase in productivity were also losing employment share (that is, their productivity growth was associated with restructuring and downsizing rather than with expansion).

- *The contribution to overall labor productivity growth of the entry and exit of firms (net entry) is generally positive in most countries,* accounting for between 20 and 50 percent of total productivity growth. While the exit effect is always positive (that is, the least productive firms exit the market, thereby helping to raise the productivity average of the firms that survive), the entry contribution tends to be negative in many countries.[1] In the transition economies, in contrast, the entry effect itself is positive and contributes directly about 10 percent to aggregate productivity growth.

Most Productivity Growth Arises from Efficiency Gains, within Existing Firms

The bulk of productivity growth arises from efficiency gains within existing businesses (figure 3.2). This is true in healthy market economies, and it is also true in transition economies. But firms improve their productivity in different ways, reflecting variations in the broader country business environment within which they operate. Among slow reformers, within-firm productivity growth is mostly driven by the utilization of excess capacity and by defensive firm restructuring, that is, shedding labor and adopting other cost-cutting strategies. In Russia, available survey data suggest that capacity utilization in manufacturing industries has increased substantially since 1999. In contrast, in advanced reformers, firms improve their productivity through strategic restructuring, which involves investing in new technologies and improving the value added content of products and exports.

Firms located in rapidly reforming regions enjoy higher productivity growth than those located in slowly reforming regions. Firms operating in rapidly reforming regions in Russia and Ukraine show higher productivity growth than those in laggard reforming regions.

FIGURE 3.2
Productivity Gains Have Arisen Primarily from Improvements within Firms

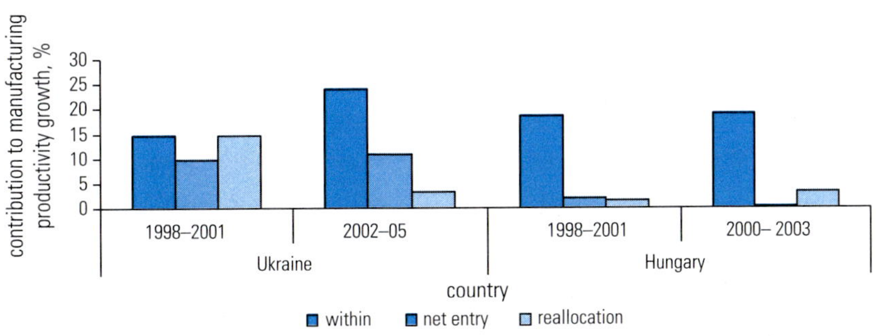

Source: Brown and Earle 2007.

Similarly, firms located in regions with better transport infrastructure tend to show higher productivity growth than those located in regions with greater transport deficiencies.

Large firms show higher productivity growth than small and medium firms; this is mostly driven by large within-firm productivity gains, but the reallocation effects are larger in smaller firms. Higher productivity growth is mostly driven by within-firm improvements, while the reallocation effects tend to be larger in industries dominated by small firms. In addition, within-firm productivity growth provides a relatively bigger contribution among large firms (250 or more employees). Though the between-firm reallocation has substantial productivity effects among large firms, the net entry contribution is often negative in this group. Among small firms (with less than 50 employees) and medium firms (firms with an average 50–249 employees), reallocation plays a more important role than within-firm productivity growth.

New private firms also show higher productivity growth than state-owned firms, and this is mostly driven by reallocation effects. Overall productivity growth is higher within new private firms. Within-firm productivity growth is nearly twice as high in this group of firms relative to old firms in Hungary and Russia, though it is lower in such firms in Romania. Reallocation contributes more among newly private firms relative to state-owned firms in Hungary and Romania, although the opposite is the case in Russia and Ukraine. In the latter two, new private entrants and exiting firms are much less productive than the average relative to their state-owned peers. The reallocation of resources among incumbent firms (the between term) is much greater among private firms in Hungary and Romania than in Russia and Ukraine. These differences are related to the modes of privatization and the degree of market competition (see the next section).

Foreign-owned firms tend to show higher productivity growth than domestic private or state firms. These findings help in addressing the endogeneity problems often found in the link between foreign entry and productivity growth. The analysis is based on time series data that allow firms to be followed before and after they have become foreign-owned. The large productivity growth enjoyed by foreign firms is driven by different factors across countries. In Russia, it is driven by higher within productivity growth. In Hungary, it seems to be related to initial productivity differences at entry.

Firms operating in ICT-related industries display better productivity performance, reflecting the presence of technological spillovers. Firms operating in ICT-related industries rely on strategic restructuring and improve their productivity by adopting new and better ways to produce goods. In contrast, firms in non-ICT industries tend to engage in defensive restructuring strategies to increase productivity, mostly by shedding labor. Overall, they tend to have lower productivity growth than firms operating in ICT industries. Firm entry also plays an important role in boosting productivity in ICT-related industries, whereas the contribution of new firms to productivity growth is negative in non-ICT-related industries. In other words, in industries with greater opportunities to innovate, a large number of new firms tend to emerge. The better performance of companies operating in ICT-intensive sectors may be considered evidence of the presence of technological spillovers. If a firm operates in a high-technology environment, it is more likely to absorb new developments quickly and to boost productivity additionally.

Likewise, firms in industries that depend on external finance tend to enjoy higher productivity growth, and this is even more the case in countries at higher levels of financial development. Productivity tends to grow more quickly in firms operating in industries that are more dependent on external finance and in countries with deeper financial markets.

Firm Churning Contributed More to Productivity Growth at the Start of Transition

The process of creative destruction encourages firms to experiment and learn; it rewards success, and it punishes failure. Healthy market economies exhibit fairly high rates of firm entry and exit. Around 5 to 20 percent of firms enter or exit the market every year. In the Region, about 20 percent of firms were created or destroyed during the past decade (figure 3.3). At the start of the transition, a large fraction of firms were closed down and replaced by new small ventures. As the transition advanced, net firm flows declined, reaching values fairly close to those observed in other countries.

The amount and timing of firm churning vary across countries and industries. Early reformers, such as Hungary, experienced a short period of large firm flows at the start of the transition process; this was dominated by the entry of firms and was mostly a response to privatization. Over time, the number of firms created or destroyed declined and then stabilized at around the rates observed in healthy market economies. In Russia, in contrast, firm flows have been remarkably low (figure 3.4), and, during the second half of the 1990s, firm exit rates exceeded the new firm entry rates. After the 1998 crisis, this trend was reversed, and the number of new firms exceeded the number of firms being destroyed.

Net entry rates are somewhat higher in services than in manufacturing. Firm turnover rates (especially if they are weighted by

FIGURE 3.3

Firm Start-Ups Have Exceeded Exits in Most Countries over the Past Decade

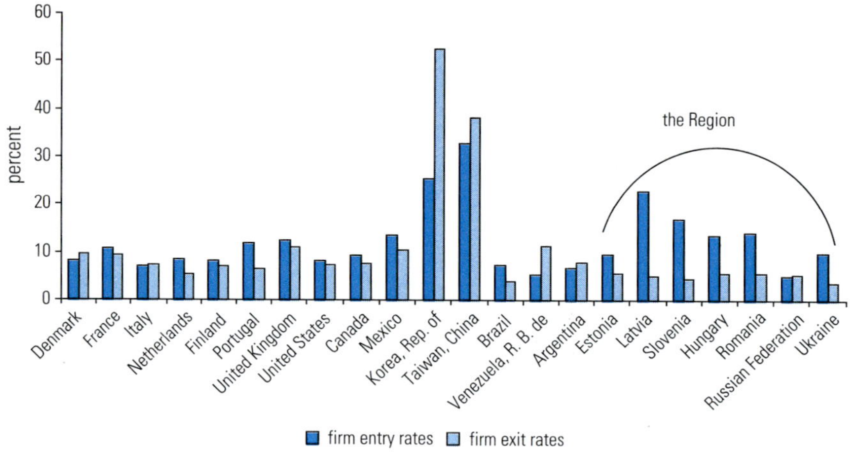

Sources: Bartelsman and Scarpetta 2007; Brown and Earle 2007.

FIGURE 3.4

Hungary and the Russian Federation Have Varied in Rates of Firm Churning

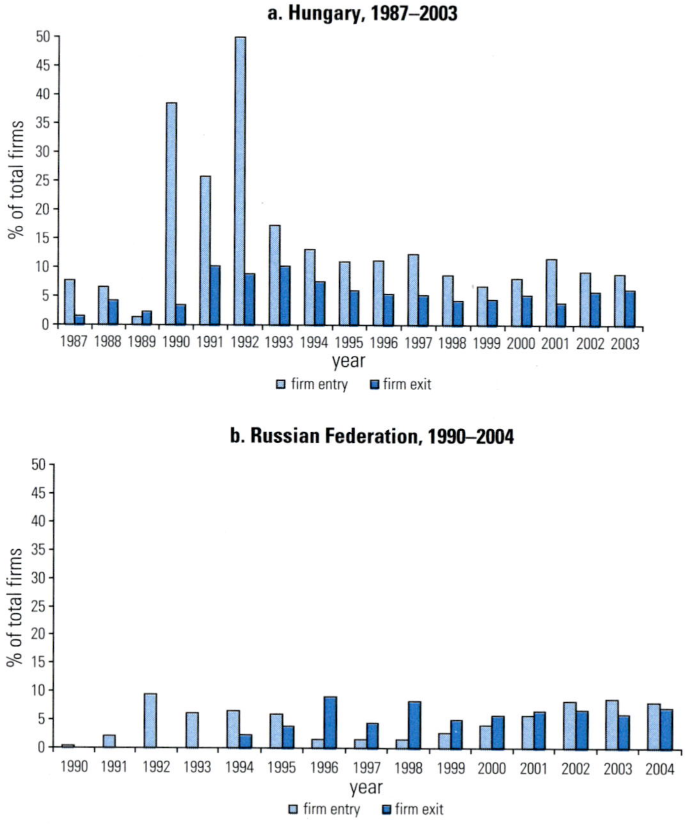

Source: Brown and Earle 2007.

employment) are higher in the service sector (especially in trade) than in manufacturing. In most countries, some high-technology industries exhibiting rapid technological change and market experimentation had relatively high entry rates in the 1990s (for example, office and computing equipment, radio and television, and communications).

The net entry effect (firm entry, plus exit) is generally positive in most transition countries, but its contribution has declined. At the start of the transition, the contribution of net entry was large and accounted for between 20 and 40 percent of total productivity growth. The effect of firm entry also tends to be larger than the effect of firm exit in slow reformers, where low-productivity firms, which are sheltered from competitive pressure, have managed to contain job destruction. This suggests that these firms may still have to undergo a period of downsizing and restructuring.

Entrants tended to show higher productivity, on average, than incumbents during the earlier phases of transition. In Hungary and Romania, entrants were less productive than the average incumbent, which might signal that there was more experimentation. This pattern is similar to the one observed in OECD countries, where entrants often lack experience, and small size often equates with less productivity among new firms. In contrast, in Georgia, Russia, and Ukraine, entrants were (on average) more productive than incumbents (see figure 3.5). They were able to occupy new market niches, mostly in market services, that had been underdeveloped or nonexistent during the central planning period.

Entrants also tended to be small relative to incumbents. Under the centrally planned system, there were relatively few microbusinesses

FIGURE 3.5

Entrants Showed Higher Productivity than Incumbents

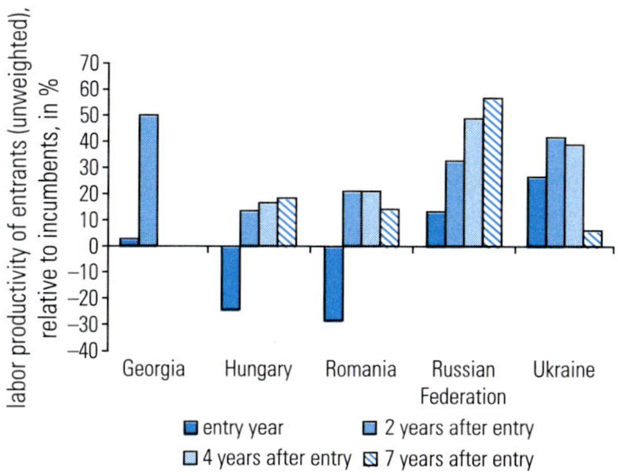

Sources: Brown and Earle 2007.

or small firms, but, after the start of the transition, the number shot up, particularly in business service activities. Many of the entrants that failed during the initial years were also small. The relative productivity of entrants has tended to rise with age.

Entrants tended to show high survival rates at the beginning of the transition. Understanding the post-entry performance of firms sheds light on the selection process in markets, which separates successful entrant firms that survive and prosper from firms that stagnate and eventually exit. Survival rates after entry are higher in Russia and Ukraine. In Estonia, Latvia, and Slovenia, but also in Romania, around 70 percent of the firms survived at least four years (figure 3.6). In contrast, in advanced market economies, firm survival is much lower, pointing toward harsher market selection or to higher variance in quality among entrants. Another possible explanation is that the entrants in the transition economies joined the market with a portion of the pretransition firms intact, that is, the new firms had employees with experience and ongoing connections with customers and suppliers. This latter effect would likely diminish over time.

As countries progress along the transition path, market competition becomes harsher, and survival rates among entrants drop. Entrants show rapidly declining probabilities of survival. In Hungary, around 35 percent of entrant firms in 1991–95 were no longer active in the market after two years, and over 50 percent after four years; only about 35 percent were still in business after seven years. In 1996–2001, survival rates dropped again: 55 percent were no longer active in the market after two years, and over 70 percent after four years; only about

FIGURE 3.6
Transition Economies Show Higher Survival Rates Than Many Advanced Economies

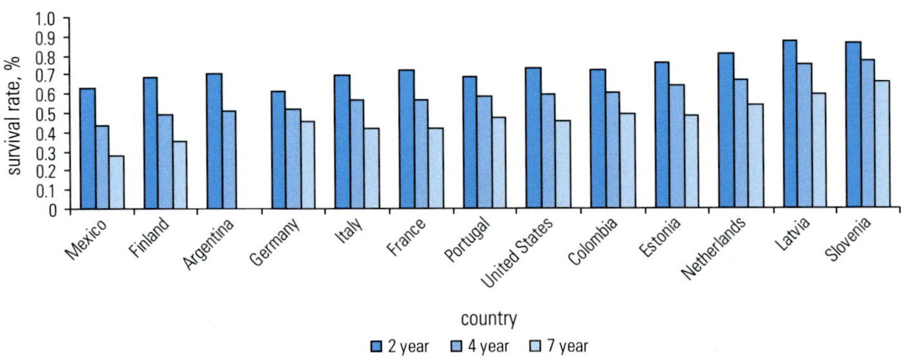

Source: Bartelsman and Scarpetta 2007.

20 percent were still in business after seven years. Opposite trends are found in countries that are relatively behind on the transition path, such as Russia and Ukraine. Survival rates in these late reformers are higher than those in Hungary, and they have increased over time (figure 3.7). In contrast, failure rates among young businesses are high in all market economies, but, in advanced industrial countries, about 40–50 percent of new firms are still in business after seven years. In the Baltic states, entrants face an environment that is slightly less harsh than the one in the EU; about 70 percent were still active after four years, and 50–60 percent survived seven years (figure 3.5).

Even successful entrants have not expanded significantly. Large firms in manufacturing have been affected the most, and the expansion of successful firms has been limited. At the start of the transition, Estonia, Latvia, and Slovenia exhibited substantial declines in firm size, especially in manufacturing, while the size of the largest firms declined post-transition and did not respond noticeably to the opportunities of the enlarged market. In Slovenia, the average size in the quartile of the largest firms had dropped from over 800 to 200 employees by the early 2000s. In the Baltic countries, no sign of any increases in the average size has been evident. The question remains whether firms in these countries are able to benefit fully from the opportunities offered by economic integration in the EU. The lack of growth among large manufacturing firms contrasts with the rapid

FIGURE 3.7

As the Transition Matures, Markets Grow Harsh, and Entrant Survival Rates Drop

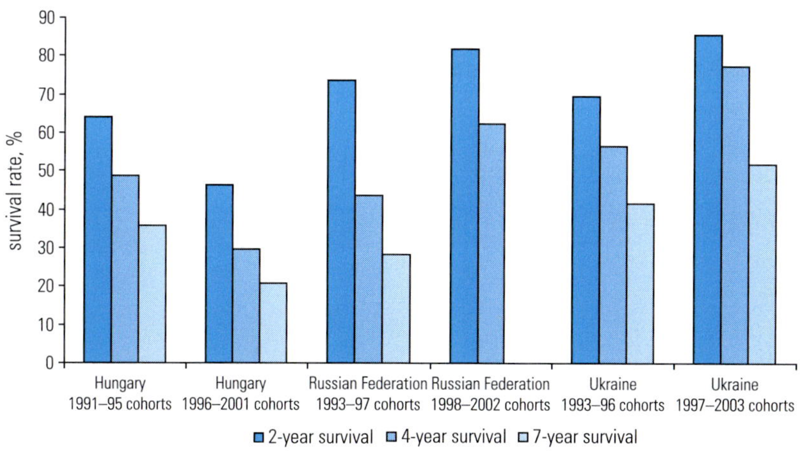

Source: Brown and Earle 2007.

expansion of comparable firms in Mexico in the few years since the establishment of the North American Free Trade Agreement. In Mexico, there has been a rapid expansion in the mean size of the quartile of the largest manufacturing firms from 80 employees to 120 employees per firm (figure 3.8).

Worker Reallocations from Less- to More-Productive Firms Contributed to Growth

The reallocation of workers across existing firms also contributed to productivity growth; its role was particularly large at the start of the transition. In countries at the early stages of transition, the between term tended to be large and positive, indicating that firms with higher than average productivity levels were tending to gain market share. At the same time, the contribution to total productivity growth of the cross term (the shift of resources toward firms with higher than average productivity growth) is negative. This means that firms experiencing an increase in productivity were also losing employment shares, that is, their productivity growth was associated with restructuring and downsizing rather than expansion.

The rapid pace of restructuring in transition economies should not yet be taken as evidence of the existence of the same competitive conditions observed in healthy market economies. The pace of firm entry and exit and the contribution of reallocation to productivity growth in mature economies point to an ongoing steady-state process that puts pressure on incumbents to perform well. In early reformers, which are less advanced in the transition process, reallocation is not so much an indicator of the overall state of competitiveness

FIGURE 3.8

Large Manufacturing Firms Are Not Expanding in Slovenia, but They Are in Mexico

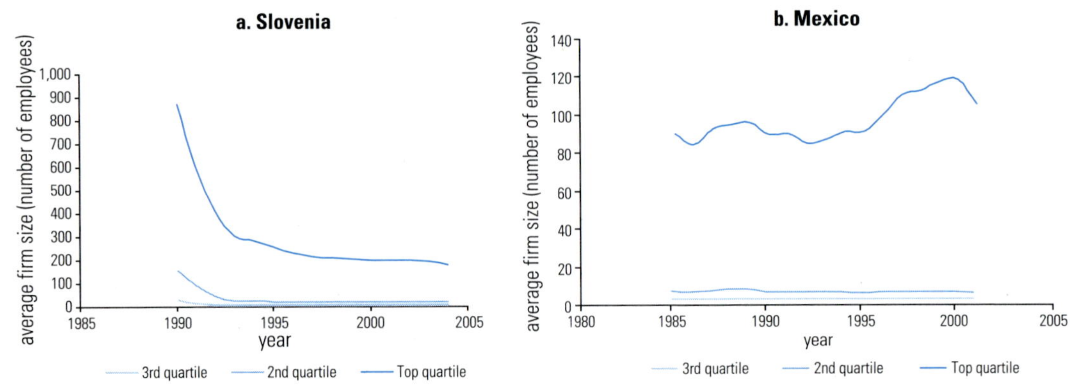

Source: Bartelsman and Scarpetta 2007.

FIGURE 3.9

Net Entry and Reallocation Are Declining, Converging toward Advanced Market Patterns

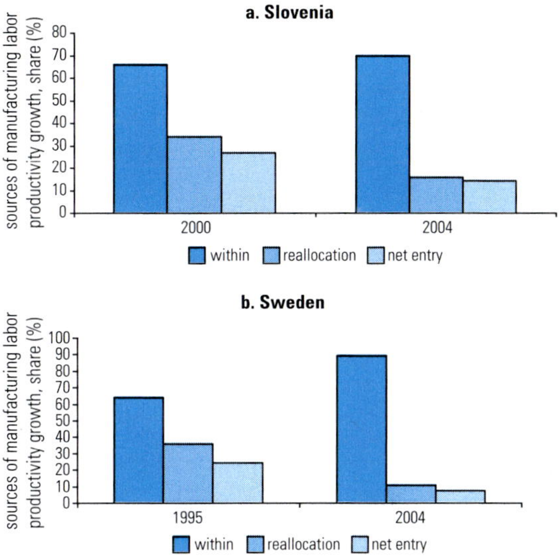

Sources: Bartelsman and Scarpetta 2007; Brown and Earle 2007.

of the market, but a reflection of a major change in the supply side of the economy.

As transition matures, the role of net entry and reallocation declines, and the pattern converges toward the patterns observed in advanced market economies. While the relative contributions of reallocation and net entry tend to decline as transition proceeds (figure 3.9), this does not mean that they do not matter in advanced market economies. In advanced industrialized economies, reallocation effects tend to be correlated with business cycles, and, during periods of restructuring, their contribution is greater. Furthermore, as countries move closer to the technological frontier, the role of entry again becomes important in fostering innovation-led productivity gains.

Under Weak Competition, Firm Churning Does Not Pressure Incumbents to Raise Productivity

The above analysis focuses on the direct contribution of the reallocation process to productivity growth either through the dynamic or the cross-sectional decomposition. But a more rapid pace of firm creation and destruction may also influence the decisions of domestic firms about efficiency-enhancing investment. In particular, the entry of productive firms may increase the contestability of the market, thereby forcing some firms to exit, but also raising the pressure on incumbents to perform more efficiently. There is a strong, positive, and statistically significant correlation between the contribution of net entries and the productivity growth of incumbents in healthy market economies. However, this relationship is weaker in the Region, particularly among the slow reformers, where market competition is also weaker.

Reallocation contributions are often interpreted in the literature as a reflection of the creative destruction process, while within-firm contributions are interpreted as a reflection of more traditional sources of productivity growth (the average firm becomes more productive as advances are achieved in technology). However, rather than alternatives, these effects (within versus reallocation) may be closely related, and the pace of the creative destruction process might be interpreted as a measure of the contestability or competitiveness of markets. Nonetheless, while there is a positive correlation in healthy market economies between the contribution of net entries and the productivity growth of incumbents, this is less clear in the transition economies (figure 3.10).

In the Region, there is a positive correlation between the contribution of net entry and the productivity growth of incumbents in some of the advanced reformers, such as Slovenia. In contrast, in later reformers (Georgia, Russia, and Ukraine), there is no association between the entry of new firms and productivity growth in existing firms (figure 3.11). The lack of pressure from new firms is partly explained by the weaker market competition. It may also be caused by large failure rates among new businesses.

FIGURE 3.10

New Firms Tend to Spur Productivity Growth in Early Reformers

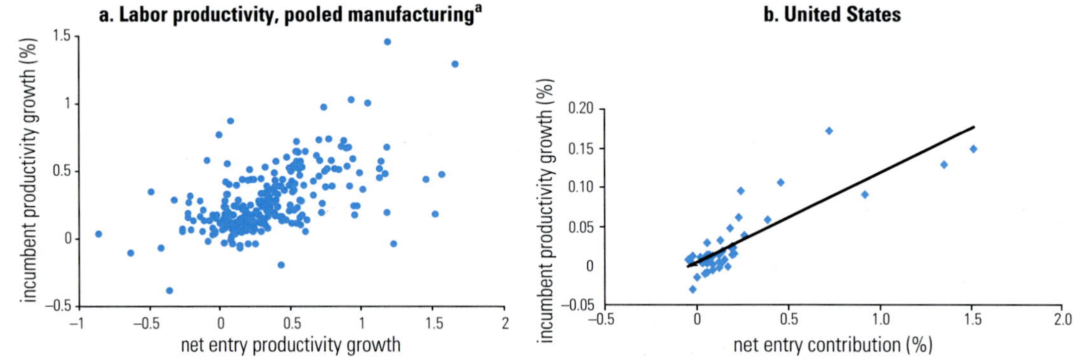

Source: Bartelsman and Scarpetta 2007.

a. Chart *a* includes Argentina, Chile, Colombia, Estonia, Finland, France, the Republic of Korea, Latvia, the Netherlands, Portugal, Slovenia, Taiwan (China), the United Kingdom, the United States, and Germany. Outliers are excluded. The chart relies on five-year differencing, real gross output, and country and industry time averages.

FIGURE 3.11

Entry of New Firms Is Not Always Correlated with Productivity Growth in Existing Firms

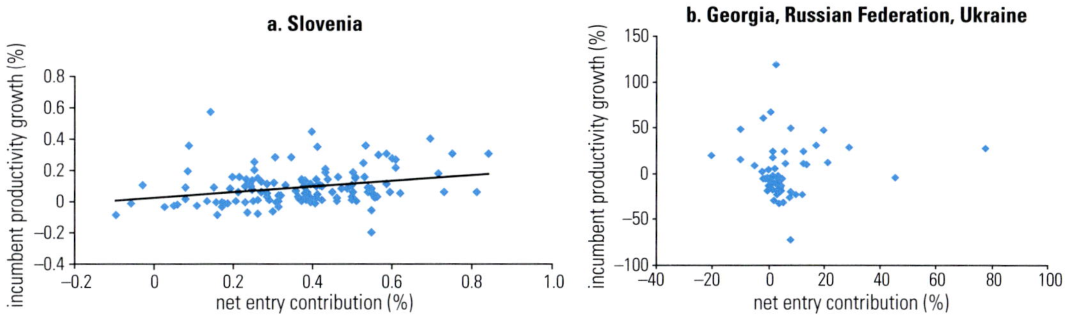

Sources: Bartelsman and Scarpetta 2007; Brown and Earle 2007.

Even in Early Reformers, Allocative Efficiency Is Less Relative to Healthy Market Economies

Distortions in market structure and institutions may affect the entry and exit margins in a variety of ways. Early in the transition, resources were locked in firms at lower productivity, on average, but the allocation rapidly improved because of the exit of less-productive firms and the movement of resources toward new more-productive firms. However, even advanced reformers (EU-10) still display lower allocative efficiency than the OECD countries, suggesting that there is room for adjustments (figure 3.12).

Firm Dynamics and Job Flows

Firm-level data on a sample of countries in the Region and several comparator countries provide insights on the dynamics of the size of firms and the nature of job markets.

The Transition Led to a Remarkable Surge in Job Flows

At the beginning of the transition, both gross and net firm flows were large compared with the flows in advanced industrial and other emerging economies. In modern economies, gross rates of job creation and destruction range from 5 to 20 percent, representing a total job turnover of up to 40 percent. A significant part of this job turnover (often 30–50 percent) is caused by firm entries and exits.

Job reallocation rates across firms were higher in transition economies relative to advanced market economies. In late reformers,

FIGURE 3.12

Labor Allocative Efficiency in Manufacturing Lags Even in Advanced Reformers

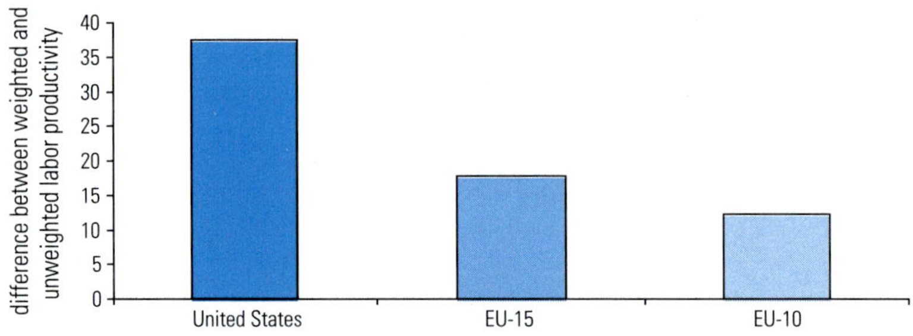

Source: Bartelsman and Scarpetta 2007.

Note: The figure shows the average Olley-Pakes cross term in manufacturing.

FIGURE 3.13

Labor Shedding at Existing Firms Was the Main Source of Job Destruction

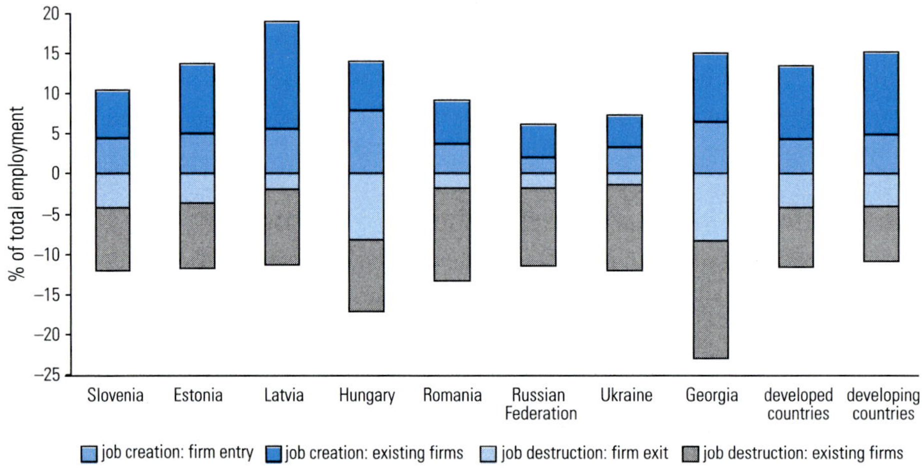

Sources: Bartelsman and Scarpetta 2007; Brown and Earle 2007.

job destruction rates exceeded job creation rates. This was in contrast to early reformers. Unlike entrant firms, existing firms resorted, on average, to defensive restructuring; that is, they improved productivity by downsizing and shedding redundant labor (figure 3.13). At the start of the transition, a large share of firms were closed down and replaced by new small ventures. Firm churning accounted for more than 10 percent of total employment in the Region. As the transition moved forward, net firm flows declined and, by the end of the 1990s, had reached values fairly close to those observed in other countries.

The Net Employment Impact of Reallocation Varied across Countries and Sectors

In countries lagging in market-oriented reforms, stringent labor market regulations discouraged job creation, and, as a result, job destruction rates exceeded job creation rates. These unsynchronized job flows gave rise to unemployment (or underemployment, that is, low-productive employment in the informal sector). Job destruction generally surged first, but it was the response of job creation that varied across countries: job creation caught up rapidly with job destruction in the early reformers, but job creation did not offset job destruction in the late reformers for any prolonged period (figure 3.14).

FIGURE 3.14

Sometimes Unsynchronized Job Flows Gave Rise to Net Employment Losses

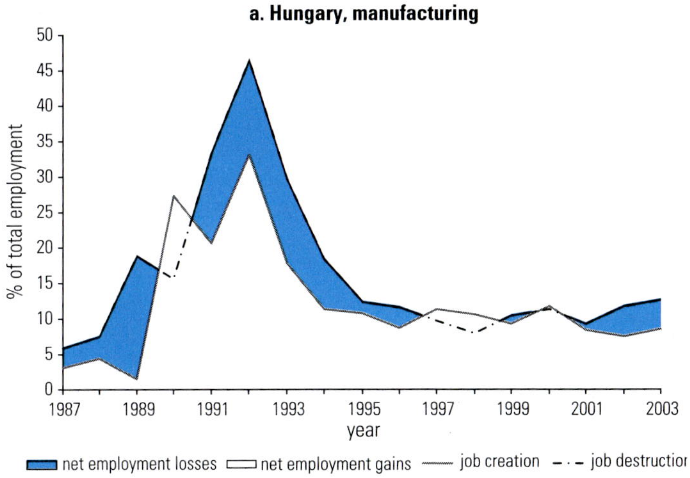

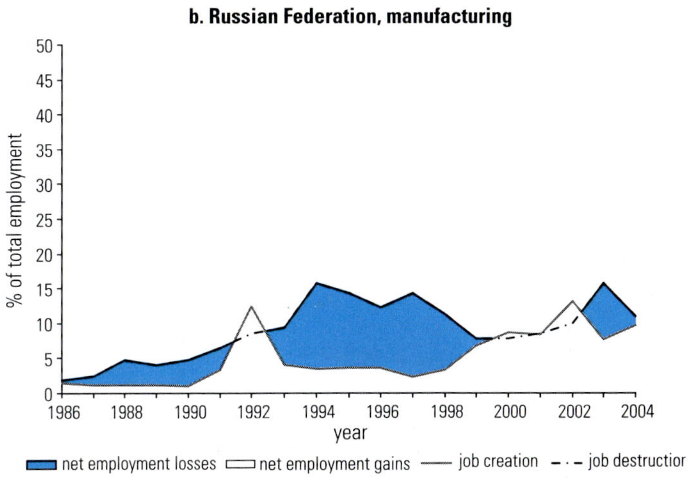

Source: Brown and Earle 2007.

The picture also varied across sectors. Thus, in services, job creation exceeded job destruction in most countries owing to the rapid growth of the sector across the Region (figure 3.15).

Firm entry outpaced firm exit at the start of the transition. During the early stages of the transition, firm entries contributed substantially to job creation (from 25 to 50 percent). New firms not only displaced obsolete incumbents, but also filled market niches that had been either nonexistent or poorly populated until then. Firm exits, in contrast, were not closely associated with job destruction. Most of the job destruction arose because existing firms were following defensive restructuring strategies. Successful entrants that showed higher initial productivity tended to create more jobs (figure 3.16).

FIGURE 3.15
Job Creation Exceeded Job Destruction in Services

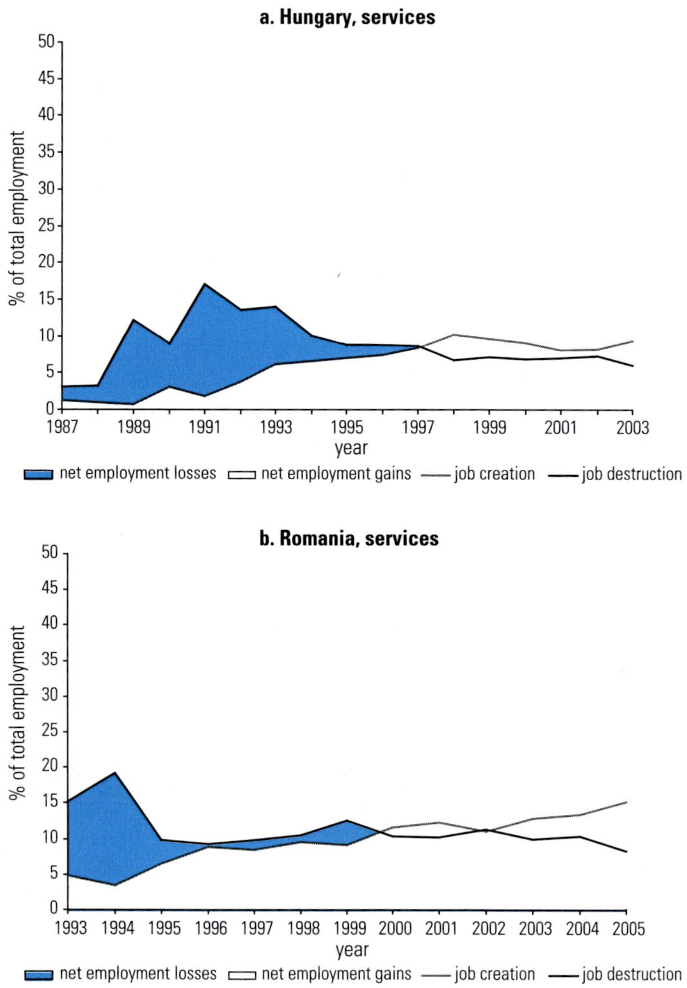

Source: Brown and Earle 2007.

FIGURE 3.16

Firms with Higher Labor Productivity Were More Successful in Creating Jobs

Source: Brown and Earle 2007.

The probability of employment growth was strongly associated with the initial productivity performance of firms.

Policy Reform Should Focus on Stimulating Productivity

In late reformers, there is still significant misallocation of resources across firms, industries, and locations. This ongoing distortion calls for policy reforms to accelerate the pace of reallocation so that resources may flow from less-productive to more-productive uses. The process of creative destruction (that is, the exit of unprofitable firms and the entry of new, more-productive ones) needs to be invigorated through privatization and stronger market competition.

Although productivity increases are now largely driven by within-firm adjustments, firm entries and exits should play an important role in sustaining productivity growth in the years to come. By continuing to protect ailing firms and to contain firm exit, late reformers have not been able to free resources from less-productive uses to apply them to more-productive uses. Similarly, restrictive product markets and uncertain business environments discourage firm entry and the adoption of available technologies.

In early reformers, the main challenges are the stimulation of innovation within firms and encouragement for the expansion of new, successful firms. These countries also need to focus on reducing any remaining barriers to entry. In this regard, credit constraints, labor market rigidities, and deficiencies in tertiary and vocational education are likely to act as barriers to entry and innovation. Restrictive product, labor, and service markets may deter the entry and growth of new firms and reduce innovative efforts and technology spillovers, and this affects productivity growth negatively.

These findings suggest that policies should focus not only on stimulating productivity growth within existing firms, but also on eliminating barriers to firm entry and exit. The high incidence of failures in Hungary and Romania and the associated job losses are a clear source of concern. While entry for small businesses may be relatively easy, firm survival seems to be more difficult. The findings of sizable labor reallocation across and within sectors and firms suggest that workers have had to adapt to changing demands for labor and skills; this calls for reforms in the education sector. In addition, even though reallocation may enhance productivity in the economy as a whole, there are clearly losers in the process. The losers include the owners of the obsolete businesses and the displaced workers. In economies with less market friction, resources are more quickly reallocated to their best uses and the adjustments take less time. The net employment losses observed in some countries of the Region are the result of policy barriers that slow the pace of the reallocation of resources. The barriers include limited factor mobility (credit market frictions and rigidities in labor markets) and other regulatory constraints affecting firm entry and firm performance. It is, therefore, not surprising to observe that, in these countries, the informal economy still plays an important role as a temporary buffer for creating (less-productive) jobs.

Policy Drivers of Firm Productivity Growth

Chapter 1 presents the outcomes of aggregate cross-country regressions: macroeconomic stability, investments in infrastructure and human capital, improvements in governance, financial sector development, and international integration are all key policy drivers of total productivity growth. This section confirms that most of the policy drivers identified in chapter 1 affect firm productivity growth.

The decisions of firms to improve their productivity are affected not only by their own ideas and capabilities, but also by the incentive framework in which the firms operate: the pressures they face to survive in a competitive marketplace and the opportunities to invest productively, create jobs, and expand. Government policies and institutions exert a strong influence on firm performance through their impact on the costs, risks, and opportunities of doing business. The analysis so far illustrates that the Region's strong productivity performance was, to a large extent, characterized by differences in firm productivity growth rates. Furthermore, those firms that performed well in a particular sector tended to be located in countries that were making the most progress in reforming the policy and regulatory environment.

This section provides empirical evidence of the link between government policies and institutions and firm productivity growth. It confirms the link between policies and productivity growth and sheds light on specific aspects of reform that had a differential impact on productivity growth across countries (see box 3.2).

While it is not possible to disentangle the productivity contribution from all factors affecting firm performance, this chapter argues that part of the rapid increase in firm productivity was driven by higher capacity utilization, sustained macroeconomic stability, investments in

BOX 3.2

Empirical Analysis of Policy Drivers of Firm Productivity Growth

The empirical analysis presented in this section draws on two data sets: the Amadeus Database and the BEEPS Database. Amadeus is a comprehensive, pan-European database compiled by Bureau van Dijk that provides firm-level accounting data in a standardized financial format on 24 balance sheet items, 25 profit and loss account items, and 26 financial ratios. It also supplies descriptive information, including trade description codes and activity codes. For the estimation of TFP, this report relies on the May 2006 edition of Amadeus and a sample that covers over 67,000 manufacturing (NACE 15–36) firms in eight countries in the Region (Bulgaria, Croatia, the Czech Republic, Estonia, Poland, Romania, Serbia, and Ukraine) from 1998 through 2004. For the econometric analysis of firm-level TFP growth and the business environment, the final sample for the analysis is limited to a panel of 22,004 firms for which data are available for 2001 through 2004, which corresponds to the 2002 and 2005 rounds of the BEEPS. BEEPS 2002 and 2005 data are assumed to capture the characteristics of the business environment in 2001 and 2003, respectively, and are, therefore, merged with Amadeus 2002 and 2004 observations on country, sector, firm size, and location.

To estimate the impact of the business environment on firm performance, we regress the change in the TFP of manufacturing firms on the lagged changes in several aspects of the business environment as measured by a wide array of BEEPS variables. To mitigate the problems of multicollinearity and endogeneity in the full model regression, we reduce the dimensionality of the BEEPS data using principal component analysis to construct indicators that summarize six distinct dimensions of the business environment: (a) infrastructure quality, (b) financial development, (c) governance, (d) labor market flexibility, (e) labor quality, and (f) competition. Each indicator varies across years and groups of manufacturing establishments of size s, operating in location l of country c at time $t-1$. In addition, changes in the level of competition in each industry m are measured by the lagged change in the four-firm concentration ratio defined at the 4-digit NACE level and calculated using the full Amadeus sample. Changes in these six business environment indicators are

(*Continues on the following page.*)

Box 3.2

Empirical Analysis of Policy Drivers of Firm Productivity Growth (*continued*)

regressed in the full model, along with changes in firm characteristics and controls for location, industry, and country effects. Formally, the model is specified as follows:

$$\begin{aligned}\Delta \ln TFP_{ijt} = {} & \alpha + \beta_1 \Delta infrastructure_{t-1}^{s,l,c} + \beta_2 \Delta finance_{t-1}^{s,l,c} \\ & + \beta_3 \Delta governance_{t-1}^{s,l,c} + \beta_4 \Delta labor\_market_{t-1}^{s,l,c} \\ & + \beta_5 \Delta labor\_quality_{t-1}^{s,l,c} + \beta_6 \Delta competition_{t-1}^{m,c} \\ & + \Delta \ln TFP_{i,t-1} + \sum_n \phi_n \Delta Z_{i,t}^n + \sum_m \xi industry_m \\ & + \sum_l \lambda location_l + \sum_c \gamma country_c + \varepsilon_{i,t}\end{aligned}$$

where $TFP_{i,t}$ is the TFP of manufacturing establishment *i*, operating at time *t*, and calculated using the semiparametric estimation technique developed by Levinsohn and Petrin (2003); $\Delta \ln TFP_{i,t-1}$ is the change in the logarithm of TFP from 2001 to 2003; $\Delta Z_{i,t}^n$ is a vector of changes in firm characteristics that include the number of employees, tangible fixed assets (thousands of 2001 U.S. dollars), and cost of materials (thousands of 2001 U.S. dollars); *LOCATION* is a vector of location dummy variables, including a capital-city dummy variable (equal to 1 if the firm is located in a capital city—that is, Belgrade, Bucharest, Kyiv, Prague, Sofia, Tallinn, Warsaw, or Zagreb—and 0 otherwise), and a large-city dummy variable (equal to 1 if the firm is located in a city with a population of 250,000 or more and 0 otherwise); *INDUSTRY* is a vector of industry dummy variables defined at the 4-digit NACE level; and *COUNTRY* is a vector of country dummy variables for Bulgaria, Croatia, the Czech Republic, Estonia, Poland, Romania, Serbia, and Ukraine.

The results of the regression analysis show that firm-level productivity growth is directly linked to each of these factors in the business environment. Data confirm that good infrastructure, financial development, good governance, and competition encourage firms to operate efficiently and promote productivity growth by lowering risks, costs, and barriers to entry. Conversely, labor market rigidity and a workforce deficient in skills and educational attainment are found to be negatively correlated with productivity growth. All empirical results are statistically significant. In a global economy where technology diffuses rapidly, the persistence of productivity differences across countries may be largely explained by differences in the business environment in which firms operate. These microeconomic foundations—infrastructure quality, financial development, governance, competition, labor market flexibility, and human capital—are critically linked to the success and growth of firms.

A complete description of the data and estimation methodology is presented in appendix 3.B.

human and physical infrastructure, stronger market competition driven by large-scale privatization, improvements in labor and financial markets, technology transfers through trade and foreign investment, and investments in R&D and new information technologies.

Improving Capacity Utilization

Chapter 1 indicates that capacity utilization contributed to TFP growth rates in Russia. In transition economies that experienced a strong growth rebound after a deep transitional recession, especially the CIS economies, it is reasonable to suspect that firms resorted to the utilization of idle assets, thereby contributing to a boost in factor productivity growth. In Russia, available firm survey data suggest that capacity utilization in manufacturing industries increased significantly beginning in 1999. In particular, the 2006 Russian Economic Barometer Survey Database suggests that there has been a U-shaped pattern, with capacity utilization falling until the 1998 Russian crisis and rising from 1999 onward (figure 3.17). The use of this productive

FIGURE 3.17

The Recovery in Capacity Utilization Spurred Productivity Growth in the Russian Federation

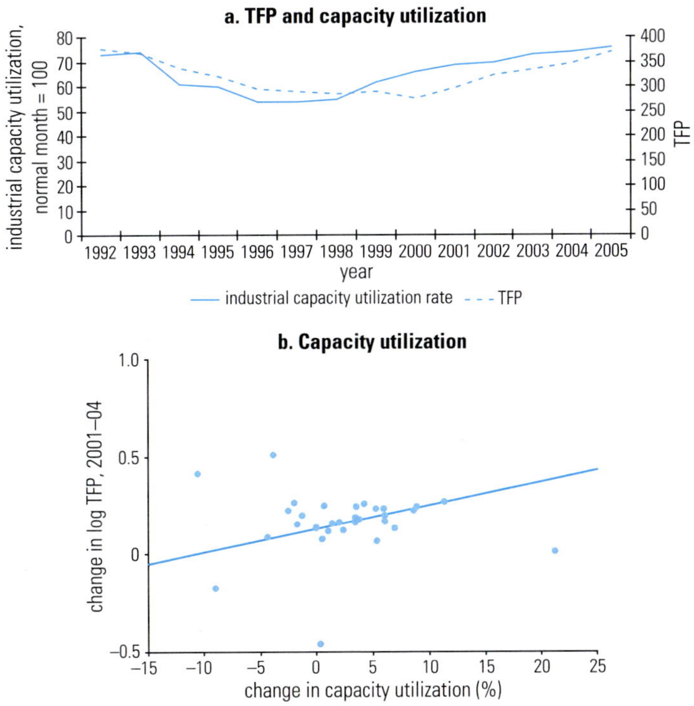

Sources: World Bank staff calculations; Russian Economic Barometer Survey Database 2006; BEEPS 2005; Amadeus Database 2006; appendix 3.B.

capacity was important in the early 2000s but, by 2005, seemed to have run its course.[2]

Implementing Large-Scale Privatization

The liquidation of inefficient state-owned companies is a phenomenon mostly unique to countries transitioning from a centrally planned to a market economy. Privatization was the main trigger of firm restructuring and productivity growth at the start of the transition. However, the net impact of privatization on productivity growth depended on the type of privatization (Brown and Earle 2007; World Bank 2005a). Transition countries have used different modes of privatization. The privatization methods used in Hungary and Romania resulted in ownership concentration at the time of privatization, while mass privatization in Russia and Ukraine led to dispersed ownership by employees and small investors (figure 3.18).

FIGURE 3.18

Privatization Raised Productivity Growth, Particularly in Countries that Attracted FDI

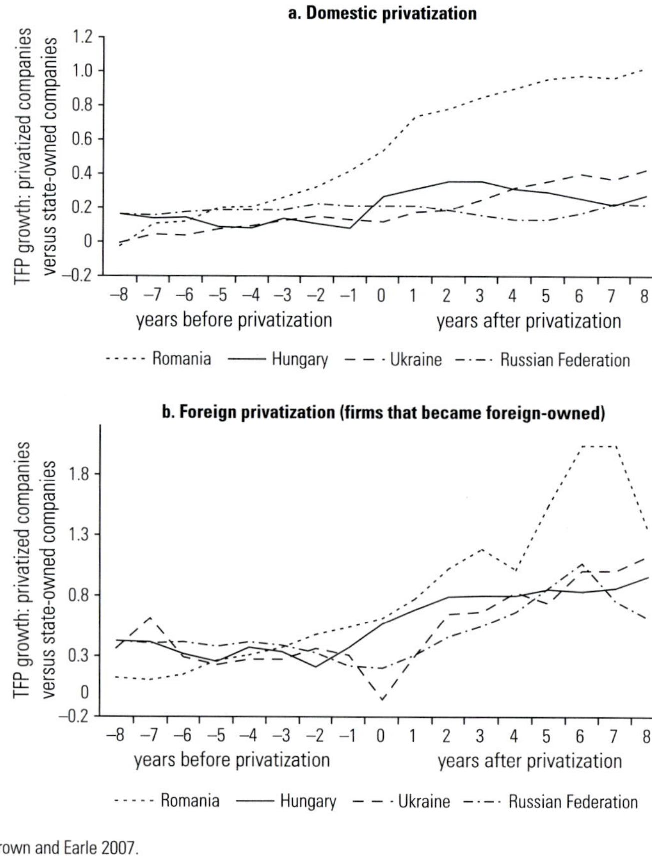

Source: Brown and Earle 2007.

In addition to affecting within-firm productivity growth, privatization also had an impact on the pace of reallocation. Privatization facilitated the process of creative destruction, leading to the emergence of new, more-productive firms and the liquidation or restructuring of obsolete state-owned companies. However, mass privatization, like the surge in capacity utilization, was mostly a one-off event. Further productivity improvements had to be sustained through other policies that aimed at accelerating the pace of reallocation and promoting innovation-led productivity gains within firms.

Strengthening Competition in Product and Service Markets

Firm-level surveys show the importance of competitive pressure as an incentive for firms to innovate and raise productivity (figure 3.19). This is not surprising since various theoretical arguments suggest that greater competition is likely to lead to increases in firm productivity. In weakly competitive markets, firm survival is not immediately threatened by inefficient practices. Managers of existing firms may maintain suboptimal use of factor inputs. In contrast, more-intense competition forces managers to speed up the adoption of new technologies to survive.

Product Market Competition

The literature has traditionally focused on static measures of product market competition such as market concentration ratios, markups, and import penetration ratios.[3] The market concentration ratio (also known as the Herfindhal index) measures the share of the total output of the largest firms in a market. The markup ratio (also known as

FIGURE 3.19

Market Competition Fosters Innovation and Productivity Growth

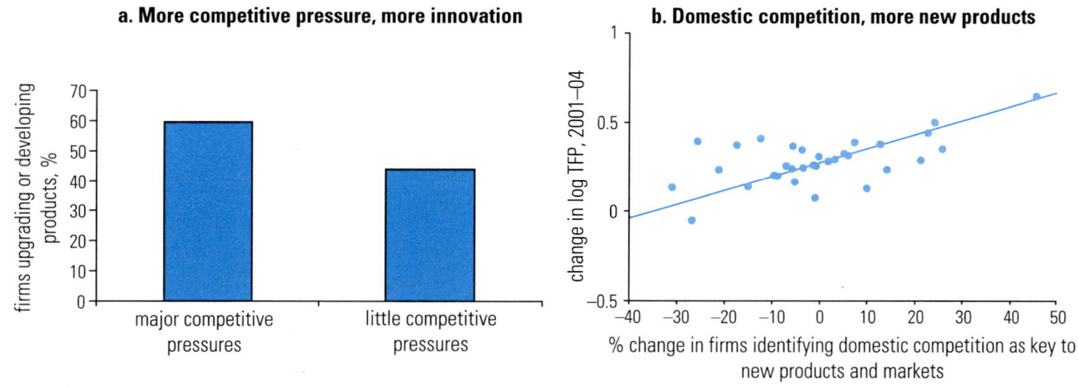

Sources: BEEPS 2002, 2005; Amadeus Database 2006; appendix 3.B.

the Lerner index) captures the degree of monopolistic markup pricing above marginal costs. In practice, because marginal cost is not readily observable, the markup is calculated as the value of sales, less payroll and material costs, divided by the value of sales. The import penetration ratio (the ratio of imports to domestic production) captures the degree of foreign competition.

Empirical evidence drawing on a sample of countries in the Region confirms that firm productivity growth is associated with market competition. The analysis starts by using these traditional indicators of product competition. It reveals that stronger competition in upstream industries is associated with higher firm productivity growth in downstream manufacturing industries. While these indicators are easy to calculate, they fail to provide a direct link to policy or regulation, making it difficult to draw policy conclusions. The empirical analysis in this report has also drawn on the role of product market regulations (proxied by the OECD index) in firm productivity growth in two countries in the Region, the Czech Republic and Poland, during 2000–04. The empirical results show a negative direct effect of the stringency of product market regulations on firm productivity growth. In both countries, product market regulations have been relaxed over the last few years, and this has been reflected in higher firm productivity growth. A recent OECD study also demonstrates that strict product market regulations have a particularly detrimental effect on productivity the more distant the country is from the technological frontier, possibly because the regulations reduce the scope for knowledge spillovers (OECD 2004).

The positive impact of competition-enhancing polices cannot be fully appreciated through measures of static efficiency gains in the short run. Competition has pervasive and long-lasting effects on economic performance by influencing the incentive structure among economic actors, by encouraging their innovative activities, and by selecting more-efficient actors over less-efficient ones over time. Earlier, we have seen how firm churning and, in particular, the role of new entrants play an important part in firm productivity growth among incumbents. The contribution of new entrants to productivity growth is especially strong in higher-technology sectors. This is consistent with recent empirical findings showing that the link between entry and productivity growth is affected by the relative distance of the industry to the world technological frontier (see box 3.3 and appendix 3.B). This also explains why EU-10 countries that are closer to the technological frontier display a stronger correlation between net firm entry and productivity growth among incumbents than do technologically laggard CIS countries. Dynamic efficiency

BOX 3.3

Competition, Productivity, and Distance to the Technological Frontier

There is an inverted-U relationship between competition and firm productivity growth. Firms have little incentive to innovate if they are not stimulated by competition, but too much competition may discourage innovation because firms are not able to reap the benefits of their efforts. There is, therefore, an optimal degree of competition.

The costs of weak market competition rise as an economy moves closer to the technological frontier. Aghion et al. (2006) draw on a panel of manufacturing firms in the United Kingdom over 1973–92 to prove this empirically. If we restrict the set of industries to those that are closer to the world technological frontier, the upward sloping part of the inverted-U relationship between competition and innovation is steeper than the shape for the whole sample. Thus, the cost of (in terms of innovation) too little competition grows as the economy develops and moves closer to the frontier.

The entry of foreign firms into the market has a more positive effect on productivity growth in industries that are close to the technological frontier than in those that are not. Similarly, R&D intensity rises as industries approach the technological frontier. Proximity to the technological frontier for an industry in a given country at a given time is defined as the ratio of TFP in that industry and the highest TFP in industry at time among all countries. Proximity varies from zero (for the most inefficient industries) to 1 (for the most efficient).

Beneficial Effects of Competition and Entry in Industries Near the Technological Frontier

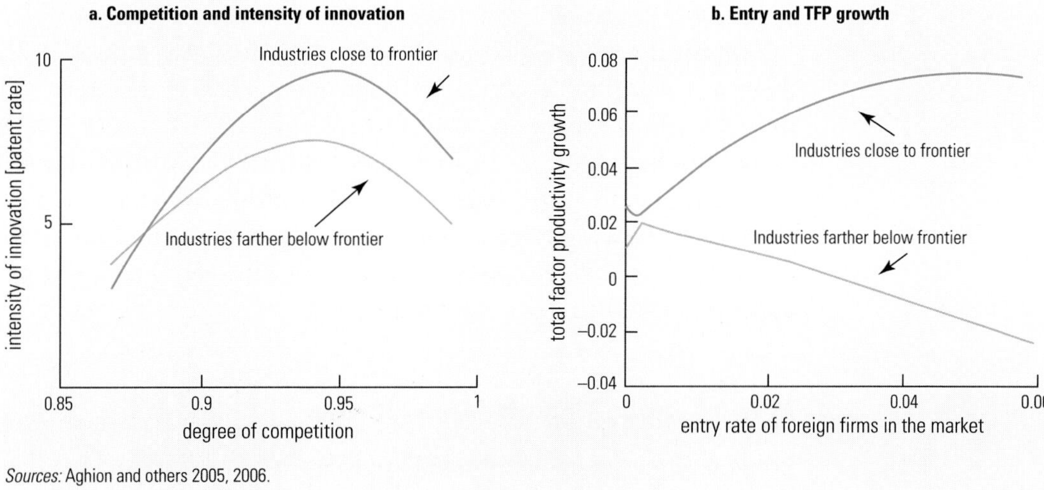

Sources: Aghion and others 2005, 2006.

gains from product market competition, however, can hardly be achieved without well-functioning service markets.

Competition in Services

Service liberalization improves the quality and availability of services through competition and economies of scale. The benefits of service liberalization are not limited to the service sectors themselves; they affect all economic activities. In view of the fact that services contribute an average of around 10–20 percent to the production cost of a product and account for all trading costs (transport, trade finance, insurance, communications, and distribution services), the savings arising from stronger competition by foreign providers and from gains in competitiveness in the international markets for services and goods may be substantial indeed.

Developing Financial Markets

Deeper financial markets provide payment services, mobilize savings, and allocate financing to firms wishing to invest. When these markets work well, they give firms of all types the ability to seize promising investment opportunities. They reduce the reliance of firms on internally generated cash flows and money from informal sources, such as family and friends, giving firms access to external equity and facilitating new entry into product markets. Barriers to the development of the financial sector—such as entry restrictions, restrictions on foreign banks, and the state ownership of banks—hurt the financial system and its ability to increase firm productivity growth.

Empirical analysis indicates that firm productivity growth in the Region is associated with deeper financial markets and better access to credit from foreign and private banks (figure 3.20). But foreign banks might select the most efficient firms. Controlling for this selection bias, we find that firm productivity growth is higher in industries showing heavy dependence on external finance and in countries in which financial sectors are more well developed (see appendix 3.B).

Making Labor Markets More Flexible

Employment protection legislation may affect firm productivity growth and the pace of the reallocation process. Empirical evidence shows that labor market flexibility is associated with TFP growth (see figure 3.21). Regulation of labor markets is usually intended to help workers, but may also represent a significant constraint on firms. Onerous labor

FIGURE 3.20

Firms with External or Private Domestic Financing Showed Higher Productivity Growth, 2001–04

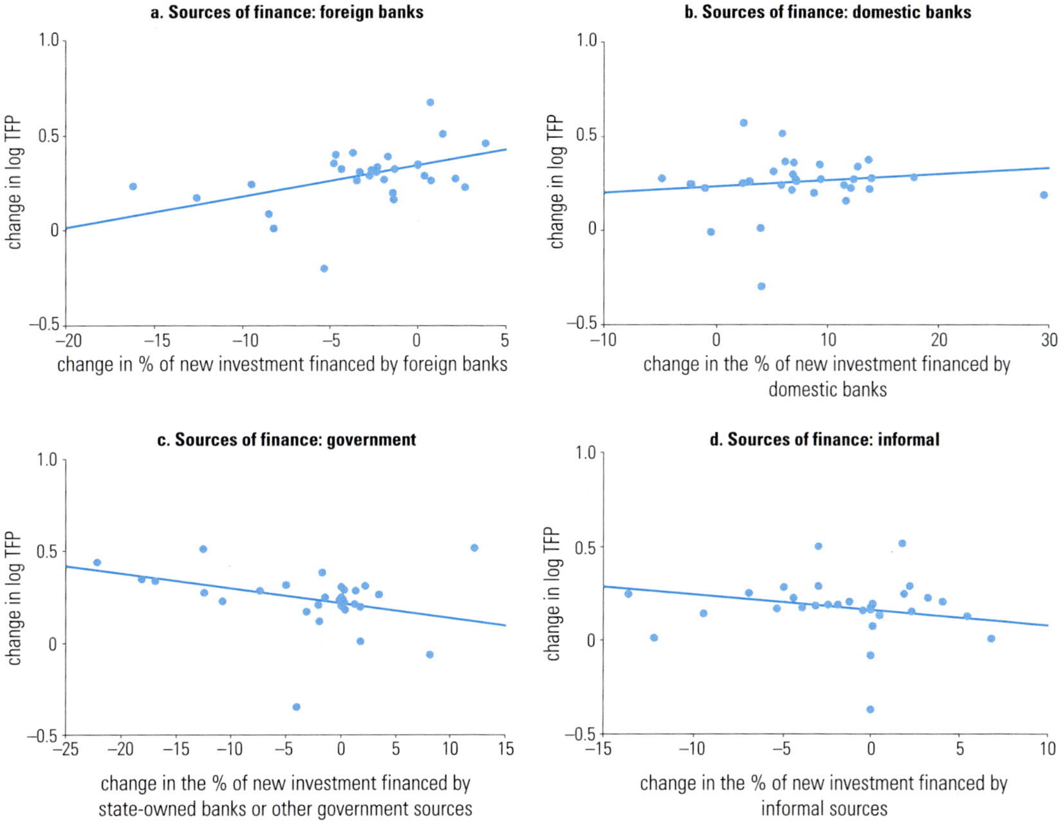

Sources: World Bank staff calculations; BEEPS 2002, 2005; Amadeus Database 2006; appendix 3.B.

FIGURE 3.21

Labor Market Flexibility Yields Productivity Gains, 2001–04

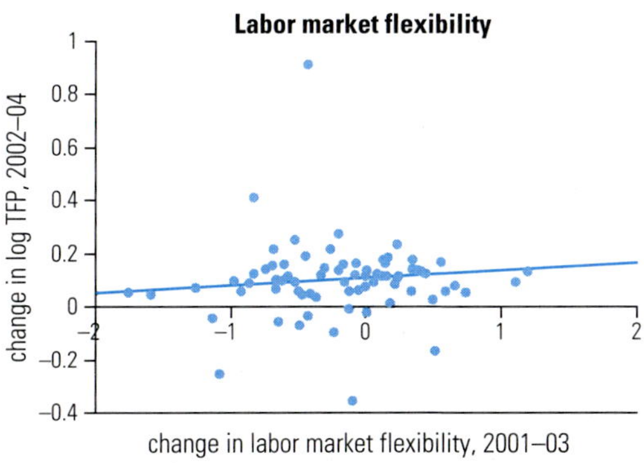

market regulations may affect firm productivity growth through their impact on the cost of doing business and the incentive to adopt new technologies. Onerous regulations may also affect the process of creative destruction by influencing the entry of new firms and the flexibility of firms in hiring and firing workers. Onerous employment protection legislation may also discourage job creation because firms will be reluctant to hire workers if they face significant costs in adjusting the workforce to changes in demand.

As we see in chapter 2, the protection offered to permanent workers is still stronger in the Region than it is in other regions. However, there is also considerable variation across the Region in the stringency of employment protection, particularly with respect to temporary employment. In laggard reformers (the CIS countries), stringent labor regulations prevented job creation in the formal economy. This meant that job destruction rates exceeded job creation rates and that there was a buildup of a large pool of unemployed or informal workers. In contrast, EU-10 countries moved toward greater flexibility in fixed-term and temporary contracts, increasing the duration of term contracts and expanding the applicability of these contracts. The liberalization of temporary contracts has favored worker mobility and accelerated the reallocation process in the EU-10 (except in Bulgaria and Romania).

Investing in Skills

A skilled workforce is essential if firms are to adopt new and better technologies. Skilled workers are more efficient at dealing with rapid changes and are more flexible in moving across jobs. A skilled workforce is useful for firm productivity growth and for the acceleration of the reallocation process. It provides job seekers with skills that will enable them to find jobs; it also helps employed workers increase their productivity and adapt to new technologies.

Innovative firms and industries are particularly in need of skilled workers. New technologies generally require significant organizational changes, which are handled more effectively by a skilled workforce. In addition, such firms are also more inclined to invest in training the workforce. While large firms have the capacity to organize internal training for their workers, smaller firms often do not (figure 3.22). Firms in the Region face an increasing shortage of skills. A recent World Bank report shows similar findings, highlighting the shortages in managerial and ICT skills in Russia (Desai and Goldberg 2007). The shortages in Russia seem to originate in deficiencies in higher education and the public research system and

FIGURE 3.22

Larger Innovative Firms Are More Likely to Provide Training

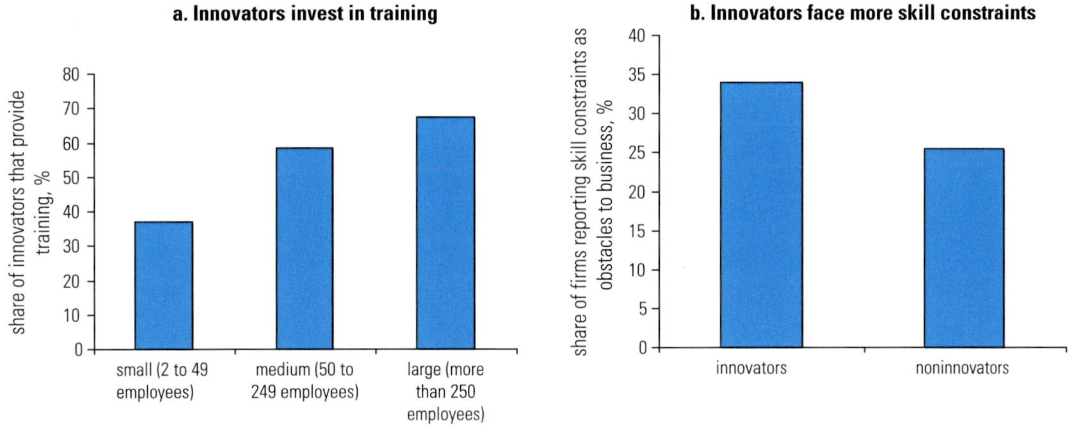

Sources: World Bank staff calculations; BEEPS 2005.

FIGURE 3.23

On-the-Job Training Yields Firm Productivity Gains, 2001–04

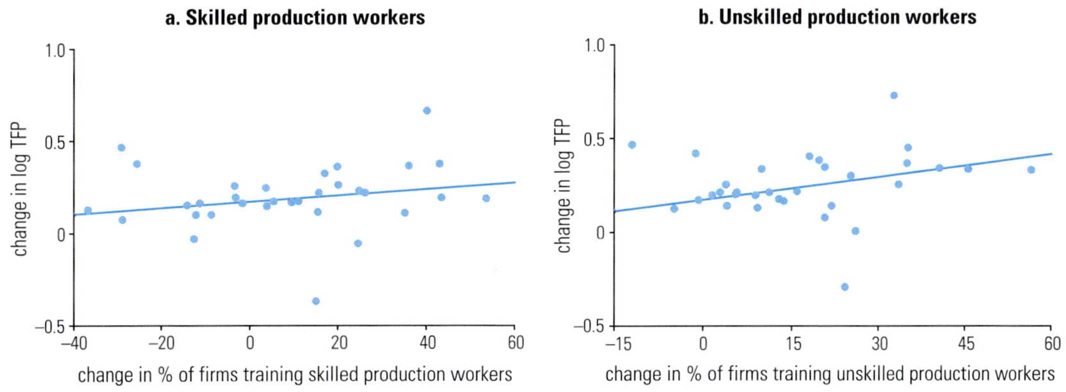

Sources: World Bank staff calculations; BEEPS 2002, 2005; Amadeus Database 2006; appendix 3.B.

underinvestment in ICT training at the firm level, factors which are common to other countries in the Region.

An enhanced supply of more highly skilled workers improves the capacity of firms to innovate. On-the-job training, particularly among unskilled workers, is associated with increases in firm productivity (figure 3.23). Data in the BEEPS Database reveal that firms in the Region are, on average, less likely to offer formal training than are firms in other regions. Controlling for firm characteristics, firms show an average probability of providing formal training at 39.0 percent in the Region compared with 63.6 percent in Latin America. Small firms are less likely to provide training. They may, therefore, be less likely to grow and become more productive. Similarly, relative to other regions, firms in manufacturing in the Region provide even less training than firms in other sectors. Consistent with what might be expected, firms in high-productivity sectors are more likely to provide training (BEEPS 2005).

Although training among workers is best provided at the level of the firm, public policies have an important role to play. Training provided by firms includes general and specific components. The first covers skills that are easily transferable to all firms, and the second includes skills that are specific to the firms providing the training (see Becker 1964). Becker's theory suggests that firms will provide training in specific skills from which they may benefit directly at low risk of not reaping the returns, while workers will invest in general skills from which they are the sole beneficiaries. Firms may have difficulty internalizing the returns to training investments because workers may move to other firms. At the same time, the incentives of workers to invest in training may be low if the workers are unable to finance their own training because of credit market inefficiencies. In these cases, government intervention may be needed to complement the efforts of firms in tackling skill imbalances.

But training alone may not suffice to improve the capacity of firms to innovate; skilled employees will still require the help of experts in adopting and improving production processes, in reorganizing company financial systems, and also in adopting new products. Such learning calls for an interaction with knowledge brokers such as consultancies, law firms, accounting firms, business incubators, and technology transfer organizations in universities. Governments may help firms, particularly smaller firms, through matching grants and support for the service providers themselves or through financing for informational mechanisms that allow for more efficient matching of the supply and demand in services.

Strengthening Governance

Firms react to incentives, costs, and constraints. Good governance, which is reflected in accountable and efficient bureaucracies, improves firm productivity by reducing transaction costs. Better governance can improve productivity by lowering the transaction costs for firms in entry, operation, and exit (figure 3.24). It does so by protecting and enforcing property rights, curbing burdensome administrative and judicial rulings, and ensuring good regulatory quality. Better governance also ensures the predictability of rules and

FIGURE 3.24

Improvements in Governance Were Associated with Higher Firm Productivity, 2001–04

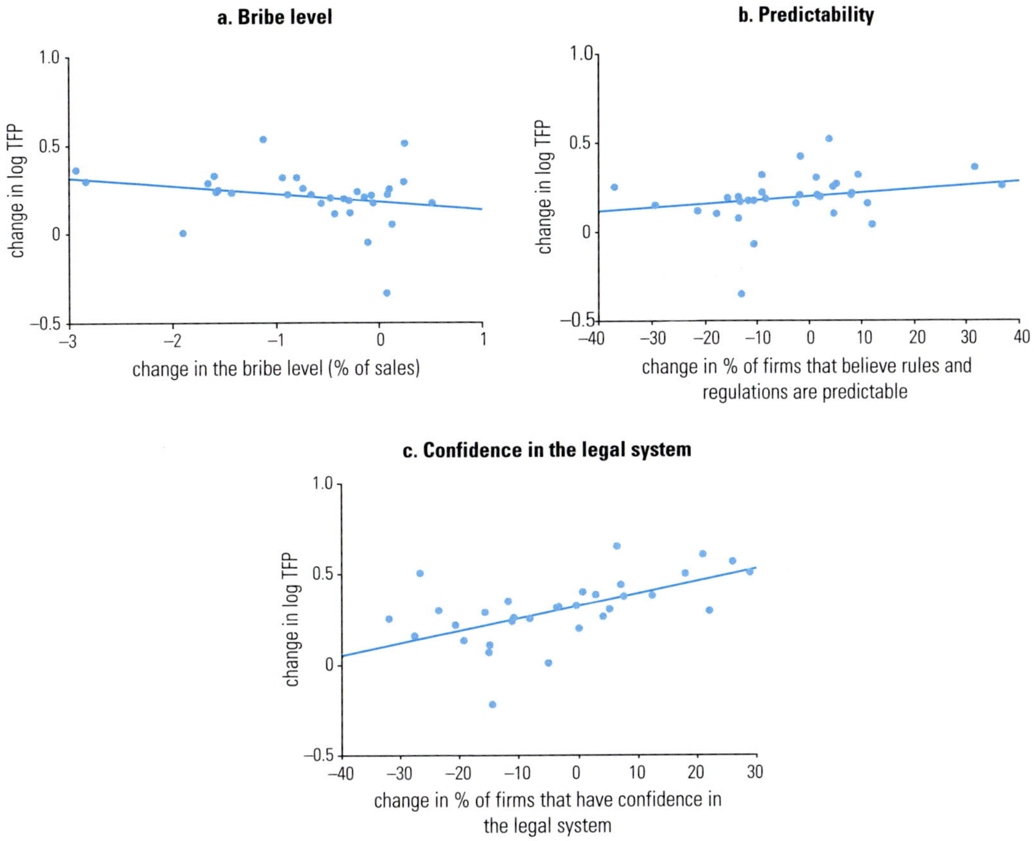

Sources: World Bank staff calculations; BEEPS 2002, 2005; Amadeus Database 2006; appendix 3.B.

regulations, thereby reducing uncertainty in investment decisions. For example, the impact of a well-functioning court system extends far beyond the number of cases the system resolves. Better courts, by providing timely and predictable rulings, reduce the risks that firms face. Firms with confidence in the courts in Poland, Romania, Russia, the Slovak Republic, and Ukraine are more likely to extend trade credit and enter into new relationships with local firms (Doing Business Database 2007).

Improvements in corporate governance also contribute to firm productivity growth. Privatization in some CIS countries followed methods that kept in power managers with little incentive to innovate, and, because financial discipline was not always in place, these laggard enterprises did not go bankrupt. Low competitive pressure in the domestic market may be a major reason for the observed low levels of innovation and effective technology absorption.

Improving Infrastructure

Firms in countries with access to modern telecommunications services, reliable electricity supply, and efficient transport links are more productive than firms operating in countries without these advantages. In many countries in the Region, infrastructure deficiencies negatively affect firm productivity growth (figure 3.25). Building and maintaining roads, ports, electricity systems, water supply systems, and telecommunications networks are expensive; so, it is not surprising that poor countries in the Region have worse infrastructure than richer countries. But the challenge of improving infrastructure is not merely one of finding financing. The problem of infrastructure provision in the Region has roots in weak competition, low levels of investments in operations and maintenance, and the inadequate regulatory framework.

Climbing the Technological Ladder through Trade and Foreign Investment

Trade and foreign investment may help increase firm productivity growth by allowing firms to tap into and benefit from the global pool of knowledge. Most firms in the Region operate in industries and countries that are far from the technological frontier. For these firms, the most cost-effective strategy for technological upgrading is to tap into technologies developed elsewhere. Imported capital goods and technological inputs may directly improve firm productivity by being used in production processes. Alternatively, firms may learn about

FIGURE 3.25

Infrastructure Quality Was Important to Firm Productivity Growth, 2001–04

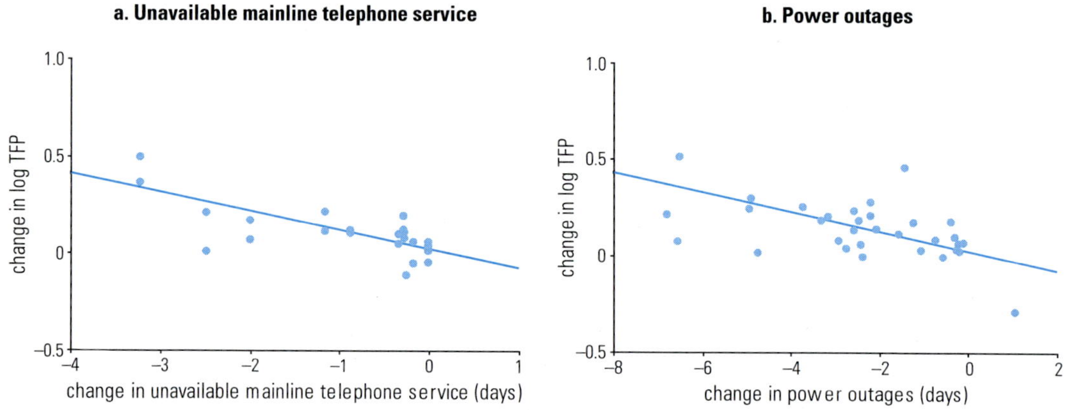

Sources: World Bank staff calculations; BEEPS 2002, 2005; Amadeus Database 2006; appendix 3.B.

technologies by exporting to knowledgeable buyers who share product designs and production techniques. Another channel is FDI. Multinational firms generally transfer technological information to their subsidiaries, directly affecting the productivity of these firms. Through trade and FDI, technology may diffuse from firms that have acquired it internationally to other firms in the same industries through demonstration effects, labor turnover, or mutual input suppliers (Hoekman and Javorcik 2006).

Trade and Firm Productivity

Trade may contribute to firm productivity directly through improved access to technologies and indirectly through strengthened competitive pressures.

Improving access to new technologies through imports. Imports may provide local firms with access to the new technologies embodied in imported machinery and equipment. Barba Navaretti, Schiff, and Soloaga (2006) find that imported technologies have a positive impact on firm productivity growth in the EU-10. In particular, they find that productivity growth in manufacturing firms depends mostly on the types of imported machinery (quality) and less on the share of imported equipment in total equipment (quantity).

Improving access to new technologies through exports. The literature suggests that there are two possible explanations for the high productivity of exporters. One is that exporting directly improves the productivity of the firms doing it (the learning-by-exporting hypothesis). Exporting exposes firms to foreign technologies and modes of production. Trading with countries that have a richer R&D stock or, more broadly, that are able to export more advanced technology goods may have positive spillovers in the form of learning. In addition, exporting allows firms to achieve greater economies of scale by expanding the potential market of the firms. The second explanation is that, because firms must be efficient to compete in international markets, only firms that are already efficient are able to export (the self-selection hypothesis). The empirical evidence on whether firms learn from exporting is mixed.[4] The two hypotheses are not mutually exclusive. Even if efficient firms are more likely to start exporting, it does not rule out the possibility that exporting might help them increase their productivity additionally. Hallward-Driemeier, Iarossi, and Sokoloff (2002) show that firms make deliberate decisions to raise productivity to serve export markets. It is not simply that more-productive firms self-select into exporting, but that firms that target export markets consistently make different decisions on investment, training, and the choice of technology, thereby raising their productivity.

The incorporation of domestic firms into international supply networks (both producer and buyer networks) may also enhance the absorption of new technology. Trading in parts and components with foreign companies that are already well integrated in the global production network may facilitate the acquisition of new technology through vertical spillovers. Empirical analyses conducted for this report confirm that these channels play a significant role in the Region: firms operating in industries that are more integrated into international supply networks display higher productivity growth (see appendix 3.B).

Enhancing competitive pressures and incentives for local firms to innovate. Import penetration may also exert competitive pressures on domestic firms operating in the same industry. The greater the export intensity of a firm, the greater the pressures to innovate and improve productivity. Firm-level studies find that trade liberalization improves productivity among firms competing with imports. In Colombia, a 10 percent decline in tariffs was associated with a 3 percent increase in firm productivity in import-competing sectors. Trade liberalization contributes directly to aggregate productivity growth through its impact on within-firm productivity growth, but also indirectly through its impact on the process of reallocation through the exit of inefficient firms, the entry of new firms, and the reallocation of workers across firms (Haltiwanger and others 2004). The empirical analysis carried out in this report confirms that import penetration in upstream sectors is associated with higher firm TFP growth in downstream sectors (see appendix 3.B).

FDI and Firm Productivity

Investments by multinational enterprises may provide domestic firms with access to more efficient technologies. Insofar as the knowledge does not remain restricted to partner firms, FDI may result in technological spillovers by operating through demonstration effects (imitation) and labor turnover. The literature distinguishes between horizontal spillover effects (within an industry) and vertical spillover effects (generated by links in the production or value chain). While the empirical evidence on intraindustry (horizontal) spillovers from FDI is mixed, the evidence on interindustry (vertical) technological transfer from multinational firms has been consistently positive. In principle, vertical spillovers are more likely to occur insofar as multinational enterprises may be expected to take actions to prevent knowledge from leaking to their competitors in the same industry. In contrast, foreign affiliates may have an incentive to reduce sourcing costs by encouraging productivity improvements among local suppliers of inputs and services.

Foreign investments may also have an indirect effect on productivity growth through their impact on net entry. Ayyagari and Kosová (2006) discover evidence of FDI affecting the entry of new firms in the Czech Republic. They find that a larger foreign presence in the Czech Republic stimulates the entry of domestic firms within the same industry, indicating the existence of possible horizontal spillovers from FDI. They also find evidence of significant vertical spillovers across industries: FDI in downstream (upstream) industries spurs entry in upstream (downstream) sectors via the presence of backward (forward) links. The empirical analysis on countries in the Region carried out for this report confirms these findings. The increased foreign presence in Czech and Polish manufacturing and service industries leads to increased firm TFP growth in these industries (see appendix 3.B).

Investing in R&D and New Technologies

While open trade and investment policies may help in attracting and accessing technology, openness alone is not sufficient. Absorptive capacity is important, as is the initial level of technological capacity of domestic firms. Investments in ICT and R&D, if combined with complementary investments in worker skills and public infrastructure, may support the innovation process, which, in turn, may help in raising productivity growth (box 3.4).

The better performance of companies operating in ICT-intensive industries may be considered evidence of the presence of spillover effects. If a firm operates in a high-technology environment, it is more likely to absorb new developments quickly and to boost productivity. More specifically, there is increasing evidence that ICT investments foster important organizational changes within firms, and such changes have an important impact on productivity performance (Black and Lynch 2001). Several studies point to an important link between the use of ICT and the ability of firms to adjust to changing demands and to innovate (Hempell 2005; Greenan and Guellec 1998). Empirical evidence in the Region shows that firms operating in industries that are more closely related to ICT display higher TFP growth (see appendix 3.B).

Another way to climb the technological ladder is to encourage domestic R&D programs. Firms in the Region perform only about 25 percent of the R&D (as a share of GDP) of firms in healthy market economies (World Bank 2006b). The literature on the relationship between R&D and firm productivity is large. The general conclusion is that R&D investments affect firm productivity positively both directly, that is, via the investments of the firms themselves, and

BOX 3.4

Innovation Leads the Catching-Up Process

Following Aghion and others (2006), let us define proximity to the technological frontier for an industry in a given country at a given time as the ratio between the normalized TFP in that industry and the highest TFP in the industry at time among all countries of the sample. Proximity varies from zero (for the most inefficient industries) to 1 (for the most efficient industries). We obtain estimates of the proximity to the frontier, as well as innovation rates (proxied by the BEEPS question about the percentage of firms that "developed successfully a major new product line/service" in the industry) for the years 2001–04.

The table reports the regression results between the speed of technological catching up (increase in the proximity to the frontier) and the number of innovators. All columns show a significant positive correlation between these two measures. These findings are consistent with the literature (Aghion and others 2006), which shows that greater innovation increases the speed of catching up with the technological frontier.

Regression	(1)	(2)
ΔInnovation	0.0006*	0.0004**
	(0.0003)	(0.0002)
Country dummies	No	Yes
Industry dummies	No	Yes
Observations	68	68
R-squared	0.042	0.781

Source: Based on Aghion and others 2006.

Note: Innovation is measured as the percentage of firms that have successfully developed a major new product line or service. Standard errors adjusted for clustering on firms are shown in parentheses.
* Significant at 10 percent. ** Significant at 5 percent.

indirectly via spillover effects (O'Mahony and Vecchi 2002). Empirical analysis in the Region shows that increased R&D (financed by the private sector) raises firm productivity growth in industries that are more closely related to ICT (see appendix 3.B).

Conclusions

In late reformers, there is still a large misallocation of resources across firms, industries, and locations. This ongoing distortion calls for policy reforms to accelerate the pace of reallocation so that resources may flow from less- to more-productive uses. The process of creative destruction (that is, the exit of unprofitable firms and the entry of new, more productive ones) needs to be invigorated through privatization and stronger market competition.

Although productivity increases are largely driven by within-firm adjustments, firm entry and exit should play an important role in sustaining productivity growth in the years to come. By continuing to protect ailing firms and contain firm exit, the late reformers have not been able to free resources from less-productive uses for more-productive ones. Similarly, restrictive product markets and uncertain business environments discourage firm entry and the adoption of new technologies. To foster labor reallocation across and within sectors and firms, policies need to encourage workers to be adaptable to changing demands for labor and skills and provide for reforms in education.

In early reformers, the main challenges are the stimulation of innovation within firms and encouragement for the expansion of successful firms. These countries also need to focus on reducing any remaining barriers to entry. Credit constraints, labor market rigidities, and deficiencies in tertiary and vocational education are likely to act as barriers to entry and innovation. Restrictive product, labor, and service markets may discourage the entry and growth of new firms and may reduce innovative efforts and technology spillovers, and this will negatively affect productivity growth.

While the entry for small businesses may be relatively easy, firm survival seems to be more difficult. In addition, even though reallocation may be productivity enhancing for the economy as a whole, there are clearly losers in the process. The losers include the owners of the obsolete businesses and the displaced workers. The high incidence of business failures and job losses in some countries, such as Romania, is a cause of concern and calls for policy reforms to improve factor mobility (reducing credit market frictions and rigidities in labor markets) so as to foster firm entry and post-entry firm expansion.

The findings of this chapter suggest that policies should focus on improving the performance of existing firms, but also facilitating the pace of the reallocation process. Countries in the Region need to strengthen competition and new entries on product markets, invest more in skills, develop financial sectors, make labor markets more flexible, and support the adoption of new technologies through trade and FDI. While the evidence presented in this chapter mostly covers the link between government policies and firm productivity growth, one should recognize that these policies may also affect aggregate productivity growth indirectly through their impact on the reallocation of labor toward higher productive activities. For example, by eliminating subsidies and price controls in previously protected agricultural sectors, trade liberalization may affect the magnitude of the shifts in employment toward higher-productivity industries in manufacturing and services. Greater financial development may also promote the movement of labor toward manufacturing and services by alleviating the liquidity constraints facing entrepreneurs who want to start up businesses. Investments in human capital and infrastructure may play a role in facilitating the sectoral shifts of workers from less- to more-productive activities. Higher skill levels increase the mobility of workers. Increased capital investments are associated with increases in the relative labor productivity of the sector.

Notes

1. A negative entry effect results if entrants are less productive than average incumbents; this does not necessarily point to a lack of dynamism. In vibrant and technologically advanced sectors, many high-risk entrants may exhibit low average productivity, while market selection weeds out all but the most productive entrant that overtakes the incumbent over time.
2. The utilization of idle capacity was an important driver of firm productivity in Russia, but not the only one. Other factors contributed to the rapid productivity surge in Russia. First, hydrocarbon export prices started to rise substantially after the 1998 collapse. Second, the 1998 crisis itself created conditions that triggered changes in relative prices and a restructuring process (changes in the input-output mix throughout the economy) that also accelerated productivity growth.
3. These traditional measures of product market conditions are used because they are easy to calculate, even though they show various shortcomings. First, they fail to capture the dynamic aspects of competition, such as the roles of future entrants or the implications of market selection effects. Second, recent research indicates that the relationship between these indicators and product market competition is not straightforward. For example, strong competition may weed out the less-productive firms and thereby increase the market share of the more-productive ones. In this case, a higher degree of market concentration would reflect higher—rather than lower—product market competition. In other words, high-productivity firms may gain market shares and enjoy innovation rents in an environment that is still highly competitive. Likewise, low market concentration does not necessarily mean a high degree of competition because less-efficient firms may maintain substantial market share in a protected market, while only the most efficient firms are able to survive under fierce competition.
4. Clerides, Lach, and Tybout (1998) find that the well-documented positive association between exporting and greater productivity is explained by the self-selection of more efficient firms into export markets. These results contrast with other studies that find evidence of learning by exporting (Van Biesebroeck 2005; Kraay 2006).

CHAPTER 4

The Future Role of Public Policy

Accelerated and sustained productivity growth is essential if the countries in the Region are to improve incomes and move rapidly toward convergence with the advanced market economies. The growing and vibrant private sector in many of these countries will drive productivity enhancements, but public policies should promote these enhancements. The barriers to and the sources of productivity growth are, of course, different in each country and will require a differentiated mix of public policies. That mix is best developed at the national level by taking into account country-specific initial conditions and institutions. How successful countries will be in moving forward on the path of prosperity will depend on how well they are able to design and implement public policies and compete among themselves to unleash the creativity of private markets.

Sustained Productivity Growth Will Accelerate the Convergence toward Advanced Economies

The productivity differentials among the countries of the Region and between them and the more advanced market economies suggest that accelerated and sustained productivity growth is essential for higher

FIGURE 4.1

A Path toward Convergence

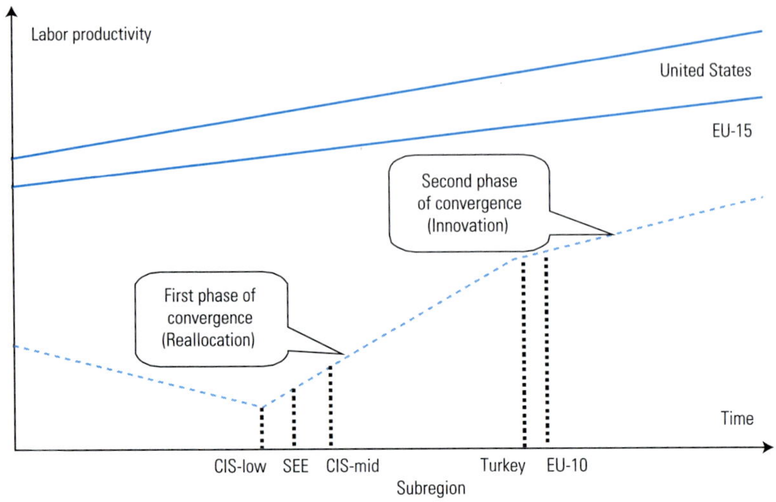

Source: Adapted by the authors from Piatkowski (2004).

living standards. Figure 4.1 suggests a conceptual view of the levels and growth of labor productivity in the Region. The countries of the Region (except Turkey) have embarked on a major economic transformation characterized by economic decline and a deep recession at the outset, followed by a strong surge in growth and productivity driven by domestic and globalizing factors. The EU-10 and Turkey are at a more advanced stage of economic transformation and incomes. The countries of the CIS and SEE have a longer road to travel even though they have shown more rapid growth rates in recent years. If these growth rates are sustained, even accelerated, then the future will be bright for the peoples of these countries.

Fostering Productivity Growth Requires a Differentiated Policy Agenda across Countries

While perseverance in reform is important for all countries, the relative importance of particular public policies in any country depends on where the country is located along the development path. Of course, the pursuit of sound economic policies is a prerequisite for growth. These policies include prudent monetary and fiscal policies (reflected, for instance, in a moderate-sized government and low inflation), an investment climate conducive to private sector growth, a relatively well-developed financial system, and an open trading system. However, beyond these broad issues, the diagnosis in this report points to a diverse set of challenges for the various groups of countries in the Region. Thus, the primary challenge for the CIS and SEE is to address the unfinished legacy of transition, while the main challenge for the EU-10 and Turkey is to sustain productivity growth and foster innovation (table 4.1). Specifically:

- For the late reformers (the CIS and SEE countries), the greater initial misallocation of resources and the slower path of transition suggest that productivity gains must still be tapped by facilitating firm restructuring, promoting the net entry of firms, easing access to credit, and taking advantage of gains in trade and greater openness by simplifying behind-the-border trade practices. While only a few of the SEE countries may have a realistic prospect of EU accession, all countries in the CIS and SEE have the opportunity to achieve greater integration with the EU and the world economies, along with the attendant benefits in productivity enhancement, new markets, and growth. The development of policies that may help maximize national benefits from regional and global opportunities needs to be a key objective of national governments.
- For the early reformers (EU-10 countries and Turkey), which have largely addressed the legacy of transition issues, gains will still accrue from efficient reallocation and firm churning, such as in even the most advanced economies. But the bulk of the productivity gains are likely to be tapped through within-firm productivity growth as

TABLE 4.1

Late Reformers Must Complete the Transition; Early Reformers Must Sustain Productivity Growth and Foster Innovation

Stage	Reforms
First phase of convergence: late reformers in which the initial level of misallocation was greater and transition reforms proceeded slowly	Address the transition legacy: • Facilitate firm entries, restructuring, and exit by improving the business environment, particularly business licensing, taxation, and legal and judicial reform, and hardening the budget constraints on loss-making public enterprises • Lower the cost of and improve access to credit • Accelerate the behind-the-border agenda to deepen the gains from trade openness, particularly the liberalization of services and the improvement of trade facilitation and logistics such as information technology, infrastructure, port efficiency, and customs regimes
Second phase of convergence: early reformers in which the misallocation of resources has been substantially corrected relative to their peers, but which are still lagging the EU-15	The second- or third-generation reform agenda: sustain productivity gains and foster innovation as a source of growth by • deepening bank and nonbank financial intermediation • adopting competitive product and labor market regulations • improving the quality of human capital (tertiary education) • investing in knowledge (R&D) and in new technologies (ICT)

Source: Compiled by the authors.

a result of boosts in competition, the fostering of technological imitation and innovation, the absorption of new skills and technologies, and the development of new products and markets. These countries are now entering into the same markets as the more advanced European economies and are catching up with the technological frontier. The success of the EU-10 and Turkey in moving ever closer to the income levels of the EU-15 will largely depend on how able their firms and workers are to advance rapidly into new products and markets and to make their production processes more efficient.

Policies need to address the relative importance of the various channels of productivity growth in a given country. This report has focused on three main channels of productivity growth at the firm level: efficiency gains within firms, reallocation across firms and sectors, and the net entry of new, more-productive firms as older, obsolete firms exit.

Encouraging the growth of new, more-productive firms and strengthening the financial discipline of existing enterprises continue to be important. Many of the former socialist economies still face significant productivity gaps across sectors and across firms. The evidence shows that new firms are typically the most productive, reflecting not only a more efficient use of resources, but also a greater capacity to innovate, adopt new technologies and business practices, and introduce new products to expand the country's set of production goods and services.

As the transition process matures and the more-advanced countries in the Region come to resemble countries with more typical economic structures, within-firm productivity growth will become more important. This channel of productivity growth is not new to Turkey, but it represents a paradigm shift in transition: the shift from reallocation and net entry to within-firm factors as the primary driver of productivity growth. As discussed earlier, this shift is not sudden and discontinuous, but a movement along a spectrum whereby reallocation issues are relatively more important in the CIS and SEE, and within-firm issues are more important in more advanced EU-10 countries and Turkey. The sources of within-firm productivity growth are likely to differ among countries at various points along the spectrum; defensive restructuring (such as labor shedding and the utilization of excess capacity) is the main driver in lagging reformers, and more strategic, market-oriented restructuring, competition, and innovation are the main drivers in the advanced reformers.

Are policies aimed at within-firm productivity growth and policies aimed at encouraging reallocation and net entry mutually exclusive?

While many policies, such as the maintenance of low inflation, trade openness, and predictable tax rates, will strengthen each of these channels, other policies, such as the enforcement of bankruptcy procedures may be more important for reallocation and net entry, while support for integration in global production networks and the development of advanced market skills may be more relevant to within-firm productivity growth.

Building on the findings of this report and the empirical literature on microlevel productivity, we may group policy measures under four broad categories: (a) governance and macroeconomic stability, (b) competition and market entry, (c) labor, infrastructure, and technology development and (d) financial development. These areas are the staple of development policies for ECA countries.

Governance and Macroeconomic Stability

The transition economies have moved a long way toward stability since the early years of the macroeconomic turbulence that eventually exploded into the financial crisis of 1998. Key aspects of the improved macroeconomic environment are the openness to trade and investment and the more rapid economic growth that has been the result. GDP is estimated to have increased 6 percent over 1999–2006. In the CIS, GDP grew even more quickly and at a higher rate, 7 percent, which makes the subregion one of the most rapidly growing in the world. Many factors have helped to accelerate output among countries in the Region: healthier growth in high-income Europe, improved private sector confidence and capital inflows (tied to EU accession for some), lower real interest rates, and massive gains in the terms of trade from increases in energy prices and other export-commodity prices, which have generated more disposable income. However, growth may yet slow down because of several factors, including declines in global energy prices, gradual increases in world interest rates, economic slowdown in the advanced economies, and capacity constraints (World Bank 2007).

While inflation decelerated from an average 9.2 percent in 1999 to 6.6 percent in 2006, inflationary and external pressures are building again as a result of the past few years of rapid growth, credit expansion, and higher energy and food prices. Several countries have inflation rates in excess of 10 percent. For several new EU member countries, achieving inflation rates in line with the Maastricht criteria remains a challenge, especially for countries seeking to adopt the euro at an early date. Current account deficits increased from an average 5.4 to 7.2 percent of GDP between 1999 and 2006.

The excess demand pressures in many countries—reflected in both external and internal disequilibriums—have generated concern over macroeconomic vulnerability. The pressures are largely caused because the open economies are experiencing strong capital inflows, extremely rapid domestic credit expansion, and, in some cases, a loose fiscal policy stance. While capital inflows are expected to remain strong, particularly those motivated by investment opportunities associated with EU accession, economic disequilibrium makes these countries sensitive to a change in investor sentiment. Even as some countries must contend with large current account deficits, the oil-rich countries, such as Russia, are facing a problem of plenty; they are running significant fiscal surpluses, accumulating large external reserves, and seeing their currencies appreciate. The challenge for them is to find a way to manage the newfound wealth so as to strengthen the productive capacity of the economy and improve economic efficiency, while limiting the erosion of potential gains from inflation and declining competitiveness.

Such risks must be addressed, especially in the middle-income countries, so as to sustain growth momentum. To this end, prudent fiscal and monetary policies must be pursued that target low and stable inflation; strong banking and corporate sector governance; effective banking supervision; sound competition policies; and prudent economic policies that permit rapid policy adjustments in response to shocks.

Moreover, as countries emerge from the transitional recession, they will need to manage the normal economic cycle. How should the structural budget deficit be managed? How might budgeting be carried out in a countercyclical manner? What is the desirable level of fluctuation in short-term interest rates over the cycle? How should government policy offset the possible negative consequences of recessions for firm investment, especially in innovative technologies? These are new questions for the emerging transition economies, that need to be addressed so as to ensure the proper management of economic cycles in a way consistent with the goal of maximizing long-term productivity growth.

Competition and Market Entry

Since the start of transition, a focus of public policy has been the promotion of the entry of new, more-productive firms and the exit of old, less-productive firms. This development has been considered a key driver of economic transformation. The approach has been based on the premise that the low productivity of obsolete firms is a drag on economic growth, with the consequence that obsolete firms either needed to be restructured to promote more rapid growth or needed to give way to new firms. (World Bank 2002 provides a fuller discussion of the policies to encourage new and discipline obsolete enterprises.)

The entry of new firms has been most effectively promoted through the development of a positive investment climate, while the exit of old firms has been best accomplished through the imposition of market discipline. A healthy investment climate provides a level playing field to attract new investment and firm growth. This requires low and stable marginal tax rates, simple regulatory procedures, secure property rights, and adequate basic infrastructure. The imposition of market discipline forces obsolete firms to restructure and become more productive and compete; otherwise, they must face closure. This discipline—for example, through the hardening of budget constraints, the introduction of market competition, the enforcement of bankruptcy procedures, and better performance measurement—forces obsolete firms to release assets and labor that can then be used by new and growing firms or to divest noncommercial operations, such as housing and other social services, and focus on creating economic value.

Policies for within-firm growth are evident from the experience of the countries of the EU-10. EU integration has provided a strong incentive to openness and competition, and this has helped industries in these countries catch up with the technological frontier. Competition policies in this context involve fostering integration with global production networks, strengthening the regulatory framework for service sector competition, and integrating domestic factor and product markets. Furthermore, as the evidence from the EU suggests, firms are more likely to innovate in the presence of competition (Aghion and others 2006).

An important new aspect of policies to promote firm-level growth is the establishment of links between upstream production and downstream services. The analysis in this report demonstrates that these links are a key factor in the shifts in sectoral patterns and a sign of the growing integration of economic sectors. While general reforms that improve the investment climate may stimulate productivity in downstream agriculture and create off-farm employment, the evidence also suggests that stronger competition in services may also boost farm profitability and productivity growth.

Labor, Infrastructure, and Technology Development

Globalizing forces provide a great opportunity for countries to acquire labor skills and technology through FDI, licensing, and imports of capital goods. A primary challenge during transition has been the shortage of skills required for a market economy. All transition economies have a positive legacy of high attainment rates in tertiary education. This suggests that these countries possess a major advantage, but, in reality, the skilled labor is often limited because of the content of that education and the lack of relevance of skills to the absorption and diffusion of the new technologies essential for the competitiveness of new market economies.

Infrastructure upgrading is necessary for within-firm and within-farm productivity growth because it enhances market access and reduces transaction costs. Infrastructure quality has suffered heavily in most transition economies through underinvestment and lack of maintenance and repairs. If firms and farms are to benefit from globalizing and domestic forces, they need high-quality infrastructure that links them with domestic and foreign markets.

Progress in innovation, as demonstrated through investments in R&D and the commercialization of technology, remains low and uneven in the Region. Average spending on R&D is now under 1 percent of GDP, well below the EU target of 3 percent. Furthermore, around two-thirds of this spending is public spending, whereas, in Western Europe, 65–70 percent of research spending is provided by the private sector. Increases in expenditure are unlikely to improve the situation until the private sector plays a bigger role (for example, see World Bank 2002; Desai and Goldberg 2007). While the new EU member states are doing fairly well in terms of knowledge economy indicators (an aggregate measure of economic incentives, the institutional regime, education, innovation systems, and information infrastructure), the rankings of other countries in the Region reveal a range of weaknesses (figure 4.2). Turkey, which has a GDP per capita that is similar to that of Lithuania and the Slovak Republic, is ranked behind these countries on the knowledge economy indicators index primarily because of low scores on education.

The Region still needs to exploit fully its fairly high human capital stock and well-developed research institutions to provide ideas for commercial applications that will lead to private sector growth. Translating R&D into commercial success is key to achieving sustained, long-term economic growth and will only occur if incentives are provided so that researchers and businesses work together. Such incentives include

FIGURE 4.2

Early Reformers Exhibit a Higher Absorptive Capacity for Innovation, 2006

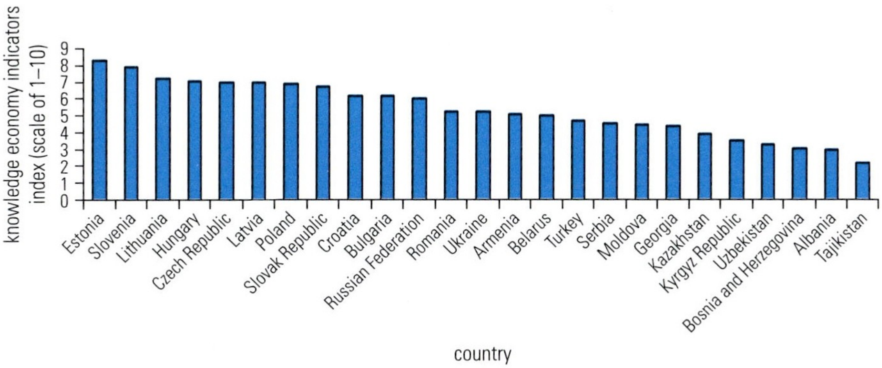

Source: World Development Indicators Database 2007.

broad public access to computers and the Internet, as well as the enforcement of rules to protect intellectual property rights.

Financial Development

Transition countries have made tremendous progress in the establishment of banks and capital markets, but the contribution of the financial sector to productivity and growth has been uneven. The financial sector in many countries remains underdeveloped relative to the financial sector in other countries at the same level of income. Financial market indicators, such as the ratio of private credit to GDP, the share of domestic credit supplied by depository banks to the private sector, the capitalization of the stock market, the level of total banking assets, and the extent of financial intermediation, are all narrow relative to per capita income (EBRD 2004). More recently, across the Region, there has been rapid growth in bank credit, much of which is highly skewed toward consumer lending. The firm lending that is taking place is concentrated among large firms. In the face of weaknesses in banking supervision and consumer risk assessment, these trends have raised concerns over potential macroeconomic risks, even as private small and medium enterprises are being starved for the credit they require to grow (World Bank 2007; EBRD 2006). Indeed, little credit has flowed to new or existing private enterprises, even though the experience of EU-10 countries and Turkey suggests that financial deepening and the development of sources of credit outside the firm are essential in promoting expansion and economies of scale within firms (Aghion and others 2006). Indeed, financial development facilitates post-entry growth, especially in sectors that are intrinsically more dependent on external financing. Financial credit for rural enterprises and farm growth is even scarcer.

A multipronged agenda needs to be followed to boost the role of the financial sector in growth. Such an agenda, which, of course, needs to be tailored to specific country situations, should cover the privatization of state banks, the strengthening of the prudential framework for bank and nonbank intermediation, the improvement of bank supervision, progress in financial reporting, greater transparency of bank ownership, and enhancement of credit information systems and collateral regimes.

Complementary policies. To support the above reforms, especially with respect to firm restructuring, adequate social safety nets that protect displaced workers are essential (see, e.g., World Bank 2002, 2005). With the transition to a market economy, the guaranteed employment, retirement security, and consumer subsidies of the socialist systems have become obsolete. In many instances, these were fiscally unaffordable as countries sought to balance expenditure demands with revenues. The best way to protect the most vulnerable workers is twofold: by removing any barriers to the entry of new enterprises, thereby creating additional employment opportunities, and by targeting social assistance to those whose skills and experience make them less likely to become employed in new enterprises.

In the CIS, where the challenge of restructuring is still relevant and poverty and inequality remain significant concerns, providing adequate levels of social assistance must be a policy priority. Where resources are limited, this needs to be accomplished through better targeting, through the use of proxy means testing, geographical criteria, or even self-targeting through public works schemes. There remains considerable scope for improving the targeting of utility and housing subsidies through, for instance, a broader expansion of lifeline tariffs, whereby utility consumption is metered and the price subsidy is restricted to the initial block of basic needs consumption. The decentralization of social assistance, as in Russia, provides another channel by delegating decisions on both the levels and targeting of social assistance to lower layers of government. In principle, this may improve targeting and move the decisions closer to the preferences of communities. But this needs to be complemented by resources to ensure horizontal equity across regions.

In the EU-10, which may afford a more generous safety net, formal unemployment insurance schemes are becoming more common and represent the best way to protect those displaced by enterprise restructuring. However, in each country, the gains from the more generous provision of benefits should be carefully assessed against the potential costs not only as a structural fiscal burden, but also as a disincentive for work.

Conclusions

How well countries are able to adapt policies to boost productivity and suit their own situations and how effectively they might implement those policies will determine their way forward on the path to prosperity. The productivity differentials among the countries of the Region and between them and the more advanced market economies suggest that accelerated and sustained productivity growth is essential in achieving higher living standards. Although reforms must continue in all countries of the Region, the relative importance of particular public policies in any country depends on where the country is located along the development path. The emphasis on policies to promote reallocation and net entry is still necessary, especially in the late reformers (CIS, SEE countries), in which the legacy of transition remains pervasive, but, for the early reformers (EU-10 and Turkey), greater productivity growth is likely to derive from within-firm improvements, much as in advanced market economies.

Appendix 1

Macro Analysis of Productivity: Data and Methodology

A. Growth Accounting

The analysis in chapter 1 relies on a growth accounting methodology to decompose the growth of real GDP into the contributions from growth in the capital stock, growth in the labor force, and TFP growth. As is widely appreciated, the measurement of TFP growth is sensitive to the measurement methodology. In transition economies, the measurement of the capital stock also presents special challenges. This appendix reports on the particular growth accounting methodology used and the techniques for addressing the challenges in capital stock measurement. The growth decompositions for individual countries in the Region are also reported in this appendix.

Methodology

We start with the following standard Cobb-Douglas production function:

$$Y_t = A_t K_t^{\alpha} L_t^{1-\alpha} \qquad \text{(a1)}$$

where Y is real GDP, K is the physical capital stock, L is the labor force, A is the level of TFP, and α is the capital share of income. Taking logarithms and differentiating, we obtain the following growth accounting equation:

$$\frac{dY}{Y} = \alpha\frac{dK}{K} + (1-\alpha)\frac{dL}{L} + \frac{dA}{A} \qquad \text{(a2)}$$

The equation shows that the growth of real GDP (the first term) may be decomposed into three sources of growth: (a) the contribution of growth in the physical capital stock (the second term); (b) the contribution of growth in the labor force (the third term); and (c) TFP growth (the final term).

Data Challenges Associated with Measurement of Capital Stock in Transition Countries

To implement this decomposition, data on GDP and the labor force have been obtained from the World Development Indicators Database, national statistical offices, and the International Monetary Fund. The basis for constructing the capital stock series is the standard perpetual inventory method:

$$K_{t+1} = (1-\delta)K_t + I_t \qquad \text{(a3)}$$

where I is the level of investment and δ is the depreciation rate. Investment data going back to 1980 for most countries have been obtained from *World Development Indicators* and *World Economic Outlook,* supplemented with data from CISStat and the Vienna Institute for International Economic Studies (see World Development Indicators Database; IMF 2007; CISStat Database; and WIIW Database). Estimates of the initial capital stock have been obtained from De Broeck and Koen (2000) for the CIS and from the Vienna Institute and national statistical offices for Eastern Europe. The commonly assumed capital share in income of 0.35 percent and a standard depreciation rate of 0.05 percent are used in the baseline analysis.

Implementing the perpetual inventory method for transition economies presents the particular challenge that, during the initial contraction, a significant portion of the communist capital stock may not only be temporarily idled, but may actually be permanently scrapped. If so, this would cause the contribution of capital accumulation to be underestimated during the subsequent recovery. To address this concern, a one-time adjustment has been applied for the permanent scrapping of a portion of the communist capital stock; in particular, the adjustment contracts the capital stock by the same rate as output during the initial contraction, so that the capital output ratio does not rise during the course of the contraction.

Extensive robustness checks were performed with alternative adjustments for the scrapping of communist capital and with alternative values of the capital share and depreciation rates. While the exact magnitudes of the contributions to growth from capital and labor force accumulation and TFP growth do indeed change, the patterns across countries and over time are robust to these alternative techniques.

B. Estimating the Impact of Structural Reforms: Cross-Country Growth Regressions

Estimating the productivity impact of potential structural improvements in a country is a two-step process. The first step involves estimating the relationship between productivity growth and the structural determinants of this growth in a cross-country setting. The second step involves using the estimated elasticities from the cross-country relationship to determine the impact on productivity growth of a potential structural improvement in the country of interest. The estimation of the cross-country relationship often proves contentious. The primary concerns have to do with the endogeneity of independent variables and the sensitivity of the estimates to omitted variables. The analysis recorded in chapter 1 has involved a number of techniques to address these concerns. (This part of the analysis in chapter 1 is based on Calderón 2007, which is a background paper prepared for this study.)

Methodology

We use a large macroeconomic panel data set of 86 countries and nine nonoverlapping five-year periods covering 1960–2005. The dependent variable is the growth rate of labor productivity, and the independent variables include a number of structural variables of interest (education, financial depth, trade openness, institutional quality, infrastructure stocks, and infrastructure quality) and a number of control variables (initial level of labor productivity, lack of price stability, government burden, and terms of trade shocks). The following equation is estimated:

$$y_{it} - y_{it-1} = \alpha y_{it-1} + \beta' X_{it} + \mu_t + \eta_i + \varepsilon_{it} \qquad \text{(a4)}$$

where y denotes aggregate labor productivity and X includes the structural variables of interest and the control variables. The terms μ_t

and η_i denote, respectively, unobserved time-specific factors affecting all countries and country effects capturing unobserved time-invariant country characteristics.

The estimation technique is the generalized method of moments estimator developed by Arellano and Bond (1991) for dynamic panel data models. This technique offers a number of advantages. First, it controls for unobserved time-specific and country-specific omitted variables. Second, it partially controls for the endogeneity of explanatory variables by using the lagged values as instruments.

Variable Definitions and Data Sources

The specific measures of the variables used in the estimation, as well as the sources of the data, are reported in table 1.B1.

It is worth pointing out that the analysis devotes particular attention to the development of indicators of infrastructure stock and quality that account for several different dimensions of infrastructure. Physical indicators of infrastructure in telecommunications, electric power, and roads are combined to construct an aggregate measure of infrastructure stock, as well as an aggregate index of the quality of infrastructure services. The aggregate index is a weighted average of the components; the weights are obtained using principal components analysis to maximize the variation of the aggregate index.

Four different aggregate indexes of infrastructure stock are created using variations in the indicators of telecommunications, electricity, and the road network. The index IK_1, which is the focus of our analysis, comprises information on main telephone lines, electricity generating capacity, and the total length of the road network. The index IK_2 uses paved roads instead of total roads; the index IK_3 uses information on main telephone lines and mobile phones, electricity generating capacity, and total roads, and IK_4 uses paved roads rather than total roads, but is otherwise the same as IK_3.

Estimation Results

Table 1.B2 reports the results of the estimates of our model of the structural determinants of productivity growth. The four columns correspond to the four aggregate indexes of infrastructure stock. The estimation technique used is the generalized method of moments (IV) estimator developed by Arellano and Bond (1991). Before we discuss the results, it is worth pointing out that the specification tests (the Sargan test and the second-order correlation test) validate our moment conditions so that we may use our regressions for statistical inference.

TABLE 1.B1

Definitions and Data Sources

Variable	Definition and construction	Source
Labor productivity	Ratio of total GDP to labor force; GDP is in US$ at constant prices	World Development Indicators Database
Education	Ratio of total secondary enrollment, regardless of age, to the population of the age group that officially corresponds to that level of education	Easterly and Sewadeh (2002); World Development Indicators Database
Financial depth	Ratio of domestic credit claims on the private sector to GDP	Author calculations based on International Financial Statistics Database and Central Bank publications; the method of calculation is based on Beck, Demirgüç-Kunt, and Levine (1999)
Trade openness	Log of the ratio of exports and imports to GDP (all in 2000 US$)	Easterly and Sewadeh (2002)
Institutional quality	*International Country Risk Guide* index of political risk (0–100), in logs; includes categories such as government stability, corruption, rule of law, democratic accountability, and quality of bureaucracy	*International Country Risk Guide* (PRS Group, various issues)
Government burden	Log of the ratio of government consumption to GDP	Author calculations
Inflation rate	Log differences of consumer price index	Author calculations using International Financial Statistics Database
Terms of trade	Log differences of the terms of trade index	Author calculations
Changes in telecommunications infrastructure stock	(a) Main telephone lines per 1,000 workers (in logs); (b) main telephone lines and mobile phones per 1,000 workers (in logs)	Author construction using Canning (1999); *World Telecommunication Development Report* (ITU, various years)
Quality of telecommunications services	Waiting time for main telephone line installation; the variable was rescaled so that it takes values between 0 and 1; higher numbers imply higher quality	*World Telecommunication Development Report* (ITU, various years); World Development Indicators Database
Infrastructure stock of the electricity sector	Electricity generating capacity (in megawatts per 1,000 workers); the variable is expressed in logs	Author construction using Canning (1999); *Energy Statistics Yearbook* (UN 2005); national sources where available
Quality of electricity services	Electric power transmission and distribution losses (as a percentage of electricity output); the variable was rescaled so that it takes values between 0 and 1; higher numbers imply higher quality	World Development Indicators Database; national sources where available
Road network	(a) Total length of the road network; (b) length of the paved road network; both variables are measured in kilometers per square kilometer of surface area of the country, expressed in logs	*World Road Statistics* (IRF, various); World Development Indicators Database; national sources where available
Quality of the road network	Share of paved roads in the overall road network; the variable takes values between 0 and 1; higher numbers imply higher quality	*World Road Statistics* (IRF, various); World Development Indicators Database; national sources where available
Aggregate index of infrastructure stock	First principal component of the three dimensions of infrastructure considered in our analysis: telecommunications, electricity and roads	Author calculations
Aggregate index of infrastructure quality	First principal component of the three dimensions of infrastructure considered in our analysis: telecommunications, electricity and roads	Author calculations

Source: Calderón 2007.

TABLE 1.B2

Structural Determinants of Productivity Growth: Panel Regression Analysis

Variable	[IK1]	[IK2]	[IK3]	[IK4]
Structural determinants				
Infrastructure stock[a]	0.885**	0.613**	0.894**	0.666**
(first principal component of stocks)	(0.13)	(0.12)	(0.15)	(0.14)
Quality of infrastructure services[b]	0.578**	0.546**	0.404**	0.272**
(first principal component of quality measures)	(0.07)	(0.08)	(0.06)	(0.10)
Education	1.323**	1.189**	0.951**	0.792**
(secondary enrollment, logs)	(0.31)	(0.22)	(0.30)	(0.28)
Financial development	0.507**	0.913**	0.381**	0.757**
(private domestic credit as % of GDP, logs)	(0.12)	(0.07)	(0.08)	(0.12)
Trade openness	0.208**	0.106**	–0.079*	–0.041
(trade volume as % of GDP, logs)	(0.10)	(0.06)	(0.05)	(0.10)
Institutional quality	1.710**	2.820**	2.239**	2.273**
(*International Country Risk Guide* index, logs)	(0.23)	(0.10)	(0.19)	(0.23)
Control variables				
Initial output per worker	–0.829**	–0.901**	–1.524**	–1.253**
(logs)	(0.14)	(0.10)	(0.12)	(0.12)
Lack of price stability	–1.793**	–0.666**	–1.769**	–1.913**
(inflation rate)	(0.19)	(0.21)	(0.16)	(0.20)
Government burden	–3.529**	–3.246**	–2.050**	–2.343**
(government consumption as % of GDP, logs)	(0.30)	(0.26)	(0.20)	(0.22)
Terms of trade stocks	0.040**	0.043**	0.052**	0.046**
(first differences of log terms of trade)	(0.01)	(0.01)	(0.01)	(0.01)
Number of countries	86	86	86	86
Number of observations	558	558	558	558
Specification test (p-values)				
(a) Sargan test	(0.488)	(0.494)	(0.499)	(0.296)
(b) Serial correlation				
First-order	(0.000)	(0.000)	(0.000)	(0.000)
Second-order	(0.570)	(0.571)	(0.571)	(0.504)

Source: Author calculations.

Note: The dependent variable is the growth rate per output of worker. The estimation is a generalized method of moments (IV) system estimation. The sample is 86 countries, 1960–2005 (nonoverlapping five-year period observations). Our regression analysis includes an intercept and period-specific dummy variables (not reported here, but available through the author). Robust standard errors are reported in parentheses below the coefficient estimates.

a. Each column uses the different aggregate indexes of infrastructure stock reported in table 1.B1.

b. Our aggregate measure of infrastructure quality uses transformations of the following variables: waiting for main telephone line installation (in years), electric power transmission and distribution losses (as a share of electric output), and the share of paved roads in total roads.

** Significant at 5 percent. * Significant at 10 percent.

The results indicate that the structural variables of our interest—infrastructure stock, infrastructure quality, financial depth, education, trade openness, and institutional quality—all have positive and statistically significant relationships with labor productivity growth. For the control variables, we notice that the coefficient on the initial level of labor productivity is negative and statistically significant, indicating that there is evidence for the conditional convergence of labor productivity. Furthermore, there is evidence that the growth of labor productivity is adversely affected by higher inflation and heavier government burden.

The analysis in chapter 1 uses the estimated coefficients from the first column to estimate the impact on labor productivity growth of potential improvements along the six structural indicators in the countries of the Region.

Appendix 2

Sectoral Analysis of Productivity: Data and Methodology

A. Benchmarking the Structural Transformation of Transition Economies

Raiser, Schaffer, and Schuchhardt (2006) propose a market economy benchmark based on regression analyses on a cross-section of 50 industrialized countries. For each sector, the share in employment is regressed on the log of GDP per capita and the respective square (table 2.A1). Since all sectoral regressions fit the data quite well, this section uses the fitted curves as benchmarks in an analysis of the distortion in economic structures and the evolution of these structures over the transition.

The analysis here relies on an updated version of an empirical analysis, performed by Mark Schaffer, that draws on the sectoral shares of employment in all countries in the Region over 1990–2004. For each of the sectors (agriculture, manufacturing, and market services), the shares of employment are regressed on the respective levels of income, and the countries in the Region are benchmarked against the average in advanced industrialized market economies.

TABLE 2.A1
Benchmarking Regressions

Independent variable	Dependent variable: share of employment			
	Agriculture	Industry	Market services	Nonmarket services
Log GDP per capita	−0.38390	0.32560	0.08198	−0.03740
	(0.036)	(0.019)	(0.576)	(0.808)
(Log GDP per capita)^2	0.01082	−0.01600	0.00058	0.00548
	(0.293)	(0.042)	(0.945)	(0.533)
Constant	2.78970	−1.37035	−0.49013	0.12316
	(0.001)	(0.023)	(0.441)	(0.853)
R^2	0.883	0.4544	0.7141	0.4784
F(2, 47)	176.4	19.57	58.71	21.55
	(0.000)	(0.000)	(0.000)	(0.000)
Number of observations	50	50	50	50

Source: Raiser, Schaffer, and Schuchhardt 2006.

Note: Standard errors are shown in parentheses.

B. Shift-Share Analysis: Decomposing Aggregate Labor Productivity Growth

Methodology

Shift-share analysis permits the decomposition of aggregate labor productivity growth for the assessment of the relative roles of (a) within-sector productivity gains, (b) shifts in employment from sectors with low productivity growth to sectors with high productivity growth, and (c) shifts in employment from sectors with low levels of productivity to sectors with high levels of productivity. The positive contribution to aggregate productivity of the high-growth sectors may be offset by their lower than average productivity levels.

The methodological approach toward shift-share analysis draws on Timmer and Szirmai (2000). Productivity for the entire economy is expressed as the sum of the productivity level of each sector weighted by the sectoral employment shares, as follows:

$$P_m = \frac{Y_m}{L_m} = \sum_{j=1}^{n} \frac{Y_j}{L_j} * \frac{L_j}{L_m} = \sum_{j=1}^{n} P_j * S_j, \qquad \text{(b1)}$$

where Y is output, L is employment by sector ($j = 1 \ldots n$) and the total economy (m), P is labor productivity (Y/L), and S is the sectoral employment share. In a discrete time perspective, the expression may be rewritten as follows:

$$\frac{P_m^t - P_m^0}{P_m^0} = \frac{\sum_{j=1}^{n}\left(P_j^t - P_j^0\right) * S_j^0}{\sum_{j=1}^{n} P_j^0} + \frac{\sum_{j=1}^{n} P_j^0 * \left(S_j^t - S_j^0\right)}{\sum_{j=1}^{n} P_j^0} + \frac{\sum_{j=1}^{n}\left(P_j^t - P_j^0\right) * \left(S_j^t - S_j^0\right)}{\sum_{j=1}^{n} P_j^0} \qquad \text{(b2)}$$

for a current year t and a base year 0.

The first term on the right-hand side is the within-industry contribution to overall productivity growth (the within term). The second term may be defined as the static shift effect, which captures the contribution arising from changes in the sectoral composition of employment (the between term). The third term represents the joint effect of changes in employment shares and sectoral productivity (the cross term). It is positive if sectors with above-average productivity growth increase their share in total employment; it is negative if expanding sectors have below-average productivity growth or if the shares in total employment of sectors with high productivity growth are also declining.

Data

The shift-share analysis conducted in this section is performed at different levels of disaggregation.

The Sectoral Shift-Share Analysis of the Region

The analysis is first conducted for the entire economy. It focuses on the relative contributions of three main sectors (agriculture, industry, and services) and covers all countries in the Region. It draws on the World Development Indicators Database.

Sectoral outputs (agriculture, manufacturing, and services) are given by GDP at PPP (constant 2000 U.S. dollars), multiplied by the respective sectoral shares of total value added.

GDP per capita based on PPP is gross domestic product that has been converted to international dollars using purchasing power parity rates. An international dollar has the same purchasing power relative to GDP as the U.S. dollar has in the United States. GDP at purchaser prices is the sum of the gross value added by all resident producers in the economy, plus any product taxes and minus any subsidies not included in the value of the products. Value added is the net output of a sector after adding up all outputs and subtracting intermediate inputs. It is calculated without making deductions for the depreciation of fabricated assets or for the depletion and degradation of natural resources. The origin of value added is determined by the ISIC (revision 3). Data are in constant 2000 international U.S. dollars.

Agriculture value added (in percent of GDP) corresponds to ISIC divisions 1–5 and includes forestry, hunting, and fishing, as well as the cultivation of crops and livestock production. Industry value added (in percent of GDP) corresponds to ISIC divisions 10–45 and includes manufacturing (ISIC divisions 15–37). It comprises value added in mining, manufacturing (also reported as a separate subgroup), construction, electricity, water, and gas. Services (and so on) value added (in percent of GDP) corresponds to ISIC divisions 50–99 and includes value added in wholesale and retail trade (including hotels and restaurants), transport, and government, and financial, professional, and personal services such as education, health care, and real estate services. Also included are imputed bank service charges, import duties, and any statistical discrepancies noted by national compilers, as well as discrepancies arising from rescaling.

The sectoral shares of total employment are taken from the Raiser Schaffer Schuchhardt (2006) data set, which has been updated for this report. The main sources of data are the CISStat *Statistical Yearbook* (for example, see CISStat 2007), the CISStat Database, and the *Yearbook of Labour Statistics* of the International Labour Organization (for example, see ILO 2006). These have been supplemented with data from various sources within countries, as well as other sources as noted below and in the country files. Data obtained from the CISStat *Statistical Yearbook* are organized according to sectors, as follows:

- agriculture, includes agriculture, fishery, and forestry
- industry, includes industry and construction
- market services, includes transport and communications, trade, catering, information and computing services, real estate, financial services, geological exploration and hydrometeorological services, and general commercial activities to support markets
- nonmarket services, includes housing, communal and personal services, health care and social security, education, culture and art, science, and general administration

Data from the *Yearbook of Labour Statistics* are aggregated in broad sectors, as follows:

- agriculture, includes agriculture, hunting and forestry, and fishery
- industry, includes mining and quarrying, manufacturing and construction, electricity, gas, and water supply
- market services, includes wholesale and retail trade; repair of motor vehicles and motorcycles; personal and household goods; hotels

and restaurants; transport, storage, and communications; financial intermediation; and real estate, renting, and business activities

- nonmarket services, includes administration and defense, education and health, social work, and other community, social, and personal service activities

The EU-8 Subsectoral Shift-Share Analysis

The shift-share analysis is performed for the entire economy, but covers nine broad ISIC sectors on a subsample of countries in the Region, specifically, the EU-8 countries: the Czech Republic, Estonia, Hungary, Latvia, Lithuania, Poland, the Slovak Republic, and Slovenia. The data have been taken from the EU KLEMS Database (2007). For a short overview of the methodology and the results relating to the EU KLEMS Database, see Timmer, O'Mahony, and van Ark (2007). For a brief description of the country-by-country results obtained from EU KLEMS growth and productivity accounts, see van Ark, O'Mahony, and Ypma (2007).

Subsectoral outputs (agriculture, manufacturing, and services) are given by gross value added measured in thousands of 1997 PPP euros for each subsector. To transform nominal value added from the EU KLEMS Database, we use production-based, subsector-specific PPPs in 1997 for country c PPP^{c}_{j2001} in the Region (relative to the euro) backdated and updated to cover our sample period, 1997–2004, using subsector-specific value added price deflators for each country c, P^{c}_{jt}, in the Region relative to Germany, P^{G}_{jt}, as follows:

$$\overline{PPP}^{c}_{jt} = \left(\frac{\dfrac{P^{c}_{jt}}{P^{c}_{j1997}}}{\dfrac{P^{G}_{jt}}{P^{c}_{j1997}}} \right) * PPP^{c}_{j199'} \tag{b3}$$

Then, we use these PPP conversion rates to transform gross nominal value added in country c, subsector j, and year t, expressed in local currency units, Y^{c}_{jt}, into real value added in 1997 PPP euros:

$$\overline{RY}^{c}_{jt} = Y^{c}_{jt} \Big/ \overline{PPP}^{c}_{jt}. \tag{b4}$$

The coverage is the EU-8 and the EU-15 in 1995–2004. For Ireland, Italy, and Latvia, the data on NACE 40 and 41 are aggregated.

Employment shares are obtained by dividing employment in subsector i by aggregate employment in the respective sample, that is, the total economy, manufacturing, and services. The coverage is the EU-8 and the EU-15 in 1997–2004. For Ireland, Italy, and Latvia, the data on NACE 40 and 41 are aggregated.

Estimation Results

Tables 2.B1, 2.B2, and 2.B3 outline the estimation results.

TABLE 2.B1

The Contribution of Sectors to Aggregate Labor Productivity
(percent)

Sector	1995–98			1999–2004		
	Within	Between	Cross	Within	Between	Cross
Agriculture, hunting, and forestry	2.2	–4.3	–1.4	6.7	–2.9	–1.8
Fishing	0.0	0.0	0.0	0.0	–0.1	0.0
Mining and quarrying	0.2	–1.5	–0.2	2.2	–0.7	–0.5
Manufacturing	15.7	–1.9	–1.4	22.6	–1.8	–0.7
Electricity, gas, and water supply	1.8	0.9	–0.4	13.0	–2.9	–2.2
Construction	17.7	1.8	0.4	6.9	0.0	–1.0
Wholesale and retail trade	9.6	6.6	2.0	10.1	4.3	0.5
Hotels and restaurants	0.7	0.5	0.0	0.8	0.5	0.1
Transport, storage, and telecommunications	14.4	–0.7	–1.1	13.6	–1.3	–0.6
Financial intermediation	–2.7	3.9	–1.7	8.9	–0.1	-0.6
Real estate, renting, and business activities	16.8	17.5	4.5	5.8	22.3	–1.0
Total	76.5	22.9	0.6	90.5	17.3	–7.8

Source: Author calculations.

TABLE 2.B2

The Contribution of Manufacturing Industries to Aggregate Manufacturing Labor Productivity
(percent)

Sector	1995–98			1999–2004		
	Within	Between	Cross	Within	Between	Cross
Food, beverages, and tobacco	0.6	7.3	–0.1	6.1	–3.2	–0.3
Textiles	3.3	–3.0	–0.4	3.3	–1.8	–0.7
Wearing apparel, dressing and dying of fur	3.1	1.0	1.3	1.2	–1.5	–0.2
Leather and footwear	–1.5	–1.6	–0.5	1.1	–1.1	–0.3
Wood and of wood and cork	5.0	1.2	0.8	5.3	1.0	0.9
Pulp, paper, and paper products	0.8	–1.2	0.0	2.5	–0.1	–0.4
Printing, publishing, and reproduction	4.6	2.4	–0.4	2.6	0.2	–0.3
Coke, refined petroleum, and nuclear fuel	5.9	–5.3	–3.8	5.6	–0.8	–1.1
Chemicals and chemical products	–6.2	–1.3	1.7	12.5	–2.0	–1.2
Rubber and plastics	3.3	7.9	1.7	4.2	4.0	1.7
Other nonmetallic minerals	14.9	–5.4	–3.4	7.7	–0.9	–0.6
Basic metals	2.3	–8.0	–1.6	6.4	–0.4	0.0
Fabricated metal	7.2	7.9	1.7	8.0	2.5	1.3
Machinery	14.6	–9.7	–4.4	12.1	–1.6	–2.1
Office, accounting, and computing machinery	1.8	0.9	4.4	1.3	0.2	–0.7
Electrical machinery and apparatus	8.8	3.2	0.9	3.6	3.7	0.8
Radio, television, and communication equipment	4.0	4.3	–2.2	3.6	1.8	1.3
Medical, precision, and optical instruments	4.6	–0.3	–0.5	1.1	0.4	–0.2
Motor vehicles, trailers, and semitrailers	12.7	4.9	4.1	1.1	4.4	–1.0
Other transport equipment	2.5	–2.3	–0.8	3.1	–0.5	–1.1
Manufacturing, recycling	3.5	3.0	–0.5	4.8	1.5	0.8
Total	95.8	6.0	–1.8	97.3	5.9	–3.3

Source: Author calculations.

TABLE 2.B3

The Contribution of Service Industries to Aggregate Service Labor Productivity

(percent)

Sector	1995–98			1999–2004		
	Within	Between	Cross	Within	Between	Cross
Electricity, gas, and water supply	2.8	–2.4	–0.4	21.4	–2.6	–4.2
Construction	29.9	–1.2	–1.1	11.8	–1.4	–1.8
Sale, maintenance, and repair of motor vehicles and motorcycles	–1.6	2.8	–0.5	1.8	0.4	0.1
Wholesale trade	13.2	0.6	0.2	6.1	0.1	0.0
Retail trade	3.3	2.3	–0.1	9.0	0.9	–0.1
Hotels and restaurants	1.2	0.2	–0.1	1.3	0.1	0.1
Inland transport	11.1	–3.2	–1.0	11.5	–1.0	–0.9
Water transport	1.4	–0.8	–1.0	0.5	–0.1	–0.3
Air transport	0.2	0.0	0.0	0.5	0.0	–0.1
Supporting and auxiliary transport activities	0.9	1.4	–1.0	3.5	0.0	–0.9
Post and telecommunications	7.3	–0.3	–0.5	6.1	–0.6	–0.8
Financial intermediation	–5.2	1.0	–0.4	9.4	–0.2	–0.8
Insurance and pension funding	0.0	1.7	–0.2	3.9	0.0	–1.2
Activities related to financial intermediation	0.5	1.5	–1.2	1.1	–0.1	0.0
Real estate activities	16.7	5.1	–7.5	18.1	1.4	–2.1
Renting of machinery and equipment	–2.1	5.1	–4.2	–0.2	0.6	–1.0
Computer and related activities	3.8	1.6	0.5	0.2	1.5	–0.5
Research and development	0.5	–2.1	–0.2	1.5	–0.2	–0.7
Other business activities	11.5	8.3	1.6	5.7	3.6	–0.1
Total	95.3	21.7	–17.0	113.2	2.2	–15.3

Source: Author calculations.

C. Estimation of Service Input Usage in the Agriculture Sector

Data

Amadeus Database 2006

The empirical analysis presented in this section is based on firm-level agriculture data in the Amadeus Database. Amadeus is a comprehensive, pan-European database compiled by Bureau van Dijk that provides firm-level accounting data in a standardized financial format on 24 balance sheet items, 25 profit and loss account items, and 26 financial ratios. It also supplies descriptive information, including trade description codes and activity codes. Combining data from over 30 specialist regional information providers, Bureau van Dijk identifies the best sources of information in each country and applies strict inclusion criteria to prevent any bias in coverage. For the estimation of TFP, we use the May 2006 edition of Amadeus and a sample that covers over 2,948 firms in agriculture (NACE 1) in four countries of the Region (Bulgaria, the Czech Republic, Estonia, and Poland) for which input-output tables are available from 2000 through 2004.

EBRD Transition Indicators

Following Arnold, Javorcik, and Mattoo (2007), we have estimated the intersectoral links between services and agriculture by weighing the extent of liberalization in the agriculture sector according to the reliance of agricultural firms on service inputs. We do not have data on service inputs among individual firms. However, we are able to apply information from the use tables of national input-output matrices to measure interindustry dependencies between the agriculture sector and the service sector. The input-output matrices for countries cover different years: Bulgaria, 2001; the Czech Republic, 2002; Estonia, 1997; and Poland, 1999. Based on the information on the relative importance of the service sector to agriculture, we calculate the measures for the agriculture sector j of country c at time t, as follows:

$$services\_linkages^{c}_{j,t} = \sum_{k} a^{c}_{j,k} liberalization\_index^{c}_{k,t}, \qquad \text{(b5)}$$

where $a^{c}_{j,k}$ is the amount of inputs sourced from service sector k, expressed as a fraction of the overall inputs used by the agriculture sector j of country c, and $liberalization\_index^{c}_{k,t}$ is one of the eight indexes of reform in service sector k at time t, that is, the services link variable captures cross effects and is obtained by multiplying the matrix of sectoral reform indicators for the service sector with a matrix of input-output coefficients.

The liberalization of service industries is captured through the indicators of policy reform (the transition indicators) published by the EBRD (2004) for seven service industries: banking reform and interest rate liberalization, securities markets and nonbank financial institutions, electric power, railways, roads, telecommunications, and water and waste water. All indicators are available for 1998 to 2004. Using these EBRD transition indicators, we construct an overall finance index that represents the average of the two finance reform indicators, an overall infrastructure index that represents the average of the five infrastructure reform indicators, and an overall service index that represents the average of the overall finance and infrastructure indicators.

The EBRD transition indicators range from 1 to 4+. A rating of 1 represents little or no change from conditions in a rigid centrally planned economy, and a rating of 4+ represents the standards in advanced industrialized market economies. The + and – ratings are treated by adding 0.33 and subtracting 0.33 from the full value. The average is obtained by rounding down; for example, a score of 2.6 is treated as 2+, but a score of 2.8 is treated as 3–. (For details, see the methodological notes in EBRD 2004, 199–204.) The scores reflect the judgment of the EBRD's Office of the Chief Economist about country-specific progress in transition. The advantage of using these measures is that they are, in principle, designed to encompass all policy aspects of liberalization. However, this broad coverage comes at the expense of limited precision, particularly with respect to the time variations in the indicators.

To exploit the panel aspect of the data set, we estimate the model in first differences (table 2.C1). Differencing takes out all unobservable (and observable) time-invariant characteristics. The second specification takes the following form:

$$\Delta \ln TFP_{i,t} = \nu + \delta \Delta services\_linkages^{c}_{j,t-1} + \sum_{n} \phi_n \Delta Z^{n}_{i,t} + \sum_{c} \gamma country_c + \sum_{t} \theta year_t + \omega_{i,t}, \quad \text{(b6)}$$

where $\Delta \ln TFP_{i,t}$ is the year-to-year changes in the logarithm of TFP of manufacturing establishment i over the period 1999 to

TABLE 2.C1

Regressions in First-Differences of Productivity in Agriculture Firms and Reform in Services, 2000–04

[Dependent Variable: ΔTFP (Levinsohn-Petrin)]

Independent variable	(1)	(2)	(3)	(4)	(5)	(6)	(7)	(8)	(9)
ΔServices*I-O coefficients	0.768*** (0.230)			—	—	—	—	—	—
ΔFinance*I-O coefficients		–0.759 (2.606)		–2.141 (2.631)	—	—	—	—	—
ΔInfrastructure*I-O coefficients			0.809*** (0.233)	0.845*** (0.236)	—	—	—	—	—
ΔElectric power*I-O coefficients	—	—	—	—	1.847*** (0.4170)	—	—	—	—
ΔRailways*I-O coefficients	—	—	—	—	—	–6.317*** (1.406)	—	—	—
ΔRoads*I-O coefficients	—	—	—	—	—	—	–23.387*** (6.689)	—	—
ΔTelecommunications *I-O coefficients	—	—	—	—	—	—	—	11.204* (6.113)	—
ΔWater and waste water *I-O coefficients	—	—	—	—	—	—	—	–	1.494*** (0.4710)
Observations	4,683	4,683	4,683	4,683	4,683	4,683	4,683	4,683	4,683
Number of firms	2,948	2,948	2,948	2,948	2,948	2,948	2,948	2,948	2,948
Overall R^2	0.038	0.037	0.038	0.038	0.040	0.040	0.039	0.037	0.038

Source: Author calculations.

Note: The dependent variable is ΔTEP (see Levinsohn and Petrin 2003). Reform is measured according to weighted EBRD transition indicators. The EBRD indicators are lagged by one year. The change in the number of employees is also included in the regressions. The I-O coefficients are derived from the use tables of national input-output matrices to measure interindustry dependencies between the agriculture sector and service sector. The input-output matrices cover four countries, but in different years: Bulgaria, 2001; the Czech Republic, 2002; Estonia, 1997; and Poland, 1999. Standard errors adjusted for clustering are noted in parentheses.

* Significant at 10 percent. *** Significant at 1 percent.

2004, estimated by the semiparametric estimation technique developed by Levinsohn and Petrin (2003); ΔZ_i^n is a vector of year-to-year changes in the number of employees over the period 1999 to 2004; and $COUNTRY_c$ is a vector of country dummy variables for Bulgaria, the Czech Republic, Estonia, Poland, and Romania.

D. Manufacturing Productivity

Data

For the data, see appendix 2B.

ICT Taxonomy, the Manufacturing Sector
The following classification is adapted from van Ark and Piatkowski (2004) for manufacturing and commercial services. (NACE 2-digit and 3-digit classification codes are noted in parentheses.)

- *ICT-producing manufacturing*: office machinery (30), insulated wire (313), electronic valves and tubes (321), telecommunications equipment (322), radio and television receivers (323), scientific instruments (331)
- *ICT-using manufacturing*: clothing (18), printing and publishing (22), mechanical engineering (29), other electrical machinery and apparatus (31–313), other instruments (33–331)
- *non-ICT manufacturing*: food, drink, and tobacco (15–16); textiles (17); leather and footwear (19); wood and products of wood and cork (20); pulp, paper, and paper products (21); mineral oil refining, coke, and nuclear fuel (23); chemicals (24); rubber and plastics (25); nonmetallic mineral products (26); basic metals (27); fabricated metal products (28); motor vehicles (34)

Skill Taxonomy, the Manufacturing Sector
The following classification is adapted from O'Mahoney and van Ark (2003) for manufacturing and commercial services. (The NACE 2-digit and 3-digit classification codes are noted in parentheses.)

- *high skilled*: mineral oil refining, coke, and nuclear fuel (23); chemicals (24); office machinery (30); radio, television, and communications equipment (32); electronic valves and tubes (321); telecommunications equipment (322); radio and television receivers (323); medical, precision, and optical instruments (33); scientific instruments (331); other instruments (33–331); other transport equipment (35); building and repairing of ships and boats (351); aircraft and spacecraft (353); railroad equipment and transport equipment (352 + 359)

- *low skilled*: food, drink, and tobacco (15–16); textiles (17); clothing (18); leather and footwear (19); wood and products of wood and cork (20); pulp, paper, and paper products (21); printing and publishing (22); rubber and plastics (25); nonmetallic mineral products (26); basic metals (27); fabricated metal products (28); mechanical engineering (29); electrical machinery and apparatus (31); insulated wire (313); other electrical machinery and apparatus (31–313); motor vehicles (34); furniture, miscellaneous manufacturing, recycling (36–37)

Export Sophistication

The level of sophistication of exports may be indirectly measured by examining wages in the countries producing the exports. The relevant measure, known as EXPY, is taken from Hausmann, Hwang, and Rodrik (2006). In that paper, the authors find that is not only how much, but also what you export that is important for growth. Countries that have a more sophisticated export basket enjoy accelerated subsequent growth. (See Klinger 2007a, 2007b for details on this and other issues in this section.)

This measure of export sophistication is constructed as follows. The authors first develop a measure of the revealed sophistication of each product, which they call PRODY; this is defined as the revealed comparative advantage–weighted per capita GDP of each country that exports the good so that:

$$PRODY_k = \sum_j \frac{(x_{jk}/X_j)}{\Sigma_j (x_{jk}/X_j)} Y_j \qquad \text{(b7)}$$

where x_{ji} equals exports of the good k by country j, X_j equals total exports by country j, and Y_j equals the GDP per capita of country j. This product-level measure is then used to measure the sophistication of a country's entire export basket (EXPY). $EXPY_i$ is simply the $PRODY_l$ of each good the country exports, weighted by that good's share in the country's export basket. It represents the income level associated with a country's export package.

$$EXPY_i = \sum_l \left(\frac{x_{il}}{X_i}\right) PRODY_l \qquad \text{(b8)}$$

Not surprisingly, the level of income implied by a country's export basket (EXPY) is higher or lower depending on the country's actual income, that is, rich countries produce rich country goods, as illustrated in figure 2.D1.

FIGURE 2.D1

Export Sophistication and GDP per Capita, 2005

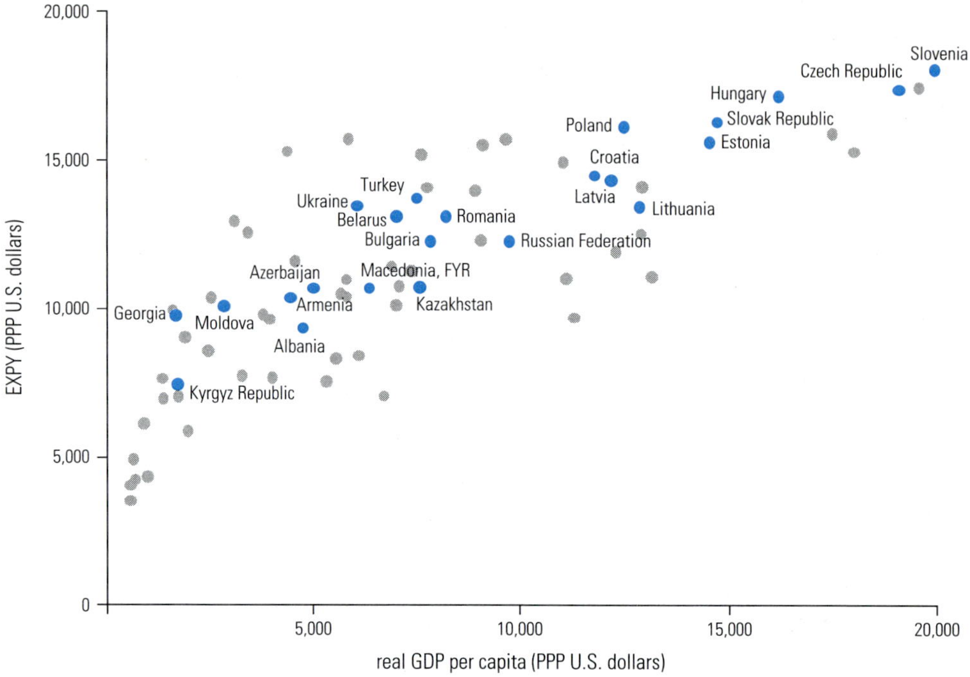

Sources: Author calculations based on UN Comtrade 2007 and World Development Indicators Database 2007; Klinger 2007a, 2007b.

Note: The countries of the Region are highlighted in blue. EXPY = Country's export basket. Grey dots represent the rest of the world.

However, there is significant variance in this relationship. Some countries have managed to discover products that are associated with a level of income much higher than their own, such as China, India, Indonesia, Malaysia, Mexico, and the Philippines. Moreover, this variance has important consequences. Thus, the authors find that countries converge to the income levels implied by their export baskets. In essence, countries become what they export. This means that, if a country has managed to begin exporting a sophisticated export basket relative to its income level, subsequent growth is higher as GDP converges to that level. However, countries specialized in relatively unsophisticated export baskets suffer lagging economic performance. Put another way, the payoff of exporting more of the same depends on the current sophistication of exports. Figure 2.D2 shows the level of export sophistication relative to subsequent GDP growth.

The Open Forest and the Product Space

The open forest is an indicator showing the degree to which a country's export basket is close to other products for the production of which

FIGURE 2.D2
Export Sophistication and Subsequent Growth

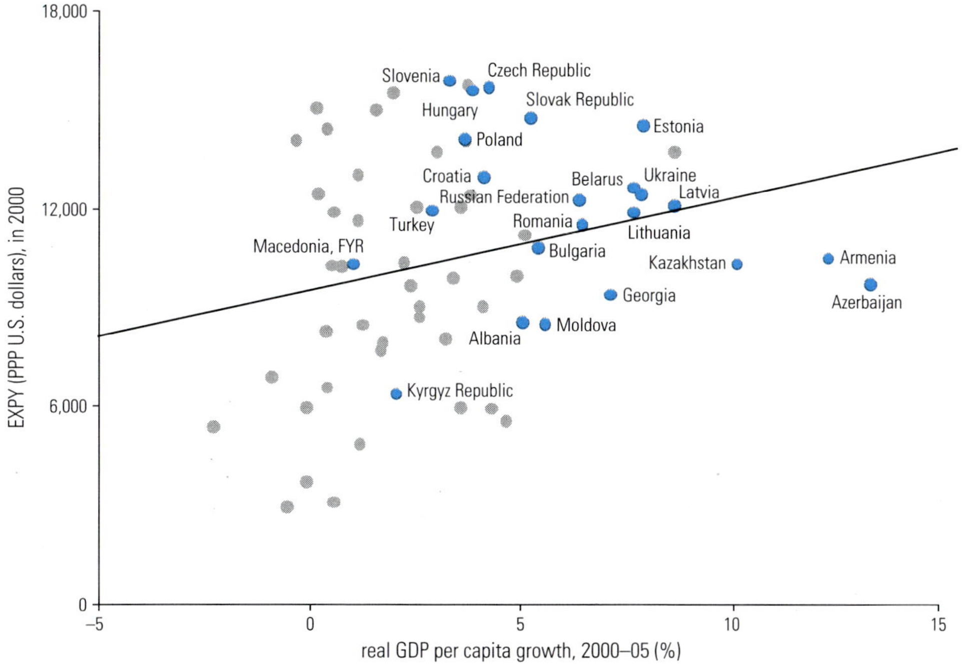

Sources: Author calculations based on UN Comtrade 2007 and World Development Indicators Database 2007; Klinger 2007a, 2007b.

Note: The countries of the Region are in blue. Grey dots represent the rest of the world.

the currently installed productive structure may be easily adapted (Hausmann and Klinger 2006). We measure the distance between each pair of such products based on the probability that countries in the world may be exporting both. If two products require the same capabilities, the result should emerge in a higher probability that a country possesses a comparative advantage in both. Formally, the inverse measure of distance between a pair of goods, *i* and *j*, in year *t*, which we will call proximity, equals:

$$\varphi_{i,j,t} = \min\left\{P\left(x_{i,t} \middle| x_{j,t}\right), P\left(x_{j,t} \middle| x_{i,t}\right)\right\}, \quad \text{(b9)}$$

where, for any country *c*:

$$x_{i,c,t} = \begin{cases} 1 & \text{if } RCA_{i,c,t} > 1 \\ 0 & \text{otherwise} \end{cases}, \quad \text{(b10)}$$

and where the conditional probability is calculated using all countries in year *t*. The calculation uses disaggregated export data across a large sample of countries from the world trade flows data in Feenstra and others (2005) and the UN Comtrade Database.

The distance between products has important implications for export growth. Shown econometrically in Hausmann and Klinger (2006), movement in this product space occurs toward products spatially nearby those already being produced. A country's opportunities of finding new export opportunities that are themselves sophisticated and allow for within-product quality upgrading, therefore, depend on the products that are nearby.

We use the pairwise distance values described above to create a measure of the distance of any particular product from a particular country's export basket as a whole. This measure, taken from Hausmann and Klinger (2006), is called density, the density of current production around any good. It is the distance of good *i* from country *c*'s export basket at time *t*. It is the sum of all paths leading to the product in which the country is active, scaled by the total number of paths leading to that product. Density varies from 0 to 1; higher values indicate that the country has achieved comparative advantage in many nearby products and therefore should be more likely to export the good in the future. It is calculated as follows.

$$density_{i,c,t} = \left(\frac{\sum_k j_{i,k,t} x_{c,k,t}}{\sum_k j_{i,k,t}} \right) \qquad \text{(b11)}$$

Hausmann and Klinger (2006) show that this measure of density is, indeed, highly significant in predicting how a country's productive structure will shift over time: countries are much more likely to move toward products that have a higher density, meaning that these products are *closer* to the country's current production capabilities.

The density measure is applicable at the country-product level, that is, there is a density for each country around each product. We may aggregate this measure to the country level to assess the degree to which the current export basket is connected with valuable new productive possibilities. This measure, called open forest, answers the questions: Is the current export basket in a part of the product space that is well connected to other new and valuable opportunities for structural transformation? Or is it in a sparse, unconnected part of the product space? The measure is calculated as follows:

$$open\_forest_{c,t} = \sum_i \sum_j \left[\frac{\varphi_{i,j,t}}{\sum_i \varphi_{i,j,t}} \left(1 - x_{c,j,t}\right) x_{c,i,t}\, PRODY_{j,t} \right] \qquad \text{(b12)}$$

Hausmann and Klinger (2006) show that open forest is highly significant in determining the future growth of export sophistication in a country. Countries with a high level of open forest enjoy more rapid subsequent growth in export sophistication and overall economic growth.

As with export sophistication (EXPY), there is also a positive relationship between income and open forest; richer countries tend to be specialized in more well connected parts of the product space (figure 2.D3).

There is variation in this relationship, and countries that have managed to move into a relatively well-connected part of the product space despite a relatively lower level of development tend to enjoy more rapid subsequent structural transformation (figure 2.D4; see also Hausmann and Klinger 2006).

Using calculated densities, we may obtain a picture of the product space from the point of view of the countries of the Region (Klinger 2007a, 2007b). Each product not currently exported in a context of comparative advantage has a particular distance from a country's

FIGURE 2.D3

Open Forest and GDP per Capita, 2005

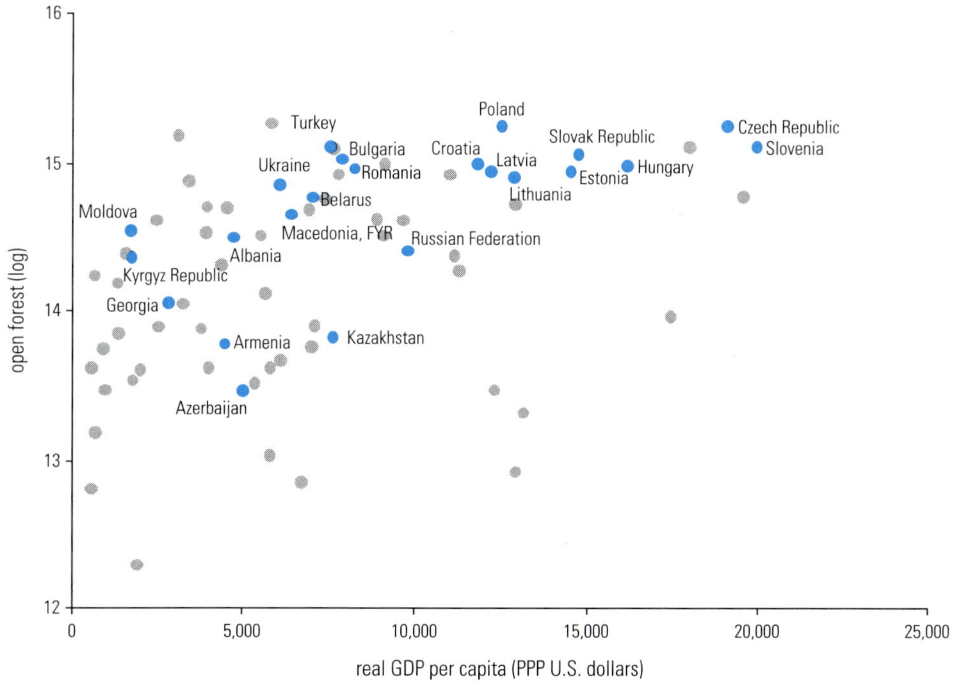

Sources: Author calculations based on UN Comtrade 2007 and World Development Indicators Database 2007; Klinger 2007a, 2007b.

Note: The countries of the Region are highlighted in blue. Grey dots represent the rest of the world.

FIGURE 2.D4

Open Forest and Subsequent Growth

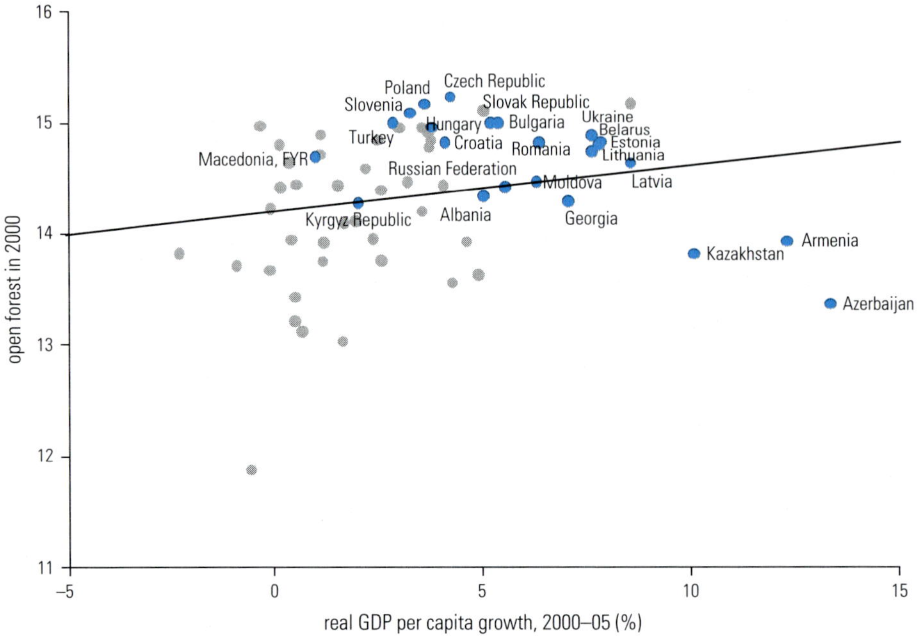

Sources: Author calculations based on UN Comtrade 2007 and World Development Indicators Database 2007; Klinger 2007a, 2007b.

Note: The countries of the Region are highlighted in blue. Grey dots represent the rest of the world.

current export basket as indicated by the country's export density. In addition, each such product has a level of sophistication measured by PRODY. We may plot each product according to its distance, meaning that a smaller value represents a product that is *closer* to the country's current productive structure and sophistication; we may also identify the corresponding Leamer commodity clusters (see Leamer 1984). See Klinger (2007a, 2007b) for details on countries.

E. Service Productivity

Data

For the data, see appendix 2.D.

ICT Taxonomy, Service Sector

The following classification is adapted from van Ark and Piatkowski (2004) for commercial services. (NACE 2-digit and 3-digit classification codes are noted in parentheses.)

- *ICT-producing services*: communications (64), computer and related activities (72)
- *ICT-using services*: wholesale trade and commission trade except motor vehicles and motorcycles (51); retail trade except motor vehicles and motorcycles; repair of personal and household goods (52); financial intermediation except insurance and pension funding (65); insurance and pension funding except compulsory social security (66); activities auxiliary to financial intermediation (67); renting of machinery and equipment (71); research and development (73); legal, technical, and advertising (741–3)
- *Non-ICT services*: electricity, gas, and water supply (40–41); construction (45); sale, maintenance, and repair of motor vehicles and motorcycles; retail sale of automotive fuel (50); hotels and catering (55); inland transport (60); water transport (61); air transport (62); supporting and auxiliary transport activities; activities of travel agencies (63); real estate activities (70); other business activities (749)

Skill Taxonomy, Service Sector

The following classification is adapted from O'Mahoney and van Ark (2003) for commercial services. (NACE 2-digit and 3-digit classification codes are noted in parentheses.)

- *high skilled*: electricity, gas, and water supply (40–41); air transport (62); supporting and auxiliary transport activities; activities of travel agencies (63); communications (64); financial intermediation except insurance and pension funding (65); insurance and pension funding except compulsory social security (66); activities auxiliary to financial intermediation (67); real estate activities (70); renting of machinery and equipment (71); computer and related activities (72); research and development (73); other business services (74)
- *low skilled*: construction (45); sale, maintenance, and repair of motor vehicles and motorcycles; retail sale of automotive fuel (50); wholesale trade and commission trade except motor vehicles and motorcycles (51); retail trade except motor vehicles and motorcycles; repair of personal and household goods (52); hotels and catering (55); inland transport (60); water transport (61)

The Effect of Services on Manufacturing

The efficiency of service subsectors is important because the subsectors are increasingly contributing to the economies in the

Region, but also because service subsectors account for important inputs for downstream sectors. Hence, liberalization-related improvements in the performance of the service sector may be crucial for the promotion of growth. Indeed, Eschenbach and Hoekman (2006) show that progress in service policy reform helps explain differences in economic growth across the Region since 1990. Arnold, Javorcik, and Mattoo (2007) find a significant positive effect from service liberalization and FDI in the service sector on the TFP of manufacturing firms in the Czech Republic. Similarly, Arnold, Mattoo, and Narciso (2006) find a significant positive effect from the regional availability of communications, electricity, and financial services on TFP for a large cross-section of manufacturing firms in 10 African countries.[1] (See Fernandes 2007 for details on this and other issues in this section.)

We apply the Arnold, Javorcik, and Mattoo (2007) approach to nine countries in the Region (Bulgaria, the Czech Republic, Estonia, Hungary, Lithuania, Poland, Romania, the Slovak Republic, and Slovenia) to examine the role of liberalization in service subsectors on downstream manufacturing productivity. Our dependent variable is labor productivity in 2-digit NACE manufacturing subsectors obtained from the WIIW Industrial Database Eastern Europe from 1997 to 2004. (Because of the use of different databases, the set of countries covered here differs from the countries covered elsewhere.) For any country and year, the labor productivity of a manufacturing subsector is expressed as a ratio to the average labor productivity of manufacturing as a whole.[2] Because labor productivity is not measured in absolute terms, but in relative terms, the problems of the deflation of real value added analogous to those discussed elsewhere for service subsectors are avoided. However, the use of labor productivity in relative terms implies that the comparison of levels across countries is not meaningful, and controlling for country and year dummies in the regressions is thus essential.

Our independent variable is a measure of liberalization in service subsectors weighted by the reliance of a given manufacturing subsector on inputs from each service subsector. Input-output matrices for each of the nine countries are used to capture the intersectoral dependencies between service subsectors and manufacturing subsectors. More specifically, the independent variable is given by:

$$services\_link^{c}_{it-1} = \sum_{k} a_{ik} * EBRD^{c}_{kt-1} \qquad \text{(b13)}$$

where a_{ik} is the quantity of inputs sourced by manufacturing subsector i from service subsector k as a fraction of the total inputs used by manufacturing subsector *i*, and $EBRD^{c}_{kt-1}$is the EBRD index of progress in policy reform in service subsector *k* in year *t–1*.[3] Considering lagged values for the EBRD index allows for the time for the effects of liberalization to materialize in the service sector.

Interestingly, we find that the use of service subsector inputs by the manufacturing sector varies greatly across the Region.

Figure 2.E1 shows the intensity of usage of each of the service subsectors (for which the EBRD index is available) by the manufacturing sector overall and by two manufacturing subsectors: textiles and textile products and electrical and optical equipment.[4] For the manufacturing sector overall, inputs of electricity, gas, and steam represent the highest share of total inputs used in almost all countries of the Region, ranging from an average of 2.3 percent of total inputs used in the Czech Republic to an average of 11 percent in Romania.[5] Across the Region, with the exception of Lithuania and Romania, inputs of electricity, gas, and steam represent a share of the total inputs used by textiles and textile products that is greater

FIGURE 2.E1

Intensity of the Use of Service Subsector Inputs in Manufacturing

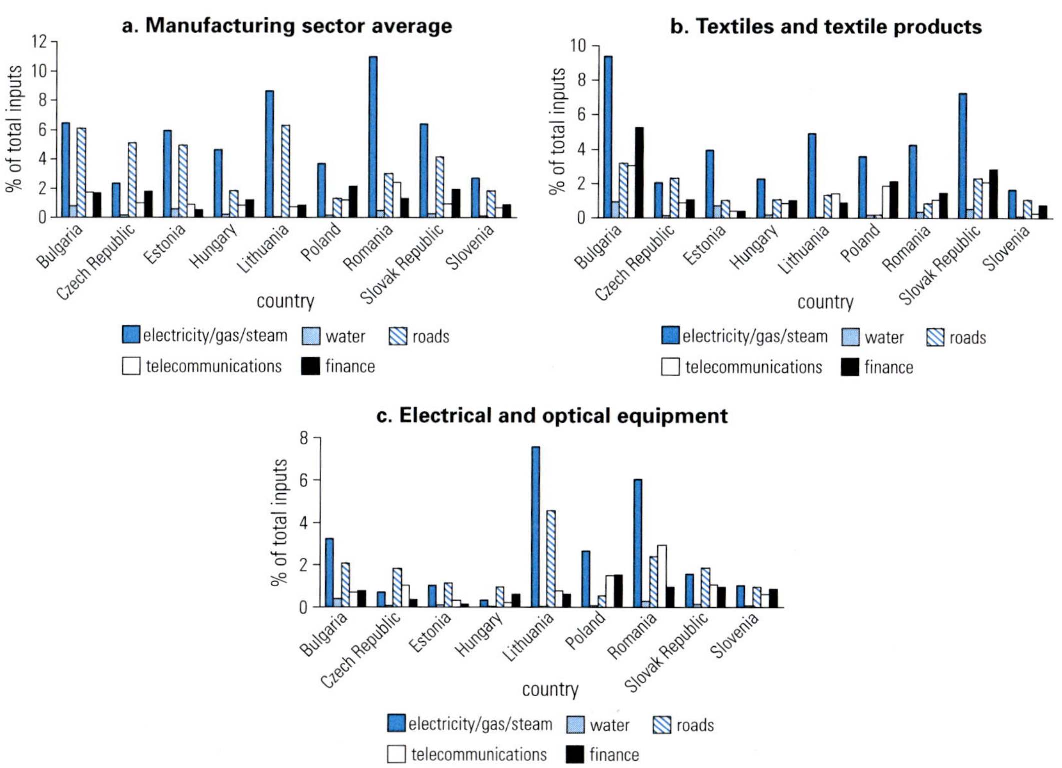

Source: Author calculations.

than the share used by electrical and optical equipment. The second most important service subsector in terms of input provision to the manufacturing sector overall is road transport, the share of which in total inputs ranges from an average of 1.3 percent in Poland to an average of 6.3 percent in Lithuania. These figures also happen to show that the production processes of the manufacturing subsector differ substantially across countries in terms of the type of service inputs used.

Our empirical strategy consists of estimating the following equation:

$$lprod^c_{it} = \beta_0 + \beta_1 services\_link^c_{it-1} + I^c + I_t + I_j + I_t * I_j + \varepsilon^c_{it} \qquad \text{(b14)}$$

where $lprod^c_{it}$ is the labor productivity of manufacturing subsector i (relative to the labor productivity of manufacturing overall) in country c and year t, I^c represents country dummies, I_t represents year dummies, I_j represents manufacturing subsector dummies, $I_t * I_j$ is an interaction of year dummies and manufacturing subsector dummies, and ε^c_{it} is an independent and identically distributed residual.

Year dummies account for policies or business cycle aspects affecting all manufacturing subsectors equally, while manufacturing subsector dummies and the interaction term account for unobservable differences in labor productivity that are constant (for example, some subsectors operate with higher capital intensity, resulting in higher labor productivity) or vary with time, respectively.[6] Table 2.E2 presents the results of the estimation of equation (b15) using ordinary least squares, fixed effects, and first-differenced regressions. Arnold, Mattoo, and Narciso (2006) argue that service liberalization in the Czech Republic may be considered exogenous to manufacturing productivity since the European Commission exerted a tight supervision on policy reform in preparation for that country's EU accession. A similar argument applies to the countries included in our analysis; thus, we are not concerned about reverse causality problems in the regressions in table 2.E2. Also, given that labor productivity is expressed in relative terms, we do not attach meaning to the magnitude of the coefficients in table 2.E2, but only to the sign and significance of the coefficients.

The estimates in columns (1) and (2) show that there is a positive and significant effect of service liberalization on the labor productivity of downstream manufacturing. More specifically, the coefficients indicate that, within countries, manufacturing subsectors that rely more heavily on inputs from more liberalized service subsectors exhibit higher productivity than other manufacturing subsectors. The

TABLE 2.E2

The Effects of Service Liberalization on Manufacturing Productivity

Independent variable	Ordinary least squares (1)	Fixed effects (2)	First differences (3)
Linkage finance, electricity, water, roads, telecommunications, to one-year lagged EBRD	2.107	2.107	0.196
	(0.368)***	(0.202)***	(0.618)
Year dummies	Yes	Yes	Yes
Country dummies	Yes		
NACE 2-digit dummies	Yes		
Year dummies*NACE 2-digit dummies	Yes		
Number of observations	820	820	695

Source: Author calculations.

Note: The dependent variable is labor productivity in manufacturing subsectors. Robust standard errors are noted in parentheses.

*** Significant at 1 percent.

coefficient in column (3) is positive, but insignificant, which is not surprising given that the first-differenced specification imposes strong demands on the data. Finally, note that the results are qualitatively similar if we consider two-year lagged values for the EBRD index.

Our findings support the idea that service liberalization in the Region is beneficial for the productivity of the manufacturing sector. Our findings use a simpler productivity measure and do not control for other determinants of manufacturing productivity (such as FDI or competition), but nevertheless mirror those in Arnold, Mattoo, and Narciso (2006) for a single country. However, note that, for the nine countries considered, the beneficial effect of liberalization occurs only if reforms occur in *both* finance and infrastructure, which are essential backbone services. In fact, unreported results on the effects of liberalization in each of the subsectors separately suggest that liberalization in a single subsector is not conducive to higher productivity in downstream manufacturing.

F. The Role of ICT in Productivity Growth

Methodology

Output and labor productivity growth may be decomposed into the contributions of various inputs by using a growth accounting framework based on the original work by Solow (1957) and Jorgenson and Griliches (1967). (See Piatkowski and van Ark 2007 for details on this and other issues in this section.) In recent years, this framework has been extended to the measurement of the separate contributions of ICT capital and the productivity of ICT production and use by Oliner and Sichel (2000) and Jorgenson, Ho, and Stiroh (2002), among others.[7] Because ICT products and services are outputs from ICT industries, as well as inputs into ICT-using industries, ICT may impact labor productivity through the following three channels:

- the use of ICT capital as an input in the production of other goods and services
- increases in the TFP of production in the ICT sector, which contributes to aggregate TFP growth in an economy
- the contribution to economy-wide TFP by increases in productivity in non-ICT-producing sectors that is induced by the production and use of ICT (spillover effects)

The growth accounting methodology may be summarized as follows. Gross domestic product (Y) is produced from aggregate factor inputs X, consisting of capital services (K), divided into ICT capital (K_{it}), non-ICT capital (K_n), and labor services (L). Productivity is represented as a Hicks-neutral augmentation of the aggregate input (A). The aggregate production function takes the following form:

$$Y = A * X(L, K_n, K_{it}) \qquad \text{(b15)}$$

where subscript n indicates services provided through non-IT capital, and subscript it indicates services provided through information technology capital (including office and computing equipment, communication equipment, and software). Under the assumption of competitive factor markets and constant returns to scale, growth accounting expresses the growth of output as the share-weighted growth of inputs and TFP, denoted by A, which is derived as a residual, as follows:

$$\Delta \ln Y = v_L \ \Delta \ Y + v_{K_n} \Delta \ln K_n + v_{K_{it}} \Delta \ln K_{it} + \Delta \ln A \qquad \text{(b16)}$$

where v denotes the average shares in total factor income; because of constant returns to scale, $v_L + v_{Kn} + v_{Kit} = 1$; Δ refers to first differences. By rearranging equation (b16), the results may be presented in terms of average labor productivity growth defined as $y = Y/L$, the ratio of output to employment, $k = K/L$, the ratio of capital services to persons employed, and TFP, as follows:

$$\Delta \ln y = v_{K_n} \Delta \ln k_n + v_{K_{it}} \Delta \ln k_{it} + \Delta \ln A \qquad \text{(b17)}$$

The analysis in chapter 2 measures the contribution of ICT capital deepening $(v_{K_{it}} \Delta \ln k_{it})$ to aggregate labor productivity growth.

Another useful distinction may be made among the TFP growth originating in industries producing ICT goods (A_{prod}), which represents the second channel above, the TFP growth originating in industries that are heavy users of ICT (A_{use}), which represents the third channel, and TFP growth in other industries (A_{other}), as follows:

$$\Delta \ln y = v_{K_n} \Delta \ln k_n + v_{K_{it}} \Delta \ln k_{it} + \Delta \ln A_{prod} + \Delta \ln A_{use} + \Delta \ln A_{other} \tag{b18}$$

However, without industry-specific data on investment, it is not possible to separate TFP growth in ICT-producing industries ($\Delta \ln A_{prod}$), intensive ICT-using industries ($\Delta \ln A_{use}$), and other industries ($\Delta \ln A_{other}$).[8]

Some clues on the distinction between productivity growth in ICT production, ICT use, and other sources of productivity growth may be obtained by decomposing aggregate labor productivity growth into the contributions of ICT-producing industries ($\Delta y_{prod} S_{prod}$), other manufacturing industries and market services that may all be marked as intensive users of ICT ($\Delta y_{use} S_{use}$), and nonmanufacturing industries and nonmarket services ($\Delta y_{other} S_{other}$) according to a shift-share methodology, as follows:

$$\Delta y = \frac{Y}{L} = \sum_{i=1}^{n} \left(\Delta \frac{Y_i}{L_i} \right) \left(\frac{L_i}{L} \right)$$

$$= \sum_{prod} \left(\Delta y_{prod} S_{prod} \right) + \sum_{use} \left(\Delta y_{use} S_{use} \right) + \sum_{other} \left(\Delta y_{other} S_{other} \right) \tag{b19}$$

where S denotes the share of each industry group in total employment.[9]

The results of these two decomposition techniques may be used to analyze the interactions between the contributors to average productivity growth and structural reform as gauged through various indicators. The reforms reflect improvements in the quality of the economic and institutional environment in the new EU members states that contribute to more rapid productivity growth relative to the EU-15 and the United States (tables 2.F1–2.F4). In this book, we develop a two-step convergence hypothesis that is based on an interaction between the investment in and the production and use of new technology (notably ICT) and the restructuring of the economy and structural reforms.[10]

TABLE 2.F1

Labor Productivity and ICT Capital, 1995–2004

Country	GDP per person employed (annual growth, %) (1)	Percentage-point contribution of Non-ICT capital intesity (2)	ICT capital intensity (3)	TFP growth (4)	Relative ICT capital share in labor productivity growth (%) (5)
New EU member states	4.0	0.9	0.5	1.8	17
Bulgaria	2.3	0.4	0.5	1.5	20
Czech Republic	2.6	1.2	0.6	0.7	25
Estonia	6.9	—	—	—	—
Hungary	2.8	0.3	0.6	1.9	21
Latvia	5.1	—	—	—	—
Lithuania	6.2	—	—	—	—
Poland	4.2	1.9	0.6	2.2	12
Romania	2.6	0.8	0.4	1.5	14
Slovak Republic	3.8	0.8	0.5	2.5	13
Slovenia	3.4	0.8	0.5	2.1	15
Russian Federation	3.5	–1.1	0.1	4.5	2
EU	1.0	0.2	0.4	0.3	44
Austria	1.5	0.5	0.4	0.6	25
Belgium	1.3	–0.1	0.7	0.7	53
Denmark	1.2	0.5	0.5	0.2	43
Finland	2.0	–0.3	0.4	1.9	21
France	1.1	0.4	0.3	0.3	29
Germany	1.0	0.2	0.3	0.5	32
Greece	2.9	0.7	0.4	1.8	13
Italy	0.2	0.4	0.4	–0.6	188
Ireland	3.5	0.7	0.5	2.3	13
Luxembourg	0.7	0.2	0.2	0.2	31
Netherlands	1.0	–0.2	0.7	0.5	73
Portugal	1.1	0.7	0.6	–0.2	56
Spain	0.1	–0.1	–0.3	0.6	–214
Sweden	2.0	0.1	0.7	1.2	33
United Kingdom	1.6	0.1	0.5	0.9	34
United States	2.1	0.3	0.7	1.1	34

Source: Author compilation based on EU KLEMS Database 2007, van Ark and Piatkowski 2004, Timmer, Ypma, and van Ark 2005.

Note: The data for the new EU member states are unweighted averages.

The Interplay Between ICT Use and Structural Reform Estimation

The analysis draws on panel data of four new EU members (the Czech Republic, Hungary, Poland, and the Slovak Republic), the EU-15, and the United States to identify structural and institutional determinants of labor productivity growth in ICT-using manufacturing industries and in the service sector during 1995–2003.

Despite the low statistical fit because of a small data set and the high volatility of productivity growth rates, the regression results show that labor productivity growth in manufacturing has been

TABLE 2.F2

Labor Productivity Growth and ICT-Producing Industries, 1995–2004

(percent)

Indicator	EU-15	United States	Czech Republic	Hungary	Poland	Slovak Republic	Slovenia	Estonia
Labor productivity growth	1.0	2.2	2.4	3.4	4.6	4.0	4.2	7.0
Contribution of ICT-producing industries to labor productivity growth	0.3	0.4	0.4	0.7	0.4	0.3	0.3	0.6
As share of labor productivity growth	29.4	18.0	15.0	22.2	9.9	8.6	7.5	9.2
Share of ICT sector in GDP	5.9	7.1	5.6	7.3	4.2	5.2	5.0	5.6

Source: Author compilation based on EU KLEMS Database 2007.

Note: Real estate has been excluded from market services. For all countries, national deflators have been used. The data for the new EU member states are unweighted averages.

TABLE 2.F3

Labor Productivity Growth, 1995–2003

(constant GDP per person employed)

Indicator	EU-15	United States	Czech Republic	Hungary	Poland	Slovak Republic	Slovenia	Estonia	Latvia	Lithuania	New EU Members
ICT production	5.6	6.1	6.5	10.2	10.1	6.6	5.9	11.5	12.3	9.1	9.0
Other production: manufacturing	1.9	3.4	3.7	3.9	8.5	6.6	6.4	9.0	2.6	9.5	6.3
Other production: nonmanufacturing	1.6	0.0	1.7	3.7	1.3	7.3	4.2	5.1	4.4	5.0	4.1
Market services	0.5	3.1	2.4	1.7	3.7	0.4	3.1	7.5	3.8	5.6	3.5
Nonmarket services	0.1	0.6	–0.3	2.8	2.9	3.9	1.3	4.3	8.6	4.7	3.5

Source: Author compilation based on EU KLEMS Database 2007.

Note: Real estate has been excluded from market services. For all countries, national deflators have been used. The data for the new EU member states are unweighted averages.

TABLE 2.F4

Contributions to Total Labor Productivity Growth, 1995–2000

(constant GDP per person employed)

Indicator	EU-15	United States	Czech Republic	Hungary	Poland	Slovak Republic	Slovenia	Estonia	Latvia	Lithuania	New EU Members
ICT production	0.3	0.4	0.4	0.7	0.4	0.3	0.3	0.6	0.8	0.4	0.5
Other production: manufacturing	0.4	0.6	1.0	0.9	1.6	1.7	1.7	1.7	0.4	1.9	1.4
Other production: nonmanufacturing	0.2	0.0	0.3	0.6	0.3	1.3	0.6	0.9	0.7	1.1	0.7
Market services	0.2	1.2	0.9	0.6	1.5	0.1	1.1	3.1	1.7	2.1	1.4
Nonmarket services	0.0	0.2	0.0	0.6	0.5	0.6	0.2	0.7	1.5	0.8	0.6
Reallocation	–0.1	–0.2	0.0	0.1	0.3	0.0	0.3	–0.1	0.1	0.1	0.1

Source: Author compilation based on EU KLEMS Database 2007.

Note: Real estate has been excluded from market services. For all countries, national deflators have been used. The data for the new EU member states are unweighted averages.

more closely correlated with basic fundamental reforms represented by the composite reform indicator, *A*1 (tables 2.F5 and 2.F6). At the same time, the analysis shows that more sophisticated reforms (represented by the composite reform indicator, *A*2) seem to be more well correlated with productivity growth in market services (tables 2.F7 and 2.F8). These findings are consistent with our hypothesis of a two-step convergence.

The Model

The following panel equations are estimated through the pooled generalized (weighted) least squares model with a common intercept for all countries and periods:

$$\begin{aligned} \Delta Y/L_{manufacturing(it)} &= \mu + \alpha \ln\left(Y_{percapita(it)}\right) + \delta A1(A2)_{it} + \varepsilon_{it} \\ \Delta Y/L_{market\ services(it)} &= \lambda + \alpha \ln\left(Y_{percapita(it)}\right) + \delta A2(A1)_{it} + \varepsilon_{it} \end{aligned} \quad \text{(b20)}$$

where *A*1 and *A*2 denote composite structural indicators for the first and second stage of structural reform, respectively; *i* and *t* denote an economy and a time period; μ_i and μ_y are constants; and ε_{it} is an error term.

The dependant variables, $\Delta Y/L_{manufacturing(it)}$ and $\Delta Y/L_{market\ services(it)}$ are the labor productivity growth rates for manufacturing and market services, respectively. The sample includes 19 countries (the United States, four countries in the Region, and the EU-15 without Luxembourg). The frequency of data is annual for the period 1996–2003.

There are three explanatory variables (see table 2.F9 for data used):

- a composite reform indicator, *A*1, represented by an aggregate of the quality of regulations and law enforcement, trade openness, macroeconomic stability, and financial system development[11]
- a composite reform indicator, *A*2, represented by an aggregate of the level or development of ICT infrastructure, human capital, labor market flexibility, and product market flexibility
- the lagged natural log of GDP per capita, which is included to capture catching-up effects

The aim of the regression is not to test the *strength* per se of the relationship between labor productivity and specific composite structural reforms, which would create a need for a much larger data sample so as to obtain robust results, but, rather, the *existence* of the relationship. This approach also lessens the importance of the omitted variables problem.

TABLE 2.F5

Panel Regression for Labor Productivity Growth in Manufacturing (*A1*)

Variable	Coefficient	Standard error	t-statistic	Probability
Constant***	49.44486	13.48175	3.667539	0.0003
*A1****	1.246516	0.362711	3.436664	0.0008
Log(GDP per capita [–1])***	–4.695648	1.337200	–3.511552	0.0006
Total panel (balanced) observations: 152				
R-squared	0.025951	adjusted R-squared		0.012876

Source: Author calculations.

Note: The dependent variable is labor productivity growth in manufacturing (A1).

*** Significant at 1 percent.

TABLE 2.F6

Panel Regression for Labor Productivity Growth in Manufacturing (*A2*)

Variable	Coefficient	Standard error	t-statistic	Probability
Constant***	28.66235	11.33914	2.527736	0.0125
*A2**	0.596429	0.342849	1.739625	0.0840
Log (GDP per capita [–1])***	–2.609090	1.121560	–2.326304	0.0214
Total panel (balanced) observations: 152				
R-squared	0.035524	adjusted R-squared		0.022578

Source: Author calculations.

Note: The dependent variable is labor productivity growth in manufacturing (A2).

*** Significant at 1 percent. * Significant at 10 percent.

TABLE 2.F7

Panel Regression for Labor Productivity Growth in Market Services (*A1*)

Variable	Coefficient	Standard error	t-statistic	Probability
Constant	7.931392	9.437073	0.840450	0.4020
A1	0.316686	0.272063	1.164018	0.2463
Log (GDP per capita [–1])	–0.734389	0.938249	–0.782723	0.4350
Total panel (balanced) observations: 152				
R-squared	–0.025095	adjusted R-squared		–0.038855

Source: Author calculations.

Note: The dependent variable is labor productivity growth in market services.

TABLE 2.F8

Panel Regression for Labor Productivity Growth in Market Services (*A2*)

Variable	Coefficient	Standard error	t-statistic	Probability
Constant***	19.24258	7.686606	2.503391	0.0134
*A2****	1.045741	0.187810	5.568081	0.0000
Log(GDP per capita [–1])***	–1.858368	0.759111	–2.448085	0.0155
Total panel (balanced) observations: 152				
R-squared	0.124791	adjusted R-squared		0.113043

Source: Author calculations.

Note: The dependent variable is labor productivity growth in market services.

*** Significant at 1 percent.

TABLE 2.F9

Data Definitions and Sources

Factor	Variable	Source
Quality of regulations and contract enforcement	Sum of World Bank regulatory quality and rule of law indicators	Kaufmann, Kraay, and Mastruzzi (2005)
ICT infrastructure	Sum of total number of telephone lines (main and cellular) and personal computers per 1,000 persons	World Development Indicators Database
Trade openness	Share of trade in GDP, percent	World Development Indicators Database
Development of financial markets	Domestic credit to private sector, percent of GDP	World Development Indicators Database
Quality of human capital	Tertiary school enrollment, percent of gross enrollment rate	World Development Indicators Database
Labor market flexibility	Rigidity of employment index	Doing Business Database
Product market flexibility	Product market regulation indicator	Conway, Janod, and Nicoletti (2005)
Macroeconomic stability	Inflation (consumer price index), percent	World Development Indicators Database
GDP per capita	GDP per capita in U.S. $, 2002	OECD

Source: Author compilation.

Note: The human capital for all countries for 1995–97 is equal to 1998, while 2002–03 is equal to 2001. The labor market flexibility for all countries for 1995–2003 is equal to 2004. For product market flexibility, 1995–97 is assumed to equal 1998, while 1999–2002 is based on the average of 1998–2003.

To mitigate the effect of heteroskedasticity typical for panel data, the analysis draws on a generalized (weighted) least squares estimator. Nonetheless, as discussed in other studies, it should be recognized that economic policy and institution variables may often be considered endogenous. However, as argued by Bosworth and Collins (2003), it is difficult to find effective instruments for each endogenous variable. Hence, the results presented, which do not control for the endogeneity problem, should be interpreted as merely showing correlation, not causality.

The weak fit of the regressions is due to the short sample period and high volatility of labor productivity growth rates. The fit might be improved by introducing country dummies. However, country dummies would significantly increase the number of estimated parameters and reduce the number of degrees of freedom. They would thus reduce the explanatory power of the *A*1 and *A*2 variables.

Separate regressions for advanced developed countries (the EU-15 and the United States) and countries of the Region are also run. While the regressions for the advanced developed countries generally show results similar to the results for the full sample, the regressions for countries in the Region show both a weak fit and statistically insignificant variables. This is not surprising given the small number of observations.

The Data Used

Results

Tables 2.F5 and 2.F6 show the results for labor productivity growth in manufacturing. The fit of the regression is weak (the adjusted R-squared is close to zero). Nonetheless, the explanatory variable *A*1 is statistically significant at the 1 percent level. The *A*2 variable is statistically significant only at the 10 percent level. The *A*1 coefficient is higher and has the expected sign. The lagged log of GDP per capita is statistically significant and has the expected negative sign.

Tables 2.F7 and 2.F8 show the results of the regression for labor productivity growth in market services. The fit of the regression is again weak. The explanatory variable *A*1 and the lagged log of GDP per capita is statistically insignificant (although it has the expected negative sign). In turn, the *A*2 variable is statistically significant at the 1 percent level. It also has the expected sign.

Notes

1. In Arnold, Javorcik, and Mattoo (2007), the panel of Czech firms covers the period 1998–2003, while, in Arnold, Mattoo, and Narciso (2006), the cross-sections of firms cover a year between 2001 and 2005 depending on the country.
2. For example, a labor productivity of 0.8 indicates that the subsector is 80 percent as productive as the manufacturing sector overall.
3. The input-output tables provide information on input usage by 2-digit NACE manufacturing subsectors from each 2-digit NACE service subsector, as well as from all sectors in the economy; this allows us to calculate a_{ik}.
4. For each country and service subsector, the intensity of the manufacturing sector overall is obtained as an average of the linkage coefficients a_{ik} across all manufacturing subsectors.
5. Note that, in the Czech Republic, inputs from road transport represent a higher share of total inputs.
6. Since the focus of this appendix is the estimation of the effect of service liberalization on manufacturing subsectors that use service inputs, the various dummies are used to control for all other determinants of the performance of manufacturing subsectors.
7. For the EU-15 countries, see, for example, Daveri (2002), Jorgenson and Vu (2005), Timmer and van Ark (2005), and van Ark and Inklaar (2005). For new member states of the EU, see van Ark and Piatkowski (2004).
8. Nonetheless, Timmer and van Ark (2005) and Piatkowski (2004) provide rough estimates of the contribution of the ICT-producing sector to TFP growth in the EU-15 and the new EU member states, respectively, during 1995–2001. Their estimates are based on TFP growth rates in the ICT-producing industry in the United States.
9. This decomposition differs somewhat from the information we used in earlier studies, including in van Ark and Piatkowski (2004). There, we made a distinction between intensive ICT-using industries and less-intensive ICT users (non-ICT industries) on the basis of ICT investment intensity measures.
10. ICT generally stands for the introduction of new technologies and modern equipment. Because ICT emerged as the key general-purpose technology

driving accelerated growth in many countries during the 1990s, we use it as a proxy for the broader phenomenon of technological change that has also accompanied the growth process in the Region.

11. In the aggregation method, the sample mean of the values of all variables is subtracted from each number, and the result is then divided through sample standard deviation. This result implies a mean of zero and a standard deviation of 1 across the countries in the sample. Hence, all results are comparable and may be aggregated. The aggregated results are submitted to the same procedure.

Appendix 3

Micro Analysis of Productivity: Data and Methodology

A. Firm Productivity Dynamics and Demographics

Methodology

Using productivity at the firm level and production factors as building blocks, one may decompose productivity for each industry into the contributions of continuing firms, new entrant firms, and firms that are exiting. One defines the sectorwide productivity level in year t, P_t, as:

$$P_t = \sum_i \theta_{it} p_{it} \qquad \text{(c1)}$$

where θ_i is the employment share of firm i, and P_t and p_{it} are a productivity measure (in this analysis, labor productivity).

We focus on a common method for decomposing productivity growth. The Foster-Haltiwanger-Krizan method (2001) breaks aggregate productivity growth into five components, commonly called the within effect, the between effect, the cross effect, the entry effect, and the exit effect, as follows:

$$\Delta P_t = \sum_{i\in C} \theta_{it-k} \Delta p_{it} + \sum_{i\in C} \Delta\theta_{it} \left(p_{it-k} - P_{t-k}\right) + \sum_{i\in C} \Delta\theta_{it} \Delta p_{it} + \sum_{i\in N} \theta_{it} \left(p_{it} - P_{t-k}\right) - \sum_{i\in X} \theta_{it-k} \left(p_{it-k} - P_{t-k}\right) \qquad \text{(c2)}$$

where Δ is changes over the k-year interval between the first year ($t–k$) and the last year (t); θ_{it} is the share of industry employment in firm i; C, N, and X are sets of continuing, entering, and exiting firms, respectively; and P_{t-k} is the aggregate (that is, the weighted average) productivity level of the sector at the first year ($t–k$).

The components of the Foster-Haltiwanger-Krizan decomposition are defined as follows:

- The within-firm effect is within-firm productivity growth weighted by initial output shares.
- The between-firm effect captures the gains in aggregate productivity arising from the expanding market of high-productivity firms or from the shrinking shares of low-productivity firms weighted by the initial shares.
- The cross effect covers gains in productivity from the expanding shares of high-productivity growth firms or from the shrinking shares of low-productivity growth firms. The term is positive if the firms that are gaining market shares are also those with above-average productivity growth; it is negative if the firms that are downsizing are the more productive ones.
- The entry effect is the sum of the differences between each entering firm's productivity and the initial productivity in the industry, weighted by the market share of the entering firm.
- The exit effect is the sum of the differences between each exiting firm's productivity and the initial productivity in the industry weighted by the market share of the exiting firm.

The Foster-Haltiwanger-Krizan method uses the first year's values for a continuing firm's share (θ_{it-k}), the firm's productivity level (p_{it-k}), and the average sectorwide productivity level (P_{t-k}). A potential problem with this method is that, in the presence of measurement errors in assessing market shares and relative productivity levels in the base year, the correlation between changes in productivity and changes in market share may be spurious, thereby affecting the within- and between-firm effects.

Data Sources on Firm Productivity Dynamics and Demographics

Data Collected by Bartelsman and Scarpetta (2007)

The analysis by Bartelsman and Scarpetta (2007) provides information on the process of creative destruction using data on firms in Estonia,

Latvia, and Slovenia, as well as similar information on firms in the Netherlands, Sweden, and other OECD countries. Comparisons are also made with developments in Mexico before and after the North American Free Trade Agreement came into effect.

The underlying data sets are constructed using confidential information at the firm level and are generally only available for use by authorized researchers at national statistical offices. In most countries, the output of the firm-level work is screened by the statistical office to ensure that no information on individual firms may be disclosed. A description of the collection methods is found in Bartelsman, Haltiwanger, and Scarpetta (2004) and Bartelsman, Scarpetta, and Schivardi (2005). For the current analysis here, updates of previously collected data have been obtained on Estonia, Latvia, the Netherlands, Slovenia, and Sweden.

The data sets for comparator countries have been collected at various times. This appendix relies on a broader set of comparator countries relative to the rest of the study because a larger set of comparable data are available. The comparator countries include transition economies in Central and Eastern Europe (Hungary, Romania, and Turkey), a few Latin American countries (Argentina, Brazil, Chile, Colombia, and Mexico), an EU average (Finland, France, Germany, Italy, the Netherlands, Sweden, and the United Kingdom), and the United States (as a benchmark). Data on comparator countries have been collected in several ways, including a recent firm-level project organized by the World Bank and an earlier OECD study. The original data sources are business registers, social security databases, and corporate tax registers.

To ensure cross-country comparability, we based all data collection and analysis on a common analytical framework. To the extent possible, the framework involves the harmonization of key concepts (such as firm entry, exit, and survival), as well as the definition of common methodologies for the study of firm-level data. The methodology for aggregating country, industry, and time panel data from underlying microlevel data sets has been referred to as distributed microdata analysis (Bartelsman, Haltiwanger, and Scarpetta 2004; Bartelsman, Scarpetta, and Schivardi 2005).

For each country, time series indicators on firm demographics have been generated on disaggregated sectors. The basic characteristics of the data are presented in table 3.A1. The classification into about 40 sectors (roughly all ISIC, revision 3, 2-digit classifications) coincides with the OECD Structural Analysis Database 2005.

The use of annual data on firm dynamics implies significant volatility in the resulting indicators. To limit the possible impact of

TABLE 3.A1
Data Sources

Country	Firm demographics and survival			Labor productivity			
	Source	Period	Threshold	Source	Period	Threshold	Sectors
Turkey	annual industrial survey	1995–2001	Emp > 10	annual industrial survey	1995–2001	Emp >10	manufacturing
United States	business register	1988–97	Emp ≥ 1	census	1987–92 to 1992–97	Emp >1	private business
Chile	annual industry survey	1979–99	Emp ≥ 10	annual industry survey	1980–85 to 1994–99	Emp ≥ 10	manufacturing
Colombia	annual manufacturing survey	1982–98	Emp ≥ 10	annual manufacturing survey	1982–86 to 1994–98	Emp ≥ 10	manufacturing
Mexico	social security	1985–2001	Emp ≥ 1	—	—	—	all
Slovenia	business register	1992–2004	Emp ≥ 1	business register	1992–97 to 1999–2004	Emp >1	all
Hungary	fiscal register	1992–2001	Emp ≥ 1	fiscal register	1992–96 to 1997–2001	Emp >1	all
Brazil	census	1996–2001	—	—	—	—	manufacturing
Sweden	—	—	—	—	1993–96 to 1999–2004	—	—
Latvia	business register	1996–2005	Emp ≥ 1	business register	1996–2001, 2000–05	Emp ≥ 1	all
Romania	business register	1992–2001	Emp ≥ 1	business register	1995–98 to 1996–99	Emp ≥ 1	all
Argentina	annual industrial survey	1990–2001	Emp ≥ 5	annual industrial survey	1990–95 to 1996–2001	Emp ≥ 5	all
Estonia	business register	1995–2004	Emp ≥ 1	business register	1995–2000 to 1999–2004	Emp ≥ 1	all

Source: Bartelsman, Haltiwanger, and Scarpetta 2005.

Note: Emp = employment level. — = no data are available.

measurement problems, we decided to use definitions of continuing, entering, and exiting firms on the basis of three time periods (rather than the usual two). Thus, the tabulations of firm demographics contain the following variables:

- Entry: the number of firms entering a given industry in a given year. Also tabulated, where available, was the number of employees in entering firms. Entrant firms (and their employees) were those observed as (*out of, in, in*) the register in time (t_{-1}, t, t_{+1}).
- Exit: the number of firms that leave the register and the number of people employed in these firms. Exiting firms were those observed as (*in, in, out of*) the register in time (t_{-1}, t, t_{+1}).
- One-year firms: the number of firms and employees in these firms that were present in the register for only one year. These firms were those observed as (*out of, in, out of*) the register in time (t_{-1}, t, t_{+1}).
- Continuing firms: the number of firms and employees that were in the register in a given year, as well as in the previous and subsequent years. These firms were observed as (*in, in, in*) the register in time (t_{-1}, t, t_{+1}).

These indicators were split into eight firm-size classes, including the class of firms without employees. The data thus allow detailed comparisons of the distributions of firm size between industries and countries.

Firm survival: available data allow entering firms to be tracked over time. This makes it possible to calculate survival probabilities over the initial life of firms and to assess changes in employment over time.

The decomposition of productivity growth: the database includes different types of productivity decomposition for manufacturing industries and some service industries. Depending on the availability of output and input measures, productivity data are available in the database with reference to labor productivity or multifactor productivity using either gross output or value added as the indicator of output (see Bartelsman, Haltiwanger, and Scarpetta 2004 for details). In this appendix, the analysis is limited to labor productivity, which is generally defined as deflated gross output per worker. Firm-level nominal values of output are deflated at the industry level.

Data Collected by Brown and Earle (2007)

The study by Brown and Earle (2007) employs annual manufacturing census-type firm-level data in each of the five countries, as well as the service sector everywhere except Russia.[1] Though the data sources and variables are similar, measures have been taken to make them sufficiently comparable to justify cross-country comparisons.

The data on Georgia cover most firms outside the budgetary and financial sectors in 2000–04. Table 3.A2 shows that the database includes roughly three-fourths of total manufacturing employment and sales reported in the statistical yearbooks.

The main sources for the Hungarian and Romanian data are balance sheets and income statements associated with tax reporting to the National Tax Authority in Hungary and to the Ministry of Finance in Romania. All legal entities that are engaged in double-sided bookkeeping have reported except in Hungary before 1992, for which the only available sample consists of most firms with at least 20 employees and some smaller firms (though the coverage in Hungary before 1992

TABLE 3.A2

Sample Coverage, Georgia

Year	Employment		Sales (lari, millions)	
	Yearbook	Database	Yearbook	Database
2000	n.a.	56,030	n.a.	489.4
2001	58,738	46,486	657.3	541.7
2002	54,135	41,253	782.4	533.3
2003	51,619	39,613	949.2	657.1
2004	52,649	38,613	1,148.1	886.5

Sources: Brown and Earle 2007; Statistics Georgia 2005.

Note: The data refer to manufacturing industries. n.a. = not applicable.

is still high; see table 3.A3). The enterprise registry of the National Institute of Statistics and the portfolio and transaction data of the State Ownership Fund provide additional information for Romania. The Hungarian data cover 1986 to 2003, and the Romanian data span 1992 to 2005. The numbers in the database on manufacturing employment and output are similar to the yearbook numbers in both countries.

The Russian and Ukrainian sources are most similar because the statistical methodologies and data collection mechanisms have been inherited from the Soviet Union, and the national statistical offices (the Federal State Statistics Service in Russia and the State Statistical Committee in Ukraine) are successors to branches of the former Soviet State Committee. The main sources in both countries are industrial enterprise registries, supplemented by balance sheet data. The data span every year between 1985 and 2004 for Russia,

TABLE 3.A3

Coverage of the Hungarian and Romanian Samples

	Hungary				Romania			
Year	Yearbook employment (1,000s)	Database employment (1,000s)	Yearbook output (billion HUF)	Database sales	Yearbook employment (1,000s)	Database employment (1,000s)	Yearbook output (billion lei)	Database sales (billion lei)
1986	1,244	1,232	1,117	1,016	–	–	–	–
1987	1,218	1,205	1,197	1,077	–	–	–	–
1988	1,179	1,156	1,258	1,119	–	–	–	–
1989	1,136	865	1,461	1,316	–	–	–	–
1990	1,074	1,092	1,585	1,510	–	–	–	–
1991	961	970	1,745	1,611	–	–	–	–
1992	812	857	1,422	1,860	2,865	2,702	5,484	4,998
1993	713	737	1,721	2,080	2,606	2,529	15,300	15,322
1994	703	694	2,134	2,691	2,456	2,283	35,247	30,516
1995	690	689	2,945	3,775	2,293	2,234	48,594	46,544
1996	654	695	3,827	4,853	2,302	2,194	76,188	72,067
1997	652	725	5,197	6,508	2,079	2,217	1,71,363	1,55,500
1998	704	754	6,616	8,068	1,964	1,976	2,05,445	1,87,106
1999	717	752	7,887	9,392	1,734	1,799	2,92,302	2,75,999
2000	734	765	10,525	11,651	1,691	1,706	5,01,554	4,18,725
2001	724	770	11,329	13,732	1,711	1,730	7,69,939	6,11,488
2002	707	716	11,442	13,621	1,835	1,677	1,001,579	8,00,197
2003	690	727	12,430	15,207	1,797	1,645	1,235,124	1,021,166
2004	676	–	13,832	–	2,051	1,591	1,483,120	1,326,285
2005	656	–	15,172	–	1,596	1,651	1,701,297	1,461,056

Sources: For Hungary: National Tax Authority and KSH 2007; for Romania: State Ownership Fund and National Institute of Statistics 2006.

Note: The employment numbers in the Hungarian yearbook for 1986–2001 are the average number of persons employed in total industry adjusted using the percentage of manufacturing employment in total industry in 1992. The data are derived from the annual institutional labor statistics survey. The 1992–2005 yearbook numbers are taken from subnational institutional labor statistics surveys and cover full-time employees in manufacturing. Yearbook employment covers firms with more than 20 employees in 1986–93, more than 10 employees in 1994–99, and more than 4 employees in 2000–05. Yearbook output covers firms with more than 20 employees in 1986–95, more than 10 employees in 1996–98, and more than 5 employees in 1999–2005. The Romanian yearbook numbers cover the manufacturing industry. – = Not available.

1989 and 1992 to 2005 for Ukrainian manufacturing, and 1999 to 2005 for Ukrainian services. The Russian registries are supposed to include all industrial firms with over 100 employees, as well as firms in which the state or legal entities that are themselves included in the registry own a share greater than 25 percent. In practice, it appears that, once firms enter the registries, they continue to report even if these conditions no longer hold. The 1992–98 Ukrainian registries cover all industrial firms producing at least one unit of output, where a unit is defined differently depending on the product. All legal entities outside the budgetary and financial sectors are included in the 1999–2005 registries. The pre-1992 Russian data and pre-1989 Ukrainian data do not include firms in the military-industrial complex. As shown in table 3.A4, the Ukrainian coverage is fairly complete except in 1989 (69 percent of employment). The Russian data cover nearly all activities

TABLE 3.A4

Coverage of the Russian Federation and Ukrainian Samples

	Russian Federation				Ukraine			
Year	Yearbook employment (1,000s)	Database employment (1,000s)	Yearbook output (million rubles)	Database output (million rubles)	Yearbook employment (1,000s)	Database employment (1,000s)	Yearbook output (1,000s UAH)	Database sales (1,000s UAH)
1985	16,950	16,019	0.43	0.344	–	–	–	–
1986	16,959	16,283	0.449	0.353	–	–	–	–
1987	16,856	16,504	0.465	0.38	–	–	–	–
1988	16,430	16,015	0.482	0.392	–	–	–	–
1989	15,949	15,165	0.49	0.392	7,288	5,044	162	98
1990	15,411	14,201	0.538	0.386	–	–	–	–
1991	20,117	19,347	1.3	1.064	–	–	–	–
1992	20,020	19,189	18.5	18.471	6,515	5,603	5,800	5,624
1993	18,864	18,706	129	129	6,012	5,642	160,100	166,045
1994	17,440	17,094	384	358	5,477	5,180	1,203,000	1,222,071
1995	16,006	14,314	1,108	983	5,035	4,907	5,882,400	5,276,831
1996	14,934	13,064	1,469	1,254	4,642	4,421	73,321,000	67,709,114
1997	14,009	11,621	1,626	1,394	4,273	4,688	75,061,000	68,344,160
1998	13,173	10,792	1,707	1,374	4,142	4,571	82,889,000	77,285,833
1999	13,077	9,322	3,150	2,551	3,932	4,217	1.08E+08	161,005,787
2000	13,294	9,703	4,763	3,762	4,064	4,396	1.44E+08	186,874,508
2001	13,282	9,699	5,881	4,472	3,811	4,004	1.84E+08	242,849,928
2002	12,886	9,955	6,868	5,166	3,578	3,853	2.03E+08	267,114,228
2003	12,384	9,157	8,498	6,390	3,416	3,550	2.6E+08	296,736,341
2004	11,977	8,765	11,209	8,596	3,941	3,478	4.01E+08	416,359,631
2005	11,563	–	13,634	–	–	3,794	4.69E+08	496,385,700

Sources: For the Russian Federation: data of the Federal State Statistics Service 2006; for Ukraine: data of the State Statistical Committee 2005.

Note: The numbers on both countries are for total industry. Because the Russian database does not include military industry employment in 1985–90, the Russian yearbook numbers for those years have been adjusted using the percentage of civilian employment and output in the total in the database in 1992. The Ukrainian database does not include military employment in 1989 either, but it is not possible to identify military firms in the database reliably in any year. The employment numbers do not include self-employed persons, with the exception of 2004 in Ukraine. The Russian yearbook numbers include the industrial divisions of nonindustrial firms. – = Not available. UAH is the ISO code for the Ukranian hryvnia.

through 1994; the coverage has declined to about 75 percent in more recent years as the de novo sector has grown.

Some truncation has been necessary to make the samples comparable across countries. The tobacco industry (NACE 16) is excluded because of insufficient observations in Hungary and Romania, and the recycling industry (NACE 37) has been removed because of noncomparability with the classification system used in Russia and Ukraine until recently. Firms in the top and bottom 1 percent of either the labor productivity distribution or the annual labor productivity growth distribution are dropped, so that outliers do not drive the results.[2]

Ideally, one would prefer to use sectors disaggregated to the level of product markets so as to compare firms only to their competitors. However, since the productivity decompositions rely on deviations from the sectoral average, it is important to have sufficient numbers of firms in each sector to ensure reliable estimates. As a compromise, sectors are divided at the 2-digit NACE level. Some 2-digit NACE sectors have been combined in cases where a single 2-digit NACE sector would show few observations in one or more countries.[3]

These data have been cleaned extensively to remove inconsistencies and to improve missing longitudinal links because of changes in firm identifiers from one year to the next (associated with reorganizations and changes of legal status, for instance). The inconsistencies have been evaluated using information from multiple sources (including not only separate data providers, but also previous-year information available in Romanian balance sheets and Russian and Ukrainian registries). The longitudinal links have been improved using all available information, including industry, region, size, multiple sources for the same financial variables, and some exact linking variables (for example, firm names and addresses in all countries except Georgia and Hungary, where this information was not available) to match firms that exited from the database in a given year and firms that entered during the following year. For Hungary, a database with direct information on longitudinal links has also been used: if a firm changed its identification number for some reason (and it appeared in the data as a new entry or an exit), the database indicated whether the firm had a predecessor or successor and, if so, that firm's identification number. Variables have also been computed so as to attain maximum comparability; the precise definitions are reported in table 3.A5.

To eliminate spurious exits and entries, we have omitted employment changes associated with firms that exit and then reenter. In Russia and Ukraine, firms in regions completely missing in the data

TABLE 3.A5

Definitions of Variables

Variable	Georgia	Hungary	Romania	Russian Federation	Ukraine
Employment	Average number of registered employees	Average number of registered employees	Average number of registered employees	The average number of registered industrial production personnel (including both production and nonproduction workers, but excluding nonindustrial personnel chiefly involved in providing employee benefits) in year t. The concept includes the full-time equivalent number of part-time workers registered at another firm (*sovmestiteli*).	The average number of registered employees
Output and sales	Sales include sales of produced goods and sales of commodities during year t, deflated by a yearly producer price index.	Sales revenue of purchased and produced products relating to the main activity of the firm, net of value added tax, deflated by producer price index at the 2-digit ISIC.	Sales include sales of produced goods and sales of commodities during year t, deflated by implicit deflators calculated by dividing the growth in nominal output at the 2-digit NACE level by a growth in the physical volume index.	The value of gross output produced in year t, net of value added tax and excise taxes, expressed in constant prices. The nominal values were deflated using implicit deflators calculated by dividing the growth in nominal output at the 3-digit All-Russia Classification of Branches of the Economy level by a growth in the physical volume index.	The value of gross output produced in year t, net of value added tax and excise taxes, expressed in constant prices. The nominal values were deflated using implicit deflators calculated by dividing the growth in nominal output at a 10-sector disaggregation by a growth in the physical volume index.
Labor productivity	Value of real sales divided by employment	Value of real sales divided by employment	Value of real sales divided by employment	Value of real sales divided by employment	Value of real sales divided by employment
New firm	Not available	Entered the data in 1990 or later and never fully or partially state-owned on the basis of exact ownership shares.	Never fully or partially state-owned on the basis of exact ownership . shares	Entered the data in 1993 or later and never fully or partially state-owned	Entered the data in 1993 or later and never fully or partially state-owned

(*Continues on the following page.*)

TABLE 3.A5 (*continued*)

Definitions of Variables

Variable	Georgia	Hungary	Romania	Russian Federation	Ukraine
Old firm	Not available	Partially or fully state-owned in at least one year in the data or is in the data prior to 1990	Partially or fully state-owned in at least one year in the data.	Partially or fully state-owned in at least one year in the data or is in the data prior to 1992	Partially or fully state owned in at least one year in the data or in the data prior to 1992
Foreign-owned	Not available	The firm is majority private, and foreign owner shareholding is larger than the domestic shareholding.	The majority of the firm's shares are owned by foreign investors.	Foreign or joint venture ownership code	Greater than 48 percent foreign share, or foreign code in 2001 or later
Domestically owned	The majority of the firm's shares are owned by private investors (includes both domestic and foreign private ownership).	The firm is majority private, and domestic owner shareholding is larger than foreign shareholding.	The firm is majority private, and foreign is less than majority.	100% private or mixed private and state ownership code	48 percent or lower foreign share, no foreign code, greater than 50 percent private share in State Ownership Fund database or nonstate code in 2001 or later

Source: Compiled by authors.

in one of two adjacent years and firms in industries with implausibly high entry or exit rates in that year (suggesting a change in sample coverage) have been excluded. Entries and exits associated with firms that were members of Soviet-era production associations or that belong to multiestablishment firms have also been excluded in Russia.[4]

B. Policy Drivers of Firm Productivity Growth

TFP Growth Estimation

Data

For the estimation of TFP in the manufacturing sector, the analysis relies on the May 2006 edition of the Amadeus Database and a sample that covers over 67,000 manufacturing firms (NACE 15–36) in eight countries of the Region (Bulgaria, Croatia, the Czech Republic, Estonia, Poland, Romania, Serbia, and Ukraine) from 1998 through 2004 (table 3.B1). TFP is estimated through the semiparametric estimation technique developed by Levinsohn and Petrin (2003). Operating revenues, tangible fixed assets, and material costs are deflated using country-level GDP deflators to express values in 2001 U.S. dollars. Data cleaning procedures include the following steps:

- Firms that are inactive, dissolved, in bankruptcy, or in liquidation have been dropped.
- Observations including data from consolidated accounts have been dropped.
- Observations including a positive number of subsidiaries have been dropped.

TABLE 3.B1

Descriptive Statistics of Log TFP Growth Estimates, 2001–04

Country	Firms	Mean	Standard deviation	Minimum	Maximum
Bulgaria	974	0.241	0.6	–3.4	4.1
Croatia	1,919	0.097	0.2	–1.2	2.7
Czech Republic	1,197	0.131	0.4	–1.4	2.6
Estonia	1,431	0.143	0.3	–1.5	1.7
Poland	1,227	0.092	0.5	–3.8	3.0
Romania	15,177	0.015	0.4	–3.0	3.3
Serbia	2,566	0.312	0.8	–2.8	4.7
Ukraine	1,939	0.102	0.6	–3.0	3.8
All countries	26,430	0.080	0.5	–3.8	4.7

Source: Compiled by authors.

- Observations involving less than two employees have been dropped.
- Observations involving negative tangible fixed assets and material costs have been dropped.
- Observations involving ratios greater than 1 between material and output or cost of employees and output have been dropped.
- Industry modifications: (a) Observations in 2-digit NACE 16 industries (tobacco products) have been dropped from the sample because there are no observations on the Croatia, Czech Republic, Estonia, Serbia, and Ukraine samples. Observations in NACE 2-digit 23 industries (coke, refined petroleum products, and nuclear fuel) have been dropped from the sample because there are no observations on the Bulgaria, Croatia, Czech Republic, Estonia, Poland, Serbia, and Ukraine samples.
- After the implementation of steps 1 through 7, observations with values for the ratios of output to labor, tangible fixed assets to labor, material costs to labor, material to output, and the cost of employees to output or TFP that are greater (less) than three times the interquartile range from the upper (lower) quartile in the corresponding 2-digit industry, country, and year are considered outliers and have been dropped.

Model: Baseline Regression

To investigate correlates of firm productivity, we regress the productivity of manufacturing firms on a set of core firm characteristics, as follows:

$$\ln TFP_{i,t} = \alpha + \sum_{n} \varphi_n X^n_{i,t} + \varepsilon_{i,t} \qquad \text{(c3)}$$

where $TFP_{i,t}$ is the TFP of firm *i* operating at time *t*, which is calculated according to the semiparametric estimation technique developed by Levinsohn and Petrin (2003), and $X^n_{i,t}$ is a vector of *n* firm characteristics. The vector includes size (that is, by definition, a small firm has 2 to 49 employees, a medium firm has 50 to 249 employees, and large firm has 250 or more employees); location in a capital city (that is, a dummy equal to 1 if the firm is located in Belgrade, Bucharest, Kyiv, Prague, Sofia, Tallinn, Warsaw, or Zagreb, and 0 otherwise); new entry (ages 0 or 1), a quadratic in age, industry, country, year; and also interactions of industry and year to account for price differences across industries and time because only national-level deflators are used (table 3.B2).

TABLE 3.B2

Baseline Regressions (Amadeus Only), 1999–2004

[Dependent Variable: ln(TFP) (Levinsohn-Petrin)]

Variable	(1)	(2)	(3)	(4)
Medium (50–249 employees)	0.398***	0.272***	0.248***	0.248***
	(0.013)	(0.012)	(0.010)	(0.010)
Large (250 or more employees)	0.726***	0.527***	0.497***	0.498***
	(0.027)	(0.023)	(0.022)	(0.022)
Located in capital city	0.417***	0.384***	0.174***	0.173***
	(0.014)	(0.012)	(0.010)	(0.010)
Age	0.007***	–0.003***	–0.001**	–0.001**
	(0.001)	(0.001)	(0.001)	(0.001)
Age squared/1,000	–0.003***	0.002***	0.001***	0.001***
	0.0000	0.0000	0.0000	0.0000
New (age 0–1)	–0.150***	–0.012***	–0.036***	–0.033***
	(0.010)	(0.008)	(0.007)	(0.007)
Constant	1.963***	2.083***	1.600***	1.323***
	(0.009)	(0.037)	(0.042)	(0.042)
Year dummies	Yes	Yes	Yes	Yes
Country dummies	No	Yes	Yes	Yes
Industry dummies	No	No	Yes	Yes
Year* industry interactions	No	No	No	Yes
Observations	202,285	202,285	202,285	202,285
Number of firms	57,774	57,774	57,774	57,774
Adjusted R^2	0.084	0.345	0.494	0.503

Sources: Author compilation; Amadeus Database 2006.

Note: The dependent variable is ln(TFP) calculated according to the technique of Levinsohn and Petrin (2003). Standard errors adjusted for clustering on firms are noted in parentheses. The countries are Bulgaria, Croatia, the Czech Republic, Estonia, Poland, Romania, Serbia, and Ukraine. The industry dummies are defined at the 2-digit NACE level for manufacturing (15–36).

*** Significant at 1 percent. ** Significant at 5 percent. * Significant at 10 percent.

BEEPS Regressions

Data

The econometric analysis of firm-level TFP growth and changes in the business environment uses a first-differences equation in firm characteristics with two-year changes. It requires a panel of manufacturing firms from the Amadeus Database with complete information on production function variables for 2001 through 2004, the period corresponding to the BEEPS rounds of 2002 and 2005. Specifically, output, labor, material inputs, and capital are given by the operating revenues, number of employees, material costs, and tangible fixed assets of firms in the Amadeus Database. Consequently, observations that are missing values in only one of these four production function variables must be dropped from the sample. Because of these data requirements, sufficient information exists in the Amadeus Database to estimate TFP for manufacturing firms in eight countries: Bulgaria, Croatia, the Czech Republic, Estonia, Poland, Romania, Serbia, and Ukraine.

BEEPS respondents were asked questions on business operations occurring in the previous year; BEEPS 2002 and 2005 data are therefore assumed to capture the characteristics of the business environment in 2001 and 2003, respectively, in order to fit the first-difference model with two-year changes in firm productivity regressed on lagged two-year changes in the business environment. BEEPS 2002 and 2005 data are match merged with Amadeus 2002 and 2004 observations, respectively, on country, sector, subnational location, and firm size. In particular, averages of variables from the BEEPS Database are first calculated for groups defined by country, subnational location, and firm size in each respective year using only the responses of manufacturing firms (NACE 15–36). There are three subnational location categories: capital city, large city (defined as a city that is not the capital and that has a population of 250,000 or more), and small city (defined as a city that is not the capital and that has a population of less than 250,000). There are also two firm size categories: small (defined as employing 2 to 49 full-time workers) and large (defined as employing 50 or more full-time workers). These country-location-size-year averages of BEEPS variables for the manufacturing sector are then match merged to each Amadeus observation on the identical set of variables. Thus, the average number of days in 2001 that large-size manufacturing firms located in small cities in Bulgaria experienced power outages or surges from the public grid is first calculated from the BEEPS 2002 database, and then this value is assigned to all observations in the 2002 Amadeus sample that operate in the manufacturing sector, employ 50 or more full-time workers, and are located in cities in Bulgaria with populations below 250,000.

The final sample that will be used for the econometric analysis of the effect of changes in the business environment on firm-level TFP growth over 2001–04 consists of 22,004 manufacturing firms in eight countries: Bulgaria, Croatia, the Czech Republic, Estonia, Poland, Romania, Serbia, and Ukraine. The distribution of the merged Amadeus-BEEPS balanced panel data set by country is as follows: Bulgaria, 221; Croatia, 1,780; the Czech Republic, 964; Estonia, 1,253; Poland, 1,133; Romania, 12,576; Serbia, 2,237; and Ukraine, 1,840. The inclusion criteria create the most comparable sample of firms across countries. Note, however, that strong conclusions at the international level cannot be derived from direct cross-country comparisons because the data requirements for the estimation of TFP result in varying sample attrition across countries, leading to nonrepresentative country samples. Nonetheless, even though sample biases may exist between countries, the basic test in this study examines within-industry differences across countries and will not be affected unless there are systematic biases in location-size-year groups within industries in each country.

Estimation Methodology

The analysis uses the cross-cell (defined by country, subnational location, and firm size) variation in the changes in the business environment variables to determine the effect on firm-level productivity. Estimated using ordinary least squares with White correction for heteroskedasticity, the full regression model is a first-differenced equation in firm characteristics with two-year changes; the main regressors of interest are lagged two-year changes in business environment indicators. It is formally specified as follows:

$$\begin{aligned}\Delta \ln TFP_{ijt} = {} & \alpha + \beta_1 \Delta infrastructure_{t-1}^{s,l,c} + \beta_2 \Delta finance_{t-1}^{s,l,c} \\ & + \beta_3 \Delta governance_{t-1}^{s,l,c} + \beta_4 \Delta labor\_market_{t-1}^{s,l,c} \\ & + \beta_5 \Delta labor\_quality_{t-1}^{s,l,c} + \beta_6 \Delta competition_{t-1}^{m,c} \\ & + \Delta \ln TFP_{i,t-1} + \sum_n \phi_n \Delta Z_{i,t}^n + \sum_m \xi industry_m \\ & + \sum_l \lambda location_l + \sum_c \gamma country_c + \varepsilon_{i,t} \end{aligned} \tag{c4}$$

where $\Delta \ln TFP_{i,t}$ is the change in the logarithm of TFP of manufacturing establishment i from 2002 to 2004, estimated by the semiparametric estimation technique developed by Levinsohn and Petrin (2003); $\Delta infrastructure_{t-1}^{s,l,c}$, $\Delta finance_{t-1}^{s,l,c}$, $\Delta governance_{t-1}^{s,l,c}$, $\Delta labor\_market_{t-1}^{s,l,c}$, and $\Delta labor\_quality_{t-1}^{s,l,c}$ are the changes from 2001 to 2003 in respective business environment indicators for groups of firm size s, location l, and country c; $\Delta competition_{t-1}^{m,c}$ is the change in the level of competition in each industry m from 2001 to 2003 (as measured by the change in the four-firm concentration ratio defined at the 4-digit NACE level, calculated using the full Amadeus sample, and multiplied by –1 so that positive changes indicate higher levels of competition); $\Delta \ln TFP_{i,t-1}$ is the change in the logarithm of TFP from 2001 to 2003; $\Delta Z_{i,}^n$ is a vector of logarithmic changes in firm characteristics from 2002 to 2004 that include the number of employees, the value of tangible fixed assets (thousands of 2001 U.S. dollars), and cost of materials (thousands of 2001 U.S. dollars); $industry_s$ is a vector of industry dummy variables defined at the 4-digit NACE level (1510 to 3663); $location_s$ is a vector of location dummy variables, including a capital city dummy variable (equal to 1 if the firm is located in a capital city—that is, Belgrade, Bucharest, Kyiv, Prague, Sofia, Tallinn, Warsaw, or Zagreb—and 0 otherwise) and a large-city dummy variable (equal to 1 if the firm is located in a city with a population of 250,000 or more and 0 otherwise); and $COUNTRY_c$ is a vector of country dummy variables for Bulgaria, Croatia, the Czech Republic, Estonia, Poland, Romania, Serbia, and Ukraine.

The above specification of the model addresses a number of econometric concerns. First, the objective of the study is to capture the effect of changes in the business environment on the productivity growth of the average firm; the regression analysis therefore opts for a balanced panel design, pooling observations across 296 NACE industries at the 4-digit level in eight countries with data on the years 2001 through 2004.

Second, the first differencing of firm characteristics and the lagging of business environment indicators by one year mitigate additonal endogeneity between unobservable firm heterogeneity and factor input choices.

Third, the inclusion of lagged changes in TFP addresses serial correlation that is not eliminated by first differencing.

Fourth, the inclusion of location, industry, and country fixed effects controls for time trends and unobserved location-, industry-, and country-specific characteristics that might affect the correlation between productivity growth and changes in the business environment.

Fifth, merging the Amadeus and BEEPS Databases on country, sector, subnational location, firm size, and year mitigates the endogeneity between firm productivity and business environment indicators (see elsewhere above). The econometric analysis in this study treats BEEPS variables as exogenous determinants of firm productivity; however, firms may be proactive in reducing the constraints they face in the business environment, producing a simultaneity bias in the estimation exercise. For example, a well-managed firm with high productivity growth may have worked with authorities to secure a more reliable power supply or to relax hiring and firing restrictions. Statistically, a balance must be struck so that the set of variables on which the Amadeus and BEEPS Databases are merged is large enough so that the resulting average values mitigate the endogeneity problem, while retaining sufficient variation for regression analysis. To the extent that subsample groupings, as defined, are sufficiently aggregated so that individual firms are less likely to influence averages, but varied enough so that heterogeneous pockets in the business environment are reflected, then the use of year-specific averages of BEEPS indicators taken across firms in the same groups according to country, sector, subnational location, and size is a valid way to instrument out the simultaneity problem (Bastos and Nasir 2004).

Sixth, to mitigate the problems of multicollinearity in the full model regression, principal component analysis (PCA) is used to reduce the dimensionality of the BEEPS data and construct indicators that summarize various dimensions of the business environment. In the BEEPS Database, there are typically several variables that address a particular issue affecting the productivity and growth of firms. Several questions collect information, for example, on the quality of infrastructure, namely, the number of days of power outages or surges from the public grid, the number of days of insufficient water supply, and the number of days of unavailable mainline telephone service. Inclusion of two or more highly correlated explanatory variables in a regression model generally leads to difficulties in ascertaining the effects of individual factors on the dependent variable. The following section explains the construction of the five business environment indicators that are used in the study.

Business Environment Indicators: Principal Component Analysis (PCA)

Synthetic indicators are constructed using PCA on the BEEPS data set for the following five distinct aspects of the business environment: (a) infrastructure quality, (b) financial development, (c) governance, (d) labor market flexibility, and (e) labor quality. All synthetic indicators are to be given by the first principal components of the respective underlying BEEPS variables. A detailed explanation of each of the underlying BEEPS variables used in the construction of the synthetic indicators for infrastructure quality, financial development, governance, labor market flexibility, and labor quality follows. Given that principal components are used to summarize a group of variables that describe a particular aspect of the business environment, the resulting indicators are expected to be correlated with the underlying BEEPS variables. Tables 3.B3 through 3.B7 show that all five indicators are, indeed, strongly associated with the corresponding BEEPS variables.

The *infrastructure quality indicator* measures the quality in the provision of infrastructure services. Underlying variables are rescaled, as explained below, so that higher values of the indicator signify higher levels of infrastructure quality. The indicator is based on a PCA of the following three BEEPS variables:

- *power outages*: the number of days over the past 12 months that each establishment experienced power outages or surges from the public grid (multiplied by –1) (question 23)

TABLE 3.B3

Correlation of the Infrastructure Quality Indicator and Underlying BEEPS Variables

BEEPS variable	Overall			2001			2003		
	Correlation	Mean	Standard deviation	Correlation	Mean	Standard deviation	Correlation	Mean	Standard deviation
Power outages	0.720	3.7	11.5	0.739	6.2	15.3	0.686	2.7	9.4
Insufficient water supply	0.362	4.6	32.9	0.466	11.9	56.3	0.184	1.7	14.9
Unavailable mainline telephone service	0.701	1.5	10.1	0.665	3.2	17.7	0.746	0.8	3.9

Sources: Author compilation; BEEPS 2002, 2005.

TABLE 3.B4

Correlation of Financial Development Indicator and Underlying BEEPS Variables

BEEPS variable	Overall			2001			2003		
	Correlation	Mean	Standard deviation	Correlation	Mean	Standard deviation	Correlation	Mean	Standard deviation
Local private commercial banks	0.574	10.5	25.1	0.462	6.3	19.3	0.635	12.1	26.7
Foreign banks	0.468	2.8	14.2	0.617	4.8	18.4	0.344	2.0	12.1
Informal (family/ friends/money lenders)	0.701	3.6	15.4	0.654	4.1	17.2	0.730	3.5	14.7

Sources: Author compilation; BEEPS 2002, 2005.

TABLE 3.B5

Correlation of the Governance Indicator and Underlying BEEPS Variables

BEEPS variable	Overall			2001			2003		
	Correlation	Mean	Standard deviation	Correlation	Mean	Standard deviation	Correlation	Mean	Standard deviation
Bribe level (officials)	0.735	0.9	2.3	0.825	1.5	3.1	0.656	0.7	1.9
Tax compliance	0.669	90.4	17.4	0.630	89.4	19.7	0.697	90.8	16.5
Confidence in legal system	0.461	3.5	1.4	0.355	3.5	1.4	0.532	3.5	1.4

Sources: Author compilation; BEEPS 2002, 2005.

- *insufficient water supply*: the number of days over the past 12 months that each establishment experienced insufficient water supply (multiplied by –1) (question 23)
- *unavailable mainline telephone service*: the number of days over the past 12 months that each establishment experienced unavailable mainline telephone service (multiplied by –1) (question 23)

The *financial development indicator* measures the reliance of firms on various sources of finance for new fixed investments (that is,

TABLE 3.B6

Correlation of the Labor Market Flexibility Indicator and Underlying BEEPS Variables

BEEPS variable	Overall			2001			2003		
	Correlation	Mean	Standard deviation	Correlation	Mean	Standard deviation	Correlation	Mean	Standard deviation
Underemployment/ overemployment	0.680	30.2	45.9	0.616	27.0	44.4	0.718	31.4	46.4
ΔTemporary workers/ permanent workers	0.509	0.3	41.5	0.690	2.1	58.7	0.356	–0.5	32.4
Labor regulations as a constraint	0.576	2.8	1.1	0.503	2.9	1.0	0.613	2.7	1.1

Sources: Author compilation; BEEPS 2002, 2005.

TABLE 3.B7

Correlation of the Labor Quality Indicator and Underlying BEEPS Variables

BEEPS variable	Overall			2001			2003		
	Correlation	Mean	Standard deviation	Correlation	Mean	Standard deviation	Correlation	Mean	Standard deviation
Skilled workers to total employees	0.640	83.0	21.5	0.568	82.5	20.4	0.674	83.3	21.9
Time to fill vacancy for skilled worker	0.689	4.0	5.4	0.765	5.1	7.6	0.646	3.6	4.2
Labor quality as a constraint	0.517	2.8	1.1	0.482	2.9	1.0	0.536	2.8	1.1

Sources: Author compilation; BEEPS 2002, 2005.

new machinery, equipment, buildings, and land). Underlying variables are rescaled as explained below so that higher values of the indicator signify higher levels of financial development. The indicator is based on a PCA of the following three BEEPS variables:

- *local private commercial banks*: the percentage of new fixed investment financed by borrowing from local private commercial banks (question 45a)
- *foreign banks*: the percentage of new fixed investment financed by borrowing from foreign banks (question 45a)
- *informal (family/friends/moneylenders)*: the percentage of new fixed investment financed by borrowing from family or friends, moneylenders, or other informal sources (subtracted from 100 percent) (question 45a)

The *governance indicator* measures regulatory quality, the control of corruption, and judicial effectiveness in resolving business disputes. Underlying variables are rescaled as explained below so that higher values of the indicator signify higher levels of good governance. The indicator is based on a PCA of the following three BEEPS variables:

- *level of bribes*: the estimated percentage of total annual sales firms typically pay in unofficial payments or gifts to public officials (subtracted from 100 percent) (question 40)
- *tax compliance*: the responses of firms to a question about the difficulties that many firms face in fully complying with taxes and regulations and the percentage of total annual sales the typical firm in the area of business reports for tax purposes (question 43a)
- *confidence in the legal system*: the responses of firm on a six-point scale (1 = strongly disagree; 6 = strongly agree) to a question about whether the legal system upholds contract and property rights in business disputes (question 27)

The *labor market flexibility indicator* measures the efficiency of employment protection legislation and the degree to which labor markets are able to adapt to fluctuations and changes in the economy or the demands of production. Underlying variables are rescaled as explained below so that higher values of the indicator signify higher levels of labor market flexibility. The indicator is based on a PCA of the following three BEEPS variables:

- *underemployment, overemployment*: the percentage of firms that either report underemployment because of labor restrictions regarding the hiring of workers (that is, seeking and obtaining permission and so on) or report overemployment because of labor restrictions regarding the firing of workers (that is, making severance payments and so on); specifically, this dummy variable is equal to 1 if the optimal level of employment estimated by the firm is equal to or greater than 120 percent (underemployment) or equal to or less than 80 percent (overemployment) of the existing workforce; the variable is equal to 0 otherwise (question 73)
- *change in the use of temporary workers*: the change in the number of part-time and temporary workers (as a percentage of permanent full-time workers) over the last 36 months (questions 66 and 67)
- *labor regulations as a constraint*: the responses of firms on a four-point scale (1 = major obstacle; 4 = no obstacle) to the question: how problematic are labor regulations to the operation and growth of your business? (question 63)

The *labor quality indicator* measures the skill level and educational attainment of workers. Underlying variables are rescaled as explained below so that higher values of the indicator signify higher levels of labor quality. The indicator is based on a PCA of the following three BEEPS variables among firms:

- *skilled workers relative to total employees*: the percentage of permanent full-time workers that are managers, professionals, or skilled production workers (question 68)
- *time to fill vacancy*: the average number of weeks it took to fill the most recent vacancy for a manager, professional, or skilled production worker (multiplied by –1) (question 70)
- *labor quality as a constraint*: the responses of firms on a four-point scale (1 = major obstacle; 4 = no obstacle) to the question: how problematic are the skills and education of available workers in the operation and growth of your business? (question 63)

Results

The results derived from the estimation of equation (c4) clearly show a positive and statistically significant effect of improvements in six aspects of the business environment on TFP at the firm level over the period 2002 to 2004 (table 3.B8). If the changes in the PCA indicators are entered one by one, the effects are statistically significant at the 1 percent level for infrastructure quality (column 1), financial development (column 2), governance (column 3), labor market flexibility (column 4), and labor quality (column 5), and at the 5 percent level for competition (column 6). If the changes in seven aspects of the business environment enter the model jointly (column 7), the effects remain strong; changes in PCA indicators are statistically significant at the 1 percent level, with the exception of the changes in the competition indicator, which remains significant at the 5 percent level. (Tables 3.B9–3.B14 show partial correlations of individual BEEPS variables and TFP.)

TFP Growth in Downstream Manufacturing and Links with Service Reform and Competition

Data

For the estimation of TFP in the manufacturing sector, the analysis has relied on the May 2006 edition of the Amadeus Database and a sample that covers over 67,000 manufacturing firms (NACE 15–36) in eight countries in the Region (Bulgaria, Croatia, the Czech Republic, Estonia, Poland, Romania, Serbia, and Ukraine) from 1998 through 2004. For the econometric analysis of firm-level TFP growth and reform, the final sample for the analysis includes 41,935 firms. For the econometric analysis of firm-level TFP growth and competition, the final sample comprises 37,411 firms. The liberalization of service

TABLE 3.B8

TFP Growth and BEEPS Full Model Regression Results, 2001–04

	(1)	(2)	(3)	(4)	(5)	(6)	(7)
ΔInfrastructure quality $_{t-1}$	0.112***	—	—	—	—	—	0.061***
	(0.018)						(0.020)
ΔFinancial development $_{t-1}$	—	0.100***	—	—	—	—	0.064***
		(0.011)					(0.012)
ΔGovernance $_{t-1}$	—	—	0.037***	—	—	—	0.023***
			(0.006)				(0.0080)
ΔLabor market flexibility $_{t-1}$	—	—	—	0.019***	—	—	0.028***
				(0.005)			(0.010)
ΔLabor quality $_{t-1}$	—	—	—	—	0.033***	—	0.048***
					(0.007)		(0.010)
ΔCompetition $_{t-1}$	—	—	—	—	—	0.117***	0.127***
						(0.057)	(0.057)
Δln(TFP) $_{t-1}$	0.253***	0.252***	0.253***	0.255***	0.254***	0.255***	0.249***
	(0.012)	(0.012)	(0.012)	(0.012)	(0.012)	(0.012)	(0.012)
Firm characteristics	Yes	Yes	Yes	Yes	Yes	Yes	Yes
Industry dummies	Yes	Yes	Yes	Yes	Yes	Yes	Yes
Location dummies	Yes	Yes	Yes	Yes	Yes	Yes	Yes
Country dummies	Yes	Yes	Yes	Yes	Yes	Yes	Yes
Observations	22,004	22,004	22,004	22,004	22,004	22,004	22,004
Adjusted R^2	0.187	0.187	0.185	0.184	0.185	0.184	0.191

Sources: Author compilation; BEEPS 2002, 2005.

Note: The dependent variable is Δln(TFP) calculated according to the technique of Levinsohn and Petrin (2003). Firm characteristics include changes in the number of employees, the value of tangible fixed assets (thousands of 2001 U.S. dollars), and the cost of materials (thousands of 2001 U.S. dollars). The industry dummies are defined at the 4-digit NACE level (1500–3663). The location dummies include a capital-city dummy variable (equal to 1 if the firm is located in the capital city—that is, Belgrade, Bucharest, Kyiv, Prague, Sofia, Tallinn, Warsaw, or Zagreb—and 0 otherwise) and a large-city dummy variable (equal to 1 if the firm is located in a city with a population of 250,000 or greater and equal to 0 otherwise). The countries are Bulgaria, Croatia, the Czech Republic, Estonia, Poland, Romania, Serbia, and Ukraine. Robust standard errors are noted in parentheses.

*** Significant at 1 percent.

industries is captured through the indicators of policy reform (the transition indicators) published by the European Bank for Reconstruction and Development (EBRD 2004) for seven service industries: banking reform and interest rate liberalization, securities markets and nonbank financial institutions, electric power, railways, roads, telecommunications, and water and waste water. (For a detailed description of the EBRD transition indicators, see appendix 2.C.)

Estimation Methodology

Following Arnold, Javorcik, and Mattoo (2007), we have estimated the intersectoral links between services and manufacturing by weighing the extent of liberalization in the service sector by the reliance of manufacturing firms on service inputs. We do not have data on service inputs among individual firms. However, we have been able to apply information from the use tables of national input-output matrices to measure interindustry dependencies between the manufacturing sector and the service sector. The input-output matrices for countries cover different

TABLE 3.B9

Partial Correlations of BEEPS Finance Variables and TFP Growth, 2001–04

	(1)	(2)	(3)	(4)	(5)	(6)	(7)	(8)	(9)	(10)	(11)	(12)	(13)	(14)	(15)
ΔLocal private banks (%)	0.003***	—	—	—	–0.002*	0.004***	—	—	—	–0.002*	0.005***	—	—		–0.001
	(0.001)				(0.001)	(0.001)				(0.001)	(0.001)				(0.001)
ΔForeign banks (%)	—	0.017***	—	—	0.018***	—	0.017***	—	—	0.018***		0.017***	—	—	0.017***
		(0.001)			(0.001)		(0.001)			(0.001)		(0.001)			(0.001)
ΔState-owned banks/government (%)	—	—	–0.008***	—	–0.007***	—	—	–0.009***	—	–0.007***	—	—	–0.010***		–0.007***
			(0.001)		(0.002)			(0.001)		(0.002)			(0.001)		(0.002)
ΔInformal (family/friends/	—	—	—	–0.009***	–0.018***	—	—	—	–0.009***	–0.017***	—	—		–0.007***	–0.016***
moneylenders) (%)				(0.002)	(0.002)				(0.002)	(0.002)				(0.002)	(0.002)
Firm characteristics	No	No	No	No	No	No	No	No	No	No	Yes	Yes	Yes	Yes	Yes
Industry dummies	No	No	No	No	No	No	No	No	No	No	Yes	Yes	Yes	Yes	Yes
Location dummies	No	No	No	No	No	Yes	Yes	Yes	Yes	Yes	Yes	Yes	Yes	Yes	Yes
Country dummies	Yes	Yes	Yes	Yes	Yes	Yes	Yes	Yes	Yes	Yes	Yes	Yes	Yes	Yes	Yes
Observations	26,291	26,291	26,291	26,291	26,291	26,291	26,291	26,291	26,291	26,291	26,291	26,291	26,291	26,291	26,291
Adjusted R^2	0.047	0.055	0.048	0.047	0.059	0.047	0.056	0.048	0.048	0.059	0.081	0.088	0.082	0.081	0.092

Sources: Author compilation; Amadeus Database 2006; BEEPS 2002, 2005.

Note: The dependent variable is Δln(TFP) calculated according to the technique of Levinsohn and Petrin (2003). BEEPS variables are constructed as averages for respective country-sector-size groups in each year. BEEPS 2002 data have been match merged with Amadeus 2001 observations, and BEEPS 2005 data have been match merged with Amadeus 2004 observations. BEEPS observations showing values greater (less) than three times the interquartile range from the upper (lower) quartile in the corresponding country and year are considered outliers and dropped before the calculation of the country-sector-size averages. Firm characteristics include changes in the number of employees, the value of tangible fixed assets (thousands of 2001 U.S. dollars), and the cost of materials (thousands of 2001 U.S. dollars). The industry dummies are defined at the 4-digit NACE level. The location dummies include a capital-city dummy variable (equal to 1 if the firm is located in the capital city—that is, Belgrade, Bucharest, Kyiv, Prague, Sofia, Tallinn, Warsaw, or Zagreb—and 0 otherwise) and a large-city dummy variable (equal to 1 if the firm is located in a city with a population greater than 1 million and equal to 0 otherwise). The countries are Bulgaria, Croatia, the Czech Republic, Estonia, Poland, Romania, Serbia, and Ukraine. Robust standard errors are noted in parentheses.

*** Significant at 1 percent. * Significant at 10 percent.

TABLE 3.B10

Partial Correlations of BEEPS Infrastructure Variables and TFP Growth, 2001–04

	(1)	(2)	(3)
ΔPower outages (days)	–0.052***	–0.052***	–0.049***
	(0.005)	(0.005)	(0.005)
ΔInsufficient water supply (days)	–0.087	–0.095*	(0.090)
	(0.053)	(0.056)	(0.056)
ΔUnavailable mainline telephone	–0.102***	–0.098***	–0.095***
service (days)	(0.014)	(0.014)	(0.014)
Firm characteristics	No	No	Yes
Industry dummies	No	No	Yes
Location dummies	No	Yes	Yes
Country dummies	Yes	Yes	Yes
Observations	26,291	26,291	26,291
Adjusted R^2	0.061	0.061	0.092

Sources: Author compilation; Amadeus Database 2006; BEEPS 2002, 2005.

Note: See note at table 3.B9.

*** Significant at 1 percent. * Significant at 10 percent.

TABLE 3.B11

Partial Correlations of BEEPS Competition Variables and TFP Growth, 2001–04

	(1)	(2)	(3)
ΔPressure from domestic competitors (% of firms that respond "important"):			
Developing new products	0.008***	0.008***	0.007***
	(0.001)	(0.001)	(0.001)
Reducing production costs	0.003***	0.003***	0.003***
	(0.001)	(0.001)	(0.001)
ΔPressure from foreign competitors (% of firms that respond "important"):			
Developing new products	0.003**	0.002**	0.002**
	(0.001)	(0.001)	(0.001)
Reducing production costs	0.002***	0.002***	0.002***
	(0.001)	(0.001)	(0.001)
Firm characteristics	No	No	Yes
Industry dummies	No	No	Yes
Location dummies	No	Yes	Yes
Country dummies	Yes	Yes	Yes
Observations	26,291	26,291	26,291
Adjusted R^2	0.063	0.064	0.094

Sources: Author compilations; Amadeus Database 2006; BEEPS 2002, 2005.

Note: See the note at table 3.B9.

*** Significant at 1 percent. ** Significant at 5 percent.

TABLE 3.B12

Partial Correlations of BEEPS Governance Variables and TFP Growth, 2001–04

	(1)	(2)	(3)	(4)	(5)	(6)	(7)	(8)	(9)
ΔBribe incidence (% of firms)	−0.002***	—	—	−0.002***	—	—	−0.001	—	—
	(0.0005)			(0.0005)			(0.0005)		
ΔBribe level (% of sales)	—	−0.048***	—	—	−0.046***	—	—	−0.034***	—
		(0.006)			(0.006)			(0.006)	
ΔPredictability of rules and regulations (% of firms)	—	—	0.002***	—	—	0.002***	—	—	0.002***
			(0.0003)			(0.0003)			(0.0003)
Firm characteristics	No	No	No	No	No	No	Yes	Yes	Yes
Industry dummies	No	No	No	No	No	No	Yes	Yes	Yes
Location dummies	No	No	No	Yes	Yes	Yes	Yes	Yes	Yes
Country dummies	Yes	Yes	Yes	Yes	Yes	Yes	Yes	Yes	Yes
Observations	26,291	26,291	26,291	26,291	26,291	26,291	26,291	26,291	26,291
Adjusted R^2	0.047	0.048	0.047	0.047	0.049	0.048	0.080	0.081	0.081

	(10)	(11)	(12)	(13)	(14)	(15)
ΔConfident in the legal system (% of firms)	0.007***	—	0.007***	—	0.007***	—
	(0.001)		(0.001)		(0.001)	
ΔTime to resolve overdue payment (weeks)	—	−0.013***	—	−0.013***	—	−0.012***
		(0.002)		(0.002)		(0.002)
Firm characteristics	No	No	No	No	Yes	Yes
Industry dummies	No	No	No	No	Yes	Yes
Location dummies	No	No	Yes	Yes	Yes	Yes
Country dummies	Yes	Yes	Yes	Yes	Yes	Yes
Observations	26,291	26,291	26,291	26,291	26,291	26,291
Adjusted R^2	0.053	0.049	0.054	0.049	0.086	0.082

Sources: Author compilation; Amadeus Database 2006; BEEPS 2002, 2005.

Note: See the note at table 3.B9.

*** Significant at 1 percent.

TABLE 3.B13

Partial Correlations of BEEPS Labor Variables and TFP Growth, 2001–04

	(1)	(2)	(4)	(5)	(6)	(8)	(9)	(10)	(12)
ΔTime to fill vacancy for a	—	−0.015***	—	—	−0.015***	—	—	−0.020***	—
skilled worker (weeks)	—	(0.003)	—	—	(0.003)	—	—	(0.003)	—
ΔTraining incidence: skilled production workers (% of firms)	—	—	0.002***	—	—	0.002***	—	—	0.002***
			(0.001)			(0.001)	—	—	(0.001)
ΔTraining incidence: unskilled production workers (% of firms)	—	—	0.004***	—	—	0.004***	—	—	0.004***
			(0.001)			(0.001)			(0.001)
ΔTraining incidence: nonproduction workers (% of firms)	—	—	−0.006***	—	—	−0.006***	—	—	−0.005***
			(0.001)			(0.001)			(0.001)
Firm characteristics	No	No	No	No	No	No	Yes	Yes	Yes
Industry dummies	No	No	No	No	No	No	Yes	Yes	Yes
Location dummies	No	No	No	Yes	Yes	Yes	Yes	Yes	Yes
Country dummies	Yes	Yes	Yes	Yes	Yes	Yes	Yes	Yes	Yes
Observations	26,291	26,291	26,291	26,291	26,291	26,291	26,291	26,291	26,291
Adjusted R^2	0.052	0.047	0.053	0.052	0.047	0.053	0.085	0.081	0.086

Sources: Author compilation; Amadeus Database 2006; BEEPS 2002, 2005.

Note: See the note at table 3.B9.

*** Significant at 1 percent.

TABLE 3.B14

Partial Correlations of BEEPS Firm Management Variables and TFP Growth, 2001–04

	(1)	(2)	(3)	(4)	(5)	(6)
ΔReorganization (% of firms)	0.002***	—	0.002***	—	0.001***	—
	(0.000)		(0.000)		(0.0004)	
ΔCapacity utilization (%)	—	0.014***	—	0.014***	—	0.011***
		(0.002)		(0.002)		(0.002)
Firm characteristics	No	No	No	No	Yes	Yes
Industry dummies	No	No	No	No	Yes	Yes
Location dummies	No	No	Yes	Yes	Yes	Yes
Country dummies	Yes	Yes	Yes	Yes	Yes	Yes
Observations	26,291	26,291	26,291	26,291	26,291	26,291
Adjusted R^2	0.047	0.049	0.048	0.049	0.081	0.082

Sources: Author compilation; Amadeus Database 2006; BEEPS 2002, 2005.

Note: See the note at table 3.B9.

*** Significant at 1 percent.

years: Bulgaria, 2001; the Czech Republic, 2002; Estonia, 1997; Poland, 1999; and Romania, 2002. Based on the information on the relative importance of the service sector to manufacturing, we calculate the measures for manufacturing *j* of country *c* at time *t*, as follows:

$$services\_linkages^{c}_{j,t} = \sum_{k} a^{c}_{j,k} liberalization\_index^{c}_{k,t} \qquad (c5)$$

where $a^{c}_{j,k}$ is the amount of inputs sourced from service sector *k*, expressed as a fraction of the overall inputs used by manufacturing sector *j* of country *c*, and $liberalization\_Index^{c}_{k,t}$ is (a) one of the eight indexes of reform and (b) competition as measured according to the Herfindahl-Hirschman and Lerner indexes in the Amadeus Database in service sector *k* at time *t*, that is, the services link variable captures cross-effects and is obtained by multiplying the matrix of sectoral liberalization indicators for the service sector with a matrix of input-output coefficients.

To establish whether a link exists between the performance of firms and the liberalization of upstream service industries, we regress the TFP growth among manufacturing firms on the lag changes of each service link measure (table 3.B15), as follows:

$$\Delta \ln TFP_{i,t} = \nu + \delta \Delta services\_linkages^{c}_{j,t-1} + \sum_{n} \phi_n \Delta Z^{n}_{i,t} + \sum_{c} \gamma country_c + \sum_{t} \theta year_t + \omega_{i,t} \qquad (c6)$$

where $\Delta \ln TFP_{i,t}$ is the year-to-year change in the logarithm of TFP of manufacturing establishment *i* over 1999–2004 estimated by the

TABLE 3.B15

First-Difference Regressions: Downstream Manufacturing Productivity and Reform in Services, 1999–2004

	(1)	(2)	(3)	(4)	(5)	(6)	(7)	(8)	(9)
ΔServices*I-O coefficients	0.008*** (0.001)	—	—	—	—	—	—	—	—
ΔFinance*I-O coefficients	—	−4.717*** (0.314)	—	−6.401*** (0.363)	—	—	—	—	—
ΔInfrastructure*I-O coefficients	—	—	0.008*** (0.001)	0.023*** (0.001)	—	—	—	—	—
ΔElectric power*I-O coefficients	—	—	—	—	0.001*** (0.0001)	—	—	—	—
ΔRailways*I-O coefficients	—	—	—	—	—	0.006*** (0.001)	—	—	—
ΔRoads*I-O coefficients	—	—	—	—	—	—	0.008*** (0.001)	—	—
ΔTelecommunications *I-O coefficients	—	—	—	—	—	—	—	0.013*** (0.002)	—
ΔWater and wastewater *I-O coefficients	—	—	—	—	—	—	—	—	0.001*** (0.0002)
Observations	119,382	119,382	119,382	119,382	119,382	119,382	119,382	119,382	119,382
Number of firms	41,935	41,935	41,935	41,935	41,935	41,935	41,935	41,935	41,935
Overall R^2	0.242	0.244	0.242	0.245	0.242	0.242	0.242	0.242	0.242

Sources: Author compilation; Amadeus Database 2006; BEEPS 2002, 2005; EBRD data.

Note: The dependent variable is ΔTFP (see Levinsohn and Petrin 2003). Reform is measured according to weighted EBRD transition indicators. The EBRD indicators are lagged by one year. The change in the number of employees is also included in the regressions. The I-O coefficients are derived from the use tables of national input-output matrices to measure interindustry dependencies between the manufacturing sector and the service sector. The input-output matrices cover five countries, but in different years: Bulgaria, 2001; the Czech Republic, 2002; Estonia, 1997; Poland, 1999; and Romania, 2002. Robust standard errors are noted in parentheses.

*** Significant at 1 percent.

semiparametric estimation technique developed by Levinsohn and Petrin (2003); $\Delta Z_{i,t}^{n}$ is a vector of year-to-year changes in the number of employees over 1999–2004; and $COUNTRY_c$ is a vector of country dummy variables for Bulgaria, the Czech Republic, Estonia, Poland, and Romania.

Herfindahl-Hirschman indexes are lagged by one year and range from 1/N to 10,000, moving from a large amount of small firms to a single monopolistic producer (table 3.B16). N is the number of firms in the respective industry, which is defined at the 2-digit NACE level.

Note that both the concentration index and market share may often be misleading measures of competition because they are related to specific classifications of the relevant sectors. The Lerner index, which measures the market power of individual firms, is more trustworthy because it is not related to specific classifications of sectors. Under the assumption that average variable cost provides a good approximation of marginal cost, the proxy of the Lerner index for each firm may be measured as sales, minus the cost of wages and the cost of intermediate inputs, divided by sales (Griffith 2001; Disney,

TABLE 3.B16

First-Difference Regressions: Downstream Manufacturing Productivity and Upstream Service Competition, Herfindahl-Hirschman Indexes, 1999–2004

	(1)	(2)	(3)	(4)	(5)	(6)	(7)	(8)	(9)	(10)	(11)	(12)
ΔServices (40–74) HHI	−0.0022***	—	—	—	—	—	—	—	—	—	—	—
*I-O coefficients	(0.0001)											
ΔTransportation (60–62)	—	0.0048***			0.0045***	—	—	—	—	—	—	—
*I-O coefficients		(0.0002)			(0.0002)							
ΔPost and telecommunicatons	—		−0.0025***		−0.0023***	—	—	—	—	—	—	—
(64)*I-O coefficients			(0.0001)		(0.0001)							
ΔBusiness-supporting services (70–74)*	—			−0.0065***	−0.0045***	—	—	—	—	—	—	—
I-O coefficients				(0.0003)	(0.0002)							
ΔLand transport (60)	—	—	—	—	—	0.0040***	—	—	—	—	—	—
*I-O coefficients						(0.0002)						
ΔWater transport (61)	—	—	—	—	—	—	−0.0161***	—	—	—	—	—
*I-O coefficients							(0.003)					
ΔAir transport (62)	—	—	—	—	—	—	—	0.0308***	—	—	—	—
*I-O coefficients								(0.001)				
ΔReal estate activities (70)	—	—	—	—	—	—	—	—	−0.0035***	—	—	—
*I-O coefficients									(0.0002)			
ΔComputer and related (72)	—	—	—	—	—	—	—	—	—	−0.0145*	—	—
activities*I-O coefficients										(0.002)		
ΔResearch and development (73)	—	—	—	—	—	—	—	—	—	—	−0.0380***	—
*I-O coefficients											(0.002)	
ΔOther business activities (74)	—	—	—	—	—	—	—	—	—	—	—	−0.0266***
*I-O coefficients												(0.0005)
Firm characteristics	Yes	Yes	Yes	Yes	Yes	Yes	Yes	Yes	Yes	Yes	Yes	Yes
Industry dummies	Yes	Yes	Yes	Yes	Yes	Yes	Yes	Yes	Yes	Yes	Yes	Yes

(*Continues on the following page.*)

TABLE 3.B16 (*continued*)

First-Difference Regressions: Downstream Manufacturing Productivity and Upstream Service Competition, Herfindahl-Hirschman Indexes, 1999–2004

	(1)	(2)	(3)	(4)	(5)	(6)	(7)	(8)	(9)	(10)	(11)	(12)
Country dummies	Yes	Yes	Yes	Yes	Yes	Yes	Yes	Yes	Yes	Yes	Yes	Yes
Year dummies	Yes	Yes	Yes	Yes	Yes	Yes	Yes	Yes	Yes	Yes	Yes	Yes
Observations	93,881	93,881	93,881	93,881	93,881	93,881	93,329	91,559	93,881	93,881	93,881	93,881
Number of firms	37,411	37,411	37,411	37,411	37,411	37,411	37,411	36,751	37,411	37,411	37,411	37,411
Adjusted R^2	0.325	0.304	0.326	0.306	0.330	0.303	0.303	0.307	0.302	0.301	0.304	0.335

Sources: Author compilation; Amadeus Database 2006; BEEPS 2002, 2005.

Note: The dependent variable is ΔTFP (see Levinsohn and Petrin 2003). Services exclude financial intermediation (NACE 65–67) because of a lack of relevant data on Romania in the Amadeus Database. They also exclude wholesale and retail trade because of a lack of relevant data on Romania in input-output tables. Herfindahl-Hirschman indexes are lagged by one year and range from 1/N to 10,000, moving from a large amount of small firms to a single monopolistic producer. N is the number of firms in the respective market. The I-O coefficients are derived from the use tables of national input-output matrices to measure interindustry dependencies between the manufacturing sector and the service sector. The input-output matrices cover five countries, but in different years: Bulgaria, 2001; the Czech Republic, 2002; Estonia, 1997; Poland, 1999; and Romania, 2002. Firm characteristics include changes in the number of employees, the value of tangible fixed assets (thousands of 2001 U.S. dollars), and the cost of materials (thousands of 2001 U.S. dollars). Standard errors adjusted for clustering on firms are noted in parentheses.

*** Significant at 1 percent.

TABLE 3.B17

First-Difference Regressions: Downstream Manufacturing Productivity and Upstream Service Competition, Lerner Indexes, 1999–2004

	(1)	(2)	(3)	(4)	(5)	(6)	(7)	(8)	(9)	(10)	(11)	(12)
ΔServices (40–74) Herfindahl-Hirschman indexes	−1.1299***	—	—	—	—	—	—	—	—	—	—	—
*I-O coefficients	(0.2462)											
ΔTransportation (60–62)	—	13.0319***			16.0374***	—	—	—	—	—	—	—
*I-O coefficients		(1.3320)			(1.8059)							
ΔPost and telecommunicatons	—		−47.1381***		−49.8542***	—	—	—	—	—	—	—
(64)*I-O coefficients			(1.2386)		(1.2280)							
ΔBusiness-supporting services (70–74)*	—			4.6573***	7.4987***	—	—	—	—	—	—	—
I-O coefficients				(0.6941)	(0.7874)							
ΔLand transport (60)	—	—	—	—	—	12.9360***	—	—	—	—	—	—
*I-O coefficients						(1.3262)						
ΔWater transport (61)	—	—	—	—	—	—	−131.1709***	—	—	—	—	—
*I-O coefficients							(34.683)					
ΔAir transport (62)	—	—	—	—	—	—	—	367.6950***	—	—	—	—
*I-O coefficients								(21.615)				
ΔReal estate activities (70)	—	—	—	—	—	—	—	—	−6.9364***	—	—	—
*I-O coefficients									(1.5022)			
ΔComputer and related (72)	—	—	—	—	—	—	—	—	—	−6.6959*	—	—
activities*I-O coefficients										(3.891)		
ΔResearch and development (73)	—	—	—	—	—	—	—	—	—	—	44.9894***	—
*I-O coefficients											(14.994)	
ΔOther business activities (74)	—	—	—	—	—	—	—	—	—	—	—	9.7937***
*I-O coefficients												(1.2528)
Firm characteristics	Yes	Yes	Yes	Yes	Yes	Yes	Yes	Yes	Yes	Yes	Yes	Yes
Industry dummies	Yes	Yes	Yes	Yes	Yes	Yes	Yes	Yes	Yes	Yes	Yes	Yes

(*Continues on the following page.*)

TABLE 3.B17 *(continued)*

First-Difference Regressions: Downstream Manufacturing Productivity and Upstream Service Competition, Lerner Indexes, 1999–2004

	(1)	(2)	(3)	(4)	(5)	(6)	(7)	(8)	(9)	(10)	(11)	(12)
Country dummies	Yes	Yes	Yes	Yes	Yes	Yes	Yes	Yes	Yes	Yes	Yes	Yes
Year dummies	Yes	Yes	Yes	Yes	Yes	Yes	Yes	Yes	Yes	Yes	Yes	Yes
Observations	93,881	93,881	93,881	93,881	93,881	93,881	93,329	86,163	93,881	93,881	93,881	93,881
Number of firms	37,411	37,411	37,411	37,411	37,411	37,411	37,311	34,891	37,411	37,411	37,411	37,411
Adjusted R^2	0.301	0.303	0.332	0.302	0.337	0.303	0.303	0.308	0.301	0.301	0.301	0.303

Sources: Author compilation; Amadeus Database 2006; BEEPS 2002, 2005.

Note: The dependent variable is ΔTFP (see Levinsohn and Petrin 2003). Services exclude financial intermediation (NACE 65–67) because of a lack of relevant data on Romania in the Amadeus Database. They also exclude wholesale and retail trade because of a lack of relevant data on Romania in input-output tables. Lerner indexes are lagged by one year and are calculated as the quantity of operating revenue, minus the cost of employees, minus the cost of materials, divided by operating costs. The I-O coefficients are derived from the use tables of national input-output matrices to measure interindustry dependencies between the manufacturing sector and the service sector. The input-output matrices cover five countries, but in different years: Bulgaria, 2001; the Czech Republic, 2002; Estonia, 1997; Poland, 1999; and Romania, 2002. Firm characteristics include changes in the number of employees, the value of tangible fixed assets (thousands of 2001 U.S. dollars), and the cost of materials (thousands of 2001 U.S. dollars). Standard errors adjusted for clustering on firms are noted in parentheses.

*** Significant at 1 percent. * Significant at 10 percent.

Haskel, and Heden 2003; Vahter 2006). Specifically, Lerner indexes are lagged by one year and are calculated as the quantity of operating revenue, minus the cost of employees, minus the cost of materials, divided by operating costs (table 3.B17).

TFP Growth and Financial Development

Estimation Methodology

Following Rajan and Zingales (1998) and Aghion, Fally, and Scarpetta (2007), we test the predictions of our stylized model by exploiting the observed industry-size and time variations in the harmonized firm-level database through a difference-in-difference approach. The difference-in-difference approach consists in identifying an industry-specific factor that affects the way financial development or other business regulations impact on the decisions of firms to enter the market or expand their activities in the early years of firm life.

We assume that industries that depend more heavily on external financing would be more affected by a weak financial market. In particular, we use the relative dependence of external financing observed in U.S. industries as the interacting factor for the different indicators of financial development. Since the *desired* amount of external financing in each industry is not observed, we may proxy this by using the *actual* amount of funds raised externally when financial markets are sufficiently developed so as to provide firms with unconstrained access to external financing. Following Rajan and Zingales (1998), we assume that U.S. financial markets come closest to providing such access and, accordingly, take U.S. listed firms to define the industry-specific need of external finance. We therefore assess whether industries that depend more heavily on external financing are disproportionately affected by weak financial market conditions.

The advantage of the difference-in-difference approach compared to standard cross-country and cross-industry studies is that the approach allows within-country differences among industry cells to be exploited based on the interaction between country and industry characteristics. We may thus also control for country and industry effects, thereby minimizing the problems of omitted variable bias and other misspecifications.

Following the stylized model of Aghion, Fally, and Scarpetta (2007), we estimate the model:

$$\Delta \ln TFP_{i,t} = \nu + \delta \Delta FinancialDevelopment * ExternalDependence^{c}_{j,t-1} + \sum_{n} \phi_n \Delta Z^{n}_{i,t} + \sum_{c} \gamma country_c + \sum_{t} \theta \, year_t + \omega_{i,t} \qquad \text{(c7)}$$

TABLE 3.B18

Financial Development and TFP Growth, 1999–2004

ΔMarket capitalization	0.0240***
× Extfin	(0.0010)
Firm characteristics	Yes
Industry dummies	Yes
Country dummies	Yes
Year dummies	Yes
Observations	108,537
Number of firms	42,061
R^2	0.267

Sources: Author compilation; Amadeus Database 2006; BEEPS 2002, 2005.

Note: The dependent variable is ΔTFP (see Levinsohn and Petrin 2003). Changes in financial development indicators are lagged one year. Firm characteristics include changes in the number of employees, the value of tangible fixed assets (thousands of 2001 U.S. dollars), and the cost of materials (thousands of 2001 U.S. dollars). The countries are Bulgaria, Croatia, the Czech Republic, Estonia, Poland, Romania, and Ukraine. Standard errors adjusted for clustering on firms are noted in parentheses.

*** Significant at 1 percent.

where *FinancialDevelopment* is measured as the market capitalization given in the World Development Indicators Database, and *External-Dependence* is proxied by the index of dependence on external finance in the NACE code in Klapper, Laeven, and Rajan (2006). The dependent variables, $\Delta \ln TFP_{i,t}$ and $\Delta Z^{n}_{i,t}$ are as previously defined in equation (c6). $country_c$ is a vector of country dummy variables for Bulgaria, Croatia, the Czech Republic, Estonia, Poland, Romania, and Ukraine. In these specifications, we examine whether the difference in industry-size entry rates among industries with high or low dependence on external financing is smaller in countries with better financial markets. Thus, by including the interactions between our variable on financial development and the industry-specific characteristic, we may control for unobserved country-size and industry-size fixed effects.

Results

The results are summarized in table 3.B18.

TFP Growth and Country-Level Variables

Data

For the estimation of TFP growth in the manufacturing sector, the analysis relies on the May 2006 edition of the Amadeus Database and a sample that covers over 67,000 manufacturing firms (NACE 15–36) in eight countries in the Region (Bulgaria, Croatia, the Czech Republic, Estonia, Poland, Romania, Serbia, and Ukraine) from 1998 through 2004.

Estimation Methodology

To establish whether a link exists between the performance of firms and country development, we regress TFP growth of manufacturing firms on the lag changes of various country-level variables as follows:

$$\Delta \ln TFP_{i,t} = \nu + \delta \Delta N_{t-1}^{c} + \sum_{n} \phi_n \Delta Z_{i,t}^{n} + \sum_{c} \gamma country_c + \sum_{t} \theta year_t + \omega_{i,t} \quad \text{(c8)}$$

where N^c is a country-level variable capturing economic development, specifically export sophistication, import penetration rates, product market regulation, and FDI inflows (table 3.B19). The dependent variable and additional regressors are as previously defined in equation (c7).

The construction of the export sophistication measure is described in appendix 2.D.

The import penetration rate is computed as the ratio of external imports to apparent consumption in the industry (gross production output, plus imports, minus exports), where production data are taken from the UNIDO Industrial Statistics Database, and trade data are taken from UN Comtrade (table 3.B20).

Product market regulation is measured by an index that has been developed by the OECD and that illustrates broad differences in product market policies. The indicators are constructed from the perspective of regulations that have the potential to reduce the intensity of

TABLE 3.B19

Export Sophistication and TFP Growth, 1999–2004

ΔIn(Export sophistication)	0.5185***
	(0.0859)
Firm characteristics	Yes
Industry dummies	Yes
Country dummies	Yes
Year dummies	Yes
Observations	102,607
Number of firms	42,061
R^2	0.310

Sources: Author compilation; Amadeus Database 2006; BEEPS 2002, 2005.

Note: The dependent variable is ΔTFP (see Levinsohn and Petrin 2003). Export sophistication indicators are lagged one year. Firm characteristics include changes in the number of employees, the value of tangible fixed assets (thousands of 2001 U.S. dollars), and the cost of materials (thousands of 2001 U.S. dollars). The countries are Bulgaria, Croatia, the Czech Republic, Estonia, Poland, Romania, and Ukraine. Standard errors adjusted for clustering on firms are noted in parentheses.

*** Significant at 1 percent.

TABLE 3.B20

Import Penetration Rates and TFP Growth, 1999–2004

	(1)	(2)	(3)	(4)
ΔImport penetration rate of own industry	0.0004*** (0.00004)	0.0004*** (0.0001)	—	–0.0009*** (0.0002)
ΔImport penetration rates of upstream manufacturing industries*I-O coefficients	—	—	0.0007*** (0.0001)	0.0023*** (0.0004)
Country dummies	Yes	Yes	Yes	Yes
Year dummies	Yes	Yes	Yes	Yes
Observations	49,130	35,376	36,753	35,376
Number of firms	25,984	20,002	20,737	20,002
Overall R^2	0.219	0.321	0.320	0.322

Sources: Author compilation; production data: UNIDO Industrial Statistics Database 2007; trade data: UN Comtrade 2007.

Note: The dependent variable is ΔTFP (see Levinsohn and Petrin 2003). Import penetration indicators are lagged one year and are computed as the ratio of external imports to apparent consumption in the industry (gross production output, plus imports, minus exports). The change in the number of employees is also included in the regressions. Column (1): the countries are Bulgaria, Poland, Romania, Serbia, and Ukraine. Column (2): the countries are Bulgaria, Poland, and Romania. Standard errors adjusted for clustering on firms are noted in parentheses.

*** Significant at 1 percent.

competition in areas of the product market where technology and market conditions make competition viable. They summarize a large set of formal rules and regulations that have a bearing on competition in OECD countries. The product market regulation indicator ranges from 0 to 6 (from the least to the most restrictive) and are available for two years, 1998 and 2003. The product market regulation indicators from 1998 and 2003 are merged with data from the Amadeus Database from 1999 and 2004, respectively (table 3.B21).

FDI, Trade and TFP Growth

FDI inflow data for the Czech Republic and Poland are provided by the Economist Intelligence Unit's World Investment Service and are derived from the International Financial Statistics Service of the International Monetary Fund and from the United Nations Conference on Trade and Development (table 3.B22). Data are available for six broad manufacturing subsectors: food, drink, and tobacco; textile and paper; petroleum and chemicals; metal and metal products; machinery and electrical equipment; and motor vehicles and related equipment.

Data for countries' participation in global production chains are provided in UNCOMTRAD statistics. The classification of export goods that are part of the buyer-driven and producer-driven networks is based on SITC (revision 2) for 4- and 5-digit products. The buyer-driven network trade covers three sub-sectors: textiles and clothing

TABLE 3.B21

Product Market Regulation and TFP Growth, 1999–2004

ΔProduct market regulation	−1.8075***
	(0.2304)
Firm characterisitcs	Yes
Industry dummies	Yes
Observations	694
R^2	0.227

Sources: Author compilation; OECD 2007b; Amadeus Database 2006.

Note: The dependent variable is ΔTFP (see Levinsohn and Petrin 2003). Firm characteristics include changes in the number of employees, the value of tangible fixed assets (thousands of 2001 U.S. dollars), and the cost of materials (thousands of 2001 U.S. dollars). The countries are the Czech Republic and Poland. Standard errors adjusted for clustering on firms are noted in parentheses.

*** Significant at 1 percent.

TABLE 3.B22

FDI Inflows and TFP Growth, 1999–2004

Δln(FDI inflows)	0.0080***
	(0.0019)
Firm characterisitcs	Yes
Industry dummies	Yes
Country dummies	Yes
Year dummies	Yes
Observations	11,304
Number of firms	5,950
R^2	0.210

Source: Author compilation based on data of the Economist Intelligence Unit, the International Monetary Fund, and the United Nations Conference on Trade and Development.

Note: The dependent variable is ΔTFP (see Levinsohn and Petrin 2003). FDI inflows by activity are lagged two years. Firm characteristics include changes in the number of employees, the value of tangible fixed assets (thousands of 2001 U.S. dollars), and the cost of materials (thousands of 2001 U.S. dollars). The countries are the Czech Republic and Poland. Standard errors adjusted for clustering on firms are noted in parentheses.

*** Significant at 1 percent.

(SITC 65+8998+84); footwear and parts: SITC 85+6123; furniture and parts (SITC 82111, 82119, 82121, 82122, 82191, 82192, 82199). The producer-driven network trade covers two sub-sectors: automotive network (SITC 6251, 6252, 6254, 7132, 7138, 7139, 7149, 71623, 7223, 7224, 74411, 74419, 77831, 77832, 7810, 7821, 7822, 7831, 7832, 7841, 7842, 7849, 7851, 78539); and ICT network (SITC 7511, 7512, 7518, 7521, 7522, 7523, 7524, 7525, 7528, 7591, 7599, 7611, 7612, 7621, 7622, 7628, 7631, 7638, 7641, 7642, 7643, 7648, 7649, 7761, 7762, 7763, 7764, 7768). Empirical evidence of the link between participation in global production chains and TFP growth in manufacturing is presented in table 3.B28.

Interaction with ICT Taxonomies

We augment equation (c8) to investigate how policy reforms affect the productivity of ICT-producing and ICT-using firms relative to non-ICT firms. Formally, we regress TFP growth on the interaction of a variable indicating that firm *i* is located in industry *j* that either produces or uses ICT, as follows:

$$\Delta \ln TFP_{i,t} = \nu + \delta \Delta M^{c}_{j,t-1} \times ICT + \delta \Delta M^{c}_{j,t-1} + ICT_{j}$$
$$+ \sum_{n} \phi_{n} \Delta Z^{n}_{i,t} + \sum_{c} \gamma country_{c} + \sum_{t} \theta year_{t} + \omega_{i,t} \qquad \text{(c9)}$$

where ICT_j is a dummy variable equal to 1 if firm *i* is located in ICT-producing or ICT-using industry *j* (see appendix 2.D for a definition of ICT taxonomy classifications); M^c is a country-level ICT-related variable, specifically R&D investment, ICT skills, labor market rigidities, and telecommunications reform; $\Delta \ln TFP_{i,t}$ is the year-to-year changes in the logarithm of TFP of manufacturing establishment *i* over 2001–04 estimated by the semiparametric technique developed by Levinsohn and Petrin (2003); $\Delta Z^{n}_{i,t}$ is a vector of year-to-year changes in the number of employees over 2001–04; and $COUNTRY_c$ is a vector of country dummy variables for Bulgaria, the Czech Republic, Estonia, Poland, and Romania.

R&D investment is measured as a percentage of GDP and is provided by Eurostat (table 3.B23).

TABLE 3.B23

R&D and TFP Growth, 2001–04

	(1)	(2)	(3)	(4)
ΔR&D financed by industry *ICT-producing or -using industry	—	—	—	0.0026*** (0.001)
ΔR&D financed by industry	0.0022*** (0.001)	—	0.0022*** (0.001)	0.0013** (0.001)
ICT-producing or -using industry	—	0.0168*** (0.002)	0.0048*** (0.002)	0.0055*** (0.002)
Country dummies	Yes	Yes	Yes	Yes
Year dummies	Yes	Yes	Yes	Yes
Observations	97,953	97,953	97,953	97,953
Number of firms	40,128	40,128	40,128	40,128
Overall R^2	0.012	0.012	0.012	0.012

Sources: Author compilation; Amadeus Database 2006; BEEPS 2002, 2005; Eurostat data.

Note: The dependent variable is ΔTFP (see Levinsohn and Petrin 2003). Firms classified as producing in non-ICT industries are the omitted comparison group. Changes in the number of employees, the value of tangible fixed assets (thousands of 2001 U.S. dollars), and the cost of materials (thousands of 2001 U.S. dollars) are also included in the regressions. The countries are Bulgaria, the Czech Republic, Estonia, Poland, and Romania. Standard errors adjusted for clustering on firms are noted in parentheses.

*** Significant at 1 percent. ** Significant at 5 percent.

ICT skills are measured based on the share of tertiary graduates in science and technology per 1,000 population aged 20–29 and are provided by Eurostat (table 3.B24).

Labor market rigidities are proxied by the index on hiring and firing provided in the Economic Freedom of the World Database (table 3.B25). The original indicator in the database has been normalized to range from 0 to 1, where 1 is the most restrictive.

TABLE 3.B24

ICT Skills and TFP Growth, 2001–04

	(1)	(2)	(3)	(4)
ΔScience and technology graduates	—	—	—	0.0067***
*ICT producing or using industry				(0.002)
ΔScience and technology graduates	0.0069***	—	0.0069***	0.0041***
	(0.001)		(0.001)	(0.001)
ICT producing or using industry	—	0.0048***	0.0048***	–0.003
		(0.002)	(0.002)	(0.002)
Country dummies	Yes	Yes	Yes	Yes
Year dummies	Yes	Yes	Yes	Yes
Observations	97,953	97,953	97,953	97,953
Number of firms	40,128	40,128	40,128	40,128
Overall R^2	0.012	0.013	0.012	0.013

Sources: Author compilation; Amadeus Database 2006; BEEPS 2002, 2005; Eurostat data.

Note: The dependent variable is ΔTFP (see Levinsohn and Petrin 2003). Firms classified as producing in non-ICT industries are the omitted comparison group. Changes in the number of employees, the value of tangible fixed assets (thousands of 2001 U.S. dollars), and the cost of materials (thousands of 2001 U.S. dollars) are also included in the regressions. The countries are Bulgaria, the Czech Republic, Estonia, Poland, and Romania. See appendix 2.D for the definition of ICT taxonomy classifications. Standard errors adjusted for clustering on firms are noted in parentheses.

*** Significant at 1 percent.

TABLE 3.B25

Labor Market Rigidities and TFP Growth, 2001–04

	(1)	(2)	(3)	(4)
ΔHiring and firing	—	—	—	–0.1138***
*ICT-producing or -using Industry				(0.016)
ΔHiring and firing	–0.0232**	—	–0.0229**	0.016
	(0.011)		(0.011)	(0.012)
ICT-producing or -using industry	—	0.0101***	0.0102***	0.0207***
		(0.002)	(0.002)	(0.003)
Country dummies	Yes	Yes	Yes	Yes
Year dummies	Yes	Yes	Yes	Yes
Observations	64,516	64,516	64,516	64,516
Number of firms	32,830	32,830	32,830	32,830
Overall R^2	0.011	0.010	0.010	0.011

Sources: Author compilation; Amadeus Database 2006; BEEPS 2002, 2005; Economic Freedom of the World Database.

Note: The dependent variable is ΔTFP (see Levinsohn and Petrin 2003). Firms classified as producing in non-ICT industries are the omitted comparison group. Changes in the number of employees, the value of tangible fixed assets (thousands of 2001 U.S. dollars), and the cost of materials (thousands of 2001 U.S. dollars) are also included in the regressions. The countries are Bulgaria, the Czech Republic, Estonia, Poland, and Romania. See appendix 2.D for the definition of ICT taxonomy classifications. Standard errors adjusted for clustering on firms are noted in parentheses.

*** Significant at 1 percent. ** Significant at 5 percent.

Telecommunications reform is measured based on the EBRD transition indicators for telecommunications, which range from 1 to 4+ whereby:

- Little progress in commercialization and regulation is represented by 1: minimal private sector involvement and strong political interference in management decisions; low tariffs, with extensive cross-subsidization; liberalization is not envisaged even in mobile telephony and value added services.
- Modest progress in commercialization is represented by 2: corporatization of dominant operators and some separation from public sector governance, but tariffs are still politically set.
- Substantial progress in commercialization and regulation is represented by 3: telecommunications and postal services are fully separated, and cross-subsidies are reduced; there is considerable liberalization in the mobile segment and in value added services.
- Complete commercialization is represented by 4: including privatization of dominant operators and comprehensive regulatory and institutional reforms; extensive liberalization of entry.
- Effective regulation through an independent entity is represented by 4+: coherent regulatory and institutional framework is established to deal with tariffs, interconnection rules, licensing, concession fees, and spectrum allocation; there is a consumer ombudsman function.

As described in appendix 2.D, the EBRD telecommunications reform indicator is weighted by the level of the reliance of a given manufacturing industry on inputs from the service industry (table 3.B26).

Innovation and Proximity to the Frontier

Following Aghion and others (2006), we define proximity to the technological frontier for an industry *i* in a given country *c* at a given time *t* as the ratio of normalized TFP in that industry and the highest TFP in the industry at time *t* among all countries of the sample. Proximity varies from zero (for the most inefficient industries) to 1 (for the most efficient industries). We obtain estimates of the proximity to the frontier, as well as innovation rates (proxied by the BEEPS question about the percentage of firms that successfully developed a major new product line or service in the industry) in 2001–04.

Table 3.B27 reports the regression results between the speed of technological catching up (increase in the proximity to the frontier)

TABLE 3.B26

Telecommunications Reform and TFP Growth, 2001–04

	(1)	(2)	(3)	(4)
ΔTelecommunications*I-O coefficients	—	—	—	0.3798***
*ICT-producing or -using industry				(0.124)
ΔTelecommunications*I-O coefficients	0.0029	—	−0.003	(0.005)
	(0.007)		(0.006)	(0.006)
ICT-producing or -using industry	—	0.0053**	0.0053**	0.0062***
		(0.002)	(0.002)	(0.002)
Country dummies	Yes	Yes	Yes	Yes
Year dummies	Yes	Yes	Yes	Yes
Observations	77,548	77,548	77,548	77,548
Number of firms	35,253	35,253	35,253	35,253
Overall R^2	0.012	0.012	0.012	0.012

Sources: Author compilation; Amadeus Database 2006; BEEPS 2002, 2005; EBRD data.

Note: The dependent variable is ΔTFP (see Levinsohn and Petrin 2003). Firms classified as producing in non-ICT industries are the omitted comparison group. The I-O coefficients are derived from the use tables of national input-output matrices to measure interindustry dependencies between the manufacturing sector and the service sector. The input-output matrices cover five countries, but in different years: Bulgaria, 2001; the Czech Republic, 2002; Estonia, 1997; Poland, 1999; and Romania, 2002. Changes in the number of employees, the value of tangible fixed assets (thousands of 2001 U.S. dollars), and the cost of materials (thousands of 2001 U.S. dollars) are also included in the regressions. The countries are Bulgaria, the Czech Republic, Estonia, Poland, and Romania. See appendix 2.D for the definition of ICT taxonomy classifications. Standard errors adjusted for clustering on firms are noted in parentheses.

*** Significant at 1 percent. ** Significant at 5 percent.

TABLE 3.B27

Innovation and Proximity to the Frontier, 2001–04

	(1)	(2)
ΔInnovation	0.0006*	0.0004**
	(0.0003)	(0.0002)
Country dummies	No	Yes
Industry dummies	No	Yes
Observations	68	68
R^2	0.042	0.781

Sources: Author compilation; Amadeus Database 2006; BEEPS 2002, 2005.

Note: The dependent variable is ΔTFP (see Levinsohn and Petrin 2003). Innovation is measured as the percentage of firms that have successfully developed a major new product line or service. Standard errors adjusted for clustering on firms are noted in parentheses.

** Significant at 5 percent. * Significant at 10 percent.

and the number of innovators. All columns show a significant positive correlation between these two measures. These findings are consistent with the literature (Aghion and others 2006), which indicates that greater innovation increases the speed of catching up with the technological frontier.

TABLE 3.B28

TFP Growth and Annual Changes in Shares of Exports in Producer and Buyer Networks, 1999–2004

ΔShare of exports in producer network	1.006***
	(0.050)
ΔShare of exports in buyer network	1.406*"
	(0.101)
Firm characterisitcs	Yes
Industry dummies	Yes
Country dummies	Yes
Year dummies	Yes
Observations	98,976
Number of firms	43,923
R^2	0.052

Note: Dependent variable: Δ lnTFP (Levinsohn-Petrin). Standard errors adjusted for clustering on firm are denoted in parentheses.

***Significant at 1 percent. **Significant at 5 percent. * Significant at 10 percent.

Share of exports are lagged one year. Firm characteristics include changes in the number of employees, tangible fixed assets, and material cost. Countries (7 total) include: Bulgaria, Croatia, Czech Republic, Estonia, Poland, Romania, and Ukraine.

Notes

1. The units of observation in these data are firms, except for multiplant entities in which individual plants are listed as subsidiaries (*dochernye predpriyatiya* or daughter companies) in the Russian registries. Apparently most, but not all cases of multiple plants are treated in this way in Russia. The 1993 registry contains a variable indicating the number of plants, which equals 1 in 99.9 percent of the 18,121 nonmissing cases. Note also that, to avoid double counting, the consolidated records of entities with subsidiaries have been dropped from the analysis.
2. Firms in the top and bottom 1 percent of either the multifactor productivity distribution or the annual multifactor productivity growth distribution are dropped from the calculations of the multifactor productivity decompositions.
3. NACE 23 has been combined with 24, and 30 with 32; 60 and 61 have been combined with 62, and 65 and 66 with 67.
4. The reason for excluding production association entries and exits during the Soviet period and multiestablishment firm entries and exits during the transition period is that many of these firms report inconsistently in the data. In one year, a consolidated entity may appear; in the next, each of the establishments may report separately, or vice versa. These exclusion rules result in a conservative bias. Of course, some production associations may be starting new establishments or closing others down, and there may be some true entries and exits in industries with implausibly high rates and in regions that enter and exit the data set.

Bibliography

Acemoglu, Daron, Philippe Aghion, and Fabrizio Zilibotti. 2006. "Distance to Frontier, Selection, and Economic Growth." *Journal of the European Economic Association* 4 (1): 37–74.

Aghion, Philippe. 2006. "A Primer on Innovation and Growth." *Bruegel Policy Brief* 2006/06 (October), Bruegel, Brussels.

Aghion, Philippe, Nick Bloom, Richard W. Blundell, Rachel Griffith, and Peter Howitt. 2005. "Competition and Innovation: An Inverted-U Relationship." *Quarterly Journal of Economics* 120 (2): 701–28.

Aghion, Philippe, Richard W. Blundell, Rachel Griffith, Peter Howitt, and Susanne Prantl. 2006. "The Effects of Entry on Incumbent Innovation and Productivity." NBER Working Paper 12027, National Bureau of Economic Research, Washington, DC.

Aghion, Philippe, Thibault Fally, and Stefano Scarpetta. 2007. "Credit Constraints as a Barrier to the Entry and Post-Entry Growth of Firms: Lessons from Firm-Level Cross Country Panel Data." Preliminary draft of a paper prepared for the 45th Panel Meeting of *Economic Policy*, Frankfurt, April 20–21.

Alam, Asad, Mamta Murthi, Ruslan Yemtsov, Edmundo Murrugarra, Nora Dudwick, Ellen Hamilton, and Erwin Tiongson. 2005. *Growth, Poverty, and Inequality: Eastern Europe and the Former Soviet Union*. Washington, DC: Europe and Central Asia Region, World Bank.

Amadeus Database. Bureau van Dijk Electronic Publishing. http://www.bvdep.com/en/amadeus.html (accessed May 2006).

Anós Casero, Paloma, Marcin Piatkowski, and Bart van Ark. 2007. "Productivity Growth, Technology, and Structural Reforms in Transition Economies: A Two-Phase Convergence Process." Unpublished working paper, World Bank, Washington, DC.

Anós Casero, Paloma, and Charles Udomsaph. 2007. "What Drives Firm Productivity Growth in Eastern Europe and the Former Soviet Union?" Unpublished working paper, World Bank, Washington, DC.

Arellano, Manuel, and Stephen R. Bond. 1991. "Some Tests of Specification for Panel Data: Monte Carlo Evidence and an Application to Employment Equations." *Review of Economic Studies* 58 (2): 277–97.

Arnold, Jens Matthias, Aaditya Mattoo, and Gaia Narciso. 2006. "Services Inputs and Firm Productivity in Sub-Saharan Africa: Evidence from Firm-Level Data." Policy Research Working Paper 4048, World Bank, Washington, DC.

Arnold, Jens Matthias, Beata Smarzynska Javorcik, and Aaditya Mattoo. 2007. "Does Services Liberalization Benefit Manufacturing Firms? Evidence from the Czech Republic." Policy Research Working Paper 4109, World Bank, Washington, DC.

Ayyagari, Meghana, and Renáta Kosová. 2006. "Does FDI Facilitate Domestic Entrepreneurship? Evidence from the Czech Republic." George Washington University School of Business Working Paper 0008, School of Business, George Washington University, Washington, DC.

Barba Navaretti, Giorgio, Maurice Schiff, and Isidro Soloaga. 2006. "The Knowledge Content of Machines: North-South Trade and Technology Diffusion." In *Global Integration and Technology Transfer*, ed. Bernard M. Hoekman and Beata Smarzynska Javorcik, 113–38. Trade and Development Series. Washington, DC: World Bank.

Bartelsman, Eric J., John Haltiwanger, and Stefano Scarpetta. 2004. "Microeconomic Evidence of Creative Destruction in Industrial and Developing Countries." Policy Research Working Paper 3464, World Bank, Washington, DC.

———. 2005. "Measuring and Analyzing Cross-Country Differences in Firm Dynamics." Draft working paper, World Bank, Washington, DC.

Bartelsman, Eric J., Stefano Scarpetta, and Fabiano Schivardi. 2005. "Comparative Analysis of Firm Demographics and Survival: Micro-Level Evidence for the OECD Countries." *Industrial and Corporate Change* 14 (3): 365–391.

Bartelsman, Eric J., and Stefano Scarpetta. 2007. "Reallocation and Productivity in Transition and Integration Phases." Background paper, World Bank, Washington, DC.

Bastos, Fabiano, and John Nasir. 2004. "Productivity and the Investment Climate: What Matters Most?" Policy Research Working Paper 3335, World Bank, Washington, DC.

Beck, Thorsten, Asli Demirgüç-Kunt, and Ross Levine. 1999. "A New Database on Financial Development and Structure." Mimeo.

Beck, Thorsten, Ross Levine, and Norman Loayza. 2000. "Finance and the Sources of Growth." *Journal of Financial Economics* 58 (1–2): 261–300.

Becker, Gary S. 1964. *Human Capital: A Theoretical and Empirical Analysis with Special Reference to Education*. Chicago: University of Chicago Press.

BEEPS (Business Environment and Enterprise Performance Survey), European Bank for Reconstruction and Development and World Bank. http://www.ebrd.com/country/sector/econo/surveys/beeps.htm (accessed June 2007).

Ben-Ari, Guy, and Nicholas S. Vonortas. 2005. "Risk Financing for Knowledge-Based Enterprises: Mechanisms and Policy Options." Department of Economics, George Washington University, Washington, DC.

Black, Sandra E., and Lisa M. Lynch. 2001. "How to Compete: The Impact of Workplace Practices and Information Technology on Productivity." *Review of Economics and Statistics* 83 (3): 434–45.

Bojnec, Stefan, and Liesbeth Dries. 2005. "Causes of Changes in Agricultural Employment in Slovenia: Evidence from Micro-Data." *Journal of Agricultural Economics* 56 (3): 399–416.

Bosworth, Barry P., and Susan M. Collins. 2003. "The Empirics of Growth: An Update." Brookings Papers on Economic Activity, September 22, Brookings Institution, Washington, DC.

Broadman, Harry G., ed. 2005. *From Disintegration to Reintegration: Eastern Europe and the Former Soviet Union in International Trade*. Washington, DC: World Bank.

Brown, J. David, and John S. Earle. 2007. "Firm-Level Components of Aggregate Productivity Growth in ECA Economies." Background paper, World Bank, Washington, DC.

Brown, J. David, John S. Earle, and Almos Telegdy. 2007. "What Makes ECA Firms Productive? Ownership, Age, Market Structure, and Import Penetration in Georgia, Hungary, Romania, Russia, and Ukraine." Background paper, World Bank, Washington, DC.

Brynjolfsson, Erik, and Lorin M. Hitt. 2000. "Beyond Computation: Information Technology, Organizational Transformation and Business Performance." *Journal of Economic Perspectives* 14 (4): 23–48.

Calderón, César A. 2007. "Infrastructure and Productivity Growth in the ECA Region: A Macroeconomic Approach." Background paper, World Bank, Washington, DC.

Campos, Nauro F., and Fabrizio Coricelli. 2002. "Growth in Transition: What We Know, What We Don't, and What We Should." *Journal of Economic Literature* 40 (3): 793–836.

Canning, David. 1999. "Infrastructure's Contribution to Aggregate Output." Policy Research Working Paper 2246, World Bank, Washington, DC.

Caselli, Francesco, and Silvana Tenreyro. 2004. "Is Poland the Next Spain?" FRB of Boston Public Policy Discussion Paper 04–8, Federal Reserve Bank of Boston, Boston.

Chawla, Mukesh, Gordon Betcherman, and Arup Banerji. 2007. *From Red to Gray: The "Third Transition" of Aging Populations in Eastern Europe and the Former Soviet Union*. Washington, DC: World Bank.

CISStat (Interstate Statistical Committee of the Commonwealth of Independent States). 2007. *The Commonwealth of Independent States in 2006: Statistical Yearbook*. Moscow: CISStat.

CISStat Database. Interstate Statistical Committee of the Commonwealth of Independent States. http://www.cisstat.com/eng/index.htm (accessed March 2007).

Clerides, Sofronis K., Saul Lach, and James R. Tybout. 1998. "Is 'Learning by Exporting' Important? Micro-Dynamic Evidence from Colombia, Mexico, and Morocco." *Quarterly Journal of Economics* 113 (3): 903–47.

Conway, Paul, Donato de Rosa, Giuseppe Nicoletti, and Faye Steiner. 2006. "Regulation, Competition and Productivity Convergence." Economics Department Working Paper 509, Economics Department, Organisation for Economic Co-operation and Development, Paris.

Conway, Paul, Veronique Janod, and Giuseppe Nicoletti. 2005. "Product Market Regulation in OECD Countries: 1998 to 2003." Economics Department Working Paper 419, Economics Department, Organisation for Economic Co-operation and Development, Paris.

Daveri, Francesco. 2002. "The New Economy in Europe, 1992–2001." *Oxford Review of Economic Policy* 18 (3): 345–362.

De Broeck, Mark, and Vincent Koen. 2000. "The Great Contractions in Russia, the Baltics, and the Other Countries of the Former Soviet Union: A View from the Supply Side." IMF Working Paper 00/32, International Monetary Fund, Washington, DC.

Desai, Raj M., and Itzhak Goldberg, eds. 2007. *Enhancing Russia's Competitiveness and Innovative Capacity*. Washington, DC: Finance and Private Sector Development Department, Europe and Central Asia Region, World Bank.

Disney, Richard, Jonathan Haskel, and Ylva Heden. 2003. "Restructuring and Productivity Growth in UK Manufacturing." *Economic Journal* 113 (489): 666–94.

Doing Business Database. World Bank and International Finance Corporation. http://www.doingbusiness.org/ (accessed June 2007).

Dollar, David, and Aart Kraay. 2004. "Trade, Growth, and Poverty." *Economic Journal* 114 (493): F22–F49.

Dorgan, Stephen J., and John J. Dowdy. 2002. "How Good Management Raises Productivity." *The McKinsey Quarterly* 4: 14–16.

Easterly, William R., and Mirvat Sewadeh. 2002. "Global Development Network Growth Database." World Bank, Washington, DC.

EBRD (European Bank for Reconstruction and Development). 2004. *Transition Report 2004: Infrastructure*. London: EBRD.

———. 2006. *Transition Report 2006: Finance in Transition*. London: EBRD.

Economic Freedom of the World Database. Fraser Institute. http://www.freetheworld.com/ (accessed June 2007).

Eschenbach, Felix, and Bernard M. Hoekman. 2006. "Services Policies in Transition Economies: On the European Union and the World Trade Organization as Commitment Mechanisms." Policy Research Working Paper 3951, World Bank, Washington, DC.

EU KLEMS Database. European Commission. http://www.euklems.net (accessed March 2007).

Federal State Statistics Service. 2005. *Statistical Yearbook of Russia 2006*. Moscow: Information and Publishing Center "Statistics of Russia," Federal State Statistics Service.

Feenstra, Robert C., Robert E. Lipsey, Haiyan Deng, Alyson C. Ma, and Hengyong Mo. 2005. "World Trade Flows, 1962–2000." NBER Working Paper 11040, National Bureau of Economic Research, Washington, DC.

Fernandes, Ana M. 2007. "Structure and Performance of the Services Sector in Transition Economies." Policy Research Working Paper 4357, World Bank, Washington, DC.

Foster, Lucia, John Haltiwanger, and Cornell J. Krizan. 2001. "Aggregate Productivity Growth: Lessons from Microeconomic Evidence." In *New Developments in Productivity Analysis*, ed. Charles R. Hulten, Edwin R. Dean, and Michael J. Harper, 303–72. National Bureau of Economic Research Studies in Income and Wealth, vol. 63. Chicago: University of Chicago Press.

Goldberg, Itzhak, Manuel Trajtenberg, Adam Jaffe, Thomas Muller, Julie Sunderland, and Enrique Blanco Armas. 2006. "Public Financial Support for Commercial Innovation." Chief Economist's Regional Working Paper 1 (1). Europe and Central Asia Knowledge Economy Study Series. World Bank, Washington, DC.

Greenan, Nathalie, and Dominique Guellec. 1998. "Firm Organization, Technology and Performance: An Empirical Study." *Economics of Innovation and New Technology* 6 (4): 313–47.

Grey, Cheryl W., Tracey M. Lane, and Aristomene Varoudakis, eds. 2007. *Fiscal Policy and Economic Growth: Lessons for Eastern Europe and Central Asia*. Washington, DC: World Bank.

Griffith, Rachel. 2001. "Product Market Competition, Efficiency, and Agency Costs: An Empirical Analysis." IFS Working Paper W01/12, Institute for Fiscal Studies, London.

Griliches, Zvi. 1988. "Productivity Puzzles and R&D: Another Nonexplanation." *Journal of Economic Perspectives* 2 (4): 9–21.

Hall, Robert, and Charles Jones. 1999. "Why Do Some Countries Produce So Much More Output Per Worker Than Others?" *Quarterly Journal of Economics* 114 (1): 83–116.

Hallward-Driemeier, Mary, Giuseppe Iarossi, and Kenneth L. Sokoloff. 2002. "Exports and Manufacturing Productivity in East Asia: A Comparative Analysis with Firm-Level Data." NBER Working Paper 8894, National Bureau of Economic Research, Washington, DC.

Haltiwanger, John, Adriana Kugler, Maurice Kugler, Alejandro Micco, and Carmen Pagés. 2004. "Effects of Tariffs and Real Exchange Rates on Job Reallocation: Evidence from Latin America." Working Paper, August 27, Inter-American Development Bank, Washington, DC.

Hausmann, Ricardo, Jason Hwang, and Dani Rodrik. 2006. "What You Export Matters." Draft, April, Center for International Development, Kennedy School of Government, Harvard University, Cambridge, MA.

Hausmann, Ricardo, and Bailey Klinger. 2006. "Structural Transformation and Patterns of Comparative Advantage in the Product Space." KSG Working

Paper RWP06-041, Center for International Development, Kennedy School of Government, Harvard University, Cambridge, MA.

Hempell, Thomas. 2005. "What's Spurious? What's Real? Measuring the Productivity Impacts of ICT at the Firm Level." *Empirical Economics* 30 (2): 427–64.

Hoekman, Bernard M., and Beata Smarzynska Javorcik, ed. 2006. *Global Integration and Technology Transfer*. Trade and Development Series. Washington, DC: World Bank.

ICRG (various). *International Country Risk Guide*.

IFS (Institute for Fiscal Studies). London.

ILO (International Labour Organization). 2006. *Yearbook of Labour Statistics 2006*. 2 vols. Geneva: Bureau of Statistics, ILO.

IMF (International Monetary Fund). 2007. *World Economic Outlook 2007: Globalization and Inequality*. Washington, DC: IMF.

International Financial Statistics Database. Statistics Department, International Monetary Fund. http://www.imfstatistics.org/imf/logon.aspx (accessed June 2007).

IRF (International Road Federation). *World Road Statistics*. Geneva: IRF.

ITU (International Telecommunications Union). Various years. *World Telecommunication Development Report*. Geneva: ITU.

Javorcik, Beata Smarzynska. 2004. "Does Foreign Direct Investment Increase the Productivity of Domestic Firms? In Search of Spillovers through Backward Linkages." *American Economic Review* 94 (3): 605–27.

Jorgenson, Dale W. 2004. "Information Technology and the G7 Economies." *World Economics Journal* 4 (4): 139–69.

Jorgenson, Dale W., and Zvi Griliches. 1967. "The Explanation of Productivity Change." *Review of Economic Studies* 34 (99): 249–280.

Jorgenson, Dale W., Mun S. Ho, and Kevin J. Stiroh. 2002. "Information Technology, Education, and the Sources of Economic Growth across U.S. Industries." Unpublished working paper, Federal Reserve Bank, New York.

Jorgenson, Dale W., and Khuong Vu. 2005. "Information Technology and the World Economy." *Scandinavian Journal of Economics* 107 (4): 631–50.

Kaufmann, Daniel, Aart Kraay, and Massimo Mastruzzi. 2005. "Governance Matters IV: Governance Indicators for 1996–2004." Policy Research Working Paper 3630, World Bank, Washington, DC.

King, Robert G., and Ross Levine. 1993. "Finance and Growth: Schumpeter Might Be Right." Policy Research Working Paper 1083, World Bank, Washington, DC.

Klapper, Leora, Luc Laeven, and Raghuram G. Rajan. 2006. "Entry Regulation as a Barrier to Entrepreneurship." *Journal of Financial Economics* 82 (3): 591–629.

Klenow, Peter J., and Andrés Rodríguez-Clare. 1997. "The Neoclassical Revival in Growth Economics: Has It Gone Too Far?" *NBER Macroeconomics Annual*, ed. B. Bernanke and J. Rotemberg, 12: 73–114. Cambridge, MA: MIT Press.

Klinger, Bailey. 2007a. "Product Space and Export Sophistication in ECA." Background note, Center for International Development, Kennedy School of Government, Harvard University, Cambridge, MA.

———. 2007b. "Export Sophistication and Structural Transformation in ECA Countries." Background note, Center for International Development, Kennedy School of Government, Harvard University, Cambridge, MA.

Klinger, Bailey, and Daniel Lederman. 2006. "Diversification, Innovation, and Imitation Inside the Global Technological Frontier." Policy Research Working Paper 3872, World Bank, Washington, DC.

KSH (Central Statistical Office). 2007. *Hungary, 2006*. Budapest: Central Statistical Office.

Leamer, Edward E. 1984. *Sources of Comparative Advantage: Theory and Evidence*. Cambridge, MA: MIT Press.

Lenain, Patrick, and Lukasz Rawdanowicz. 2004. "Enhancing Income Convergence in Central Europe after EU Accession." Economics Department Working Paper 392, Economics Department, Organisation for Economic Co-operation and Development, Paris.

Lerman, Zvi. 2007. "Agriculture Productivity in CIS Countries." Background paper, World Bank, Washington, DC.

Levine, Ross, and Sara Zervos. 1998. "Stock Markets, Banks, and Economic Growth." *American Economic Review* 88 (3): 537–58.

Levinsohn, James, and Amil Petrin. 2003. "Estimating Production Functions Using Inputs to Control for Unobservables." *Review of Economic Studies* 70 (2): 317–41.

National Institute of Statistics. 2006. *Statistical Yearbook 2005*. Bucharest: National Institute of Statistics.

OECD (Organisation for Economic Co-operation and Development). 2001. *Measuring Productivity, OECD Manual: Measurement of Aggregate and Industry-Level Productivity Growth*. Industry, Services and Trade Series 2001 (26): 1–156. Paris: OECD.

———. 2004. *Understanding Economic Growth: A Macro-Level, Industry-Level, and Firm-Level Perspective*. General Economics and Future Studies Series. Paris: OECD.

———. 2005. *Micro-Policies for Growth and Productivity*. Paris: OECD.

———. 2006. *OECD Compendium of Productivity Indicators*. Economics Department. Paris: OECD.

———. 2007a. *Economic Policy Reforms: Going for Growth*. Economics Department. Paris: OECD.

———. 2007b. "Indicators of Product Market Regulation Homepage." Economics Department. Paris: OECD.

Oliner, Stephen D., and Daniel E. Sichel. 2000. "Information Technology and Productivity: Where Are We Now and Where Are We Going?" Unpublished working paper, Board of Governors of the Federal Reserve System, Washington, DC.

O'Mahony, Mary, and Bart van Ark, eds. 2003. *EU Productivity and Competitiveness: An Industry Perspective; Can Europe Resume the Catching-Up Process?* Luxembourg: Office for Official Publications of the European Communities, Luxembourg.

O'Mahony, Mary, and Michela Vecchi. 2002. "Do Intangible Investments Affect Companies' Productivity Performance?" NIESR Discussion Paper 201, National Institute of Economic and Social Research, London.

Oomes, Nienke, and Oksana Dynnikova. 2006. "The Utilization-Adjusted Output Gap: Is the Russian Economy Overheating?" IMF Working Papers 06/68, International Monetary Fund, Washington, DC.

Perminov, Sergey, and Elena Egorova. 2005. "ICT Impact on Labor Productivity and Employment in Russia." TIGER Working Paper 73, Transformation, Integration and Globalization Economic Research, Warsaw.

Piatkowski, Marcin. 2004. "Does ICT Investment Matter for Growth and Labor Productivity in Transition Economies?" Development and Comp Systems 0402008. EconWPA. http://129.3.20.41/.

Piatkowski, Marcin, and Bart van Ark. 2007. "Productivity Growth, Technology, and Structural Reforms in Transition Economies: A Two-Phase Convergence Process." Draft chapter, Knowledge and Innovation Institute, Warsaw.

PRS Group. Various issues. *International Country Risk Guide*. Monthly, PRS Group, East Syracuse, NY. http://www.prsgroup.com/ICRG.aspx.

Raiser, Martin, Mark E. Schaffer, and Johannes Schuchhardt. 2006. "Benchmarking Structural Change in Transition." World Bank, Washington, DC.

Rajan, Raghuram G., and Luigi Zingales. 1998. "Financial Dependence and Growth." *American Economic Review* 88 (3): 559–86.

Röller, Lars-Hendrik, and Len Waverman. 2001. "Impact of Telecommunications Infrastructure on Economic Growth and Development." *American Economic Review* 91 (4): 909–23.

Russian Economic Barometer Survey Database. Institute of World Economy and International Relations. http://www.imemo.ru/en/period/barom/ (accessed December 2006 and March 2007).

Rutkowski, Jan J., and Stefano Scarpetta. 2005. *Enhancing Job Opportunities: Eastern Europe and the Former Soviet Union*. Washington, DC: World Bank.

Schadler, Susan, Ashoka Mody, Abdul Abiad, and Daniel Leigh. 2006. "Growth in the Central and Eastern European Countries of the European Union." IMF Occasional Paper 252, International Monetary Fund, Washington, DC.

Schumpeter, Joseph Alois. 1911. *Theorie der wirtschaftlichen Entwicklung*. Leipzig: Duncker and Humblot.

Solow, Robert. 1957. "Technical Change and the Aggregate Production Function." *Review of Economics and Statistics* 39: 312–320.

State Statistical Committee of Ukraine. 2005. *Statistical Yearbook of Ukraine 2004*. Kyiv: State Statistical Committee of Ukraine.

Statistics Georgia. 2005. *Statistical Yearbook of Georgia*. Tbilisi, Georgia: Department of Statistics, Ministry of Economic Development.

Swinnen, Johan F. M., and Liesbet Vranken. 2007a. "Patterns of Land Market Developments in Transition." LICOS Discussion Paper 17907, Centre for

Institutions and Economic Performance, Katholieke Universiteit Leuven, Leuven, Belgium.

———. 2007b. "Agriculture Productivity in Transition Economies." Background paper, Katholieke Universiteit Leuven, Leuven, Belgium.

Timmer, Marcel P., Mary O'Mahony, and Bart van Ark. 2007. "The EU KLEMS Growth and Productivity Accounts: An Overview." EU KLEMS Net. http://www.euklems.net/data/eu_klems_productivity_report_overview.pdf.

Timmer, Marcel P., and Adam Szirmai. 2000. "Productivity Growth in Asian Manufacturing: The Structural Bonus Hypothesis Examined." *Structural Change and Economic Dynamics* 11 (4): 371–92.

Timmer, Marcel P., and Bart van Ark. 2005. "Does Information and Communication Technology Drive EU-US Productivity Growth Differentials?" *Oxford Economic Papers* 57 (4): 693–716.

Timmer, Marcel P., Gerard Ypma, and Bart van Ark. 2005. "IT in the European Union: Driving Productivity Divergence?" Research Memorandum GD-67, Groningen Growth and Development Center, University of Groningen, Groningen, the Netherlands.

Transition Indictors Database. European Bank for Reconstruction and Development. http://www.ebrd.com/country/sector/econo/stats/index.htm (accessed June 2007).

UN (United Nations). 2005. *2002 Energy Statistics Yearbook*. New York: United Nations Statistics Division.

UN Comtrade (United Nations Commodity Trade Statistics Database). Statistics Division, United Nations. http://comtrade.un.org/ (accessed March 2007).

UNIDO Industrial Statistics Database. Research and Statistics Branch, United Nations Industrial Development Organization. http://www.unido.org/doc/3474 (accessed June 2007).

Vahter, Priit. 2006. "Productivity in Estonian Enterprises: The Role of Innovation and Competition." Bank of Estonia Working Paper 2006–07, Bank of Estonia, Tallinn, Estonia.

van Ark, Bart, and Robert Inklaar. 2005. "Catching Up or Getting Stuck? Europe's Trouble to Exploit ICT's Productivity Potential." Research Memorandum GD-79, Groningen Growth and Development Center, University of Groningen, Groningen, the Netherlands.

van Ark, Bart, Mary O'Mahony, and Gerard Ypma, eds. 2007. *The EU KLEMS Productivity Report* 1 (March). EU KLEMS Net. http://www.euklems.net/data/eu_klems_productivity_report.pdf.

van Ark, Bart, and Marcin Piatkowski. 2004. "Productivity, Innovation and ICT in Old and New Europe." *International Economics and Economic Policy* 1 (2): 215–46.

Van Biesebroeck, Johannes. 2005. "Exporting Raises Productivity in Sub-Saharan African Manufacturing Firms." *Journal of International Economics* 67 (2): 373–91.

White, Halbert. 1980. "A Heteroskedasticity-Consistent Covariance Matrix Estimator and a Direct Test for Heteroskedasticity." *Econometrica* 48 (4): 817–38.

WIIW (Vienna Institute for International Economic Studies). 2005. *wiiw Handbook of Statistics 2005: Central, East and Southeast Europe*. Vienna: WIIW.

WIIW Industrial Database Eastern Europe. Vienna Institute for International Economic Studies. http://www.wiiw.ac.at/e/industrial_database.html (accessed November 2006).

World Bank. 2002. *Transition, the First Ten Years: Analysis and Lessons for Eastern Europe and the Former Soviet Union*. Washington, DC: World Bank.

———. 2005a. *Enhancing Job Opportunities: Eastern Europe and the Former Soviet Union*. Washington, DC: World Bank.

———. 2005b. *From Disintegration to Reintegration: Eastern Europe and the Former Soviet Union*. Washington, DC: World Bank.

———. 2006a. "Turkey: Investment Climate Assessment." World Bank, Washington, DC.

———. 2006b. "Russia: Investment Climate Assessment." World Bank, Washington, DC.

———. 2006c. *Migration and Remittances in Eastern Europe and the Former Soviet Union*. Washington, DC: World Bank.

———. 2007. *Global Economic Prospects 2007: Managing the Next Wave of Globalization*. Washington, DC: World Bank.

———. Forthcoming. *Productivity Growth, Job Creation and Demographic Change in Eastern Europe and the Former Soviet Union*. Washington, DC: World Bank.

World Development Indicators Database. World Bank. http://go.worldbank.org/B53SONGPA0 (accessed March 2007).

Index

Boxes, figures, notes, and tables are noted by b, f, n, and t, respectively.

A

agriculture, labor shedding in, 13, 16, 73, 77, 78, 108
agriculture reform index, 78
agriculture sector, 14–15
  farm efficiency, 76–77
  farm restructuring, 78
  labor shedding in, 13, 16, 73, 77, 78, 108
  labor shifts back to in CIS countries, 67
  performance in, 75–77, 110*n*4
  productivity growth in, 73, 74–80, 108, 110*n*4
  role as social safety net, 15
  service input usage in, 181–84
  shift-share analysis of, 176–81
  shifts away from, 16–17
allocative efficiency, 88, 129, 130*f*3.12
Amadeus Database, 4–5, 135–36*b*3.2, 181, 217, 225

B

backbone services, 80, 109
Baltic states, patterns of growth in, 48
BEEPS (Business Environment and Enterprise Performance Survey) Database, 5, 135–36*b*3.2, 145, 152*b*3.4
BEEPS regressions, 217–25, 226*t*3.B8, 227–30*tt*3.B9–3.*B*14
business environment indicators, 221–25
business start-ups, 22, 23*f*4
  See also firms
buyer-driven production chains, 90–92, 239–41

C

capacity utilization, 53, 53*f*1.4
  and adjusted TFP growth rates, 53, 53*f*1.4, 64*n*2
  link to firm productivity growth, 137–38, 154*n*2
capital stock, 1
  decomposition of, 116–17
  inflows of, 160
  link to economic growth, 10–13
  measurement of, 48–52, 64*n*2, 168–69
capital-to-labor ratios, 110*n*2
CIS. *See* Commonwealth of Independent States (CIS)
CISStat, 50–51*b*1.1, 168, 178
Cobb-Douglas production function, 16–68, 50*b*1.1
commercialization, 243
Commonwealth of Independent States (CIS), 2, 7–8
  and decomposition of firm–level data, 117–18
  firm productivity growth drivers, 140–42
    improving capacity utilization, 137–38, 154*n*2
    strengthening governance, 146–47
  GDP growth in, 52
  labor force, sectoral shifts in, 14, 67
  land use in, 75
  manufacturing employment in, 66
  productivity growth in
    impact of policy reforms on, 61–63
    outlook for, 42–43
    overview of within sector growth, 42–43
    patterns of, 9–13
    policies to foster, 157
    sustainment of, 155–56
    within–sector productivity, 70
  reforms in agricultural policy, 79–80
  social safety nets, 164–65
  See also low income CIS countries; middle income CIS countries
competition, 239
  in backbone services, 80
  fostering innovation and, 8–9
  and imports, 150
  international integration of, 8–9
  policy approaches to, 78, 160–61
  relationship of firm churning to productivity, 127–28, 129*f*3.11
  strengthening of, in product and service markets, 139–42, 154*n*3
  strengthening of, to increase productivity growth, 37–39
corporate farms, 79
creative destruction, 22, 32–33, 121, 128
  information on process of, 206–07
and privatization, 139

D

decomposition
  of aggregate labor productivity growth, 68–71, 176–81

of capital stock, 116–17
of gross domestic product, 49–52, 64*n*1, 167–69
of productivity growth, 19–20, 44*n*5, 114–17
defensive restructuring, 18
deficits, 160
demographics, analysis of firm productivity dynamics and, 205–15, 245*nn*1–4
density measure, 188
difference-in-difference approach, 236

E

East Asia and Pacific region (EAP), 14*f*9*b*, 51*f*1.3, 55*f*1.7
and computing productivity growth, 49, 51–52
GDP growth rate of, 52
impact of policy reform on, 58–63
Eastern Europe and Central Asia region (ECA)
economic overview (1999–2005), 1–9
firm productivity growth
link of FDI to, 151–88
link to competition in product and service markets, 139–42, 154*n*3
GDP growth in, 41–42
impact of policy reforms in, 58–63
labor market flexibility of, 88*f*2.19
productivity growth in, 47–48, 49, 51–52, 55–56
firm churning as source of, 23–27
within–sector productivity, 70–74
shifts in resources to services, 65–68
See also EU-8 countries; EU-10 countries; EU-15 countries
EBRD. *See* European Bank for Reconstruction and Development (EBRD)
ECA. *See* Eastern Europe and Central Asia region (ECA)
economic cycles, management of, 160
economic disequilibrium, 160
Economic Freedom of the World Database, 242
economic growth
overview, 46–47
role of productivity in, 48–56, 64*nn*1–2
Economist Intelligence Unit, 239
educational attainment, 58–63, 85–87
and firm productivity growth, 144–45
policy approaches to, 162
efficiency gains, 13, 109
as driver of productivity growth, 20–22
in industries with high capacity innovation, 73–74
from product market competition, 28
and productivity growth within existing firms, 119–21
within sector vs. cross-sectoral shifts, 16
efficiency of service industries, 79
electricity, 79

employment
 growth in, 26
 impact of reallocation of jobs on, 129–32
 net employment losses, 134
 rates of, 11–12
 sectoral shares of, 65–71, 72–74, 110*nn*1–2, 178–79, 197
 worker training, 145–46
 See also job reallocation; labor force; shift-share analysis
equity markets, 89
EU-8 countries
 ICT-related industries, 83, 85*f*2.15, 98–99, 105–06, 112*n*17
  impact of ICT capital in, 4, 103, 112*n*16
  impact of ICT use, 106–08, 112*n*18
 labor productivity
  in ICT industries, 98–99
  in service industries, 97–98
 performance of manufacturing sector in, 80–81
 subsectoral shift-share analysis of, 179–81
EU-10 countries, 8
 agriculture productivity in, 75–77, 78
 allocative efficiency in, 88
 backbone services in agriculture markets, 80
 educational opportunities in, 87
 expansion of trade and FDI in, 89–90, 91*f*2.21
 exports, 92
 financial development and innovation in, 89, 110–11n6, 163–64
 firm-level data, decomposition of, 117–18
 firm productivity growth in, 140–42
 and global production chains, 90–92
 ICT industries, 105–06, 107, 112*n*17
 income disparities in, 3, 3*f*1
 labor
  flexibility in labor market, 144
  liberalization of labor markets in, 87–88
  shifts to services, 67, 68*f*2.3
 patterns of growth in, 52–54
 polices for competition and market entry, 161–62
 and producer-driven networks, 92*f*2.23
 productivity growth in, 5–6
  impact of policy reforms on, 61–63
  outlook for, 42–43
  overview of, within sector growth, 42–43
  patterns of, 9–13
  policies to foster, 157–58
  and reallocation of resources toward services, 14–15
  and reform progress, 5–7, 61–63
  sources of, 16
  sustainment of, 155–56
 R&D spending in, 88
 service liberalization, 100–01
 shifts in resources to services, 66
 social safety nets in, 164–65
 and transition indicators, 57

EU-15 countries
allocative efficiency in, 88
ICT-related industries, 85*f*2.15, 98–99, 100*f*2.29, 105–06, 112*n*17
impact of ICT capital in, 4, 103, 112*n*16
impact of ICT use, 106–08, 112*n*18
income disparities in, 3, 3*f*1
labor productivity
gains in, 72–73
in ICT industries, 98–99, 100*f*2.29
in service industries, 97–98
manufacturing performance, 80–81, 82*f*2.12
productivity growth in
outlook for, 42–43
overview of within sector growth, 72–74
sources of, 18
shift-share analysis of, 179
EU KLEMS Database, 70–71, 110*n*3, 111*n*12, 179
European Bank for Reconstruction and Development (EBRD), 56–57, 78, 101, 111*nn*13–14, 193
policy reform indicators, 226
transition indicators, 182–84, 226, 243
European Union, 125, 157, 161
export baskets, 94, 111*n*7, 186, 188–89
export sophistication, 83, 185–86, 238, 238*t*3.B19
gaps in, 94*f*2.25, 95–96
measure of, 94, 189
and productivity growth, 187*f*2.D2, 189
and TFP growth, 84*f*2.14*f*
exports
growth in, 188
hydrocarbon export prices, 154*n*2
link to productivity growth, 89–90, 91*ff*2.21–2.22, 149–50, 154*n*4
and product space, 94, 95*b*2.2
strategies for, 92–97, 111*n*7
technology, 90, 91*f*2.12
and TFP growth, 243*t*3.B28
EXPY measure, 185, 189
See also export sophistication
external financing, 121

F

factor mobility, 8
FDI. *See* foreign direct investment (FDI)
finance index, 182
financial depth, 58–63
financial services, 79
development of for firm productivity growth, 142, 143*f*3.20
external finance, 121
financial development indicator measures, 222–23
and financing of innovation, 89, 110–11*n*6
increased development of, 41
policy approaches to financial development, 163–64
TFP growth and financial development, 236–37
firm churning, 19, 22–27, 44*n*6
and productivity growth, 28–30, 31*f*21, 33, 121–26
under weak competition, 127–28

firm dynamics, 2
analysis of firm productivity dynamics and demographics, 205–15, 245*nn*1–4
and job flows, 129–34
and productivity growth, 114–29
contribution to, 18–20, 44*nn*5–6
as source of, 30–32, 33*f*23, 34*f*24
firm entry, 8, 31, 117
contribution to labor productivity growth, 119, 121–26, 154*n*1
foreign firms, 141*b*3.3
net entry effect, 123
policy approaches to, 160–61
and productivity growth, 22–23, 44, 118, 153
and worker reallocation, 126–27
firm exit, 8, 31, 117
contribution to labor productivity growth, 119, 154*n*1
and productivity growth, 33, 118, 121–26, 153
and worker reallocation, 126–27
firm productivity growth
analysis of firm dynamics and demographics, 205–15, 245*nn*1–4
policy drivers of
developing financial markets, 142, 143*f*3.20
implementing privatization, 138–39
improving capacity utilization, 137–38, 154*n*2
improving infrastructure, 148
investing in skills, 144–46
making labor markets flexible, 142–44
overview, 134–37
R&D investment and new technologies, 151–52
strengthening competition in product and service markets, 139–42, 154*n*3
strengthening governance, 146–47
trade and foreign investment, 148–51, 154*n*4
sources of, 117–29, 154*n*1
efficiency gains within firms, 20–22
firm churning, 22–27
firm dynamics, 30–32, 33*f*23, 34*f*24
firm dynamics versus sectoral changes, 18–20, 44*nn*5–6
link of labor reallocation, firm turnover, and within-firm growth, 21*f*21, 28–30
recourse allocation across existing firms, 27–28
within-firm, 119–21
See also productivity growth
firm turnover, 19, 22–27, 44*n*6
and job creation, 31
rate of, 7–8, 117, 121, 123
role in productivity growth, 28*f*19, 29, 30*f*20
See also firm churning
firms
business environment indicators, 221–25
demographics of, 208–09

efficiency gains in, 20–22
financial development of, 163–64
increasing financial sector opportunities for, 41
investments in infrastructure, 40–41
investments in labor and technology, 39–40
ownership of, 21
policies for competition and market entry, 160–61
policy reforms as source of expansion of, 32–35
productivity growth in
BEEPS regressions, 217–25, 226*t*3.B8, 227–30*tt*3.B9–3.B14
outlook for, 42–43
policies to boost, 35–41
size of relationship to, 120
TFP growth in, 215–17
and country-level variables, 237–39, 240*t*3.B21
link to FDI and trade, 239–43
manufacturing sector with links to service reform and competition, 225–26, 230–36
foreign direct investment (FDI), 38, 39*f*26, 192
and global production networks, 92
and ICT industries, 105
link to firm productivity growth, 148–51, 154*n*4
and promotion of innovation, 89–90, 91*f*2.21
and TFP growth, 239–43
foreign-owned firms, 21, 120
Former Soviet Union
drivers of firm productivity growth in
development of financial markets, 142, 143*f*3.20
improving capacity utilization, 137–38, 154*n*2
link to competition in product and service markets, 139–42, 154*n*3
strengthening governance, 146–47
economic overview (1999–2005), 1–9
employment protections in, 144
exports, 92
financing innovation, 89, 110–11*n*6
firm productivity growth in, 55–56, 74–80, 110*n*4
link of labor reallocation, firm turnover, and within-firm productivity, 28–30, 31*f*21
link to increase in trade and foreign investment, 148–51, 154*n*4
link to infrastructure, 148
link to investing in R&D and new technologies, 151–52
relationship of firm dynamics to, 30–32
GDP, 45–46
and global production chains, 90–92
impact of policy reform on, 58–63
infrastructure, 40–41, 148
innovation in, 162
patterns of growth in, 46–48

productivity growth in, 48–56, 64*nn*1–2, 102–03
efficiency gains vs. cross-sectional shifts, 16–18, 44*n*4
and firm churning, 121–26
firm dynamics and job flows, 129–34
outlook for, 42–43
patterns of, 9–13
polices to foster, 158
and reallocation of resources toward services, 14–15
role of ICT in, 85–87, 103–08, 112*nn*16–17
shift-share analysis of, 68–71, 110*n*2
sustainment of, 155–56
within sector overview, 72–74, 110*n*3
service industries
effect of services on manufacturing productivity, 101–03
potential for productivity growth in, 102–03
service liberalization, 100–101, 111*nn*13–14
shifts in resources into, 65–68
and skilled workers, 144–46
Foster-Haltiwanger-Krizan method, 115–16*b*3.1, 205–06

G

G-7 countries, 103
GDP. *See* gross domestic product (GDP)
Georgia, firm-level data for analysis of productivity in, 209–15, 245*nn*1–4
global production chains, 90–92
governance
as driver of firm productivity growth, 37, 146–47
governance indicator measures, 223–24
policy approaches to, 159–60
government institutions and policies, link to firm productivity growth, 134–37
gross domestic product (GDP), 45–46, 177
convergence of, in Region to industrial country levels, 47–48
decomposition of, 49–52, 64*n*1, 167–69
and export sophistication, 185–86
growth of, in ECA region, 51
increase in, 9–10, 10*f*3, 159
link of growth in to financing innovation, 89, 110–11*n*6
and measures of structural determinants of productivity, 60*b*1.2
and open forest, 189*f*2.D3
and venture capital, 89
growth accounting methodology, 49–52, 167–69

H

Herfindahl-Hirschman indexes, 139–40, 154*n*3, 231, 232–33*t*3.B16

high-skilled workers, 85–87, 99–100, 184, 191
high-technology industries, 17
contributions of, 140–42
exports in, 92–93
human capital, 162–63
accumulation of, 64*n*1
high-skilled workers, 85–86

I

ICT. *See* information and communication technology (ICT)
ICT-related industries, 83, 85*f*2.15, 151, 241
contributions of, 105–06
as drivers of manufacturing productivity, 80–81, 82*f*2.12
productivity growth in, 120
strategic restructuring of, 21–22
See also labor productivity; labor productivity growth
ILO. See International Labour Organization (ILO)
IMF. See International Monetary Fund (IMF)
import penetration rate, 140, 238, 239*t*3.B20
imports, of new technologies, 149
income levels, 3, 9–10, 11, 47, 186
industrial countries
changes in sectoral employment shares, 66–68
GDP in, 47–48
and productivity growth, 54–56
structural reforms in, 59*f*1.9
and transition indicators, 57
inflation, 159–60
information and communication technology (ICT), 2–3
contribution of ICT capital to productivity growth, 103–04, 112*n*16
and efficiency gains, 21–22
ICT taxonomy
in manufacturing industries, 184
in service sector, 190–95, 203*nn*1–6
ICT-using industries, 106–08, 112n18, 198, 200, 204*n*11
investments in, 13, 13*f*8, 151–52
link to labor productivity, 197, 198–99*tt*2.F1–2.F4
production of ICT goods, 105–06, 112*n*17
reform in, 243, 244*t*3.B26
role in productivity growth, 195–203
and structural reform, 198, 200, 204*n*11
See also ICT-related industries; technology industries
infrastructure
indicators of, 170–73, 221–22
investments in, 40–41
policy approaches to, 162–63
quality and stock of, 58–63
transport, 120, 203*n*5
innovation, 133
absorptive capacity for, 162, 163*f*4.2
financing of, 89, 110–11*n*6
and incentives for local firms, 150
link to ICT use, 151, 152*b*3.4
in manufacturing sector, 73–74

progress in, 162
promotion of through trade and FDI, 89–90, 91*f*2.21
and proximity to frontier, 243–45
institutional quality, 58–63
International Financial Statistics Service, 239
International Labour Organization (ILO), 178
International Monetary Fund (IMF), 50*b*1.1, 168
International Standard Industrial Classification of all Economic Activities (ISIC), 70–71, 178, 179
international supply networks, 150
investments
in capital-intensive industries, 83
climate for, 161
by firms in labor and technology, 39–40
to foster macroeconomic stability, 159–60
in infrastructure, 40–41
policy reforms in, 78
and productivity growth, 12–13, 13*f*8
in skills, 85–87
ISIC. *See* International Standard Industrial Classification of all Economic Activities (ISIC)

J

job creation and turnover, 129–32
job reallocation, 30–32

K

KLEMS Database, 70–71, 110*n*3, 111*n*12, 179
Krugman, Paul, 1

L

labor allocative efficiency, 1, 129, 130*f*3.12
labor force
investment in, 39–40
reallocation of labor, 30–32
rigidities in labor markets, 242
sectoral shifts in, 14
value added per worker, 68*f*2.4
worker mobility, 87
See also employment; shift-share analysis
labor market flexibility, 9, 87–88, 142–44, 224–25
labor productivity, 4, 108, 192, 203*n*2
in agriculture sector, 74–76
in EU-8 vs. EU-15 countries, 80, 81*f*2.11
gains in EU-15 countries, 72–73
in ICT industries, 98–99, 101*f*2.29, 197, 198–99*tt*2.F1–2.F4
impact of service liberalization on, 102
link to economic growth, 10–12
link to job creation, 132–33
in manufacturing industries, 81–83
service industries, 97–98, 111*nn*9–12
labor productivity growth, 199–202

in ICT-using manufacturing industries, 107
role of ICT capital to, 103, 104*f*2.33, 197, 198–99*tt*2.F1–2.F4
shift-share analysis of, 68–71, 176–81
within firm, 117
labor shedding, 130
in agriculture, 13, 16, 73, 77, 78, 108
and job destruction, 31, 32*f*22, 130*f*3.13
in late reforming countries, 7
LAC. *See* Latin America and the Caribbean region (LAC)
land use, 75
Latin America and the Caribbean region (LAC)
GDP growth in, 47*f*1.1
impact of policy reform on, 58–63
structural reforms in, 59*f*1.9
TFP, 11*f*4, 14f9, 51*f*1.3, 55*f*1.7
worker training, 145–46
Lerner index, 139–40, 213, 234–35*t*3.B17
liberalization index, 182, 230
low income CIS countries, 2, 44*n*1
GDP growth in, 52
market services share of employment, 67, 68*f*2.3
patterns of growth in, 48
relationship of productivity to progress of reform in, 7
technology exports, 90, 91*f*2.12
TFP, 11*ff*4–5, 14*f*9, 51*f*1.3
transition indicators, 57
See also Commonwealth of Independent States (CIS)
low-skilled workers, 99–100, 185, 191

M

macroeconomic stability
to increase productivity growth, 37
policy approaches to, 159–60
manufacturing industries, 14–15, 66, 184
effect of services on, 191–95, 203*nn*1–6
and firm turnover rate, 123, 125–26, 126*f*3.8
ICT-using, 106–08
and job flow, 131–32
and labor allocative efficiency, 129, 130*f*3.12
labor productivity growth in, 199–202
link of competition to technological frontier, 141*b*3.3
performance of, 80–81, 82*f*2.12, 83*f*2.13
productivity growth in, 17, 19–20, 44*n*4, 109
analysis of, 184–90
decomposition of firm-level data, 118*f*3.1
drivers of, 73–74
effect of services on, 101–03
patterns of, 20–22
policy drivers of, 81, 82–97, 110–11*nn*5–7
TFP growth estimates in, 215–17
shift-share analysis of, 176–81

skill taxonomy of, 184–85
TFP growth in, 135–36*b*3.2
and country-level variables, 237–39, 240*t*3.B21
and financial development, 236–37
link to FDI and trade, 239–43
with links to service reform and competition, 225–26, 230–36
market concentration ratio, 139–40, 154*n*3
market economies, 2
and allocative efficiency, 129, 130*f*3.12
benchmark for, 175–76
market entry, policy approaches to, 160–61
market services
labor productivity growth in, 199–202
labor shifts to, 67, 68*f*2.3
markup ratio, 139–40
methodology
and aggregate productivity growth, 115*b*3.1
for analysis of firm productivity dynamics and demographics, 205–6, 219, 226
for analysis of growth accounting, 167–68
for analysis of role of ICT in growth, 195–98
for analysis of structural reforms, 60*b*1.2
cross-country growth regressions, 169–70
data sources used in growth accounting methodology, 49, 50–51*b*1.1, 170–73
shift share analysis, 176–77, 179
and TFP growth, 236–37
Mexico, 126, 126*f*3.8
and firm churning, 25*f*16, 27
middle income CIS countries
GDP growth in, 52
labor shifts to services, 67, 68*f*2.3
relationship of productivity to progress of reform in, 7
TFP, 11*ff*4–5, 14*f*9, 51*f*1.3
transition indicators, 57
See also Commonwealth of Independent States (CIS)

N

NACE sectors and subsectors, 70, 111*n*11, 135–36*b*3.2, 179, 203*n*3, 212, 245*n*3
net entry, 19, 21*f*13, 22–29, 30, 44*n*6
and productivity growth, 119, 120, 123, 127–29, 151
rates of, 121–22
See also firm churning; firm entry; firm exit
non-ICT related industries, 120–21
North American Free Trade Agreement, 126, 126*f*3.8

O

OECD. *See* Organisation for Economic Co-operation and Development (OECD)
open forest measures, 94, 111*n*7, 186–90

Organisation for Economic Co-operation and Development (OECD), 24, 29, 76
  and firm exit, 31
  and product market regulation, 238–39, 240*t*3.B21
  worker protection in, 87–88
output growth, 1, 2, 9–13, 44*n*3
ownership of firms, 21

P

PCA. *See* principal component analysis (PCA)
Poland, product space in, 95*b*2.2
policies
  and agricultural productivity, 77–80
  for competition, 160–61
  drivers of firm productivity growth
    developing financial markets, 142, 143*f*3.20
    implementing privatization, 138–39
    improving capacity utilization, 137–38, 154*n*2
    improving infrastructure, 148
    increase in trade and foreign investment, 148–51, 154*n*4
    investing in R&D and new technologies, 151–52
    investing in skills, 144–46
    making labor markets flexible, 142–44
    overview, 134–37
    strengthening competition in product and service markets, 139–42, 154*n*3
    strengthening governance, 146–47
  for financial development, 163–64
  to foster productivity growth, 35–41, 133–34, 156–59
    in manufacturing, 81, 82–97, 110–11*nn*5–7
    in services, 98–101, 111*nn*13–14
  to increase financial opportunities for firms, 41
  for infrastructure, 40–41, 162–63
  to invest in labor and technology, 39–40
  for macroeconomic stability, 159–60
  for market entry, 160–61
  to promote governance, 159–60
  for skilled workers, 162–63
  for social safety nets, 164–65
  in support of innovation, 95–96
  for technology development, 162–63
policy reforms, 32–35
  as challenge to productivity growth, 4
  in the Region, 46
  impact of, 58–63, 133–34
  overall record of, 56–57
  as source of productivity growth, 32–35
poverty, and GDP, 10*f*3
PPP. *See* purchasing power parity (PPP)
price liberalization, 46, 78

principal component analysis (PCA), 221–25
private firms, 120
privatization, 21, 38, 39*f*26
  in CIS countries, 147
  as driver of firm productivity growth, 138–39
  of land, 78
producer-driven networks, 91–92, 239–40
product markets
  competition in, 139–42, 154*n*3
  regulation of, 101, 238–39, 240*t*3.B21
product space, 94, 95*b*2.2, 186–90
productivity growth, 48–56, 58, 64*nn*1–2
  cross-country growth regressions, 169–73
  cross-sectoral shifts in, 65–71, 110*n*2
  data used to assess and analyze, 4–9, 44*n*2
  and distance to technological frontier, 141*b*3.3
  drivers of, 2–3
    policy drivers, 35–41, 77–80
    within sector productivity improvements, 68–71, 110*n*2
  estimating impact of structural reforms on, 169–73
  exports link to, 89–90, 91*ff*2.21–2.22
  and firm dynamics, 114–29
  link to competition, 127–28, 129*f*3.11
  outlook for, 42–43
  overview (1999–2005), 1–9
  patterns of, 9–13
  relationship of labor shifts to services, 67, 68*f*2.4
  role of ICT in, 103–08, 112*nn*16–18, 195–203, 203–4*nn*8–10
  sources of
    efficiency gains within sectors vs. cross-sectoral shifts, 16–18, 44*n*4
    overview, 13–14
    policy reforms, 32–35, 56–57
    reallocation of resources toward services, 14–15
  sustaining to promote higher standard of living, 155–56
  within sectors
    agricultural productivity, 74–80
    improvements in, 68–71, 110*n*2
    manufacturing productivity, 80–97, 110–11*nn*5–7
    overview, 72–74, 110n3
    service productivity, 97–103, 111*nn*8–14
  See also firm productivity growth; labor productivity; labor productivity growth; methodology
PRODY, 185, 190
purchasing power parity (PPP), 1–2, 110*n*3, 177, 179

R

R&D. *See* research and development (R&D)
RCA. *See* revealed comparative advantage (RCA)
real estate, 98
real income per capita, 1–2
reallocation of jobs, 129–32

reallocation of labor, 29, 126–27, 134
across existing firms, 126–27
rates of, 19–20
role in firm productivity growth, 153
reallocation of resources
across existing firms, 27–28
impact on productivity growth, 118
into service sector, 65–68
and privatization, 139
to services, 108
toward services, 14–15
reforms
in education, 86
and firm churning, 23–24
in ICT-related industries, 243, 244*t*3B.26
and ICT sector convergence with non-ICT sectors, 107
relationship of productivity and progress of reform, 5–7
See also policies; policy reforms; structural reforms
the Region. *See* Former Soviet Union
regulations, 243
in labor market, 142, 144
product markets, 101, 140, 238–39, 240*t*3.B21
research and development (R&D)
investments in, 88–89, 111*n*5, 241–42
spending on, 162
resource reallocation. *See* reallocation of resources
restructuring of firms, 42–43
revealed comparative advantage (RCA), 91, 94, 96, 185
road transport, 203*n*5
Romania, firm-level data for analysis of productivity in, 209–15, 245*nn*1–4
Russia, product space in, 95*b*2.2
Russian Economic Barometer Survey Database, 137
Russian Federation, firm-level data for analysis of productivity in, 209–15, 245*nn*1–4

S

SAP. *See* South Asia and Pacific (SAP) region
SEE. *See* Southeastern Europe (SEE) countries
service industries
and competition, 38
definition, 111*n*8
growth in, 14–15, 18
ICT-using, 106–08
productivity growth in, 74, 97–103, 109, 111*nn*8–14
resource reallocation into, 65–68
TFP growth in manufacturing with links to service reform and competition, 225–26, 230–36
service liberalization, 79, 100–01, 111*nn*13–14, 192, 195, 225–26
service sectors
analysis of productivity in, 190–95, 203*nn*1–6
competition in, 142
and decomposition of firm-level data, 118*f*3.1
effect on manufacturing industries, 191–95, 203*nn*1–6

estimation of use in agriculture sector, 181–84
firm-level data for, 209–15, 245*nn*1–4
and firm turnover rate, 123
ICT taxonomy of, 190–91
and job flows, 132–33
shift-share analysis of, 176–81
skills taxonomy, 191
shift-share analysis, 68–71, 176–81
skilled workers, 85–87, 99–100, 144–46, 162
skills
skill taxonomy in manufacturing sector, 184–85
skills taxonomy in service sector, 191
social safety nets, 8, 15, 42–43, 164–65
South Asia and Pacific (SAP) region, 47
Southeastern Europe (SEE) countries
agriculture productivity in, 75, 77
patterns of growth in, 48, 53–54
productivity growth in
outlook for, 42–43
overview of within sector growth, 42–43
patterns of, 9–13
policies to foster, 157
sources of, 16
sustainment of, 155–56
relationship of productivity to progress of reform in, 7
shifts in resources to services, 66
transition indicators, 57
within-sector productivity, 70
specification tests, 170
stock market capitalization, 89
strategic restructuring, 18, 21–22, 119
structural reforms, 58–63, 169–73, 198, 200, 204*n*11
subsidies, 78

T

technological frontier, 141*b*3.3, 148, 152*b*3.4, 243–45
technology industries
and export markets, 90, 91*f*2.22
investments in, 39–40, 110*n*5
policy approaches for development of, 162–63
and productivity growth, 3–4, 148–51, 154*n*4
See also information and communication technology (ICT); skilled workers
tertiary education, 85–87, 242
total factor productivity (TFP), 2, 74
in agriculture sector, 75–76
and BEEPS regressions, 217–25, 226*t*3.B8, 227–30*tt*3.B9–3.B14
growth of
and capacity utilization-adjusted TFP
growth rates, 53, 53*f*1.4, 64*n*2
and country-level variables, 237–39, 240*t*3.B21
and financial development, 236–37

link to FDI and trade, 239–43
in manufacturing sector with links to service reform and competition, 225–26, 230–36
and high-technology industries, 17, 104, 196
link to flexibility in labor market, 142–44
in manufacturing sector, 83, 84*f*2.14, 215–17, 225–26, 230–36
measurement of, 167
policy drivers of, 83, 84*f*2.14
and privatization, 39*f*26
and proximity to technological frontier, 141*b*3.3, 243–45
relationship to economic growth, 10–11, 11*ff*4–5, 44*n*3
and shares of exports, 243*t*3.B28
and use of growth accounting methodology to compute growth in, 48–56, 64*nn*1–2
trade
to foster macroeconomic stability, 159–160
liberalization of, 78
link to firm productivity growth, 148–151, 154*n*4
openness of, 58–63
promoting innovation through, 89–90, 91*f*2.21
and TFP growth, 239–43
training programs, 145–46
transition economies
benchmarking transformation of, 175–76
data challenges in measuring capital stock in, 50–51*b*1.1, 168–69
financial sector in, 41
and firm churning, 22–27
firm productivity growth drivers
implementing privatization, 138–39
improving capacity utilization, 137–38, 154*n*2
impact of firm entry vs. firm exit, 119, 123
and job reallocation rates, 129–32
labor shifts in, 67, 68*f*2.3
productivity growth in, 49–52
and firm churning, 121–126
outlook for, 42–43
patterns of, 7–8
and reallocation of resources across existing firms, 27–28
relationship of firm dynamics to, 30–32
relationship of worker reallocation to, 126–27
transition indicators, 56–57
transport infrastructure, 120, 203*n*5
transport services, 79
Turkey, 162
exports, 92
financial development in, 163–64
growth in, 52
and producer-driven networks, 92*f*2.23
productivity growth in, 5–6, 16, 54–55
outlook for, 42–43

overview of within sector growth, 42–43
sustainment of, 155–56
within-sector, 70
relationship of productivity to progress of reform, 5–7

U

Ukraine, firm-level data for analysis of productivity in, 209–15, 245*nn*1–4
UN Industrial Development Organization (UNIDO), 238, 239
United Nations Conference on Trade and Development (UNCTAD), 239–240
United Nations Food and Agriculture Organization, 76
United States, ICT-using industries, 106–09

V

value added, 14–15, 32, 66, 111*n*11, 209, 243
per worker, 15, 67, 68*f*2.4, 178
of products and exports, 20, 119, 177
sectoral shares of, 72–74, 177
and shift share analysis, 179
venture capital, 89
Vienna Institute for International Economic Studies, 50–51*b*1.1, 168

W

Western European countries, research spending, 162
WIIW Database, 110*n*3, 111*n*13
World Bank, 78
World Development Indicators, 50–51*b*1.1, 168
World Development Indicators Database, 70, 110*n*3, 168, 237
World Economic Outlook, 50–51*b*1.1, 168

Y

Yearbook of Labour Statistics, 178

ECO-AUDIT

Environmental Benefits Statement

The World Bank is committed to preserving endangered forests and natural resources. The Office of the Publisher has chosen to print ***Unleashing Prosperity*** on coated, recycled paper with 30 percent post-consumer waste, in accordance with the recommended standards for paper usage set by the Green Press Initiative, a non-profit program supporting publishers in using fiber that is not sourced from endangered forests. For more information, visit www.greenpressinitiative.org.

Saved:

- 13 trees
- 9 million BTUs of total energy
- 1,098 lbs. of net greenhouse gases
- 4,558 gallons of wastewater
- 585 lbs. of solid waste

green press INITIATIVE